Methodism and Society:
Guidelines
for Strategy

METHODISM AND SOCIETY

Volume IV

Methodism and Society: Guidelines for Strategy

Herbert E. Stotts
and
Paul Deats, Jr.

Edited by the Board of Social and Economic Relations
of The Methodist Church and Published by

Abingdon Press

NEW YORK   •   NASHVILLE

METHODISM AND SOCIETY: GUIDELINES FOR STRATEGY

Copyright © 1962 by Abingdon Press

Library of Congress Catalog Card Number: 62-9997

SET UP, PRINTED, AND BOUND BY THE
PARTHENON PRESS, AT NASHVILLE,
TENNESSEE, UNITED STATES OF AMERICA

Introduction

In the conclusion of his classical study of *The Social Teaching of the Christian Churches*, Ernst Troeltsch made the remark: "Faith is the source of energy in the struggle of life, but life still remains a battle which is continually renewed upon ever new fronts." If Troeltsch were alive today, he would find ample confirmation of this statement in the upheavals of the twentieth century. The arena of the social struggle has become global. Myriads of human beings in Asia, Africa, and Latin America have seen a glimpse of a better life and are rising to claim their share in the resources of the earth. Revolutions in expectations are breeding revolutions of the social order. Changes which once took centuries are now telescoped into decades. Modern science and technology are providing unprecedented opportunities for the enhancement of life or for totalitarian regimentation of human ants. The entire globe is an explosive "area of rapid social change" from which no country is exempt. In an interdependent world, the battle for freedom from hunger and misery, from diseases and illiteracy, from injustice and tyranny, from the threat of atomic annihilation, is everybody's concern and everybody's responsibility.

Does the Christian faith furnish a "source of energy" and a sense of urgency and direction in this new battle for the dignity and welfare, no longer of particular groups of underprivileged alone, but of every member of the human race? It must frankly be acknowledged that the churches, as often in the past, are disappointingly slow in their response to swiftly changing situations and weak and divided in their social witness. For many Christians, the world-transforming power of the gospel is reduced to the virtue of social respectability.

5

Yet, in the longer perspectives of history, it must also gratefully be recognized that this century has witnessed an almost miraculous upsurge of social concern in widening Christian circles. The labors of the pioneers of the American social gospel movement and related endeavors in Europe, though often decried by advocates of a theological and economic status quo, have not been without fruit. From an irritant, the movement has turned into a ferment. From an act of prophetic revolt, it has developed into an impressive range of official and unofficial program activities of the churches—largely reformist and educational, it is true, yet not insensitive to the urgings of the prophets to translate "social creeds" into bolder and more costly deeds.

Acceptance of social responsibility on the part of the churches, however variously conceived, has to such an extent become a part of American culture that it is easy to overlook its comparative novelty. A glance at the international scene furnishes an even more telling indication of the truly amazing growth of social awareness within the short span of a few decades. When the Methodist Episcopal Church and the Federal Council of the Churches of Christ in America in 1908 adopted the "Social Creed," such a step would have been unacceptable to most Protestant and Eastern Orthodox bodies on other continents. The first ecumenical world conference on Practical Christianity, held in Stockholm in 1925, was above all a stirring confession of the failure of the Christian churches to live up to their mission in society. But one needs to have only the slightest acquaintance with the program of the World Council of Churches, a generation later, to become aware of the extent to which the struggle for a responsible society has become a commonly accepted obligation. The huge project currently undertaken by the World Council on "The Common Christian Responsibility Toward Areas of Rapid Social Change" is a very instructive illustration of this change of mind.

The progressive leavening of the life of the denominations and the growth in sensitivity and professional expertness, which characterize the movement of social Christianity at home and abroad today, are doubtless in part a response to the pervasive pressures of history. But they also reflect profound changes in the Church's understanding of its own life and mission. A few of these changing emphases may be listed in summary fashion:

(1) There is a new emphasis on the Church—the people of God, the

body of Christ—as a corporate agent of social criticism and redemption. Its primary impact on society does not reside in its social teachings and program activities. Its impact derives above all from its very existence in the world as a community of believers and from the redemptive radiance of their life in prayer and worship, in Christian self-discipline, and in care for the neighbor near and afar. (2) The gospel of salvation is the opposite of religious individualism; it is social because it is personal. Its concern is not with disembodied souls nor with material progress without soul, but with the wholeness of man-in-community. (3) The Christian social witness becomes relevant and effective in the myriads of decisions and actions of laymen and lay women as they seek to live out their faith in the rough-and-tumble of everyday life. The Evanston Assembly of the World Council of Churches in 1954 offered a pointed formulation of this view: "The real battles of the faith today are being fought in factories, shops, offices, and farms, in political parties and government agencies, in countless homes, in the press, radio and television, in the relationship of nations." (4) There is also a growing recognition that social prophecy, in order not to remain a pious but ineffectual gesture, must be instrumented by social and political realism and translated into strategic planning. In the complexities of an increasingly organized and technicized society, the scattered efforts of individuals and small groups in immediate situations do not suffice. Christian efforts need to be co-ordinated in an all-inclusive strategy—a strategy which rests on an incisive diagnosis of national values and evils, which projects Christian imperatives into captivating and realizable goals, and which knows how to utilize the decision-making processes in an organized society.

The last point is worth stressing. Despite its flourishing busyness, the Christian social witness is caught up in a grave though mostly unavowed crisis. The root cause of the crisis lies, no doubt, in the fact that the "source of energy in the struggle of life" (to quote again Troeltsch's phrase) for many Christians has lost its transforming dynamism. But there is also a disturbing feeling that much of the Christian social witness is "beating the air"—not only because it is often hesitant and weak but because it has become uncertain of its target. Hampered by social and ethical myopia, Christian groups are slow to recognize that the battle-field of social responsibility has become vastly expanded and more complex. A missionary strategist once remarked: "The devil never laughs so heartily as when he succeeds in luring devout Christians to concentrate their efforts on secondary fronts. For then he has the central front, unguarded, all to himself." Though some may take exception to the language, no one can deny the pertinency of this observation in a time when the configuration of the battle is undergoing such swift and extraordinary changes.

It is not without reason, therefore, that Christian leaders are paying increasing attention to broader questions of aims and goals and the attendant problems of long-range planning. What are the purposes of this nation? What are the purposes of the Christian Church in and beyond the nation? To be sure, there is a legitimate place for particular "causes" and "emphases." But, in the opinion of many, the present situation calls for an imaginative attempt to rethink larger priorities. To take an illustration, are those right who suggest that the overriding Christian social concerns in the years ahead should be world peace under law, a more equitable partnership in utilizing the abundant material and technological resources of the earth, and the population explosion?

It is in this world context that the project on *Methodism and Society* is set. Like other Christian bodies, Methodism is challenged to ponder the lessons of its heritage, to redefine its social motivations and ideals, to assess its present activities and resources, and to project adequate strategies for more vigorous advance. The MESTA[1] study is an exploratory contribution to this task. Although it is chiefly concerned with the interaction of Methodism and American society, its broad Protestant approach, it is hoped, will commend it to the attention of social-minded Christians in other denominations as well.

Following the invitation from the Board of Social and Economic Relations, the committee appointed by the Boston University School of Theology faculty prepared a prospectus which was approved by the Board in September 1957. The committee has worked as a team in the general planning and in the definition and constant review of scope and research procedures. While the designated authors have carried primary responsibility for the writing of the individual volumes, these also include, in varying degrees, contributions of other members.

The preliminary survey of source materials indicated that such a

[1] The term "MESTA," frequently used in these volumes, is an abbreviation of the original working title, "Methodist Social Thought and Action."

study, to fulfill its purpose, would require a far greater amount of primary research than had been originally anticipated. Hence the committee carried out a series of specialized projects covering such sources as Annual Conference Journals and regional periodicals, files of boards and agencies of The Methodist Church, educational curriculum materials, and personal records. Limitations of time and resources have prevented more than a sampling of representative periods, regions, and types of data. The largest single project—on "The Beliefs of Methodists" (designated MR [2])—is described in Appendix B of the present volume. A full account of this particular inquiry is given in a mimeographed monograph by Herbert E. Stotts. Correlations are in Appendix C.

The findings of the whole project have been condensed in a series of four volumes appearing under the general title of *Methodism and Society*.

Volume I, *Methodism and Society in Historical Perspective*, traces the social history of Methodism up to 1908, when the adoption of the "Social Creed" by the Methodist Episcopal Church and subsequently by the Federal Council of Churches of Christ in America opened up a new period. Beginning with a consideration of British Methodism from John Wesley to 1850, it recounts the checkered history of Methodism's interaction with the American environment.

Volume II, *Methodism and Society in the Twentieth Century*, brings the story up to the present time, correlating the growth of social concerns with major developments in national life. In further parts, the volume examines the contributions of specific agencies and groups, both official and unofficial, and gives a topical presentation of Methodism's stand on major issues.

Volume III, *Methodism and Society in Theological Perspective*, pursues a twofold aim. After analyzing the social implications of John Wesley's thought, it discusses major trends and emphases in relating religious convictions and social conduct as they appear in twentieth-century Methodism in the United States. The constructive part suggests in broad outline a theology of society which is both rooted in the truths of the Christian faith and relevant to the contemporary social scene.

The present volume, *Methodism and Society: Guidelines for Strategy*, relates the findings of the preceding studies to the insights of social science into the processes of decision-making and planning. Against this background it seeks to develop a framework of principles and considerations which may serve as guidelines for a realistic strategy of social education, leadership, and action. Although this volume is the product of a co-operative research and writing venture, there has been division of labor. Herbert E. Stotts exercised major responsibility for Chapters VI through X, and Paul Deats, Jr., was primarily responsible for Chapters I through V and for Chapter XI.

Some of the general features, and limitations, of the project should be pointed out. As the reader of the volumes will notice, the study pays major attention to the institutional manifestations of Methodist social concern. Such an approach may tend to create the one-sided impression that the social witness of Methodism is to be seen chiefly in its institutional activities and in deliberate efforts of clergy and lay professionals to promote social change. The committee was, of course, aware of the fact that the social radiation of a church is an expression of its total life as it interacts with the environing culture, and especially of the countless decisions of individual Christians in the run of everyday life. It has therefore sought to probe also these elusive realities at certain points—particularly through the inquiry into the actual religious beliefs and social attitudes of Methodists, referred to above as MR [2].

The fact is often overlooked that The Methodist Church as a denomination is not limited to America alone. It is world-wide in structure and polity, as evidenced by the composition of its top legislative and executive organs, the General Conference and the Council of Bishops. A study of the varied relations existing between Methodism and society around the globe would be of great benefit in fostering a deeper sense of fellowship and a mutual understanding of the widely differing conditions under which Methodists are called to bear their social witness. The present volumes, however, are focused on the religious and social scene of the United States, with some notable exceptions. Thus Volume I includes an account of the social history of British Methodism from John Wesley to 1850. The narrative of twentieth-century developments in Volume II suggests the influence of international perspectives on General Conference resolutions and Board actions. The deliberative parts of Volumes III and IV possess, in the nature of the case, a transcultural reference.

The ecumenical aspirations and affiliations of Methodism pose a somewhat similar problem, especially with respect to Volumes III and IV.

It would have been theoretically possible to attempt to define a distinctive Methodist theology of society and a corresponding social strategy. Both theological and pragmatic reasons led the committee to adopt a different course. Methodism is officially committed to the cause of Christian unity. Methodist pronouncements and attitudes today are more expressive of the common outlook of social-minded Protestantism than of a separate tradition. Moreover, in the realm of strategy and action, it would clearly be self-defeating to seek to do in isolation what can be accomplished more effectively by a pooling of resources. Guided by such considerations, the committee has deliberately chosen to place its discussion of Methodist social responsibility in the broader framework of co-operative Christianity. Especially in the constructive parts, emphases of the Methodist heritage have been freely combined with the experiences and insights of the ecumenical community. It is hoped that this approach not only will be recognized as congenial to Methodism, but also will enhance the contribution of the project to a common task.

As previously indicated, the research phase of the project has been a co-operative venture of high order. It has benefited from the assistance of hundreds of correspondents, collaborators, and advisers across the country—denominational and interdenominational executives, liaison persons with the boards of The Methodist Church, ministers and laymen engaged in social work, academic scholars, social researchers, theological students, and so forth. Altogether over six thousand persons participated in the inquiry on "The Beliefs of Methodists." Drafts of the manuscripts were reviewed by members of the subcommittee of the Board of Social and Economic Relations as well as by outside experts.

Substantial reviews of the manuscript of the present volume on *Methodism and Society: Guidelines for Strategy* were contributed by Kenneth D. Benne, Saul Bernstein, James Bristah, Robert Chin, Georgia Harkness, F. Ernest Johnson, Franklin H. Littell, and C. Arild Olsen.

William Clifton Moore of the Boston University School of Theology served as editorial consultant for this volume. Members of the committee have used the opportunity of exploring aspects of the project in seminars. The following students of the school furnished resource materials in the form of term papers, research memoranda, and, in a few instances, doctoral dissertations on related topics: Donald W. Anderson, C. Philip Bosserman, John C. Campbell, John H. Cartwright,

Lloyd E. Chorpenning, Ivan N. Clark, John T. Dahlquist, James B. Darcy, Richard L. Deats, Dewey R. Findley, Harold W. Garman, Ronald H. Goetz, John H. Graham, Hugh E. Haggard, Richard L. Hamilton, Donald H. James, Pierre M. Kempf, C. Travis Kendall, C. Eric Lincoln, Robert Paul Lisensky, Robert C. Mezoff, Leslie H. McKeown, Orloff W. Miller, Ralph T. Mirse, Charles H. Moore, Robert W. Musil, Joseph A. Perez, Charles M. Prestwood, F. Warren Rempel, C. Allyn Russell, Robert L. Shelton, John J. Shephard, James A. Smith, Robert E. Snyder, Henry J. Stonie, Duane F. Stroman, Harry G. Swanhart, Alfred H. Tracy, Mark C. Trotter, John G. Wall, Douglas E. Wingeier, and J. Philip Wogaman.

The voluminous material thus assembled is deposited in the library of Boston University School of Theology, which has established a repository of documents and publications on Methodism and society. A portion of the data has also been transcribed and coded in a punched-card file.

The committee wishes to express its deep gratitude to all those, named and unnamed, who in various ways so generously contributed to this undertaking. A special thanks is due to the librarian of Boston University School of Theology, Jannette E. Newhall, who, with her staff, not only unsparingly assisted the committee in its researches but also provided office space in a congenial atmosphere.

NILS EHRENSTROM
PROJECT DIRECTOR

Foreword

THIS VOLUME IS PART OF A LARGER STUDY OF "METHODISM and Society" undertaken by the Board of Social and Economic Relations of The Methodist Church in co-operation with the faculty of the Boston University School of Theology.

It is the hope of the Board that the four volumes of the project will serve as a foundation for study and action in the church, with the aid of forthcoming study guides and interpretive materials, and that it will be used extensively by professors and students in colleges, universities, and seminaries, and by scholars doing independent study. The volumes should find their place as a significant contribution to ecumenical interests and research in the broader reaches of the total Christian impact upon society.

The interest of The Methodist Church in social matters goes back to its founder, John Wesley. It was an integral part of the thought, life, and activity of early Methodism. This interest in the welfare of people and the direction which society takes has been of increasing concern to The Methodist Church in the United States of America.

"The Social Creed" of the Methodist Church was adopted by the General Conference of the Methodist Episcopal Church in 1908. This was a turning point in the life of Methodism and for all the churches associated together in the Federal Council of the Churches of Christ in America. For it was the "Social Creed" of The Methodist Church which was adopted with little change as the social ideals of the Federal Council of Churches in 1908.

The Board of Social and Economic Relations was established by the General Conference of The Methodist Church in 1952 and received as its mandate the implementation of the "Social Creed."

13

As the new board began its work in race relations, economic life, and social and civic welfare, it soon became apparent that there was no systematic, objective survey and evaluation of the historical involvement of Methodism in the United States in social issues and the realization of social justice by the society.

Such questions as the following seemed to require answers:

Has The Methodist Church actually been a determining factor in the achievement of social justice in the United States?

Has The Methodist Church largely reflected advances made by secular and political institutions or has it actually been a pioneer for social justice which is the assumption that most Methodists make?

What has been the relationship of Methodist social action to Methodist theological beliefs?

Is there a well-defined Methodist theology for social action?

What has been the relationship of Methodist social action to that of other churches?

What have been the special social action emphases characteristic of Methodism in the United States?

What should Methodist social action be and do in the future?

The board decided to undertake a study of Methodism and the social scene in the United States of America and applied to the Fund for the Republic for a grant to undertake the project. The fund made a grant which has been supplemented by the board's own funds and by a research grant from Boston University to bring the project to conclusion. We are grateful to the fund for its support.

The board consulted with various educational institutions of our connection and decided that the project would be well done at the Boston University School of Theology. We are especially glad that Nils Ehrenstrom, professor of ecumenics at Boston, and for many years the director of studies for the World Council of Churches, consented to become the chairman of the committee and project director. The other members, appointed by the faculty, were Dean Walter G. Muelder; Paul Deats, Jr., associate professor of social ethics (secretary of the committee); Richard M. Cameron, professor of church history; Allan K. Chalmers, professor of preaching and applied Christianity; S. Paul Schilling, professor of systematic theology; and Herbert E. Stotts, professor of church and community. They have discharged their responsi-

14

bilities with imagination and diligence and have worked in the closest co-operation with the board and its sub-committee for the project.

The board's own committee consisted of:

> Mr. Samuel W. Witwer, Chairman
> Mrs. T. J. Cottingham, Secretary
> Bishop Lloyd C. Wicke
> Bishop Willis J. King
> Dr. Georgia Harkness
> The Reverend Frank M. Templin

They were the responsible representatives of the board in the formulation, organization, and carrying out of the undertaking.

The board extends its deepest thanks to each member of the committee for doing so well a task which consumed many hours of detailed and hard work. We are especially grateful for the work of Mr. Witwer who spent many days with the faculty committee to bring the project into formulation and fruition.

The books were written by members of the faculty committee as follows:

Volume I *Methodism and Society in Historical Perspective—*
Richard M. Cameron
Volume II *Methodism and Society in the Twentieth Century—*
Walter G. Muelder
Volume III *Methodism and Society in Theological Perspective—*
S. Paul Schilling
Volume IV *Methodism and Society: Guidelines for Strategy—*
Herbert E. Stotts and Paul Deats, Jr.

To these authors we express our thanks and commend their work to the church.

Another group of persons actively participated in the undertaking. These were the expert critics who reviewed the books. At least four critics were chosen for each book (including one non-Methodist). These critics examined and evaluated the books carefully from the vantage point of their own specialized technical skills. To these critics we are indebted for incisive, objective, and constructive suggestions which improved the early drafts of the manuscripts greatly.

15

We are especially happy to acknowledge the work of Charles H. Seaver of White Plains, New York, who for many years has worked in similar projects and who in this connection edited for style and content.

All concerned with the project are conscious of the special responsibility which the office staff, both in Boston and in Chicago, assumed in bringing the entire undertaking to completion.

The board and the faculty of Boston join in hoping that this project will be a forerunner of other larger and more penetrating analyses of the total social scene and the part of Methodism in it.

Above all, it is the earnest desire of all those who participated in any way in the project that the work will be an honor to the Lord whom we serve and be one of his instruments to sharpen the social witness of his Church in the world.

The project has been a co-operative one. The gathering and selection of the material, the interpretations and evaluations, and the method of presentation have been the primary responsibility of the faculty committee and the individual authors to whom the board extended great freedom. In no sense, therefore, can or should any statement in the books of this project (except direct quotations from official actions) be regarded as an official declaration of The Methodist Church or of the Board of Social and Economic Relations.

Alfred Dudley Ward
General Secretary
Board of Social & Economic Relations
and General Editor of the Project

Contents

PART TWO: THE STRATEGIC RESPONSE OF METHODISM TO THE CHALLENGE.. 107

Synopsis

METHODISTS ARE INEVITABLY ENGAGED IN SOCIAL ACTION. THEY act, alone and in concert, and their actions affect the future of their society by chance or by design. If this is true, and this volume proceeds upon the assumption that it is, then it is imperative that Methodists take counsel together to make their social action purposive rather than accidental, to make their social witness a wise, faithful, and strategic response to the God and father of Jesus Christ.

The challenge of responsible social action comes not to Methodism alone. As indicated in the "Introduction," this discussion of Methodist social responsibility is placed deliberately within the broader framework of co-operative Christianity. Much of the social science theory and most of the insights regarding strategy are thought to be applicable to all Protestant churches (and may well apply to Orthodox, Roman Catholic and Jewish institutions also). Thus Parts I, II, and IV are cast in an ecumenical frame of reference, even though many illustrations are Methodist.

In Part I the challenge of social action is interpreted as the viewing of social problems in the light of Christian theological and ethical norms. Part II gives attention to the necessity for and nature of a strategic response to the challenge and places social action goals within the larger system of goals of the church. Part IV seeks to move from theory to the practice of strategy at the national and local levels, with a final chapter on the limits of strategy.

In Part III Methodism is taken as a case study, with special attention being paid to its power structure and to those obstacles and resources peculiar to its social action tasks. Throughout the volume the church is treated as a social institution, but there is also a pervading sense (most explicit in Chapter II) of the divine purpose of the church and of the need for prophetic voices which will enable Methodism to serve as a vehicle for that gospel which seeks the increase of the love of God and man in the world.

23

There is thus a dimension of moral judgment throughout the volume. The authors will move back and forth between two positions in the pages which follow. On the one hand, they will use the methods of social science to describe the church and its functions. This will involve criticism and questioning, presenting an array of almost overwhelming problems. But the authors are not outsiders, observing casually and writing with detachment, even when they attempt objectivity. They write, as they live, as Methodist Christians, with deep personal and professional commitments to the church. They engage in social criticism because they care about the church, and because they believe it can respond strategically to the challenges facing it. They seek dispassionate appraisal in order that commitment may be more adequate. They try to shake loose ordinary thinking about values, norms, and social action in order to urge more rational, more purposeful commitment and action.

PART ONE

The Challenge
of Methodist Social Action

Synopsis

THE GREATEST SOURCE OF ETHICAL TENSION IN METHODISM LIES in the gap between acknowledged goals and their embodiment in the institutional forms and practices of church and society. When theologians set forth Christian norms, affirming the kingdom ideal for society, the God-given purpose of the church, and the Christlike ideal of personality, there is no necessary tension. Nor is there tension when social scientists describe and analyze the social situation, for institutional structures are neither good nor bad apart from some system of norms.

The challenge to social action comes as institutional forms and practices are judged in the light of transcendent norms. Then at least three major points of tension emerge: (1) There are tensions in ethics itself as Christians face competing goals and purposes, not all of which can be realized in a given situation, and as choices have to be made between goods. (2) At the level of the social situation there are conflicts between and among institutions, as these compete for resources to accomplish their tasks or as they overlap in functions chosen or assigned. (3) The continuing tension between the norms of theology and ethics and the institutions described by functional analysis provides the challenge for social action and the focus of the discipline of social ethics. The chart which follows shows these tension areas in the setting of the challenge to social action and the response to that challenge. The attempt in this study is to make the response to the challenge a strategic one.

Chapter I will explore the dilemmas that face the church and its leadership in social action. Chapter II will deal with the ethical dimensions of the challenge, providing theological perspective for understanding the challenge. Chapter III will focus on the social situation, identifying the most critical social problems for action in the next decade.

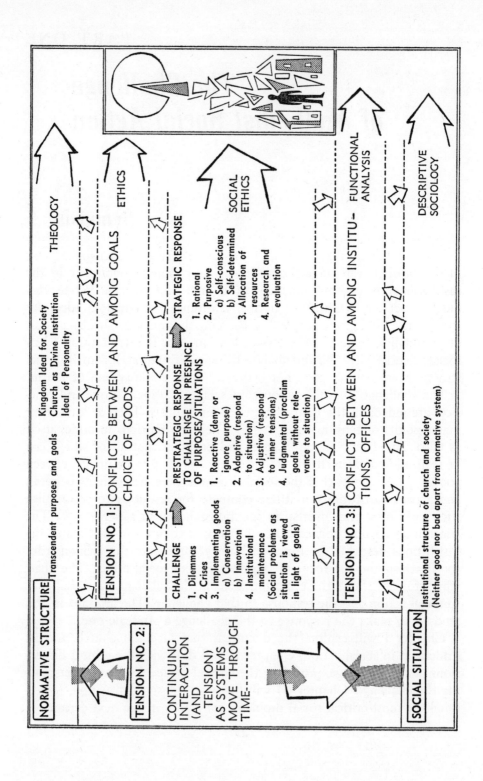

NORMATIVE STRUCTURE — Transcendent purposes and goals

Kingdom Ideal for Society
Church as Divine Institution
Ideal of Personality

THEOLOGY

TENSION NO. 1: CONFLICTS BETWEEN AND AMONG GOALS
CHOICE OF GOODS

ETHICS

TENSION NO. 2:

CONTINUING
INTERACTION
(AND
TENSION)
AS SYSTEMS
MOVE THROUGH
TIME------

CHALLENGE

1. Dilemmas
2. Crises
3. Implementing goods
   a) Conservation
   b) Innovation
4. Institutional
   maintenance
(Social problems as
situation is viewed
in light of goals)

PRESTRATEGIC RESPONSE
TO CHALLENGE IN PRESENCE
OF PURPOSES/SITUATIONS

1. Reactive (deny or
   ignore purpose)
2. Adaptive (respond
   to situation)
3. Adjustive (respond
   to inner tensions)
4. Judgmental (proclaim
   goals without rele-
   vance to situation)

STRATEGIC RESPONSE

1. Rational
2. Purposive
   a) Self-conscious
   b) Self-determined
3. Allocation of
   resources
4. Research and
   evaluation

SOCIAL
ETHICS

TENSION NO. 3: CONFLICTS BETWEEN AND AMONG INSTITU-
TIONS, OFFICES

FUNCTIONAL
ANALYSIS

SOCIAL SITUATION — Institutional structure of church and society
(Neither good nor bad apart from normative system)

DESCRIPTIVE
SOCIOLOGY

The Dilemmas of Methodist Social Action

A. Introduction

I talk to the young ministers and I ask them why they aren't saying any-thing. They say no one will listen to them; they aren't known and their churches are small. But wait, they say, until we get big churches and are widely known. We won't be silent then. Then I turn to the ministers in the big churches and I listen to them trying to explain why they have done so little. Their answer is a simple one; they say they have too much to lose. Only recently, one such man said to a group I was in, "I've spent seventeen years of my life in building up that church, and I'm not going to see it torn down in a day."

—A YOUNG MINISTER [1]

THE LOCALE IS LITTLE ROCK, ARKANSAS, IN A PERIOD OF RACIAL crisis in 1957. But the dilemma has a wider setting as one facing all ministerial leadership: how to attain power and influence without sur-rendering the ideals and purposes for which one wishes the power.

In a still wider setting the question becomes: how does the Christian community express its social witness in faithful obedience amidst the complexities of modern society and in wise stewardship of its institu-tional resources? The dilemma of the minister is posed only to illustrate the problem facing the church. Campbell and Pettigrew, in a study of ministerial behavior in Little Rock, point to the anomaly that those ministers most qualified for effective leadership in crises are least willing to risk defeat of a program or discord and dissension in their member-ship. They quote another minister:

[1] Quoted in E. Q. Campbell and T. F. Pettigrew, *Christians in Racial Crisis* (Wash-ington, D. C.: Public Affairs Press, 1959), pp. 120-21.

To advance your career in the ministry today you must succeed in an organizational way. You must get for your church a bigger building, more members, and more money. But to do this you have to dilute the gospel enough to secure its appeal for everybody—even sinners. As you advance, then, you must go out of God's favor. It looks like the way up is the way out.[2]

The problem is not limited to ministerial leadership. It is the dilemma of any person who seeks to exercise responsible leadership and to give more than lip service to the ideals to which he is committed. Thus it faces the layman who expresses his vocation in politics, management, the trade union, teaching, the arts, or homemaking. Further, there is an institutional as well as individual dimension to the dilemma. Whenever an organization, religious or political, engages in social action, it faces two alternatives, the idealistic and the organizational. The idealistic alternative involves refusal to compromise, even though potential supporters are lost; it tends toward ineffectiveness and utopianism. The organizational alternative comes to terms with the necessity for supporters and support, even when this means sacrifice or modification of aims. This is peculiarly the Christian dilemma: the sect-type religious group corresponding to the idealistic approach and the church-type group to the organizational alternative. Campbell and Pettigrew follow Troeltsch and Yinger in distinguishing the sect, with its small and disciplined membership living in defiance of the world, from the church, with its larger membership and responsibility, dominating and thus dominated by the world.[3]

1. THE NATURE OF THE DILEMMA

The crucial point of a dilemma is not the matter of choice itself, but rather the situation of choice between unsatisfactory alternatives. The church must be loyal to its goals; but it must also have members, none of whom, clerical or lay, is completely committed to its goals. When a decision is clear-cut between right and wrong, there is no real dilemma. Strategy must deal, not only with dilemmas, but also with meeting crises, with implementing clear-cut choices, and with the normal processes of maintaining an institution. But the critical problem is the unresolved

[2] *Ibid.*, p. 127.
[3] *Ibid.* See the Foreword by Walter G. Muelder. See also pp. 151 ff., below.

choice, the dilemma; for here the challenge of goals in tension with the social situation is most acute and here concrete choices always involve compromise between the idealistic and organizational alternatives.

Gunnar Myrdal, in his classic *An American Dilemma*, builds upon a slightly different definition, "the conflict between . . . moral valuations on various levels of consciousness and generality."

The "American Dilemma" . . . is the ever-raging conflict between, on the one hand, the valuations preserved on the general plane which we shall call the "American Creed" where the American thinks, talks, and acts under the influence of high national and Christian precepts, and, on the other hand, the valuations on specific planes of individual and group living, where personal and local interests; economic, social, and sexual jealousies; considerations of community prestige and conformity; group prejudice against particular persons or types of people; and all sorts of miscellaneous wants, impulses, and habits dominate his outlook.[4]

Myrdal's study is incisive precisely because he highlights the moral tension inherent in the idealistic alternative, the choice between competing conceptions of the good. He insists that the same person holds conflicting valuations, that "the moral struggle goes on within people and not only between them."[5] There is ground for unity despite diversity and for hope that transcends divisions if moral issues do not only separate groups of persons but have their locus within the heart and conscience of individual persons.

This study will be concerned with the moral tension in which there is a clash between more inclusive and more restrictive moral values. In these the judgment should become clear. But this study is also concerned with the larger conflict between the transcendent norms and the possibilities of securing support and influence enough to realize these norms in a resistant social situation.

From this point of view not all dilemmas can or need to be resolved. The norms serve as reminders of points that must be held in tension: transcendent ideals and social power. There is some real virtue in learning to live with the tension, in refusing to settle for "the irrelevance of noble but unimplemented ideas" on the one hand or for "the betrayal

---

[4] Gunnar Myrdal, *An American Dilemma* (New York: Harper & Brothers, 1944), p. xlvii.

[5] *Ibid.*, p. xlviii.

of ideas through accommodation to the world" on the other.[6] Living with this tension is the dilemma not only of ministerial leadership; it is the Christian dilemma, and in it Methodism shares.

A. Dudley Ward writes of a typical letter from a well-educated pastor, complaining sincerely and bitterly that the Dallas Human Relations Conference (1959) and its message "are making it harder to collect the pledges on his church's $80,000 debt, and to go from door to door in evangelistic work seeking new members."[7] This pastor has "found it necessary to explain away the position on human relations of the General Conference, the General Boards, and now the Dallas Conference." Here the tension is relieved by weakening one horn of the dilemma.

But dilemmas are found in other areas than race and human relations. A Massachusetts pastor attempted a discussion of the dangers of continuing tests of nuclear weapons and of the Christian concern for disarmament. The critical response from some members of his congregation reflected not simply a disagreement on principle. These parishioners earned their livelihood in defense plants, and their ability to support a growing church, to say nothing of their families, depended on their employment. And some of them grounded their criticism in a larger issue of survival, survival of "the democratic way of life." Here the pastor faces a conflict between faithfulness to his own understanding of God's will and responsibility to maintain his relationship to people who need the church's ministry. The people also face the moral tension between more inclusive and less inclusive loyalties (concern for all men vs. service to one's nation) and the choice between supporting their families in defense jobs and living in faithfulness to their ministry of reconciliation and peace.

Pressures to conform, to do the acceptable thing, come from within the church ("You want to get ahead in your chosen profession, don't you?") and, more insidiously, from society. Ministers are tempted to preach rousing sermons on safe issues rather than to tackle the primary evils of society.[8] If there is such a thing as a "demonic strategy," it

---

[6] Muelder, "Foreword," in Campbell and Pettigrew, *Christians in Racial Crisis* (Washington, D. C.: Public Affairs Press, 1959).

[7] "An Analysis of a Problem: America and Its Churches," *Contact* (December 15, 1959), p. 5.

[8] See Merrimon Cuninggim, "A Commencement Address," *The Perkins School of Theology Journal* (Spring 1953), pp. 3-9.

surely includes getting Christians to devote their energies to secondary matters.[9] Ministers seem very much aware of one horn of this dilemma, the danger of losing "good churchmen" by dealing with "controversial issues." [10] They do not always seem so aware of the number of former or potential churchmen who are committed to humanitarian action and need desperately the fellowship of the church, but stay outside because they feel the church is preoccupied with trivialities.

The choice faces the seminary student who is a pastor. Presumably his primary task is intellectual and spiritual growth, with the pastorate an opportunity for field experience and, for many, a financial necessity. Occasionally ecclesiastical leaders, concerned to keep "pulpits occupied, the treasuries filled, and the membership growing," counsel the student "to let his studies go so that he may build up his church and keep his name before the church leaders as a promising young pastor." [11] Here the dilemma does not necessarily involve social action but the conflict between intellectual and spiritual integrity and the importance of the "conference ladder."

The Christian dilemma inheres in the tension between the achievement of power and loyalty to purpose. Power[12] may be defined as the discretionary control of resources and the influence over the decisions of persons and groups. Power may be arbitrary or reasonable, coercive or persuasive, manipulative or democratic, but it seems a necessary part of social life. Power conflicts develop as persons seek to exercise influence and as institutions compete for resources to accomplish their goals, or as they overlap in functions. These conflicts exist within as well as outside the church and are faced acutely by ecclesiastical leaders.

Ministers and seminarians and even seminary professors usually think of bishops as having security of tenure (elected for life) and virtually unlimited power and authority. But the bishop has a more explicitly recognized administrative role than a local pastor and he is charged with institutional maintenance and advance. The bishop who has a social

[9] See C. S. Lewis, "Screwtape Proposes a Toast," *The Saturday Evening Post* (December 19, 1959). Screwtape closes his address, "Nowhere do we tempt so successfully as on the very steps of the altar."

[10] A famous *New Yorker* cartoon shows a well-fed cleric in a sumptuous study counseling a neophyte: "If you would seek preferment in our profession, there are two topics you must avoid, religion and politics."

[11] Don Cramer, "The Student . . . and His Church," *The Log*, Perkins School of Theology (January 14, 1960), p. 3.

[12] See pp. 37, 194, 219.

31

passion is acutely aware of the dilemma he shares with his fellow-ministers and of the limitations upon his support of courageous pastors under his supervision. As we will note later, the Methodist connectional system offers in principle splendid protection for the minister who would seek to engage in social action in controversial areas. There have been outstanding cases of such support by connectional leaders. But all too many instances of inadequate support suggest that some bishops and district superintendents either lack power commensurate with their authority or lack sympathy with the pastor who has sought, even though at times without being as wise as a serpent, to stand on principle.

This dimension of the dilemma comes to special focus in a church committed to democratic procedures and lay involvement in church government. The district superintendent in his role as a connectional officer can be frustrated in his attempt to support a minister who has taken a position based on action of the authoritative General Conference but is impeded by lay control over financial affairs of a congregation.[13]

2. THE POWER OF THE LAITY

Earlier volumes in this series have recounted the struggle over the rights of laymen[14] (as in representation in the system of Annual and General Conferences) and the rising concern with the "ministry of the laity." [15] The former growth, in lay rights, reflects the democratic temper of American society and, in part, some aspects of anticlericalism. This is a necessary basis for the development of the ministry of the laity, a concept in which laymen are no longer seen as a "cheering section" for ministers who are doing the real work of the church. Muelder has written of the layman not being "primarily a consuming unit of spiritual goods distributed by the clergyman," but "a productive agent of Christian values." [16] The Protestant belief in the priesthood of all believers means not only equal access to God in prayer without a priestly mediator being required, but also the common responsibility of ministering to one's neighbor.[17] Every Christian is called to be a minister and a missionary where he lives and works, in this sense, with the ordained person a minister to the ministering community.

[13] See Chap. V.
[14] See Vol. I, *Methodism and Society in Historical Perspective*, by Richard M. Cameron.
[15] See Vol. II, *Methodism and Society in the Twentieth Century*, by Walter G. Muelder.
[16] *Ibid.* See also Chap. II, below.
[17] L. Harold DeWolf, *The Case for Theology in Liberal Perspective* (Philadelphia: The Westminster Press, 1959), p. 185.

This becomes a tragic development when the power of the laity is used not to enable but to thwart the expressed purpose of the larger church. This is especially true in the issue of desegregation. Lay associations have been formed for the explicit purpose of "preserving Methodism" from some decisions of its General Conference and for the seeming purpose of penalizing ministers who voiced their accord with General Conference action.[18]

Part, but only a part, of this problem is the lack of communication of church pronouncements among the members. When a Congressional committee was considering renewal of the draft in 1959, an effective testimony based on official actions was being presented by a minister representing The Methodist Church through its Board of World Peace. The testimony was interrupted by a member of the committee who challenged: "I've been a Methodist for forty-one years and I've never heard of this attitude on the part of my church before." Many laymen feel that they never hear from the church except when they are being "promoted" or when their support is sought for a "program." They do not sense that they are being asked to engage in genuine dialogue concerning real issues, to bring their own competence into play on social decisions under the judgment of Christian norms and loyalties. The minister's image of lay resistance may on its reverse side be lay frustration at not being responsibly involved. Both ministers and laymen must take initiative in ending this impasse.

The "power of the laity" is even more crucial outside the institutional life of the church. It is laymen exercising political responsibility who must stand on principle and seek to stay in office in our divided society. Other aspects of dilemmas in economics and education will be explored later.

3. THREE DIMENSIONS OF THE DILEMMA

There are at least three dimensions of the predicament we have been considering. One involves conflicts of judgment concerning which goal is more important or urgent. A second involves the action requirements of achieving a goal, once it is chosen. The third involves disagreement over which office or institution assumes responsibility. The 1960 General Conference debate over the jurisdictional system and the Central Jurisdiction illustrates all three dimensions. There was conflict between the

[18] See pp. 120-21.

explicit goal of achieving racial justice by eliminating the segregated Central Jurisdiction and the often unstated goal of preventing a split into a Northern and a Southern church. The second dimension focused on the method: decisive action by the General Conference or voluntary and permissive action, church by church, annual conference by annual conference. The third dimension related to the role of leadership assumed by the church in relation to society. The General Conference, with frank facing of the conflicts, kept open the dilemma, although it chose temporarily unity over desegregation, permissive over decisive action, and a supportive rather than prophetic role for the church in relation to action by public institutions.

B. The Social Setting of the Dilemmas

1. DIVIDED CHURCH IN A DIVIDED SOCIETY

Methodists are divided by many of the same issues that divide their society. Over 40 per cent of them believe that the federal government in labor legislation should aim primarily at controlling unethical union practices, but almost 30 per cent favor passage of "right to work" laws. Nearly a fourth oppose public power projects such as the TVA. Almost a third take a position on alcoholic beverages other than personal abstinence.[19] Similarly, Methodists find themselves on different sides of the fence regarding abolition of capital punishment, the pace of extending civil rights, and the limits of free speech for Communists, to say nothing of various foreign policy questions.

One such question is of special significance, for men of good faith have had honestly and deeply felt convictions concerning China. Following World War II the question of the admission of Communist China to the United Nations was before one of the boards of the church. A staff person of the Board of World Peace reported to the board that someone in an official government position had asked the board's help in mobilizing public sentiment so that mainland China would be admitted into the forum of world debate.[20] But Methodism's share in Protestantism's financial and ideological investment in the missionary enterprise in China, and the identification with the persons of Generalissimo and Madame Chiang Kai-shek stood in the way of action. Widespread re-

[19] See Appendix B.
[20] Interview with a former officer of the board, 1958.

sistance to dealing responsibly with the problem of the two Chinas continues to plague the nation and the churches.[21]

In 1959-60 Methodists shared in the National Council of Churches' Nationwide Program for Peace. This program was launched with the fifth World Order Study Conference in November 1958. The Conference's "Message to the Churches" dealt with nuclear weapons and disarmament, the cold war and aid to underdeveloped countries, and then, in one paragraph, spoke to the China question:

> With reference to China, Christians should urge reconsideration by our government of its policy in regard to the People's Republic of China. While the rights of the people of Taiwan and of Korea should be safeguarded, steps should be taken toward the inclusion of the People's Republic of China in the United Nations and for its recognition by our government. Such recognition does not imply approval. . . . The exclusion of the effective government on the mainland of China . . . from the international community is in many ways a disadvantage to that community.[22]

In one state there was an episcopal warning to ministers not to relate themselves to the Council of Churches during the year of the Nationwide Program for Peace.

Much of the misunderstanding may have come from failure to distinguish official pronouncements of the General Board from the unofficial findings of a study conference and from lack of familiarity with study conference purposes. On February 25-26, 1959, the General Board of the National Council of Churches first received the Report of the Fifth World Order Study Conference and then dealt with its critics in a declaration of freedom:

> Our nation faces dilemmas, at home and abroad, which are difficult enough to resolve even with the benefit of full and forthright public debate. There is little reason to hope these dilemmas will diminish or disappear in the foreseeable future, or that they will make lesser claims upon our wisdom and fortitude. Accordingly, the right of free discussion becomes ever more essential, not as a private privilege but as a public necessity, and attacks upon it must be vigilantly resisted.
>
> The National Council of Churches reminds the churches that its pro-

[21] See also p. 246.
[22] "Christian Responsibility on a Changing Planet," National Council of Churches, Department of International Affairs, 1959, pp. 22-23.

nouncements, policy statements, and findings of Study Conferences are designed to help our members in the free process of finding the truth and acting upon it. They are not to be interpreted as beyond thoughtful criticism.[23]

The problem of achieving responsible discussion of this vital foreign policy question is a part of the larger social apathy which David Riesman calls "the enemy that doesn't fight back, the lack of debate." [24] Some persons are no longer willing to be identified with action groups. Families which do not drink may provide alcohol for guests rather than provoke an argument. Junior executives sometimes have difficulty securing clearance from headquarters to speak at church-sponsored conferences on industrial relations. Schoolteachers in some sections are advised not to discuss integration.

But when some issues are raised they may call forth vigorous and partisan debate. Methodist Bishop John Wesley Lord, in July 1959, posed questions to be put to a Roman Catholic candidate for public office, including queries on support of the public school system, adherence to the principle of separation of church and state, and participation in public religious services. *The Boston Pilot*, organ of the Roman Catholic archdiocese, replied in an August 1 editorial, "Sauce for the Goose." A Methodist running for high public office should be asked about racial segregation within his church, respect for the rights of others to consume alcoholic beverages, and variance from national policy concerning recognition of Red China.

Although Methodists and Roman Catholics differ on which aspects of the heritage they would emphasize, both are in a sense heirs of a Puritan era and its concern for public morals. Leo Pfeffer points to three differences between the Puritan era and our own which contribute to the dilemmas we face in social action: (1) the Puritan church had no strong secular competitors; (2) none of the competing forces can achieve goals by command but only by persuasion; (3) where once the

[23] Quoted in A *Christian Newsletter on International Affairs* (NCC Department of International Affairs), Vol. 7, No. 1 (February-March 1959).

[24] "Private People and Public Policy," *Bulletin of the Atomic Scientists*, XV, 5 (May 1959), 203-208. Riesman sees "fear of idealism" as another barrier to debate and concludes that now as "we are aware of the strength of irrational forces in man, and are sometimes tempted to try to appeal to those forces when, for instance, we try to scare people into wisdom only to discover, in many cases, that they lack the imagination to be frightened."

church controlled, it must now convince.[25] Methodist leaders are eager for religious influences to find expression in the lives of citizens and statesmen, but their eagerness turns to anxiety when the religious influence has overtones of the institutional authority of a hierarchical church.

Thus Methodism faces a paradoxically divided society, one that is profoundly divided on both institutional loyalties and ultimate convictions in the religious field, but one that is "remarkably homogeneous" [26] in values and social attitudes. Much of the homogeneity may be due to the restriction of debate in our obsession with Communism, to the bureaucratization of American society, and to the distaste for dealing with problems of power as such. The homogeneity may well be a façade to hide deep and publicly unacknowledged differences. To the extent that this is true, with a divided society waiting for the churches to help articulate issues which have been muted or ignored, there is opportunity for social education and action.

2. THE PROBLEM OF POWER [27]

Methodists share with Americans generally a special problem in the responsible use of power. Numerous political commentators have noted our reluctance as a people to face the implications of the United States' emergence as a world power in this century. Some have resisted on principle the extension of power of the federal government, even as a check or "countervailing power" against other concentrations in the economic domain. Few have gone as far as William F. Buckley, Jr.: "I will not cede more power to the state. I will not willingly cede more power to anyone, not to the state, not to General Motors, not to the CIO. I will hoard my power like a miser, resisting every effort to drain it away from me." [28] Such an extreme attitude refuses to accept the necessary corporate expressions of power in the modern complex world and so to use them responsibly.

[25] *Creeds in Competition* (New York: Harper & Brothers, 1958), pp. 6-7.

[26] The phrase comes from Philip E. Jacob's *Changing Values in College* (New York: Harper & Brothers, 1957), pp. 3-7. Jacob describes college students as "gloriously contented," "unabashedly self-centered," cheerful conformists who need religion but not to govern important decisions—"the unconscious ushers of an essentially secular (though nominally religious), self-oriented (though group-conforming) society."

[27] See Chap. VII.

[28] *Up from Liberalism* (New York: McDowell, Obolensky, Inc., 1959), pp. 202-3. See John K. Galbraith, *American Capitalism: The Concept of Countervailing Power* (Boston: Houghton Mifflin, 1952), on the larger issue.

37

If power is the discretionary control of resources and influence over the decisions of persons and groups, then it is an essential ingredient of political life. Most Western theologians have sanctioned the power of the state as "ordained of God." Certainly there is more than one institution to which God has granted power and the crucial issue is responsible rather than arbitrary use of power, whether in church institutions or in secular organizations.

Only by awareness of the problem of power and of our own power can we use it in the service of purposes. Institutional self-consciousness has led many persons to a new awareness of the problem in the church as well as in society. Religious institutions are especially prone to ignore the struggle for power within their own ranks. Methodism's frankly connectional system has its formal power structure more open to view than have many free churches—and therefore more subject to control. New attention must be paid to, and new controls found for, the operation of the informal power structure, such as the selection of key personnel, the assignment of committees, the drawing up of agenda.

Most social science analyses of power have been made of secular institutions rather than churches, and, while these are instructive, they are not always useful from the standpoint of strategy. Analysts often assume that the organization of power is more unified and solid than it may be in fact. The result of this self-fulfilling prophecy is that the centers of power are accepted and so strengthened rather than challenged. One consequence is that, by separating techniques from moral issues, the focus of power encourages manipulation in contrast to education, persuasion, and direct opposition on moral grounds.

For many Protestants the problem of power has centered in the political state. For both historical and theological reasons they have seen the main task to be maintaining freedom from the state, opposing every extension of state power. But Protestants are becoming aware of a changing conception of the democratic state and of the usefulness of state power in counterbalancing other concentrations of power. The questionnaire on "The Beliefs of Methodists" [29] indicates that three-fifths of the Methodists sampled approved public power projects such as the TVA, with fewer than one-fourth directly opposed. Over 70 per cent indicate approval of government action on agricultural surpluses and soil conservation, with almost half of the total favoring price

[29] See Appendix B.

38

stabilization. This is further reflected in the following paragraph on "Responsible use of power" added to the Social Creed in 1960.

The Christian point of view demands that concentrations of power in government, labor, business, and religious organizations be used responsibly. The task of the Church in this regard is to help people in positions of power and the organizations which they serve to achieve and exercise a high level of social responsibility.[30]

3. "PRISONERS OF THE MORE ABUNDANT LIFE"

As we move from an economy of scarcity to one of abundance, we face dilemmas similar to those resulting from our unaccustomed possession of power. We have thought that when we solved the problem of production all would be well.

Our cities rise higher. Our suburbs spread afar. Streams of people move from place to place across the land. Astounding inventions provide abundance of goods, swiftness of communication, miracles of healing, and relief from many burdensome tasks. Opportunities for educational and cultural enrichment are multiplied.

In the midst of this abundance, we are beset by much that is trivial, dehumanizing, and vulgar. Prodigious plenty tempts us to selfish indulgence while millions of people in our land and abroad live in want. Private consumption has reached unprecedented levels while public services on which all of us depend are starved. Concentrations of power, controlling the channels of information, beguile masses of people into unthinking conformity and slavish striving for goods that do not satisfy. Much of our leisure time is devoted to forms of entertainment and escape that dull us to the world's problems and our neighbor's need. We are tempted to love things and use people when we should love people and use things. And even in the midst of crowds our lives are often empty, anxious, and alone.[31]

Edward Heimann is only one of the social analysts who have warned that the "fabulous success" of our economy may have dangerous by-products, tending to lull the critical faculties of even Christian moralists, reducing them "to the always valid insistence on the immeasurable distance between our relatively best achievements and the Kingdom of God." From the perspective of centuries of struggle against scarcity, the

[30] *Doctrines and Discipline of The Methodist Church*, 1960, ¶ 2020.
[31] "Call to Christian Action in Society," adopted by the Second General Synod of the United Church of Christ, July 8, 1959, *Social Action*, XXVI, 1 (September 1959), 7-8.

achievement in production seems a remarkable accomplishment. But Heimann cautions against seeing any achievement as final, needing "nothing but constant watching, repairing, and readjusting in matters of detail." [32] This is a persistent danger of the American pragmatic temper.

The moral problem remains in the elimination of "pockets of persistent maldistribution," which may derive from such noneconomic causes as racial discrimination. There is also the shift from an ethic of production, with its emphasis upon frugality and the discipline of work, to an ethic of consumption, with an economy based in part on installment buying. Persons face constructive use of increasing leisure and at the same time increasing automation of their work. Irresponsible advertising tends "to create unlimited wants, to overemphasize material values and to appeal to motives of social pride, envy, and lust." [33] The increasing number of older citizens in our society raises questions of the adequacy of health services and housing facilities for the aging.[34]

American abundance cannot be treated apart from the population explosion, which may be the chief enemy of the free society in the world today. The countries which are more highly developed face an increase of 64 per cent between 1955 and 2000. But the two thirds of the human race living in underdeveloped areas anticipate an increase of 168 per cent in the same period.[35] "Within the next eleven years China will add as many people to her population as now live in the United States." [36]

The economy of abundance is at least partially dependent upon defense expenditures. Many persons have come to feel a vested interest in the "cold war," since they are not sure we can prevent a depression if peace should come. Several economists have recently indicated the possibility of reconversion from defense to peacetime production without drastic economic dislocations. Military expenditures other than aid to veterans and interest on war debt amount to approximately 10 per cent of our gross national product, and about 5 per cent of our labor force is in the armed forces or in civilian defense work. It is suggested, for

[32] "The Economy of Abundance," *Social Action*, XXIII, 5 (January 1957). See also Chap. III, below.

[33] *Evanston Speaks: Reports of the Second Assembly* (New York: World Council of Churches, 1955), p. 31. See also Heimann, *op. cit.*, pp. 5 ff.

[34] "Churches and the Aging," *Social Action*, XXVI, 5 (January 1960).

[35] "The Population Explosion," *Social Action*, XXV, 4 (December 1958). See also R. M. Fagley, *The Population Explosion and Christian Responsibility* (New York: Oxford University Press, 1960).

[36] *Social Action*, XXVI, 6 (February 1960), 27.

example, that much of this money and personnel could be used to meet the need for more adequate highways, national parks, education, and international development.[37]

4. Rapid Social Change

Modern military preparation with its advances in weaponry represents only one aspect of the technological programs which makes rapid social change a phenomenon not only in underdeveloped countries but even more in countries already industrialized. A report of the World Council of Churches points out that while the Reformation, the Enlightenment, the Industrial Revolution, and the Proletarian Revolution occurred over a four-hundred-year period in European countries, with changes still in progress, in newer lands these revolutions are telescoped and become simultaneous. "In the span of a single lifetime men are forced to grapple with immense unprecedented revolutions, affecting every aspect of national as well as most realms of personal life." [38] The report also points out that the changes occur not only in technology but also in family life, education, standards of living, traditional patterns of authority, and the relations between employers and employees. There is increasing cultural contact as well as the growth of science. The process of scientific discovery is irreversible, it contains an inner dynamic of its own with a built-in accelerator, and its application is ambiguous. If these complex processes were "inert" or "merely neutral; capable of use which had no moral consequences," there would be less urgency. But dynamic forces, ambiguous in moral results, pose "a permanent moral problem for mankind . . . to find ways of bringing [them] under the control of moral purpose." [39]

The most obvious and urgent dilemma is posed by the development

[37] See Albert L. Gray, Jr. and Byron L. Johnson, "If the Arms Race Ends" (Board of World Peace, The Methodist Church, n.d.); Emile Beloit, "Ethical Issues in the Economic Impact of Defense Spending and Disarmament" (National Council of Churches: Department of the Church and Economic Life, August 1960—mimeographed study document); Harrison Brown and James Real, The Community of Fear (Santa Barbara, Calif.: Center for the Study of Democratic Institutions, 1960).

[38] Dilemmas and Opportunities: Christian Action in Rapid Social Change (Geneva, Switzerland: World Council of Churches, 1959), p. 7. Richard La Piere writes: "The difficulty is that we must keep on changing our society . . . at a constantly accelerating rate if we are to keep it going; for a modern industrial society constantly changes the conditions on which it thrives and in order to survive must be dynamic technologically, organizationally, and otherwise. "The Apathetic Ethic," Saturday Review (August 1, 1959), p. 45.

[39] Ibid., p. 18.

41

and testing of weapons of overwhelming destructiveness: "The dread nuclear weapons cannot be used without destroying the moral fabric of the nation. And yet they cannot be simply disavowed without courting surrender." [40] Norman Cousins has urged that twentieth-century man is being "desensitized" by preparation for nuclear war and that natural reactions against violence are being blunted. The individual's moral imagination is dulled and he is relieved of "essential indignation over impersonal hurt . . . is becoming casual about brutality." [41]

Less obvious is the pervasive influence of modern methods of persuasion and communication. "The Invasion of Privacy" [42] may range from wire tapping to insidious manipulating of opinion by pressure groups and may call forth paradoxical responses. It may re-enforce the tendency to define such things as drinking and religion as "purely personal affairs" and so further the distinction between private and public realms which Reinhold Niebuhr calls "particularly unfortunate in a democratic society in which every private citizen has public responsibilities." [43] David Riesman notes the temptation of "noncomplacent minorities," whether pacifist or interventionist, "to move people by arguments in which they do not really believe in order to achieve ends in which they do believe." Since Americans are hard to move by good or bad arguments, "there is always the terrible temptation to move them by events." [44]

5. URBANIZATION AND BUREAUCRACY

Improvement of communication and transportation has made possible our urbanized society. More and more people move into the heterogeneous city and then, continuing on the move, with one fifth of our people changing residence each year, drift outward into suburbs where neighbors are typically of the same class and color. City-dwellers depend less upon the whims of nature and seem oblivious to new perils of conservation of natural resources, such as the pollution of streams and

---

[40] Reinhold Niebuhr, "The Problem of a Protestant Social Ethic," *Union Seminary Quarterly Review*, XV, 1 (November 1959), 8.

[41] "The Desensitization of Twentieth Century Man," *Saturday Review* (May 16, 1959), p. 32.

[42] See two articles in *The American Scholar* (Autumn 1958, and Winter 1958-59).

[43] *Op. cit.*, 4. Professor C. Northcote Parkinson raises the question of whether new technical developments make democracy incapable of expanding or even existing in the modern world. See "Can Democracy Survive?" *The Saturday Evening Post* (February 6, 1960), pp. 38 ff.

[44] "Private People and Public Policy," p. 207.

the rapidly dwindling water supply. Methodist work faces special problems in the city, where its gains in membership in the working classes do not keep up with general population gains.[45]

But the larger issue is not the movement of people to the cities but the increasing urbanization of all life, as newspapers, television, and access to educational opportunities wipe out many of the differences between urban and rural ways of life. The Methodist Church, like many other Protestant churches, has its basic orientation in rural life.

Hand in hand with urbanization and industrialization has gone the process of bureaucratization, seemingly necessary in a large and complex society. This process involves the management of organizations, public and private, "by the book," by rules that are set up according to a rational purpose. It operates with a hierarchical order of professional, trained specialists, who are advanced according to seniority and performance. Bureaucracy is evident in the government, the economic system, education, and even in the church. In the last it may mean the widening of the gap between the minister, who acts like an official, and his flock, who may be treated more like clients than like sheep. Norman Washburne notes that "bureaucracy carries with it penalties in the form of a growing unwillingness to innovate or to tamper with what has become established routine. [It] nearly always implies standardization, rigidity, and often mediocrity."[46] This, along with the production of what Robert M. Hutchins calls "interchangeable men,"[47] poses special problems for a strategy of social action.

C. The Church and Society

1. ACCEPTANCE OF RESPONSIBILITY

In the study of "The Beliefs of Methodists,"[48] 7.6 per cent of the respondents indicated that "social change is no responsibility of the church, since if individuals are soundly converted social problems will take care of themselves." Forty per cent saw social change as "a partial responsibility, but secondary to the transformation of individuals."

[45] See Walter G. Muelder, *Methodism and Society in the Twentieth Century*, Ch. XX, for discussion of the movement of Negroes to the city and the resulting challenge to churches.

[46] *Interpreting Social Change in America* (New York: Random House, 1954), p. 47. See also p. 42.

[47] Interchangeable men bear the uniform stamp of a common imprint and lack individuality.

[48] See Appendixes B and C.

Forty-six per cent agreed that it is of equal or greater importance than individual conversion. Of those who think social change is no responsibility of the church, almost twice as many (44.7 per cent as opposed to 24.8 per cent) are in favor of the segregation of races, for whatever reason, as is the total population of Methodism. Almost 80 per cent of Methodists claim direct guidance of conduct from religious beliefs or guidance on the basis of moral principles in reference to the drinking of intoxicants. But only 63 per cent of them check a position on temperance in accord with the traditional Methodist teaching. Over 55 per cent claim either direct guidance or guidance from moral principles as to whether to participate in war. But almost half feel "obligated to support my country in war when its continued existence is at stake, *apart from considerations of justice.*" [49] Over two thirds of Methodists support a free pulpit, believing that their minister "should be free to take on controversial issues any position which he regards as Christian."

Such a confused, but certainly not hopeless, picture suggests how deeply Methodists are involved in the dilemmas of responsible social action. They are more and more aware of the ways in which personal decisions are influenced by group loyalties and group norms, yet in a religious frame of reference they rely mainly upon individual conversion. Methodists, traditionally fearful of state power, have in the case of prohibition been willing to call for drastic action on the part of government; but they have typically been less willing to use legal means to deal with problems of racial discrimination. Methodists have found it very difficult to train persons in disciplined abstinence from the use of alcoholic beverages and at the same time to help them to have genuine compassion for the alcoholic. The image of Methodism in the nation's capital has often in the past been that of concern with prohibition to the exclusion of other interests. Just so in the church there has been a pacifist image of the Board of World Peace. This may have been due to the pacifist orientation of its leaders, to its opposition to war and conscription or to its war-time concern with conscientious objectors. The lack of a coherent social strategy reflected in education and action has led to unfortunate images both inside and outside the church. The united Board of Christian Social Concerns established by the 1960 General Conference offers hope for such a strategy.

[49] Italics not in original questionnaire.

The current absence of a coherent social strategy is furthered by the goals of particular individuals and groups. Some Methodists lament their church "lagging behind" secular institutions in achieving racial justice. The authors of this study join this lament, but they are constrained to remember that the goal of a desegregated church in a desegregated society comes to local focus as a specific church tries to provide an inclusive fellowship in a community with few or no Negro residents.[50] There is at least a sense in which the church can deal adequately with its internal problem only by coming to grips with the problem in society.

There are other Methodists who call for a strategy to make this a "Christian nation." These would seem to agree with John Courtney Murray that "Religious pluralism is against the will of God," although he adds, "it is written into the script of history." [51] Reinhold Niebuhr takes issue with Father Murray, insisting that peace and creativity in community life require cultural pluralism, and that "cultures in which there is no secular criticism of historic religions become moribund." [52] Participants in a World Council of Churches study conference on rapid social change agree:

Christians and non-Christians belong together in their communities and face the same necessities of life. They often share common goals and concern for the same values. Frequently sensitivity to the same human values is a consequence of Christian influence on the culture but this is not the only factor. Such shared goals and values have other sources in human experience under the providence of God. The problem is that the significance of such co-operation is only rarely considered and is often given in a grudging or patronizing spirit. Co-operation . . . should be governed by respect for them as persons, respect for the sincere conviction and integrity of spirit that we find in them. Christians can learn from them, not only because they may have special knowledge and experience for which Christian insight is no substitute, but also because Christians can often be corrected by the response of outsiders to their ways of understanding and implementing their faith.[53]

[50] See Chap. X.
[51] "America's Four Conspiracies," in Religion in America, ed. John Cogley (New York: Meridian Books, Inc., 1958), p. 40. Father Murray urges that we can "limit the warfare" and "enlarge the dialogue."
[52] "A Note on Pluralism," Religion in America, p. 44.
[53] Dilemmas and Opportunities, p. 48.

Thus, as Methodists come to realization of their collective rather than individual responsibility for social action, they must face the necessity for exercising this responsibility in a divided and pluralistic society.

2. FREEDOM FROM ILLUSIONS

In 1937 J. H. Oldham wrote: "The churches will accomplish their purposes in proportion as they are free from illusions regarding the ability of the church to mold the economic, political, and international life of our time." [54] Volume II in this series has sought to analyze the interaction of Methodism and American society in the twentieth century.[55] It concludes that The Methodist Church "has made a significant transition from the individualistic evangelism of the nineteenth century to the inclusive personal and social evangelism of the present." Obviously the transition is not complete. The church finds itself in the world, participating in the sin of society and in the saving power of God. This conclusion is set against the background of the development of social Christianity, understood as a movement belonging to the churches rather than to the radical social revolt of the sects. Methodism has retained some of its sectlike qualities as it has become more churchlike. Its growth of social concern is in part a churchlike recognition of and response to changes already partly accomplished by secular forces. The church did follow behind the action of labor unions and of "cause" organizations, and often only a minority followed at all. But Muelder argues that its response to challenges has steadily grown, that what was begun as an unofficial Methodist Federation for Social Service in 1907 has become a major aspect of the life of the church. He does not think it helpful to try to sort out in general the influence of Methodism upon society except as a part of a broader movement. At times Methodist agencies and leaders have initiated action, at times supported, rejected, or adapted the efforts of others.

In seeking to understand the Methodist response, one must see the church not only in a sociological perspective but also as it "stands under a divinely ultimate judgment and within a divinely ultimate mercy." Methodism has all the limitations and possibilities of a social institution, but its hope is that within the worship of the church men

[54] W. A. Visser 't Hooft and J. H. Oldham, *The Church and Its Function in Society* (New York: Harper & Brothers, 1937), p. 100.
[55] This material is drawn from Walter G. Muelder, *Methodism and Society in the Twentieth Century,* Ch. XX.

"experience a vision of God . . . are transformed into a community of love, and . . . are sent out into the world as a community of service." [56]

3. THEOLOGICAL PERSPECTIVE

Theology today, in the opinion of H. Richard Niebuhr, "is not simply an affair of translating ancient ideas into modern language, but of wrestling with ultimate problems as they arise in contemporary forms." [57] In the third volume of this series, S. Paul Schilling treats *Methodism and Society in Theological Perspective* in just this way, noting shifts in the theological climate within and surrounding Methodism and in ethical guide-lines for strategy as the church has wrestled with social issues. Existentialism, which stresses involvement and decision rather than reflection, and which has its own diagnosis of the ills of our society, has been especially critical of "Methodist moralism." [58] There has been a changing conception of what is possible in terms of redeeming social institutions, as well as of the basic relevance of religion to economic and political issues (defined as "technical" problems).

Some aspects of these changes are seen as a shift from social ideals to norms for guidance.[59] Methodism has at times tended to codify its ideals and to define the ethical life in terms of conformity to specific injunctions. Many Methodists are now going beyond acceptance of a code to consider together the basis of ethical judgment, the range of application, and the means of persuasion used to secure consensus. The ethical judgments must be concerned with the possibilities of the growth of persons, the achievement of a responsible society, and the adequate functioning of religious institutions. Significant changes have taken place in the conception of the church. One aspect lies in the shift from the idea of the church as ministering to its members to that of a fellowship of ministry to a needy world.

4. SALVATION: INDIVIDUAL AND SOCIAL[60]

A Methodist social ethic centers in grateful response to the redemptive love of God and issues in trust, love, and obedience. Salvation involves

[56] Muelder, *Methodism and Society in the Twentieth Century*, p. 387. See Chap. II, below.
[57] *The Purpose of the Church and Its Ministry* (New York: Harper & Brothers, 1956), p. 3.
[58] See p. 60.
[59] Robert Handy, "From 'Social Ideals' to 'Norms for Guidance'," *Christianity and Crisis*, XIV, 24 (January 24, 1955), 187-91.
[60] See S. Paul Schilling, *Methodism and Society in Theological Perspective*, pp. 197-210 ff.

both personal regeneration and social transformation, in what should be a continuing and growing experience. God's action initiates salvation but fulfillment depends upon man's faithful response. The social dimension is inevitable, because men are saved not in isolation but in the community of the church and through the church fulfilling its mission in society. Men are persons-in-community and their group relations and institutions stand in need of redemption. This social theology of salvation is true to the deepest meaning of the gospel, develops major emphases of the Wesleyan tradition, and serves as an integrating center for ecumenical thought.

When Methodism was a small sectarian movement, it could well afford to focus its strategy in the ethical discipline of its members' lives. This need for ethical discipline thoroughly grounded in devotional practices continues. But Methodism is no longer a sect, and the world in which Methodists live and vote and work and play is increasingly baffling and complex. It is no accident that Methodism has realized that it must become aware of itself and of its social context.

Methodists no longer live in a homogeneous, predominantly rural, largely Protestant, directly governed society. We live this side of the industrial revolution,[61] with people moving rapidly into the cities and more rapidly out into the suburbs. We live with religious pluralism and cultural heterogeneity. Representative government assumes a larger role in our lives to offset and control other forces. Our country is no longer isolated but must make all its decisions in the light of conflicts between nations. Social and moral codes are not shaped by a Puritan ethos alone; there are secular forces bent on shaping society to their own interests or value judgments—the liquor industry, the medical profession, labor unions, associations of businessmen, organized minority groups, publishers, political parties, and so on. In such a world, with change so rapid and mistakes so costly, Methodists need guidance concerning their roles as citizens, workers, parents, and concerning their action through

[61] Cameron P. Hall has observed that it is not a coincidence that the modern missionary movement and the industrial revolution struck full stride at the same time. The eyes of some churchmen became fixed on paganism abroad. See *The Younger Churchmen Look at the Church*, ed. Ralph H. Read (New York: The Macmillan Co., 1935), p. 46. Since that time we have come to a new understanding of an inclusive mission of the church, ministering to persons in need and sin wherever they live.

the church. Methodists, like other Protestants, need to learn how to exercise power responsibly and to face ethical problems corporately.

In 1935 John C. Bennett discussed salvation as "a condition of the lives of persons in all their relationships which is directly experienced in this world." He pointed to three half-truths which had wide currency in that decade and which still hold much of Protestantism to an individual ethic:

I. The claim that individuals can rise above any conceivable combination of social circumstances and that therefore it is misplaced zeal to become deeply concerned about changing those circumstances.

II. The assumption that since individuals control institutions and social systems the strategy of Christians should be confined to the task of creating a new heart in as many of those individuals as possible.

III. The belief that it is possible to change society without at the same time making a direct attempt to change individuals.[62]

Each of these is a half-truth rather than a complete error. Bennett pointed to the effects of poverty, wealth, great power, war, and greed, suggesting that only the spiritually developed person can rise above circumstances. The second half-truth fails to recognize that individuals are seldom changed in directions relevant to social situations and that institutionalized evil requires an organized attack. The third half-truth fails to come to terms with the roots of evil in human nature; Bennett argued that a changed system could provide better opportunities for self-realization.[63]

Some Christians who have seen reliance upon an individual ethic as inadequate have turned to communitarian experiments. Such an experiment may be a work-study-residential community such as the Brook Farm in early New England or Koinonia in today's Georgia. In terms of institutional religion the church is interpreted as a gathered community, withdrawn from the world in order to achieve purity and wholeness of life, but also in close relationship to the world so that the example of holiness may serve as a model for the world.[64] One difficulty

[62] John C. Bennett, *Social Salvation* (New York: Charles Scribner's Sons, 1935), p. 44.
[63] *Ibid.*, pp. 45-61. See also Margaret Mead, "Christian Faith and Technical Assistance," *Christianity and Crisis*, XIV, 23 (January 10, 1955), 179-82.
[64] Such groups as the Mennonites have held this position, although there are sectarian tendencies in much Methodist history, especially in the early societies. See, for example, Guy F. Hershberger, *The Way of the Cross in Human Relations* (Scottdale, Pa.: Herald Press, 1958), for a recent presentation.

of such a strategy is the temptation to preoccupation with the life of the group and loss of contact with the world. J. Milton Yinger has argued that the religious group must to some extent accommodate to society and must accept responsibility for the larger society if it is to have real influence.[65]

The social gospel movement in American Protestantism, in which Methodism has played a responsible role, sought to move beyond strategies for changing individuals and for making the church a "colony of heaven," although there was continuing concern with regeneration of persons and with renewal of the life of the church. This movement brought ethical demands to bear upon institutions, urging that the Kingdom ideal required Christianizing the state, economic institutions, the family, education, international relations, and so forth. The social gospel recognized the force of environment and social conditioning in determining character. Its context was a world in which awareness of the evils of urbanization and industrialization was leading people to expect radical social changes. It was increasingly sensitive to the viewpoints of oppressed classes and races, especially during the Depression and the racism of World War II.[66]

5. DENOMINATIONAL LOYALTIES AND ECUMENICAL MISSION

The social gospel movement also brought a new awareness of the institutional life of the church and contributed to the growth of the ecumenical movement. Wrestling with problems of society and of church unity brought the church from the periphery into the center of attention as both a social institution and a theological institution. On the one hand was a realization of the responsibility of a large and powerful institution not only in terms of resources and members but also of representatives in positions of influence.

Methodism shares in the emerging ecumenical consensus which takes the church into account as a social institution with resources and responsibilities for dealing with its own problems and with the institutional problems of the society in which it lives. The authors of the

[65] See J. Milton Yinger, *Religion in the Struggle for Power* (Durham: Duke University Press, 1946). See especially pp. 32-33 for a brief discussion of Methodism's change from a sect to a church.

[66] See John C. Bennett, *Christian Ethics and Social Policy* (New York: Charles Scribner's Sons, 1946), pp. 1-14.

Oxford Conference volume, *The Church and Its Function in Society,* wrote in 1937:

There is widespread agreement that, whatever limitations there may be on the action of the church as an organized society, Christians must give expression to their faith not only in what one may call the prepolitical sphere of the aims, standards and values that determine political action, but also in the field of concrete political decision and political struggle. To doubt this would be to deny the sovereignty of God over the whole of life and to surrender large areas of life to the unfettered control of the forces of evil.[67]

Arthur Holt once made a crucial distinction which is still applicable: "The modern church is working at the task of being influential in a social order which it does not desire to manipulate, but for which it feels a moral responsibility.[68]

There are, of course, obstacles to the ecumenical consensus, especially in relation to social action. One such obstacle is the very success of denominational programs. In our age religion is a popular movement. "All of us are doing so well in our various strings of service stations," as James A. Pike puts it,[69] that we feel no sense of urgency in achieving unity or even in working together. Truman B. Douglass cites a related obstacle:

Every minister is under more pressure to receive ten new members of his church than to make certain that ten old members who have moved to new places have formed association with some church in their new home. This may very well be, in a majority of instances, a church of some other communion—which will not help denominational statistics one whit. Yet the real task of evangelism and renewal in our time probably depends more upon the ability of the Church to follow its ever-moving members with a real sense of pastoral care than upon the relatively easy job of recruiting new members.[70]

Mobility is only one issue that blurs the traditional conception of

[67] Visser 't Hooft and Oldham, pp. 199-200.
[68] Quoted in Harold A. Bosley, *Preaching on Controversial Issues* (New York: Harper & Brothers, 1952), p. 176.
[69] "That They May Be One," *The Christian Century,* LXXVII, 2 (January 13, 1960), 47.
[70] "The Relevance of Long-Range Planning to the Task of the Church," mimeographed address to a National Council of Churches consultation, November 1959.

the parish in both a geographical and a denominational sense. M. Moran Weston, in a study of Episcopal social action, has indicated that in the "Good Samaritan" stage of development, service to individuals is pastoral in nature and so parochial.[71] But in an urban and industrial society work is done mainly away from the home and the neighborhood, and the church must somehow learn to minister to the needs of people who spend their working day (or night) outside the local parish.[72] A rapidly rising proportion of college-age persons are in colleges and universities and ministers must learn to work with more highly educated congregations. The tremendous increase in college population will largely be felt in urban universities and community colleges, with more and more students commuting to their studies. Truman Douglass insists that the minimal meaning of this educational "revolution is that the mission to the college and university, which for most denominations has been peripheral and optional, must become central and mandatory." [73] And in whose parish will commuting students be ministered to—the home community where educational issues are not crucial or the educational community which is in many ways neither a campus nor a community? Alvin Denman suggests one campus approach that may have wider applicability when he writes of "the chaplain as having denominational authorization but an ecumenical mission." [74]

Perhaps none of the fundamental ministries of the church can be directed any longer by isolated denominational strategy or supported by appeal only to denominational loyalties. Certainly each denomination must set its strategy in relation to an ecumenical strategy. Together the churches must face challenges to civil liberties and the stifling of discussion of controversial issues. Divisions of churches along economic and cultural lines can partly be overcome by participation in the larger church that transcends these lines. The inclusiveness of the ecumenical movement makes consensus on concrete social issues difficult, but it

[71] "Social Policy of the Episcopal Church in the Twentieth Century," unpublished study, 1951, p. 65.

[72] Dilemmas and Opportunities, p. 102.

[73] "The Relevance of Long-Range Planning to the Task of the Church."

[74] "Standing Between—The Role of the College Chaplain," Nexus, III, 1 (Boston University School of Theology, November, 1959), 11. See other articles in this issue and also, Higher Education in a Decade of Decision (American Council on Education, 1957), and Max Wise, They Come for the Best of Reasons (American Council on Education, 1958).

also provides correction for the blind spots of each denomination.[75] Muelder concludes: "As a denomination with a world-wide membership and an inclusive mission, The Methodist Church cannot afford in theory or in practice to take a view less than truly ecumenical." [76]

Just as Methodism has learned that it cannot face its social task alone, so it knows that it cannot deal with any social issue in isolation, but only as part of a larger complex of interrelated problems. We no longer think we can settle an issue and leave it alone, but realize that problems persist, though in new and different forms. Some issues once seen as regional, such as the "race problem" belonging to the South and urbanization to the North, are now at least national in scope. The focus of concern has shifted over the years from economic problems to political issues.[77] Social action continues to be pragmatic and flexible, although it is more sensitive to theological issues and is concerned with a more penetrating criticism of society. During half a century Methodism has brought into existence a structure of boards and agencies focusing upon social relations.[78]

Emerging patterns point to a recognized need for strategic planning and action, for a new philosophy of administration and leadership, for consolidation of functions and probably for new institutional forms. Methodists by and large are ready to go further in social action than the church has yet moved, or than they themselves realize they are ready to go. On many issues there is not the gap between clergy and laity so often suggested, nor are Methodist conservatives so far to the right as might be expected.[79] Recognition of these trends may shift the burden of proof to those who oppose social action, rather than resting as it does upon those who think that change is necessary, possible, or desirable. Methodism would seem to be ready to pool its ethical heritage and institutional resources in a new concern for strategy in social education and action.

[75] John C. Bennett, "Christianity in Civic and Political Life," mimeographed document for the National Council of Churches, Division of Christian Life and Work, 1956.

[76] *Methodism and Society in the Twentieth Century*, p. 334.

[77] John C. Bennett, *Christians and the State* (New York: Charles Scribner's Sons, 1958), p. xv. The "Beliefs of Methodists" study shows that, while four fifths of Methodists vote regularly (slightly more in national elections), only one sixth participate regularly in nonchurch organizations concerned with social problems on the national level and one third in such organizations in the local community. Material in the next paragraph refers to this study.

[78] See Muelder, *Methodism and Society in the Twentieth Century*. Ch. X.

[79] See Appendix B.

6. THE DILEMMA RESTATED

This chapter began by confronting specific dilemmas of Christian leadership and social action. It is within the framework of such dilemmas that strategy must be devised and carried out. We have seen that Methodism shares in the basic problem and dilemma of all social movements. The problem is gaining sufficient power to influence decisions without surrendering the principles and purposes for which the power has been sought. The dilemma is that a church can maintain the purity of its principles, refuse to compromise, and so cut itself off from potential members and the society it would influence, or it can so compromise its principles in the attempt to build membership and influence that the distinctiveness of its witness is lost.

There have been three major proposals for dealing with the dilemma. The first is the continuing effort to root social objectives and methods in a fundamental understanding of the Christian faith to help prevent the church being merely a reflection of its culture.[80] The second is the continuing effort to face each social problem in the context of inter-related issues and of rapid social change. The third proposal is that responsible participation in the ecumenical movement can contribute to the enrichment of Methodist social witness and correct its blind spots. Other proposals will be considered in terms of the specific resources for and obstacles to change within Methodism and of the requirements of strategy itself.

J. Milton Yinger concludes that awareness of the dilemma itself is one resource for dealing with it:

Religious influence on the course of social change will be greatest when the strategic decisions of religious individuals are made with clearest recognition of "the dilemma of the churches," when prophetic or charismatic leadership is most abundant, when religious institutions are most effectively autonomous from the secular institutions of power.[81]

The pages which follow will continue to take serious account of the dilemma of the church. There is an underlying assumption of the effective autonomy of religious institutions in contemporary American society. We will focus attention upon the problem of cultivating,

[80] See Schilling, *Methodism and Society in Theological Perspective*, pp. 197-98.
[81] *Religion, Society and the Individual* (New York: The Macmillan Co., 1957), p. 307.

disciplining, liberating, and supporting prophetic ministerial and lay leadership. These will be persons who can combine integrity and social passion with the ability to work in the structure and program of a bureaucratized church. There is no inherent reason why Methodism cannot accept both the necessity of bureaucracy and the prophetic tension and conflict equally essential to its task. We turn now to consider the theological goals which illumine the social problems and make of them a challenge to social action.

CHAPTER TWO

Theological and Ethical Guidelines for Strategy

A. Changing Ethical Perspectives

ETHICAL PERSPECTIVES CHANGE NOT ONLY FROM THEIR OWN inner development, but also in response to new situations and to shifts in theological climate. The changes that took place in the social gospel movement in the era from Walter Rauschenbusch to Reinhold Niebuhr reflected not only different theological insights and emphases but also global changes in economics and politics.[1] Observers have variously sought the clue to the cutting of the nerve of social action in the new mood of theological pessimism [2] and in the complacency and comfort of our own relatively isolated existence. S. Paul Schilling has traced within Methodism in the twentieth century a greater concern with theological issues, a search to relate social thought to religious beliefs, a new emphasis on the sovereignty of God and the sinfulness of man. Some would, on the basis of principle, separate theological depth and social concern. For example, a critic writes in *Christianity Today:* "Perhaps because of this lack of theological training and interest, Methodism so easily turned to schemes of world betterment and social uplift as a substitute for the declining evangelistic urge." [3]

[1] See *Methodism and Society in Theological Perspective* for a complete treatment. See also James Gustafson, "Christian Ethics and Social Policy," in Paul Ramsey (ed.), *Faith and Ethics* (New York: Harper & Brothers, 1957), p. 122. See Chap. III for an analysis of changing problems.

[2] See the "Message to The Methodist Church from the Council of Bishops," April 10, 1958, charging Neo-orthodoxy with defeatism and inactivity.

[3] R. P. Marshall, "Trends in Modern Methodism," *Christianity Today,* IV, 7 (January 4, 1960), 11.

Other critics pose the question as between an ethic of principles and one of inspiration or faith:

Does the Christian have positive spiritual principles to give him the answers to public problems; or is he rather given in faith a personal purpose for wholeheartedly participating in political situations in a search for answers— answers which are certainly aided by reference to the history of principles and virtues which have been a part of the Christian life but which can still come only out of acceptance of responsible participation in public life? [4]

The problem of an adequate social ethic reflects social conditions (the loss of causes, the therapeutic mood, the complexity of issues) and also such theological emphases as the realistic appraisal of human sinfulness, the revolt against moralism, the questioning of philosophical ethics, and the awareness of involvement in, rather than detachment from, social evils.

1. LOSS OF SHINING CAUSES

In the early days of the social gospel emphasis, problems stood out in bold relief, issues seemed to be clear, and crusades seemed more in order. We have experienced disillusionment about "shining social causes," and solutions no longer seem so clear-cut and assured of success. The "war to end war" [5] turned out to be the prologue to more devastating conflicts, and the "rights of labor" incite less moral fervor when a strike can cripple a nation than when workers were still struggling to establish the right to organize. It is not that issues are settled or that there are no more problems; it is rather that causes are no longer so clear and shining.[6] Some problems have been solved, at least in terms of the way they were seen in 1910. We are aware of new dimensions, increasing complexity, and greater urgency.[7] In this process we have become less sure that we can identify the "devils" against whom we fight.

The other side of this aspect of the changing ethical scene is that we

[4] Kenneth Underwood, "The Social Responsibility of the American Politician." (To be published.)
[5] This was not a social gospel "cause" and some leaders were critical of American participation.
[6] For many, the sit-in demonstrations of 1960 provided a "shining cause."
[7] See Chap. III for identification of present problems.

now have an all-encompassing devil upon whom we can blame all our ills! A current Civil Defense pamphlet argues in this vein.

Civil defense has a moral foundation in that all our trouble stems from the presence in the world of an atheistic, materialistic philosophy which is out to conquer the world and to destroy all other forms of government. This is a moral issue and there is no agency better than the church in our way of life to effectively deal with this issue.[8]

Such a definition of the global conflict not only desensitizes us to moral issues *within* our society, but it tends to make criticism of social evils almost the same as treason, in so far as the criticism is similar to Soviet criticism or is supposed to divide the nation and weaken our defenses.

William Lee Miller notes American preference for either a crusade or complete noninvolvement and reminds us that we can no longer have either of these.[9] Some persons argue that Methodist thought is clear on the issue of alcoholic beverages, but recent studies indicate a real difference of opinion (or at least of practice). Others hold that there is no general disagreement over the rights of minorities, but it is precisely in the spelling out of these rights in schools, lunch counters, and churches that we are most divided as a people. We do lack shining causes—or sufficient will to do something about those causes we have.

2. THE THERAPEUTIC MOOD

Another element in changing ethical perspectives is what might be called "the therapeutic mood." This mood is probably not wholly the result of Freudian psychoanalysis, but certainly the two re-enforce each other in creating what Richard LaPiere calls "The Apathetic Ethic."[10] LaPiere says that, to Freud, men are not villains or heroes but neurotics, not to be praised or blamed but accepted and understood and treated. The ethic is one of adaptation, bordering on irresponsibility, and willing-

---

[8] *The Religious Affairs Service*, Office of Civilian Defense Mobilization. See the brilliant critique by Harold J. Berman, "The Devil and Soviet Russia," *The American Scholar* (Spring, 1958).

[9] "Religion and Responsibility," *Worldview*, 2, 10 (October, 1959), 4. See John C. Bennett, "Faith and Responsibility," *The Christian Century*, LXXV, 49 (Dec. 3, 1958), 1394-97.

[10] See *Saturday Review* (August 1, 1959), pp. 40-45. It is only fair to note revisions of the theory in such works as Erich Fromm, *The Sane Society* (New York: Rinehart, 1955) and Lawrence K. Frank, *Society as the Patient* (New Brunswick: Rutgers University Press, 1948).

ness to interpret social criticism as the expression of hostility. The mood is one of seeking "security" in a permissive environment, assurance that there must be a "cause" somewhere in the patient's past that is the seat of trouble. Social science determinism, attempting causal explanations of behavior in such factors as social class, also contributes to explicit and implicit denials of human freedom—and consequent loss of a sense of responsibility. Psychological determinism is invoked and prejudice is explained in terms of "the authoritarian personality," with patterns fixed in childhood. Many ministers find an increased demand for counseling with some persons hoping, consciously or unconsciously, that their difficulties can be attributed to factors beyond their conscious control. Thus it will not be necessary to confess and repent. Whatever its complex social origins, in theory or in crisis, the therapeutic mood is a challenge to responsible social action and to critical ethical reflection.

3. COMPLEXITY OF ISSUES

A third dimension of perplexity concerning ethics takes its forms in the complexity of issues facing the person today. At one pole this involves application of the Marxist theory of socialization of production to the whole realm of human action. Marx argued that with the shift from handicraft to mass industrial processes, no laborer could identify the product of his own effort, all labor being inextricably intermixed. So it is with personal responsibility in a huge, interconnected, and depersonalized society, say the critics; and the individual disclaims his responsibility other than as an agent of the corporation or state. At the other pole this stresses "technical competence" in economics, politics, city administration, military affairs, and so forth, with theological and ethical concern separate and remote from the real issues and with nontechnical responsibility diminished.[11]

4. REALISM AND HUMAN SINFULNESS

The stress upon realism and human sinfulness must be taken into account also in the changing ethical perspective. "Realistic" ethics stresses both the importance of technical competence and the depth of human sinfulness. Especially since the publication of Reinhold Nie-

[11] A hopeful sign is that leaders occupying strategic decision-making positions are becoming aware of ethical issues. See, for example, Paul H. Nitze, The Recovery of Ethics (New York: The Church Peace Union, 1960).

buhr's *Moral Man and Immoral Society* in 1932, the emphasis has been on the sinfulness and immorality of human groups, which inevitably transmutes the individual altruism and morality of the members into group egoism. In 1959 Niebuhr continued to assert that "the Christian message of grace is more directly relevant to individuals in their sins and sorrows, their hopes and frustrations, than it is to nations and civilizations in the throes of earth-shaking revolutions." [12] There is thus a tendency to accept a double or dual morality, with a more rigorous personal standard and a less rigorous one for organized groups from the family and trade union to the nations and their alliances. It is obvious that this tendency leaves the decisions of groups to be made more in terms of calculation of consequences, less in terms of a transcendent frame of reference. That this leaves the interest of any group unchallenged by a more inclusive interest and tends to sanction the existing state of affairs should also be obvious.

5. REVOLT AGAINST MORALISM

The revolt against moralism is a crucial aspect of the changing ethical perspective. Moralism is usually identified as legalism, casuistry, the reliance upon codified and predictable ethical judgments. The revolt is often extended to include reaction against natural law concepts or against emphasis upon the human freedom of the moral will. Joseph Sittler defines moralism as "longing for ethical clarity, unambiguous moral demands as divinely accredited in quasi-legal form: a built-in longing to get rid of the indeterminable and imperial requirements of faith active in love." He sees a continuing threat in efforts "to transform the flexibility of faithful obedience into the rigidities of law." [13] Here the stress is upon conformity to social mores as equivalent to the moral life. Some moralists lack proportion in judgments, overlook the fact that the sources of self-discipline are gifts of grace, and ignore the destructiveness of self-righteousness.[14] There is special indignation against "middle class

[12] "The Test of the Christian Faith Today," *The Christian Century*, LXXVI, 43 (October 28, 1959), 1239-43. See the criticism of double morality in W. E. Hocking, *Strength of Men and Nations* (New York: Harper & Brothers, 1959), pp. 70 ff.

[13] "Some Concepts of the Church and the Division of Life and Work," mimeographed. Thomas O'Dea describes moralism as the "tendency to see the world as devoid of ontological value and spiritual significance but instead to regard it almost exclusively as a place of moral danger to the Christian soul." *American Catholic Dilemma* (New York: Sheed and Ward, 1958), p. 160.

[14] John C. Bennett, "Morality and Moralism," *Union Seminary Quarterly Review*, XI, 4 (May 1956), 39-40.

moralism" and its stress upon ambition, individual responsibility, achievement, planning ahead, respect for property, and good manners.[15] We will note later that identification with a class may not be an adequate criterion for dismissing moral values. But we should here note the danger to the church when, in the name of middle-class morals, it seeks to protect its fellowship from corruption by "rotten apples," and so forfeits its opportunity to be a redemptive community. Moralism may also be interpreted, not as a response of individuals alone, but as the posture of a church. Some denominations once had the prerogative of dictating the morals of a community. Even in today's pluralistic society these groups are tempted to act as if they spoke for the community. The question here becomes that of who is speaking, in whose name and to what audience is the message addressed.[16]

6. AN ETHIC OF FAITH

Another dimension of the shift in ethical thought is seen in the quest for an ethic of faith, whether defined as one of inspiration or as a situational ethic. J. H. Oldham set such an ethic of inspiration over against an ethic of ends or purposes to be realized. Its primary concern is with the source of action, not in ends or programs or codes calculated in advance, but in faith and obedience, in living relationship to God.[17] Others phrase the quest as one for an ethic to eliminate all ethics, for an emphasis on neighbor-regarding love rather than principles. Principles may even be a barrier to the response to neighbor. Still others stress the response of faith rather than love. Sittler calls for a re-enactment of God's self-giving deed.

God does the redemptive and restorative deed, and God creates the response which is man's reception of it. So adequate are the God-initiated vitalities there deployed that evangelical ethics is under no necessity to import into its basic structure presuppositions from the rich and ennobling tradition of philosophical thought about the good, the valuable, etc.[18]

[15] See Albert K. Cohen, *Delinquent Boys* (Glencoe, Ill.: Free Press, 1955), pp. 88-95. This indignation may be confined to social workers and theologians; many people seem quite satisfied with middle-class morals.

[16] See pp. 123 ff.

[17] *The Church and Its Function in Society*, pp. 220-21. See also Schilling, *Methodism and Society in Theological Perspective*, pp. 247-51.

[18] "The Structure of Christian Ethics," in Harold C. Letts (ed.), *Life in Community*, (Philadelphia: Muhlenberg Press, 1957), p. 10.

The dismissal of philosophy is typical of some authors, who are not always so courteous as Sittler. The situational ethic stresses the requirements of acting within a specific context, without prejudgment from abstract and ideal principles except as these are internalized in the actor. One is able to make the loving or faithful response only when one is in the situation. The absolutism is of loyalty rather than of principles. Paul Lehmann describes such an ethic as *koinonia*, starting from the reality of the church, always concrete, always indicative rather than imperative.[19]

7. FROM DETACHMENT TO INVOLVEMENT

A final dimension of the problem takes its cue from this emphasis on context or existential involvement. Traditional philosophical ethics is criticized as objective, detached, neutral, encouraging a spectator attitude toward the ethical life. But the Christian is not outside or above the moral conflict; rather he is in it, facing actual decisions, and his moral life consists in his choosing as well as in his reflections *about* how he ought to choose.

In different ways, each of the above changes in perspective challenges ethics as a system of moral principles, challenges the adequacy of philosophical criteria in Christian ethics, and even challenges the relevance of theological reflection. These challenges are even more acute in the search for an adequate social ethic, for many of the challenges presuppose a radical individualism despite some protests to the contrary. Yet the quest for ethical enlightenment continues and the critics of philosophy employ philosophical arguments to demonstrate the inadequacy of philosophy.

B. The Continuing Quest for Principles

1. INTERACTION BETWEEN THEOLOGY AND ETHICS

There is need for greater theological awareness in dealing with social issues as well as for more incisive theological criticism of ethical perspectives. But the interaction between theological and ethical study should be genuine, two-way interaction. Just as theology should not be used as a polite invocation to give an aura of sanctity to otherwise pru-

---

[19] "The Foundation and Pattern of Christian Behavior," in John A. Hutchison (ed.), *Christian Faith and Social Action* (New York: Charles Scribner's Sons, 1953), pp. 104-10. Lehmann insists that such an ethic makes an inseparable connection "between a theology of the 'right' and a politics of the 'left.'"

dential considerations, so theology should not be developed apart from ethics and then applied to ethical issues. Nor should theological reflection be used as a device to evade responsibility to act. Roger Shinn insists that "Just as there can be no Christian ethics without theological foundations, so there can be no theology without ethical foundations." If bad doctrine produces bad ethics, so too does bad ethics produce bad doctrine. He suggests that theologians "should talk less about problems of theology, do more talking theologically about the problems of God's children in human societies." [20]

Against this background what has been learned from the critical perspectives briefly outlined above? It may be morally healthy that we lack shining causes, that we are "disillusioned about all-embracing social solutions." John Bennett urges attention to more modest tasks, dealing with particular forms of injustice and corruption, but not in complete isolation from one another. He adds that "Much of our effort must be aimed at checking the drift to disaster." [21] No single cause can be elevated to the status of a crusade to "bring in the kingdom," though this should not relieve any valid cause of its urgency.

If there is some dimming of the causes and limiting of grand schemes for social betterment, there is nevertheless a broadening attention to the whole man. If man has been seen as only a rational being, for whom to know the right is to do it, he is no longer so seen. Men must not only use God-given reason to discover the right amid changing circumstances, but they also must come to terms with problems of motivation and deal with nonrational vested interests and irrational fears. The purpose of therapy is not to release one from responsible action but to release one for responsible action. Schilling points to the tendency in the church to see evangelism and social action as separate if not opposed concerns.

[20] "Some Ethical Foundations of Christian Theology," Union Seminary Quarterly Review, XV, 2 (January 1960), 101, 102, 109. Shinn credits liberal Christianity at its best with "a grand social passion and a desire to realize Christian love," but sees it at its worst as a "tamed idealism with deceptive hopes for society and misunderstanding of selves." Neo-Orthodoxy at its best reflected disturbed consciences aware of the need of a gospel of salvation, but at its worst, "it decides that sin is here to stay and to be acknowledged in liturgy, while sinners rest at ease in Zion, or the suburban community, or the society of the intellectuals." 104.
[21] "How My Mind Has Changed," The Christian Century, LXXVI, 51 (Dec. 23, 1959), 1501.

As a result, much evangelism has proceeded with little conception of the reality and seriousness of men's social sins, and little or no awareness that Christian commitment involves the acceptance of social responsibility. On the other hand, much social action has ignored the pervasive sway of individual sin in the social evils it attacks; forgotten the need for personal transformation; urged men to act uprightly without relating them to the power of God.[22]

In the face of complex issues, the Christian faith offers no substitute for technical competence or for attention to causal factors. Faith provides no direct and simple answers in a single source for the troubling issues we face. We need empirical analysis, rational reflection and foresight, the illumination provided by theology, and deep spiritual motivation. Theological insights, of course, must be presented "not as a simple panacea for all collective ills but as the frame of meaning for the tragic facts and awful responsibilities of the day." [23]

Paul Schilling has reminded us that the question is not whether we have theological presuppositions for ethical judgments, but whether these are unconscious, implicit, accidental, and ill-defined, or carefully wrought and interrelated. A clear conception of the relation of theology to ethics helps us to deal with ethical inconsistencies and cultural accommodation, with individual whims, limited interests, and partial perspectives.[24] Theology and ethics are a part of man's grateful, repentant and loving response to God. The central social goal of the Christian ethic is a redeemed society: the release of persons from all those aspects of group relationships which corrupt life, obstruct personal growth, and hinder the divine purpose; the establishment among groups of relationships which promote the maximum concern of persons for each other's welfare, further the realization of their highest potentialities, and facilitate their communion with and service of God. Man's salvation is in-

[22] *Methodism and Society in Theological Perspective*, p. 210.

[23] Reinhold Niebuhr, "The Test of the Christian Faith Today," *The Christian Century*, LXXVI, 43 (October 28, 1959), 1243.

[24] *Methodism and Society in Theological Perspective*, pp. 197-98, 207-8. H. Richard Niebuhr sees the task of theology today not as "translating ancient ideas into modern language, but of wrestling with ultimate problems . . . in contemporary forms." One might justifiably change "educator" to "moralist" and "educational" to "ethical" in the following passage: "The theologian as [moralist] or the [moralist] as theologian cannot carry on his theological and his [ethical] critiques separately and independently, nor can he reduce them to one method in the hope of gaining one single answer." *The Purpose of the Church and Its Ministry*, pp. 3, 5.

evitably social, concerned with redeeming corporate and institutional life as well as individual, and realized within the fellowship of a redeemed and redeeming community.[25]

2. LIFE IN THE CHURCH

The Christian begins neither his theological nor his ethical quest "from scratch" but from within the experience of the church, "with its longer history and more universal consensus." [26] Thus that part of the response to God which is repentance is, in principle, not just ritual or "repentance in general," but repentance against a background of the requirements of life in the community of the church, in the light of knowledge about God's will and purpose. Persons may first enter the life of the church in a basic response of repentance for their sin or of gratitude for God's forgiveness. Certainly a genuine entrance is a response and both repentance and gratitude are necessary. Whatever revival of religion and increase in church membership and attendance we may have had recently has involved numerous motives: persons who have discovered the inadequacy of individualism or of intellectual belief alone; persons who feel socially unrelated and desire to "belong"; persons with anxieties who seek security; and others.

The church, then, is a gathering of *people*, a fellowship of those who have experienced the love of God in Jesus Christ, who in repentant and grateful response receive his forgiveness; who in worship express together their praise and deepen their understanding of God's purposes; who, in faithful life and work, seek to increase in the world the love of God and man. The church is people, a human society with limitations and frailties; but it is also that which God intends "as the instrument for the fulfillment of his purpose." [27]

It is in the *purpose* of God that the nature of the church is discovered.

[25] Schilling, *Methodism and Society in Theological Perspective*, pp. 236, 207-8.
[26] Reinhold Niebuhr, "The Test of the Christian Faith Today," 1239. H. Richard Niebuhr writes: "I do not see how we can witness to the divine sovereignty without being in the church nor how we can understand what God is doing and declaring to us in our public and private experience without the dictionary of the Scriptures, but it seems to me that in our new orthodox movements we are moving dangerously near to the untenable positions against which the Reformation and the 18th Century revival had to protest." "Reformation: Continuing Imperative," *The Christian Century*, LXXVII, 9 (March 2, 1960), 250.
[27] Visser 't Hooft and Oldham, *The Church and Its Function in Society*, pp. 2-3. See pp. 142 f. of this study; H. R. Niebuhr, *The Purpose of the Church and Its Ministry*.

The church does not become what it is in essence without the working together of persons who share in God's intention.[28] There is a perennial problem of boundaries in defining the church: who is entitled to membership and the sacraments? [29] The concern for discipline must always be balanced by a sense of responsibility for a parish defined not in terms of present quality of life but of need to find fulfillment.

The mission of the church is the expression of God's purpose, the increase of the love of God and man, in whatever situation it exists. The mission is not an outpost overseas, in an urban slum, or in the mountain country, although the mission which begins where a church is must extend to all these. The renewal of the church comes as its members become aware of God's purpose as their mission and so become united in a fellowship of ministry to the world.

3. THE MORALITY OF GROUPS

This ministry to the world involves not only the choices of individuals but also the morality of groups. We are in many ways being led to question whether there are any purely individual choices, or whether a person can exercise moral judgment in isolation. We choose from among the competing claims of groups, those in which we are members and those to which we would belong, groups ranging from the family to the beloved community of Josiah Royce. And our choices lead us into action within a network of group relationships. There would seem to be no way for individuals to live out their salvation apart from their involvement in groups. Further, groups enable men to attain goals as well as frustrate them in the attainment.[30] There is an inherent communitarian dimension to all ethics. *Persons and groups stand under the judgment and mercy of God.* Although one may not attribute consciousness to groups in substantive terms, there is some degree of group awareness

[28] DeWolf, *The Case for Theology in Liberal Perspective*, pp. 153-59. This section draws heavily upon DeWolf and upon John Deschner, "Methodism's Thirteenth Article," *The Perkins School of Theology Journal*, XII, 2 (Winter 1960), 5-14.

[29] See George W. Webber, *God's Colony in Man's World* (Nashville: Abingdon Press, 1960), esp. pp. 128 ff., but also pp. 70 ff.

[30] George Wald, a biologist, has suggested that even biologists tend to think of environment as given, to which organisms must adapt or die, but that one of the most important features of the environment is the product of living organisms ("The Origins of Life," lecture, March 17, 1960). In the same way we take the *social* environment of man as fixed, given; whereas to see groups as the product of the interaction of human persons keeps the group from being a given but rather subject to the continuing action of persons.

and common purpose. This does not mean that persons can shed moral responsibility by invoking group membership.[31] Rather, the individuals who compose a group may so share purposes with respect to their action that they achieve group purposes. It is precisely our life in groups (family, corporation, white majority, nation) that requires judgment by moral principles.

The crucial issue in a double morality usually arises to the degree that a group has defined its interests as over against the interests of some other group. The argument concerning conflicts of interest usually assumes that "good" emerges only as one interest triumphs or as a least common denominator or compromise is worked out. Traditional natural law doctrine has assumed, on the other hand, that there is an objective, moral order which transcends the claims of any group and with which both individuals and groups must come to terms. Regardless of the formulation of a law of nature, the Christian would seem bound to affirm the existence of a transcendent and inclusive interest, in terms of which conflicting lesser interests can find reconciliation in a good greater than any lesser good.[32] The corollary assumption concerning the responsibility of an officer (ruler, legislator, or even citizen) is often put in terms that refuse to admit that a group can choose self-sacrifice, although such a choice is laudable for an individual. Such an assumption ignores the fact that groups can and do choose self-sacrifice in war. In point of fact, the distinction would seem to be that a nation (the crucial group in such an argument) can choose the risk of sacrifice in war, but not the risk involved in refusing war. Certainly the church, when it is true to its nature, must refuse identification with any nation's interest as ultimate. John Bennett acknowledges: "The church can do much

[31] Adolf Eichmann was chief of the Jewish office of the Nazi Gestapo in World War II. He was in 1961 convicted of having directed the massacre of five million Jews. His memoirs give a hint concerning his defense: "It was really terrible but quite necessary. Anyhow, the Fuhrer ordered it, and I did not have anything to do with the annihilation. I was not a killer but a man who executed orders. . . . I carried out with clean conscience and faithful heart the duty imposed upon me. I was always a good German." Quoted in Quentin Reynolds, et al., *Minister of Death* (New York: The Viking Press, 1960), pp. 100, 204.

[32] See John H. Hallowell, *The Moral Foundation of Democracy* (Chicago: University of Chicago Press, 1954). Edward Heimann calls attention to the dangerous error of pragmatism in social policy divorced from transcendent standards of judgment. Pragmatism "presupposes a given and somewhat stable structure and improves its operation but cannot explain the structure itself" or recognize necessary fundamental changes. "Niebuhr's Pragmatic Conservatism," *Union Seminary Quarterly Review*, XI, 4 (May, 1956).

simply by being the community of Christ that never allows us to be merely Americans or people of the political West." [33]

4. THE DISCIPLINED LIFE

The revolt against moralism noted earlier has been valid in so far as the emphasis has been on an individualistic set of behaviors or upon a rigid code of prescriptions and proscriptions.[34] But, as Roger Shinn puts it, "The answer to a misguided religious ethic is not a less ethical, but a more profoundly ethical faith." [35] Bennett poses the argument in these terms:

Those who stress moral discipline are most concerned about the sins of weakness, the sins of inertia, of personal disorganization and irresponsibility. Those who stress grace and the limits of morality are most concerned about the sins of strength, about the more subtle sins of the well-organized effective man who is righteous according to usual standards but whose righteousness so easily leads to hardness and self-sufficiency and a lack of charity.[36]

The moral life requires discipline and reflection; society cannot live without integrity of word, loyalty, responsible use of time and resources, inhibition of appetites in the interests of purposes. In fact, some conception of principle and purpose is required even at the minimal level of harmonious satisfaction of appetites. DeWolf concludes, "An ethic not dependent upon rules is not therefore an ethic without principles." [37] The ethical objection to what have been called "Puritanical" answers is not that the questions were improper (May a Christian drink or gamble?), but that particular answers were rigidly conceived and were often viewed as a way of winning one's salvation. The law of the Christian is "not a system of rules, with instructions for every situation, and not a sys-

[33] "How My Mind Has Changed," *The Christian Century*, LXXVI, 51 (Dec. 23, 1959), 1502.
[34] L. Harold DeWolf notes: "Curiously, then, liberal and neo-orthodox Christians in America tend increasingly to accommodate to the world in personal ethics though they challenge it on social issues, while conservative Christians usually accommodate on social issues, though some of them are nonconformists in personal practice. Neither position adequately represents Christian ethics." *The Case for Theology in Liberal Perspective*, pp. 147-48.
[35] "Some Ethical Foundations of Christian Theology," 108.
[36] "Morality and Moralism," *Union Seminary Quarterly Review*, XI, 4 (May 1956), 39.
[37] *The Case for Theology in Liberal Perspective*, p. 139.

tem by which we can qualify to make demands upon God," but the law of love as an inclusive principle.[38]

Such a conception of the moral life requires both philosophical reflection and a transcendent point of reference, as well as expression in concrete acts and attitudes. There is need for continuing interaction between philosophical ethics as the critical, rational interpretation of experience and theological ethics as the guidance of life in existential situations in accordance with Christian norms. Joseph Sittler, quoted earlier as proposing an ethic of faith and re-enactment, insists on the relevance of the philosophical enterprise to the concrete tasks of Christian ethics, provided that "the faculty of reflection when functioning within the structure of the Christian ethical life must not betray that structure." [39] The question would seem to be whether the Christian, by living in obedience to the truth he knows and living within the nurture of the Christian fellowship, can revise *his idea* of the structure. Even the ethic of inspiration operates with some conception of the character of God. When the Christian responds, he does so, not *to* faith conceived in terms of content, but *in* faith—in faithful trust, loyalty, and obedience[40] to the God whose nature is never exhausted in any knowledge of him. The opposite of faith is not reason but unfaith, disloyalty to the highest known. Such faith needs continuing nourishment in experiences of corporate and private worship, as well as testing in critical discussion and practice in occasions of obedience.

The Christian maintains a theoretical openness to rational reflection and to new evidence from experience, but he is also—and at once—practically committed, obedient to the truth already known, involved in living out his faithful response. His obedience is not to an outer compulsion, but to an inner acceptance of moral principle, for only an uncoerced response can be a moral one. There is an imperative quality to such an ethic of response, but there is also an element of purpose, of working with God to achieve his purposes. Paul writes: "As God's fellowworker, I appeal to you, too, not to accept the favor of God and then waste it" (II Cor. 6:1 Goodspeed). And the author of III John urges

---

[38] *Ibid.*

[39] "The Structure of Christian Ethics," p. 11.

[40] Roger Shinn writes: "The Christian Message has from its beginning said that obedience is a way to knowledge." "Some Ethical Foundations of Christian Theology," 101.

us "to show that we are ready to co-operate with the truth" (III John 8 Goodspeed).

A Christian social ethic is always to be related to the requirements of a specific situation, but there are elements that transcend the situation. "Each present moment in which we decide is filled with memories and anticipations; and at each present moment there is present to us some other whom we have met before and expect to meet again." [41] Against the background of an integrated structure of conviction the Christian seeks middle axioms, "attempts to define the directions in which, in a particular state of society, Christian faith must express itself. They are not binding for all time, but are provisional definitions of the type of behavior required of Christians at a given period and in given circumstances." [42] A middle axiom mediates between universal ethical principles and specific programs of action. John C. Bennett illustrates in terms of the principle of co-operation and mutual concern applied to world order in 1945. The middle axiom deals with the need for a political framework within which the United Nations can continue co-operation. The specific strategy calls for critical support of the San Francisco Charter and the resulting organization.[43] Such middle axioms are the meeting place of theology and social action for individual judgments and corporate decisions. The strategic concern is with the basis of the principles, the range of their relevance, and the way in which others may be persuaded of their validity.

5. DISCRIMINATE AND INDISCRIMINATE CRITICISM

In the continuing quest for ethical principles, an important factor is criticism—which may be either discriminate or indiscriminate. Knowledge of human sinfulness calls forth humility, but by itself it may be a "principle of indiscriminate criticism," with all human judgments seen as *equally* far from the will of God. The Christian knows something also of the sovereignty of God as creator and sustainer, of the love of God as redeemer, of the hope of the coming Kingdom, of the inclusive character of the Christian concern, of the *relative* goodness of all human institutions. Such theological insights illumine Christian ethical understanding.

[41] H. Richard Niebuhr, *Christ and Culture* (New York: Harper & Brothers, 1951), p. 247.
[42] Visser 't Hooft and Oldham, *The Church and Its Function in Society*, p. 194.
[43] *Christian Ethics and Social Policy*, pp. 77-78.

It is not sufficient to be able to repent of past known sins; we need also principles of discriminate criticism, ethical illumination for situations presently faced and to be faced, some of them different from any we have faced before. It is imperative that we have foresight as well as hindsight, that we learn from history, that we reflectively anticipate decisions. Normative principles must become a part of persons' interior orientation, since the context of decision is concrete and existential, and since decision-makers act less rationally and abstractly than we assume.[44] But for social action (that which takes into account the behavior of others), it would seem essential not only that principles be internalized, but also that they be made explicit in policy statements. The very process of formulating statements brings the principles to the foreground, opens the way for awareness of inconsistency, and provides an opportunity for reconciliation of differences. Publicly made commitments are not static or inflexible but they do provide a firmer base of co-operative endeavor.

Ernest W. Lefever seems to oppose principles and calculation of consequence as mutually exclusive. Beginning with a statement with which we can surely agree, "No statesman can make policy from principles alone," he goes on to insist that goals and ideals must be related to the "political facts of life." But the crucial question comes when he asks, "What factors shall we take into account when we calculate?" He concludes that "control and restraint in international politics, and human relations generally, do not depend mainly on the 'goodness of men' but rather on a balance of forces and interests among sinful men." [45] One receives the impression that ethical principles become the factors left out of account [46] and that the only relevant theological insight is the sinfulness of man. One critic suggests that such a completely future-oriented calculation amounts to a suspension of ethics. "Prudence" must be "understood to be in the service of some prior principle";

[44] See James Gustafson, "Christian Ethics and Social Policy," op. cit., pp. 126-29. John C. Bennett reminds us that decisions for war or peace may have to be made in a few minutes, thus making foresight crucial. "Faith and Responsibility," 1396.

[45] "The Ethics of Calculation," Worldview, 2, 10 (October 1959), 6, 7.

[46] John Bennett, commenting on Lefever's article, thinks the author has lost the ethics in the calculation, resulting in a complacent conclusion. Bennett urges as other factors to be considered in calculation of consequences of a nuclear war (in addition to the statistics): the effect on the fabric of community, the results in moral and emotional health, and the survival of institutions of political and spiritual freedom. Worldwide, 2, 11 (November 1959), 7, 8.

morality or immorality cannot be "wholly swallowed up in consequences." [47]

There is no need to set calculation over against consideration of principles, or to set principles over against action in the presence of God. Schilling has interpreted a theology of salvation as the foundation of a dynamic Christian social ethic, with the Christian's social concern "implicit in and an outgrowth of his experience of redemption." The response of the Christian is to the "expectations, judgment, love, and power of God," understood in the light of Jesus Christ, and made in humility and in the awareness that his perspective may warp his judgment.[48]

6. AN ETHIC OF RESPONSE

The Christian life arises as a grateful and repentant response to God's action and continues in trust, love, and obedience.[49] Just as there is no gratitude without some conception of God's action, so there is no true repentance without some conception of God's righteous will, without principles or a reasonable facsimile thereof. Roger Shinn calls attention to sophisticated Christians who develop "exquisite skill in repentance" but do not repent "of anything in particular." The vocabulary is existential and concrete but concrete wrongs are rarely righted.[50] Schilling outlines a conception of social repentance after stating that without awareness of need there is no redemption.[51] Social repentance helps save us from passive acquiescence or indifference (e.g., the illusion of economic prosperity with a base of military armament production); from insensitivity to the problems, needs, and aspirations of the less fortunate; from an easy assumption of superior worth.

Social repentance is preparation for reconciliation, so that we act, not to merit favor, but in response to God's forgiveness.[52] Accepting in faith the forgiving grace of God, we are released and empowered to act, saved from anxiety, from fearful avoidance of responsibility, and from

[47] Paul Ramsey, "Right and Wrong Calculation," *Worldview*, 2, 12 (December 1959) 6-9. He quotes Robert L. Calhoun: "Christian conscience in war time seems to have chiefly the effect . . . of making Christians do reluctantly what military necessity requires."

[48] *Methodism and Society in Theological Perspective*, p. 207; see also pp. 253 ff.

[49] *Ibid.*, p. 199.

[50] "Some Ethical Foundations of Christian Theology," p. 104.

[51] *Methodism and Society in Theological Perspective*, pp. 216-21.

[52] *Ibid.*, pp. 221-35.

vain regret. The conception of social holiness reminds us that there is no limit set to the extension of God's redemptive purpose, nor to what God can accomplish in and through us. The kingdom of God is forever a challenge to smug, ingrown piety and to complacency.

C. Love, Justice, and Compromise

It is possible for the conception of the Kingdom to be so transcendent and abstract that it becomes irrelevant to present decisions. In such views the kingdom of love becomes an impossible ideal, leaving men in the world to work out their compromises in the name of justice. The pitting of love against justice fails to deal adequately with either concept. When the love ethic is exalted so far above human achievement that it becomes an "impossible possibility," then love is reduced to a norm, or a motive, or an attitude. Love seen only as a norm becomes a transcendent absolute incapable of realization in history. Love viewed only as motive lacks concern for consequences. If love is only an attitude, it leads to no principles immediately relevant to concrete action.

DeWolf thinks such definitions of love as *caritas*, or disinterested benevolence, or *agapé*, all assume a "basically atomistic, individualistic society." He goes on to define love as a "dynamic intention," establishing the supreme goal—the "community of grateful sharing in God's blessings," keeping the actor in proper perspective; with justice as the "right ordering of love's expression." [53] Love breaks through the principle of equality with regard for the one who is in need; it is both personal—to each man, and discriminate—to all men.[54] It prevents justice from protecting the *status quo* and from being rigid and fixed, as sometimes happens in the writing of Reinhold Niebuhr: "The relatively satisfactory solution of the problem of economic justice . . . has given us a complicated system of balances, preservation of which requires discriminate judgment rather than a passion for justice or religious sensitivity." [55]

Some writers distinguish love as a vague and subjective term from the clear and distinct concept of justice. John Ferguson, on the contrary, suggests that justice "has become a political catchword whose effectiveness is in inverse proportion to its clarity of definition." He traces

[53] *The Case for Theology in Liberal Perspective*, pp. 142, 150-51.
[54] See John Ferguson, "Justice and Love," in *Studies in Christian Social Commitment*, ed., John Ferguson (London: Independent Press, 1954), pp. 64-65.
[55] "The Test of the Christian Faith Today," 1240.

its complex derivation to: (1) personal righteousness, response to the will of God; (2) social custom, the right ordering of citizens' relations in a state; and (3) law which can be formulated and followed, is binding and obligatory. The Christian is obligated to fulfill the demands of society, even to go beyond legal demands in the "second mile," but he is also to say "no" when the social custom conflicts with the personal righteousness of response to God's will. Ferguson notes that "it is the very people who claim that 'love' must give way to 'justice' who also claim that 'justice' must give way to something else." [56]

The conception of compromise would seem to indicate an absolute and abstract "best," apart from any situation, which is enjoined in a situation, but which cannot be accomplished, and so is debased, or compromised. There is a basic difference between this and seeking illumination from ethical principles. However, from such principles one cannot deduce the "right" action in the abstract. Rather the principles must be brought into integral relationship with concrete situations in such a way that the "right" or ethical action is the "best possible" in the specific circumstances, inclusive of the greatest possible good and reconciling the relevant principles.[57] In such calculation love is not one among several competing principles. Instead of conflicting duties, we have conflicting evidence of what our duty is.[58] Over against a conception of compromise as disobedience we need to set the more positive conception of *obedience seeking relevance*.

D. Principles of Christian Ethics

Let us look briefly at five principles in terms of which the Christian seeks to define his ethical obedience. In doing so, it is well to remember that the ethics of response, though guided by principles, is grounded in the living reality of God as creator and sustainer, moral governor and judge, redeemer of men and societies, strengthener and life-giver.[59] Principles are derived from and corrected by the Christian's understanding of God's will as he lives in the church and in the world and engages in critical reflection and disciplined living. As formulations of men's

[56] Ferguson, "Justice and Love," pp. 56-58, 63, 67.
[57] See Edgar S. Brightman, *Moral Laws* (New York: The Abingdon Press, 1933), pp. 156 ff., 171 ff., 183 ff.
[58] See Albert C. Knudson, *The Principles of Christian Ethics* (Nashville: Abingdon Press, 1943), p. 184.
[59] Schilling, *Methodism and Society in Theological Perspective*, pp. 199-200.

experience in responding to God in concrete situations, they are inevitably abstract. The Christian is obedient, not to the principles, but to God, whose will is to be followed in actual circumstances, under the guidance of principles. No one principle is involved in ethical decision without due regard for other relevant principles.

1. HUMAN WORTH

The first principle is the dignity and worth of the human person as a child of God. The Christian ethic is one of response to a God who creates and values persons, seeks their fullest growth and fulfillment in love, and thus imparts to them through creation and redemption the status of infinite worth. All institutions, including the church and the sabbath, are judged in terms of their effect on persons.

2. HUMAN FREEDOM

A second principle, closely related, is that these persons cannot be fulfilled in love apart from their freedom to choose (and so to err) and from the responsibility that inheres in moral choice. Persons are redeemed not in isolation but in community. The community life in which persons can become what they are intended to be through responsible use of their freedom is one in which differences are respected and encouraged, in which diversity is valued. The limits of such freedom must always be set by the requirements of maintaining the community life and of preserving responsibility—for one's own realization and for the impact of one's choices on the freedom of others.

3. THE INCLUSIVE COMMUNITY

A third Christian principle, binding despite its repeated violation in practice, is the inclusiveness of the human community in which Christian concern for neighbor is expressed. Love knows no barriers of geography, of color, of age, of sex, or even of creed. H. Richard Niebuhr warns against the idolatrous temptation of the church—the worship of "the God of an ingroup rather than the ground of all being." [60] The most dangerous modern ingroup is the nation-state.

[60] "Reformation: Continuing Imperative," p. 250. See also Nitze, The Recovery of Ethics, pp. 23-24.

4. SOCIAL SALVATION

The next principle has to do with social salvation—the transformation of institutional life. Within any community the Christian is concerned not only for the freedom of the church but also for the freedom and proper functioning of other institutions—family, school, business, theater, government at various levels, the mass media. "Since amid the complex interconnections of modern culture [the church] cannot fulfill its mission without the co-operation and utilization of agencies outside of the church, it must be concerned with the transformation of those agencies." [61] This is not to imply domination by the church, for each institution has its own purpose and relative autonomy.

5. THE COMMUNITY OF THE FORGIVEN AND THE FORGIVING

A fifth principle deals with the church as a barrierless community transcending all man-made divisions, as a human and divine institution always judged and renewed by God, as a fellowship of those who, needing forgiveness, seek to live in obedience and forgiveness.[62]

Pervading all these principles, and yet identical with no single principle, is the goal of the Kingdom of God, "the actualization in all human relations of God's righteous, loving will, but also his reign in judgment even when his will is violated." [63] John Bennett acknowledges:

Many of our predecessors were wrong in believing that society itself would become the Kingdom of God as the goal of human progress. But they were not wrong in believing that society was created to be invaded by the Kingdom, to be touched and inspired by the gospel.[64]

The Kingdom thus conceived is both present demand and future hope.

E. Supporting Sanctions: The Social Creed

Methodism has given its own expression to these principles in the continuing revisions of its Social Creed and other pronouncements of its General Conferences. Methodist statements correct and are corrected by, support and are supported by the actions of other churches and by the

[61] Schilling, *Methodism and Society in Theological Perspective*, p. 233.
[62] See pp. 55-56.
[63] Schilling, op. cit., pp. 140-41.
[64] "How My Mind Has Changed," p. 1395.

growing ecumenical consensus on social issues. The Methodist Federation for Social Service began in 1908 to present a statement on "The Church and Social Problems" for action by the General Conferences of the Methodist Episcopal Church. The story of how this statement became the "Social Creed" of the Federal Council of Churches and was adopted by the Southern church is told in Volume II: *Methodism and Society in the Twentieth Century*. Methodist statements are also influenced by increasing awareness of the requirements of the American Creed [65] and of the pervasive democratic ethos (itself reflecting Christian rootage) seeking extension into all of our political, economic, social, educational, and family life. Social positions find not only institutional support; they are also corrected and strengthened by the individual person's response of compassion or sense of injustice, that which is both a human endowment and a delicate achievement.

In 1908 the Methodist Episcopal Church opened its statement on "The Church and Social Problems" with these words:

When the spirit of Christ shall pervade the hearts of individuals, and when his law of love to God and man shall dominate human society, then the evils which vex our civilization will disappear.

We recognize the gravity of the social situation and the responsibility of the Church collectively, and of its members severally, for bringing about better conditions, through the practical application of the ethics of the New Testament. (1908, p. 479.) [66]

At this date, and for several years, primary attention was paid to industrial problems. The church expressed its approval of conciliation and arbitration, its recognition of the right of labor to organize and bargain collectively, and its concern for the protection of the worker, the abolition of child labor, and safeguards for employed women.

The General Conference of 1912 expanded its concern in several areas. It stood for "the fullest possible development of every child, especially by the provision of proper education and recreation," as well as by abolishing child labor. It opposed the "social, economic, and moral waste of the liquor traffic." There was a concern for security in old age and

---

[65] See Gunnar Myrdal, *An American Dilemma*.

[66] Selections for illustration will be taken from the *Doctrine and Discipline* of the Methodist Episcopal Church through 1939, and from that of The Methodist Church for 1940. They will be noted at the end of the quotation in parentheses.

"for that degree of leisure for all which is a condition of the highest human life." Especially noteworthy was the attention given to the church's own life:

In its capacity as employer the Church should set Christian standards as to hours and wages, provision for sickness and old age, and in developing the principle of coöperation and profit-sharing. Relations with employees should be in harmony with the utterances of the General Conference. (1912, pp. 512-14.)

In 1916 and 1920 there was urging of the application of Christian principles to the acquisition and use of property; also for provision for a living wage and for equitable division of the product of industry. Co-operative control and ownership of industry and natural resources were espoused. Concern was expressed regarding farm labor and tenancy. New sections were added on "The Church and the Community," "Community Services," "Training for Service," and "Industrial Democracy."

The 1928 "Social Creed of the Churches" stated: "We believe in making the social and spiritual ideals of Jesus our test for community as well as for individual life." Positive suggestions were made for translating these ideals into education, into industry and economic relationships, into agriculture, into racial relations ("the elimination of racial discrimination"), and into international relations. In the last area the church supported removal of trade barriers, aid to "backward nations," and abolition of military armaments except for internal police. Responsibility was affirmed for local moral and economic conditions as well as for world problems. (¶ 597) The extension of the church's concern beyond industrial problems is evident from this point on.

As might be expected the conference of 1936 gave detailed attention to the depression and provided some of the most radical statements Methodism has made on social issues. Science offered the possibility of plenty, but multitudes suffered privation; so the church called for "reconstruction of society." There was frank recognition of divergences of opinion in the church. Some Christians urged that the economic problem be solved by increased production, others by the spread of co-operative societies, and others by replacing the struggle for profit with a "planned social economy." The final test for each solution was its effect on personality. The conference also took its stand against violence and the rising dictatorships. (¶ 1463)

The 1940 statement reflected the social conscience of the united church. There was still the call to subordinate the profit motive to the creative and co-operative spirit. New emphases emerged in concern for juvenile delinquents and for the application of the redemptive principle to the treatment of older offenders against the law. Of special importance was the stand "that The Methodist Church as an institution cannot endorse war nor support or participate in it." The church gave its support to conscientious objectors to military service and called for "recognition and maintenance of the rights and responsibilities of free speech, free assembly, and a free press."

We stand for the right of every individual and group of individuals to believe in and to advocate any peaceful method for the solution of any and all problems that may confront society. (¶ 1712)

Several concerns of the 1960 Social Creed are worth noting here. The increase in services provided by other institutions is noted in the call for high standards of institutional care. Planned parenthood is supported. The church refuses to identify Christianity with any economic system. Christians are urged to vote their convictions and to participate in political action. There are new concerns for the responsible use of power and for dealing with the perils of prosperity. Labor and its employers are both obligated to work for the common good. There is a special section on Christian vocation, with daily work regarded "as a sphere of service to God for the advancement of His Kingdom." [67]

F. The Ministry of the Laity

It is in the light of such a social ethic as that expressed in the creed that the Christian finds the response which is his vocation. The ethics of response with its community orientation make many discussions of "personal morality" seem petty. In the true ministry of the laity, typical arguments for indulgence are transcended and set aside. The responding Christian does not ask, "Can I get by with this?" but rather "How can I live out my response to the continuing action of God?" The committed Christian is a practical absolutist in his faithful, obedient response, but he knows that persons are both the goals and the instruments of change. He loves and respects those with whom he differs,

[67] *Doctrines and Discipline of The Methodist Church,* 1960, ¶ 2020.

even while he attempts to live by his convictions, interpret them to others, and seek to persuade. He welcomes into the fellowship of the church the alcoholic, the divorced person, and the paroled prisoner, who are sometimes shunned, affirming at once the ethical obligation which presses upon him. As a part of a ministering fellowship he exercises his ministry.

Paul wrote to the Christians of Rome: "Don't let the world around you squeeze you into its own mold, but let God remold your minds from within, so that you may prove in practice that the plan of God for you is good, meets all his demands and moves toward the goal of true maturity." (Rom. 12:2 Phillips.) Changed—and changing—ethical and theological perspectives help Christians today to refuse to identify any shining cause with the kingdom of God. We are aware of the awful power of human sin in personal and institutional life and of our own involvement in evil. But we are allowed neither to enter uncritically into the world's struggles nor to hold ourselves aloof. Our grateful and repentant response to God's love involves rational reflection upon a structure of moral principles, obedience to God as we seek to discover his will in relating principles to social situations, and continuing renewal within the life of the church.

We turn now to the social scene—to identify the issues and problems in which our obedience becomes relevant, in both personal discipline and institutional strategy.

CHAPTER THREE

Areas of Concern for Methodist Social Action: The Identification of Social Problems

A. Asking the Right Questions: Criteria for Identifying Social Problems

1. THE NORMATIVE FRAME OF REFERENCE

IN SEEKING CRITERIA FOR ANY PURPOSE, IT IS IMPORTANT THAT one ask the right questions—and ask the questions in the right way. C. Wright Mills insists that one cannot escape value judgments in defining social problems, "for we cannot very well state any problem until we know whose problem it is." [1] One may put the question, "For whom?" and be interested in the numbers and types of persons involved in or affected by a social problem.

One may also ask, "For whom?" and want to know "according to whose criteria or norms?" or "Who says so?" This chapter follows "Theological and Ethical Guidelines" because the challenge of Methodist social action comes as the social situation is seen in the light of transcendent norms and as social problems emerge against the background of social goals. Henry Kissinger points to the need for such an orientation, holding that "in the absence of well-understood goals each problem becomes a special case." [2] We have set forth in Chapter II a structure of ethical norms which builds upon human worth and human freedom. These require a quality of community life in which no artificial and arbitrary barriers restrict opportunity for the growth of persons. In

[1] *The Sociological Imagination* (New York: Oxford University Press, 1959), p. 76. See Don Martindale, "Social Disorganization," in Howard Becker and Alvin Boskoff (eds.), *Modern Sociological Theory* (New York: Holt, Rinehart & Winston, Inc., 1957), p. 340. This treatment is indebted at several points to Martindale's review.
[2] "The Policymaker and the Intellectual," *The Reporter*, XX, 5 (March 5, 1959), 32.

such a community there is not only respect for personal differences but also provision for diversity of institutions, judged by their contribution to the growth of persons. Essential to the proper functioning of persons and community is the life of the church as it seeks to witness to the purpose of God in his world.[3] These principles will be explored in relationship to four categories of Christian concern: (1) the development of freedom and responsibility in community life, (2) stewardship of the created world, (3) introducing forgiveness and reconciliation into the treatment of deviants, and (4) the achievement of trust.[4]

2. APPROACHES TO SOCIAL PROBLEMS

The normative frame of reference, however important, is not the only one that is needed in identifying social problems. Sister Mary Chisholm has outlined four main approaches that sociologists have used in defining social problems.[5] (1) The first approach was general and moral, issuing in moral exhortations, with some social welfare concern. Social evils were seen to root in personal selfishness, injustice or ignorance, against a commonly accepted value framework. There was little causal analysis. (2) The second approach emphasized causation, but it looked for single factor explanations, whether biological (with stress on eugenics), or geographic (with concern for environment), or economic. In terms of a single factor Charles A. Ellwood defined the social problem in 1915 as how to live amicably and avoid conflict. Others today might tend to identify work, or education, or race, or peace as the problem. (3) A third approach was more empirical, stressing facts and many causes, though these were seldom related to each other in systematic form. There was concern with institutional dislocations, value conflicts, with "society as the patient," rather than individual selfishness. (4) The fourth approach sought some principle or principles of integration, some unified body of theory, recognizing the interdependence of problems. Harvey Swados illustrates this orientation in referring to work:

In this country today the problem of satisfying work is indissolubly linked with that of fruitful leisure. The problem of leisure is interlocked with that

[3] See pp. 65-66.
[4] See pp. 100-106.
[5] *Ideological Implication of Current Definitions of a Social Problem* (Washington, D. C.: The Catholic University of America Press, 1948), pp. 1-21.

of the content and control of the mass media; which problem in turn cuts to the heart of a commercially oriented culture. In short, the probing of what at first consideration may seem a comparatively limited problem, is actually nothing less than a revolutionary act calling into question our very social structure.[6]

Most persons today look for specific rather than general moral issues in approaching social problems. However, few accept a single-factor approach. Increasingly there is attention to the interrelatedness of social problems and acceptance of some such conception as cumulative causation.[7] According to this theory the result in a sequence of events becomes in turn a cause of further events, thus re-enforcing patterns or trends in what may be a "vicious circle"; or it may, on the other hand, work toward social goals.

3. INADEQUATE CRITERIA

Still many current definitions of social problems propose criteria which are less than adequate when taken in isolation. We shall consider the criteria of size (or number of people affected by a problem), of social disorganization (or disruption of order), and of conflicts in values.

Quantitative considerations identify as social problems those conditions which affect a significant proportion of the population. Such criteria are important. Recent debates over continuing nuclear tests have made a central issue out of the numbers or percentages of persons who are actual victims of present fallout rates or potential victims of further testing or of indirect genetic effects in later generations.

But numbers alone do not provide a basis for judgment. Are the conditions important, as the problem of fallout damage certainly is, or trivial, as the increase in male baldness might be considered? Is the direction in which the conditions point desirable (a lowering of the infant mortality rate due to X rays of the position of the fetus), or undesirable (a possible increase in mutations due to exposure to radiation)? Are the conditions such that something can be done about them, whether preventive action to lower the incidence of blindness in children or ameliorative action to help children who are blind deal with their situation? Further, what happens to one man may be symbolic or

[6] "Work as a Public Issue," *Saturday Review* (December 12, 1959), p. 45.
[7] See Myrdal, *An American Dilemma*, Appendix 3.

portentous. Willard Uphaus in a New Hampshire jail for refusing to release to the state Attorney-General a conference guest list involved only one man actually, although many potentially. But he also symbolized the problem of restriction of civil liberties which cannot be evaluated in terms of statistics.

Definition of problems in terms of social organization may hinge on humanitarian criteria (the awareness of pain or suffering on the part of persons) or utilitarian criteria (the awareness of the social costs).[8] Alcoholism may be viewed as a problem because of concern for the alcoholic or because of concern for absenteeism and lowered production, to say nothing of taxes for institutional care and family services. Usually problems of social disorganization are set against a background of stability and order that seems to have been disturbed or upset. The problem is an element of instability and the concern is to restore order. The remedial or adjustive action may be directed toward symptoms or toward repressing efforts toward change. There is little understanding of forces in motion or of challenges to the existing order as different aspects of culture change at different rates, with conflict between the norms of different groups. A crime ring may be viewed as a problem of disorganization by the larger society, but it is itself highly organized, with norms and rules. Robert K. Merton sees social structure as defining goals and enforcing ways of achieving these goals, thus providing stress and conflict (and so, social problems) when groups of persons cannot achieve the goals with the approved means and turn to deviant behavior.[9]

In such terms juvenile delinquency becomes a problem not only for youngsters who engage in deviant behavior (and who cannot ultimately escape responsibility), but also for the society which restricts access to socially desirable goals and which also "solves" its own problems with violence and threats of violence. The problem is not fully understood unless the focus includes the conflict of norms between parts of the society, all against the background of goals of equal opportunity for self-realization. With reference to the church, when does juvenile delin-

[8] Jessie Bernard, *Social Problems at Midcentury* (New York: Holt, Rinehart & Winston, Inc., 1957), pp. 104 ff.

[9] Don Martindale, "Social Disorganization," pp. 349-65. See also Robert K. Merton, *Social Theory and Social Structure*, rev. (Glencoe, Ill.: The Free Press, 1957), pp. 131-94; Albert K. Cohen, "The Study of Social Disorganization and Deviant Behavior," in Merton, et al. (eds.) *Sociology Today* (New York: Basic Books, 1959), p. 365.

quency become a problem? Is the church concerned with what is happening to growing persons, or with protection of society, or only when young toughs upset a church-planned program or try to crash a Youth Fellowship dance?

Each of the previous criteria has been qualified by considerations of value. Definitions of a social problem change according to the degree of consensus on values in a given society. Some would identify as a social problem conditions which clash with the values of a large part of the population. Such conceptions, in so far as they assume uniformity either as fact or as ideal and so devalue diversity, may be "propaganda for conformity," [10] criticizing divergence from older agrarian mores on the one hand or the refusal to accept "progress" on the other.

But such conceptions may just as well assume that diversity is a fact and a "good" and that conflict over values is not itself necessarily a social problem but may indicate the presence of a problem. There is, for example, real difference of opinion and conflict of value whether one phrases a problem as "getting the people out of the slums" or "getting the slums out of the people." That people live in slum conditions is one dimension of a social problem, but why they live there and why others think they should or should not be concerned are also dimensions of the problem.

There is no single criterion for identifying social problems. We will attempt in our identification to operate within a framework of explicit norms; neither change nor order, conflict nor harmony will be valued in itself but only as it serves the larger goals. We will consider both the effects of social patterns on persons and the number of persons affected. We will try to keep in focus the conflicts of values within and between persons and groups. We will also take account of the possibility of doing something about the conditions.

James Coleman suggests that the type of event or condition helps to determine "whether a crisis will unite a community, defeat it, or cause controversy" [11] A flood pits men against a common enemy; a school desegregation pronouncement affects different groups in different ways and may divide the community. In either case there are things that men can do.

[10] Mills, The Sociological Imagination, pp. 90-91.
[11] Community Conflict (Glencoe, Ill.: The Free Press, 1957), pp. 4 ff.

B. The Shifting Focus of Social Problems

We turn now to consider the shifting forms of social problems, the sources of change, and the way in which some problems are solved and new ones emerge. Byron Fox points to the troubled conscience of the sociologist in a rapidly changing society:

It may be that as we continue to study social problems as conventionally defined, our society will slide toward destruction. As we make the fatal slide, the sociologist of social problems, also a passenger, may find that he can do no better than to take a detached pose and make careful observations until the final awful moment.[12]

Social problems change in focus and in urgency in a mobile and technological society; America is not always willing either to face problems frankly or to reconstruct. We need to become aware of the crucial problems that emerge as new forces modify older concerns. Few, if any, social problems are "given"; rather they occur within the context of change. People face many kinds of crises—factory shutdown and unemployment, increased incidence of crime, struggles over school taxes, floods, explosions, crop failures, oil discoveries, religious tensions, and political disputes.[13] What are the sources of change which give rise to crises and problems?

1. SOURCES OF CHANGE AND SOCIAL CONSEQUENCES [14]

We are concerned with those sources of change which have social consequences. Not all natural disturbances precipitate social crises, although there may be natural crises which result from social causes. For example, the creation of the dust bowl in the Plains States was a natural event, but it was contributed to by the way men cleared fields, plowed and planted crops. The following outline classifies sources of change under the headings of natural crises and social crises.

Sources of Change
1. Natural crises (nonmanipulable in the first instance)
   a) PHYSICAL (E.G., FLOOD, EARTHQUAKE, EROSION)

---

[12] Byron Fox, "American Social Problems in a World Setting," *Social Problems*, 6, 2 (Fall, 1958), 106.

[13] Coleman, *Community Conflict*, p. 4.

[14] See Irwin T. Sanders, "Approaches to Social Change," in *Education for Social Work*, Proceedings of the 8th Annual Program Meeting of the Council on Social Work Education (New York: 1960), pp. 1-23. See also Arnold M. Rose, "Theory for the Study of Social Problems," *Social Problems*, 4, 3 (January 1957). See p. 167.

    b) PHYSIOLOGICAL (E.G., PUBERTY, DISEASE)
2. Social crises
    a) RATE (OR TIMING OF CHANGE)
        (1) CATACLYSMIC (E.G., WAR, CLOSING OF FACTORY)
        (2) RECURRENT (E.G., AUTOMATION, MOBILITY)
    b) Process (or *how* change occurs)
        (1) DRIFT (E.G., INCREASED SCOPE OF GOVERNMENT)
        (2) PLANNED (E.G., OVERPRODUCTION)
        (3) CONFLICTS OVER VALUE (E.G., MIXED COMMUNITIES, RELIGION IN THE SCHOOLS)

It is useful to understand the sources of change, although a natural crisis and a social crisis may each have similar consequences. There are common problems in cataclysmic events, whether from natural or social sources. An earthquake or a flood may require immediate help for the victims, the restructuring of social relationships due to death, and the rebuilding of cities or sections of them. Or the catastrophe may be social in nature, the closing of a factory necessitating relief, movement of peoples, search for new employment, adjustment of family patterns. War may involve not only destruction of life and property, but also increased regimentation (and loss of civil liberties), disruption of normal vocational patterns, refocusing of education and science, and deterioration of moral values. It may also bring shifts in population, from rural to urban, from farm to factory, and toward new patterns of racial and ethnic composition of communities. These long-range consequences are much like the results of such recurrent crises as automation, although automation is a part of planned or purposive action.

Social change may also have its source in a process of gradual drift. In the physical environment this can mean the erosion of the soil and the pollution of rivers, with resulting social dislocations. Ralph Linton has called attention to such processes in social terms, contrasting them with technological forces:

The most drastic differences between the thematic values involved in our own economic system and those common to primitive societies in general seem to derive less from the technical developments which have taken place in our own civilization during the last 200 years than from the lessening of intimate social relations and enduring association which has accompanied these developments. The extraordinary degree of both social and spatial mobility . . . has resulted in the breakdown of extended kin groups and in the progressive concentration of populations in cities where opportunities for the establishment of close and continuing social contacts are minimal. A considerable part of the modern industrial population passes its life as transients with both the freedom for individual activity and the psychological insecurity which this condition entails.[15]

Washburne illustrates drift in terms of the impact of mobility on courtship practices. The availability of a family car and the anonymity of a more urban way of life, combined with love-making portrayed on movie screens and increased sex education—all of these modified considerably youth's "definition of socially acceptable behavior and their expectations of one another's responses." [16] Industrialization has had many unpremeditated effects in the South, including its long-run effect on patterns of segregation. Rural electrification and farm-to-market roads have contributed to breaking down distinctions between rural and urban ways of life.

A second source of change is planned or purposive action. Flood control may involve the transplanting of villages, the removal of farm-land from cultivation, and the rerouting of traffic patterns. Tax policy can be used for redistribution of wealth or for spreading purchasing power, and may also result directly in public works or indirectly in inhibiting investment. A Supreme Court ruling on desegregation affects not only the schools but also political alignments, segregation in department store lunch counters, and foreign policy. Or the initial issue in a school controversy has been increased budget and a consequently higher tax rate, but before long the crisis concerned "progressive education." [17]

A third source of change lies in conflicts over values. As men move about more freely and old barriers are broken down, peoples face sets of values and ways of life that diverge sharply from their own. Families from different cultural backgrounds have different ways of rearing children and place different values on formal education. Side by side in a community are congregations with contrasting beliefs, ideas of right and wrong, and ways of worship. Meeting together in the deliberations

[15] "An Anthropological View of Economics," in A. Dudley Ward (ed.), *Goals of Economic Life* (New York: Harper & Brothers, 1953), p. 333.
[16] Washburne, *Interpreting Social Change in America*, p. 21.
[17] Coleman, *Community Conflict*, p. 10.

of the United Nations and in the travels of individual citizens are representatives of competing ways of organizing societies, with different values placed on freedom. The presence of such contrasts and the possibilities of communication across formerly closed borders provide the stimuli for borrowing and innovation—for change.

2. THE CHANGING DIMENSIONS OF SOCIAL PROBLEMS

The church must be aware of and responsive to such changes. There must be realistic appraisal of accomplishments so that we do not waste energies in retaking the same territory, marching up the hill to march back down again, as Walter Rauschenbusch put it. New problems arise and old problems assume new forms. In race relations, the question in the twenties was the ending of lynching; then came campaigns against the poll tax; and in the forties a concern for desegregation itself. With the achievement of desegregation new and different problems will arise in working toward a genuinely integrated (but not regimented) society. Progress has been notable in extended coverage of social security legislation. There is a general sense of public responsibility for minimum decencies (care of the mentally and physically ill and education of handicapped persons, for example) even though there is disagreement on specific details of action. Labor has achieved power in its own right so that countervailing powers of public interest must be set over against those of employer and employee. Let us look at ways in which the dimensions of social problems have changed in context and in goal.

(1) The *application of rationality* to industrial and scientific problems, itself a matter of planned and purposive action, has had effects that have reached far beyond immediate increases in power and productivity. We are hesitant to attempt to use rationality equally in facing problems of human relationships. We rely upon tradition or chance to cope with the challenge of Marxism—"the most large-scale effort to introduce rationality into human affairs." [18] We face also the criticism of our wastefulness from less privileged people, and at once the fact that our resources are dwindling at a rapid rate because of unplanned exploitation. But we fear that manipulation might creep in under the guise of planning.

(2) Tremendous *increases in power*, partly a matter of planned change and partly one of drift of cumulative scientific discoveries, have

[18] Sanders, "Approaches to Social Change," pp. 25-26.

had very mixed consequences. Nuclear power, when put to work in a peacetime economy, may well bring a new revolution in transportation, utilities, work patterns, and leisure. Meanwhile, this power is being used primarily for destructive purposes, or for strategy purposes as a threat of destruction. There is thus an unprecedented possibility of violence along with an unprecedented acceptance of the "tragic necessity" of readiness to use weapons of destruction. This factor, most obvious in the concentration upon nuclear fission and guided missiles but equally violent in the potential reliance upon chemical and bacteriological warfare,[19] stands in paradoxical relationship to the fact of increasing reliance by minorities upon nonviolent means for achieving social justice.[20] There are also shifting concentrations of power. Mills warns of an alliance between military, political, and industrial leaders producing a "power elite," over which ordinary political processes will exercise little control.[21]

(3) We live in an *economy of abundance:* Most of our social problems have been described and defined against the background of an economy of scarcity. Much of our ethical thought has been concerned with production. We have been able to solve many problems by sheer increase in productivity and now must redefine ethical responsibility in an economy of plenty, where we face problems of consumption, distribution, status, and waste more than problems of production.

(4) Social problems emerge in a *vast network of interrelationships.* Problems formerly considered national in scope now have world-wide dimensions and significance. America's treatment of minorities is watched closely by the two thirds of the world that is dark-skinned; juvenile delinquency cannot be considered apart from our acceptance of violence in international relations; many persons fear an "outbreak of peace" because of its possible economic effects.[22]

(5) *Growth in government* has taken place both in sheer size and cost and in range of functions. The country has grown in population and productivity. Many problems have proved to be beyond the scope

[19] Brig. Gen. J. H. Rothchild refers to these weapons as potentially "more effective and more humane" than nuclear ones. "Germs and Gas: The Weapons Nobody Dares Talk About," *Harper's Magazine* (June 1959), p. 29.
[20] See Martin Luther King, Jr., *Stride Toward Freedom* (New York: Harper & Brothers, 1958).
[21] C. Wright Mills, *The Power Elite* (New York: Oxford University Press, 1957).
[22] See Stuart Chase, "Peace, It Could Be Wonderful," *The Progressive* (February 1960), pp. 15 ff.

of local or state action. A mobile society demands highways. We are protected by food and drug laws. Education is a function of government at various levels and many persons see a necessity for federal aid to education without federal control. Conduct of foreign policy is a task of national government.

(6) *Mobility*, whether it be spatial with one family in five moving each year or social with the stresses and strains incident to anxiety about status, strikes at the roots of community life. We have yet to learn how to nurture a sense of responsibility which can find expression quickly and easily as we move from community to community. We are not always aware of the ways in which we use community institutions and offices of leadership as part of our search for status rather than our expression of responsibility. Population shifts also mean heterogeneous communities, with different religious groups and different occupational groups living side by side.[23] We have yet to learn to explore the full riches of cultural pluralism.

(7) We have little disturbing "sense of problem" or mood of concern. Harvey Swados notes that "we have come by insensible stages to the point of denying that serious problems still exist in this nation." Except for juvenile delinquency,

> We have resolutely determined—influenced perhaps more than we realize by the ceaseless cajoling of an advertising culture—to look only on the sunny side of things, to believe indeed that if there is a dark side it exists only in the shadow cast by the Iron Curtain, or in the pathetically underdeveloped lands.[24]

Byron Fox points to two restrictions upon social problem analysis, the limitation of geographic boundaries to our own land and the acceptance without question of the assumptions of our economic system.[25] America lacks a clear sense of moral purpose and a consensus on what its values are. What is for some groups a moral issue becomes for others a matter of taste or manners. There are competing conceptions of what is good ranging from birth control to foreign aid (and these two may be combined in one issue). *The Christian Century* has distinguished between

[23] Coleman, *Community Conflict*, p. 7.
[24] "Work as a Public Issue," pp. 13-14. See also Edward Heimann in the *Union Seminary Quarterly Review* for May 1956.
[25] "American Social Problems in a World Setting."

national *purpose* and national *interest:* "If our aim is to serve nothing higher than our national interest, we cannot creditably serve even that." [26]

C. Emerging Problems

Against the background of these changes we lift up eight emerging issues for future action.

1. INDUSTRIAL RELATIONS

The early concern of the social gospel movement was with problems related to the industrialization of this country. The problem was at first defined in terms of securing the workers' right to organize for collective bargaining and to strike, of protection against unemployment, and of distributing of income (with attacks upon the profit system in the thirties). The areas of concern have been redefined since labor's right to organize has been established and accepted (although the right to strike operates under some limitations) and since social security coverage and unemployment compensation provisions have been made available to more people.

Emerging issues include the responsibility of industry for some kind of "Guaranteed Annual Wage," the responsibility of organized labor for ethical practices of its leaders, and the responsibility of government for preserving the interest of the public and for dealing with inflation. There is also the fact that our economy has been based upon an armaments program for two decades. Economic planning for conversion of productive capacity to peaceful purposes as we work toward reduction of armaments might well enable us to deal more adequately with school facilities, provisions for public health, and expansion of foreign aid.

We face other economic problems. Increasing automation not only challenges us to plan for full employment but it also raises questions of the use of leisure time, standards of success in a status-conscious society, and the meaning of work. Automation affects the work process itself. Harvey Swados contends:

The fact that Americans are spending billions annually on "hobbies" does not mean to me that they are living richer lives, but rather that they are seek-

[26] Editorial, "National Purpose and Christian Mission," LXXVII, 1 (January 6, 1960), 3-4. See also *Life Magazine* issues of May and June 1960; *Goals for Americans* (New York: Prentice-Hall, Inc., 1960).

ing elsewhere for the satisfactions of personal fulfillment that formerly came from the job of work itself.[27]

He relates this question of vocation to leisure, asking whether we can "really believe that workers who increasingly hate what they do will make intelligent use of their increasing leisure time?" His answer is that, "half-numb on the job, they will settle off the job for those mass opiates which render them wholly numb." As lesiure time increases, there will be corresponding competition by commercialized recreation for people's time and money. The churches may need to join with the schools in educational programs for creative use of leisure and may have to provide more opportunities for family-centered instead of age-group-centered activities.

The productivity and plenty of our economy tend to blind us to the needs of such neglected groups as migrant laborers, the aged, and the handicapped. Christian norms preclude consideration of industrial problems in the context of American prosperity without reference to the tremendous needs of underdeveloped areas. Solutions must include sharing our present production and our technology in international economic development.

Finally, the conception of Christian vocation raises for us the question of women at work. While only 6.9 per cent of Methodists think "Woman's place is in the home," there is division whether men and women have equal and identical rights (34.1%), or complementary but different roles (23.7%), or whether full equality is modified by woman's responsibility to home and children (30.6%).[28]

2. FAMILY DISORGANIZATION

Family disorganization is the label given to an array of problems which range from the changing economic function of the family (no longer a producing unit) and working mothers to the problems of housing precipitated by older persons living in the home (returning again in many instances to a three generation family pattern). One is not sure whether divorce rates reveal greater family conflict or less repression of conflicts than have been present in earlier generations.[29]

[27] "Work as a Public Issue," p. 14.
[28] See Appendix B.
[29] See Gibson Winter, Love in Conflict (Garden City: Doubleday & Company, Inc., 1958).

Family stability is challenged by the demands of work patterns (movement at the will of the company, pressure of getting ahead, and so forth) as these affect family community roots and ties. Different members have conflicting expectations of family life. Probably juvenile delinquency belongs more in family disorganization and in the broken home than in crime as such.

Disorganization of family life both shares in and contributes to the larger patterns of social disorganization. The service tasks of the church involve it in social welfare work in dealing with the causes and results of disorganization. In this field there is a continuing need for the churches to improve their standards and facilities in their own church-related agencies and institutions: hospitals and homes, family service agencies, rehabilitation centers, neighborhood houses, and so forth. Churches also share in the civic responsibility for standards and facilities in public agencies and institutions and for providing special ministries in these. In addition there is a preventive and protective dimension to church civic responsibility, in seeking legislation to protect family life, encourage law enforcement, and strengthen community life.

3. POPULATION PROBLEMS

No institution has failed to feel the impact of what in world terms is called the "population explosion." Pressure upon educational facilities has been given dramatic focus as the proportion of the college-age group seeking higher education moves toward 50 per cent. The pressure felt in other countries upon food supply is felt most immediately in this country in dwindling water resources and inadequate housing, and in the long-term effects of soil erosion and depletion of natural resources. A shifting population pyramid (with larger proportions of the aging and of the young) has its impact upon the relatively smaller proportion of persons in their productive years. The concentration of persons in vast urban areas brings problems of transportation, urban renewal, and breakdown of community institutions. Population problems are closely related to increasing mobility.

Discussion of population pressures also brings moral and political questions relating to planned parenthood. Although two states have laws prohibiting dissemination of birth-control information and materials, the acute focus of the problem is in terms of foreign policy. The significant difference of opinion between religious groups in the United

States over whether any foreign aid funds shall be used for the control of population by underdeveloped countries where the population explosion is greatest is at once a moral issue, a church-state question, a political problem, and a question of foreign policy. Debate over such an issue may be the prelude to more controversy to come when religious groups bring conflicting interpretations of policy matters into the political arena. Certainly here is one crucial problem for the next decade.

4. EDUCATION

Educational problems have come to be redefined under the pressure of increasing enrollments, in terms of Soviet competition in science, and in terms of value conflicts in a pluralistic society. "For whom is higher education intended?" is an urgent question as we debate quality vs. quantity. Given the resources of our country and given the necessity of an educated citizenry in a democracy, there would seem to be no inherent reason why the vision of equality in opportunity should rule out the vision of excellence. An economic issue is also raised in so far as rising education costs discriminate against lower income groups. The problem of women at work is often related to the necessity of additional funds for education. It has been possible in higher education to use indirect scholarship funds and loans for dormitories without infringing on academic freedom (except in the Loyalty Affidavit requirements) or favoring sectarian groups.[30]

Increasing emphasis upon science must be set in the framework of the "Cold War." Christians must somehow think in terms of moral values so that science and education can be considered against the background of universal human purpose rather than the national interest alone. There must be free and responsible moral inquiry rather than sectarian indoctrination. A major challenge to formal education comes from the mass media of communication, potentially able to raise cultural standards but today suffering from "payola," manipulation of tastes, and other problems relating to advertising and isolation from a genuine educational concern.

Christians need to share in developing criteria for assessing the arts and to encourage health and vitality of the arts by helping artists resist vulgarization and commercialization. Churches have a special responsi-

[30] See Douglas M. Knight (ed.), The Federal Government and Higher Education (Englewood Cliffs, N.J.: Prentice-Hall, Inc., 1960).

bility for the quality of religious programming on radio and television and for the support of educational TV.

5. ETHNIC RELATIONS

Many nationality and language groups have been effectively assimilated into American life. However, the melting pot as a solution to all minority problems is being challenged by some religious and cultural minorities who seek, not assimilation, but equality of treatment within a pluralistic society. Some also seek special privileges. In different ways the Roman Catholic and Jewish groups pose the questions of providing freedom for religious differences either through a separate system of parochial schools or within the public schools. The problem relating to persons whose differences are of color rather than of culture has also been redefined in several ways. Problems once seen as regional are now national, with desegregation of schools the focus in the South and open occupancy housing the crucial issue in the North. As Haselden expresses the issue, it is not only the *right* of the Negro (and the Indian as well) *to have* (freedom from discrimination) but also his *right to belong* (freedom from segregation) and his *right to be* (freedom from prejudice).[31] Two crucial issues emerge for the decade ahead: one is the role of government in bringing better relations through law, the other is the challenge of secular institutions to the segregation policies and practices in the life of the church. It is worth noting that Methodists seem willing to end segregation in the life of the church more quickly than in the community at large.[32]

6. POLITICAL ISSUES

Christians have concern for both the structure of the political processes and the substantive issues with which these processes deal. We have already noted the shift from a basically economic to a political definition of problems and the redefinition of the role of government in respect to the rights of minorities, to conflicts between labor and management and to education. Paradoxically, as there has been recognition of the relevance of political or governmental action, there has been less clarity and distinction in the issues and principles separating the

[31] Kyle Haselden, *The Racial Problem in Christian Perspective* (New York: Harper & Brothers, 1959), pp. 90-154.
[32] Compare Questions 28 and 29 in Appendix B. Some question whether this would be reflected in behavior.

major parties. The overriding consideration has become accession to or perpetuation in positions of power. Many are urging re-examination of the present system in which both primaries and national conventions are used to nominate candidates for president and vice-president, and of the electoral college system of voting for these high offices. By balancing tickets geographically and by balancing platform pronouncements with regional compaigning, parties seek to win, in the same national election, both the "Negro vote" of the Northern cities and the vote of the Southern conservatives. Likewise in many areas other than civil rights principle is adjusted to appeals to special interest groups.

The lack of clear issues has also been in part a result of bipartisan foreign policy in the face of the threat of Communism. Such an external threat has tended to make for government restriction upon political freedom, civil liberties, and the right of persons to know. The abrogation of the citizen's right to information, even when done in the interest of security, has profound implications for a democratic society. The collaboration of reactionary political leaders and of similarly oriented church groups was evident in the controversy concerning the Air Force Training Manual in early 1960. When Congressional investigating committees have sought to weaken civil liberties, churchmen (such as Bishop G. Bromley Oxnam) acting alone or through the American Civil Liberties Union have taken the lead in opposing arbitrary government action.

On the state political level the balance of power is often held by rural areas, with cities underrepresented in legislative bodies. Irwin Sanders interprets the "ruralite" task as seeking to hold back resources from the city and to secure benefits at the expense of the city. The suburbanite who "refuses to let the affairs of his well-run town be contaminated by any contact with the 'politics-ridden city' [say, in a joint transportation authority] is taking on much of the same coloration as the ruralite." The "urbanite" voice is that of the metropolitan planner who must deal with the drain of talent to the suburbs and the loss of tax revenue through expansion of nontaxpaying educational and recreational facilities.[33]

Many political issues of a substantive nature concern the development of the welfare state.

[33] "Approaches to Social Change."

At one extreme social welfare is defined in terms of an intense collectivism or totalitarianism. On the other hand social welfare is being defined in terms more compatible with pluralistic democratic goals. In this latter conception the state is seen as the legal instrument of the politically organized community, but not as the total community, a legal association which is the instrument, not the master, of the community.[34]

Through the state the community seeks adequate medical care for the aged, social security, unemployment compensation, family services, and education, by protecting the freedom and proper functioning of voluntary agencies and by such state action at various levels as seems required. The state is also responsible for the administration of penal justice, for the related matter of capital punishment, for encouraging economic growth, and for conservation of natural resources—to name only a few issues on which public opinion is divided.

The action of the state is accomplished through the enactment, interpretation, and administration of law, through the maintenance of political order. Christians have a stake in an orderly society governed by law and have often used Romans 13 as sanction for respect for government. Civil disobedience is interpreted by some as disruptive of law and political order.

But Christians have perspectives which enable such action to be seen rather as a protest in the direction of a transcendent law. A communique from the Central Committee of the National Student Christian Federation, dated March 6, 1960, and addressed to Campus Christian Student Groups, states in part:

The law and custom which undergird the civil order are not, descriptively speaking, the embodiment of absolute values, but the manifestation of a particular fabric of social relationships . . . they cannot be disobeyed recklessly. . . . However, God also continually brings their injustice under judgment, and calls Christians to work toward changing the law and custom in the direction of his will.

Civil disobedience and passive resistance in response to what we feel to be an unjust civil order are, to the extent we are willing to accept the legal punitive consequences of our disobedience, an affirmation of the rule of law.

We must distinguish challenges to the law made in the name of a

[34] Muelder, *Foundations of the Responsible Society* (Nashville: Abingdon Press, 1959), p. 144.

higher law and those which stem from self-interest or irresponsibility for actions. Crime is seldom seen as simply a matter of personality disorganization. Increasingly we recognize the responsibility of the community in the act of the criminal, without erasing his own moral responsibility. Such recognition has accompanied attempts to abolish capital punishment and to make penal institutions serve to protect society and rehabilitate offenders rather than to exact punishment.[35] Alcoholism is related not only to traffic accidents and family disorganization but also to crime and to physical and mental health problems.

7. WAR AND PEACE

One cannot adequately face the political problem without recognition of the overwhelming issue of war and peace. This is the most urgent issue of the 1960's. Not only does three fourths of our federal budget go for past wars and preparation for defense, but all other issues tend to be redefined in terms of "the free world vs. the totalitarian world." [36] The Christian must challenge the definition of community in in-group or national terms, whereby any action becomes a moral necessity if it can be shown to contribute to defense. Just as Christians testify to the precedence of the inclusive good over the special interest within a nation, so they must oppose the tendency to define all morality in terms of the national interest, however freighted such an interest may be with the invoking of Christian and democratic values.

There are ethical as well as scientific and political issues at stake in the cessation of nuclear testing and in the negotiations for disarmament. There are moral as well as expediential considerations in the support of dictatorial regimes and the refusal to admit Communist China to membership in the United Nations. The sending of foreign aid requires response to human suffering and understanding of developing economies as well as strictly political assessment. The church can contribute to problems of war and peace out of its fund of understanding through its missionary outreach and through its transcending of any divisive barriers.

[35] Almost 70 per cent of Methodists see the main purpose of a prison as the rehabilitation of offenders. See Appendix B.

[36] See *Foreign Policy and the Free Society* (New York: Oceana Publications, 1958); Muelder, *Foundations of the Responsible Society*, Ch. XIV.

8. PUBLIC VS. PRIVATE POLICY INITIATIVE

Finally, we are divided between a conception of private and public responsibility for attacking social problems. Individualism and evolutionism have reinforced beliefs that individuals, or at the most voluntary associations, should work out their problems without government help. We are reluctant to accept the changed nature of the democratic state and trust it in solving some social problems. John Kenneth Galbraith has focused attention on the distrust of public initiative: "At best public services are a necessary evil; at worst they are a malign tendency against which an alert community must exercise eternal vigilance." He goes on to point out interesting contradictions:

Automobiles have an importance greater than the roads on which they are driven. We welcome expansion of the telephone services as improving the general well-being but accept curtailment of postal services as signifying necessary economy. We set great store by the increase in private wealth but regret the added outlays for the police force by which it is protected. Vacuum cleaners to insure clean houses are praiseworthy and essential in our standard of living. Street cleaners to insure clean streets are an unfortunate expense . . . public services rarely lose their connotation of burden.[37]

A pre-eminent question for the future is the proper role of public initiative and public services in solving our complex problems.

This is a major problem on the world scene, where new nations turn to the principles of "guided democracy" in dealing with problems of economic development and capital accumulation. We rightly fear manipulation as a possible consequence of such efforts. On the other hand, condemnation out of hand of practices that differ from ours may ignore the fact that certain types of action may be more appropriate at early stages of economic and political development than at later ones. Struggling regimes may need our critical co-operation rather than our withdrawal.

D. Social Problems and Christian Social Action

1. CHURCH AND STATE

The churches must recognize both the extent and the limits of Christian social action upon social problems. The churches cannot themselves deal adequately with all problems with the same degree of

[37] *The Affluent Society* (Boston: Houghton Mifflin Co., 1958), pp. 133-34.

responsibility. In some areas of concern the churches have initiated action and established institutions when no other agencies were acting. The churches have exercised a major responsibility for the care of unfortunates (the blind, the physically and mentally ill) through hospitals and welfare institutions. With the seeming necessity of turning to the federal and state governments for funds for hospitals, the churches may have to redefine their conception of state responsibility and of their task.

With their belief in the separation of church and state and their more pluralistic approach to the community, Protestants tend to be more hospitable than Roman Catholics to the assumption of welfare responsibility by secular institutions. At the same time the right of sectarian agencies to protect their own vested interests and therefore to oppose certain public assumption of welfare responsibility must be affirmed.[38]

Muelder calls for research in redefining the meaning of separation in the expanding area of public welfare. In this area, as in education, there is a role for church action in maintaining the diversity of institutional life, in pioneering in new areas, and in encouraging sensitivity to need and achievement of standards in both public and private agencies. Methodists may feel that they can use public funds on behalf of the entire community while a sister church might pursue sectarian ends. They should consider whether their responsibility is not to maintain their institution with their own resources and to encourage supplementary community institutions.

The use of foreign aid funds for birth control information and material by countries facing the population explosion raises especially critical issues. The United States would seem to have no moral ground for refusing such aid to nations requesting it, despite the opposition of some religious groups, any more than it would be justified in curtailing shipments of vaccines because some denominations protest immunization.

In some areas of concern the churches have acted to arouse the public conscience, so that appropriate legal or institutional action could be taken by other agencies. Here the continuing responsibility is to maintain sensitivity, to be responsive to new needs, to help laws and agencies adapt to changing dimensions of problems. In the matter of desegregation of schools, the role of the church should be to create the mood of

[38] Muelder, *Foundations of the Responsible Society*, p. 251.

acceptance of justice, to strengthen the agencies of enforcement of law, to keep alive channels of communication and reconciliation, and to remind men of the needs and hopes of all of God's children. As we have noted, for some social problems, the church must accept responsibility within its own life, not in added institutions. Alcoholics, for example, need not only professional treatment but also acceptance within a redemptive community.

2. FREEDOM AND RESPONSIBILITY

The solving of urgent social problems requires rationality and planning. The critical questions are: "Planning by whom?" and "In the service of what purposes?" We have stressed the proper role of public initiative, the necessity to recognize the government as an agency of freedom as well as of repression. This is not to say that all planning should be by government agencies. It would seem essential in our society for there to be a variety of centers of planning, with freedom and responsibility insured by providing limits on the power of any one center and by more open discussion of purposes, goals, and consequences. We have already referred to the concept of the responsible society as an instructive guide in this connection.

Man is created and called to be a free being, responsible to God and his neighbour. Any tendencies in State and society depriving man of the possibility of acting responsibly are a denial of God's intention for man and His work of salvation. A responsible society is one where freedom is the freedom of men who acknowledge responsibility to justice and public order, and where those who hold political authority or economic power are responsible for its exercise to God and the people whose welfare is affected by it.

... For a society to be responsible under modern conditions it is required that the people have freedom to control, to criticise and to change their governments, that power be made responsible by law and tradition, and be distributed as widely as possible through the whole community.

We therefore condemn:

1. Any attempt to limit the freedom of the Church. . . .

2. Any denial to man of an opportunity to participate in the shaping of society. . . .

3. Any attempt to prevent men from learning and spreading the truth.[39]

[39] *Man's Disorder and God's Design,* "The Church and the Disorder of Society," Volume III of the Amsterdam Series, World Council of Churches (New York: Harper & Brothers; London: SCM Press, 1949), pp. 192-93 of one volume edition. See also Muelder, *Foundations of the Responsible Society,* Ch. I ff.

Persons must be protected against arbitrary political power. Democratic government rests upon the right of the people to know.[40] A vicious circle is created if people are denied certain information and then told they cannot criticize government action because they are not informed. There is also a concern for the responsible use of power on the part of labor leaders, industrial officers, the mass media, and ethnic majorities. Freedom is endangered in the uninhibited conflict of interests by various pressure groups. There is a danger of the church acting simply as a pressure group rather than reminding all of the inclusive interest (which may be especially threatened by some pressure groups).

Freedom rests on at least two emphases in Christian thought: (1) the human personality as somehow requiring the exercise of moral choice, and (2) the redeemed man as set free to love and serve his neighbor. The churches are interested not only in the foundations of freedom and its exercise by individuals but also in religious liberty itself. Harold C. Letts suggests that this involves four concerns in a pluralistic society:

1) No religious group and no adherent to any system of belief should be treated as a second-class citizen because of his belief.

2) In a pluralistic society there should be widespread understanding of the outlook and traditions of various groups.

3) There should be a deeply grounded unity that respects differences but supports a spirit of acceptance of each other.

4) The religious element in a pluralistic society must not be lost or so watered down as to lose its significance.[41]

3. STEWARDSHIP

Another area of concern is the stewardship of all resources, natural and human. Stewardship has often been interpreted as financial provision for church institutions rather than as the more broadly conceived responsibility for conserving the gifts of the creator God. A proper conception would center in a doctrine of Christian vocation, dealing on the one hand with the problem of meaning in work for all men, not just those in church-related jobs, and on the other hand calling for restructur-

---

[40] Readers will recall the early 1960 controversy over the *Air Reserve Center Training Manual* (45-0050), which on page 15-4 read: "Another rather foolish remark often heard is that Americans have a right to know what's going on."

[41] *A Case Book on Christian Responsibility for Freedom*, ed. Harold C. Letts, National Council of Churches, 1960, pp. 75-76.

ing the world of work as well as for individual rethinking of vocation. Problems of "personal" morality, such as drinking of alcoholic beverages and gambling, find their solution in such a positive conception rather than in a negative asceticism. Stewardship must come to terms with standards of consumption, with the creative use of leisure time, with the waste of advertising, and with standards of success based on genuine achievement and social contribution rather than on conspicuous consumption. Stewardship involves conservation of the family, not with any predetermined list of functions but with continuing concern for the nurture of growing persons at all stages of development. Stewardship also involves conservation of natural resources, protection of soil from erosion, water supplies from pollution and exhaustion, and forests and areas of natural beauty from exploitation. George Kennan has shown the relevance of the doctrine of creation to dealing with the destructive forces of nuclear weapons and nuclear testing. He asks whether we have a right to despoil the heritage—natural and biological—of coming generations, even in defending ourselves against a presumed enemy.[42]

4. FORGIVENESS

The concern in stewardship calls for commitment and discipline in caring for and in increasing God's created good. Forgiveness brings together man's failures and refusals with God's redemptive action. The concern is to restore relationships, to rehabilitate persons, to reclaim commitments. It finds its focus in the conception of the inclusiveness of the community of concern. Some persons stand outside the community of concern of any one group simply because of geography, color of skin, or some other "accident of birth." Others stand outside the community of concern because they have grown old or have given themselves to an unpopular ideology. The Christian concern must include in its community of caring the member of the ethnic minorities, seeking equal justice for all, the child or the aged person who cannot care for himself completely, the person whose opportunity is restricted by poverty, whatever the cause. But the redemptive community extends also to those who have forsaken commitments or violated norms. Without diminishing his concern for enforcement of law, stability of family life, or commitment to abstinence, the Christian seeks in personal relationships and social institutions to deal redemptively rather than

[42] "Foreign Policy and Christian Conscience," *Atlantic Monthly* (May 1959), p. 48.

censoriously with the juvenile delinquent, the criminal offender, the unmarried mother, the divorcee, the alcoholic.

5. TRUST

Forgiveness is in one dimension the expression of trust and confidence in advance of justification by behavior.[43] Many social problems dealt with in the preceding section reflect in one way or another a crisis of confidence. Several aspects of the problem of church-state relations have been mentioned. In different ways these are problems of trust. How far can the churches trust the state to deal sensitively in its caring for education, for mental health, and so forth? How far can the state trust the churches to use public funds and public power in the services of community rather than for sectarian purposes? How far can the churches trust one another, as each desires religion to be an influential factor in public morals and policy and none presumably wants ecclesiastical control for itself or others.[44] One implication of such questions would be that no church should ask special privilege for itself, but rather that it should forego seeking for itself influence or funds which it would not want other churches to share equally.

The crisis of confidence is at the center of the quest for international community. Many persons have believed that men and nations would be driven to peace through their fears of nuclear destructiveness or of chemical and biological warfare. But the fear of the consequences of war (or of the threat of war) does not overbalance the fear of the enemy, so that the only trust is in a balance of terror. Reinhold Niebuhr has written: "Terrible as would be the use of the nuclear weapons, the possibility of their use cannot be disavowed without running the danger of capitulation to the adversary by the destruction of the 'balance of terror.' " [45] The late Senator Neuberger urged in protest against hydrogen bomb testing: "Why not err—if err we must—on the side of husbanding human life." [46] Murray Kempton once wrote of a controversial scientist, and his dismissal by the Atomic Energy Commission, words that have a wider relevance:

[43] See Paul Schilling's treatment of the social implications of justification by faith: *Methodism and Society in Theological Perspective*, pp. 221-26.

[44] See A. F. Carillo de Albornoz, *Roman Catholicism and Religious Liberty* (Geneva: World Council of Churches, 1959); Cardinal Lercaro, "Religious Tolerance in Catholic Tradition," *Catholic Mind* (Jan.-Feb. 1960), pp. 12-24.

[45] "The Test of the Christian Faith Today," p. 1241.

[46] Quoted in *The Christian Century*, LXXVII, 12 (March 23, 1960), 341.

We forget . . . [him] at our peril if only because his case was one more of the way stations from which we have retreated on the road down from our ancient sense that trust in each other was an act of faith and a risk worth accepting because its reward was life. The end of that road is the end of community.[47]

Methodists as individual citizens and in voluntary groups will wish to concentrate attention on various specific social problems. As Methodists seek to select specific problems on which to work they will consider (1) urgency of need, (2) clarity of normative issues, (3) others at work on the problem, (4) other claims upon resources, and (5) possibilities of effective action. But whatever specific issues are selected, a church cannot afford to ignore the broader issues of creating a climate of trust in which freedom and responsibility can be exercised through planning, stewardship of God's creation can be expressed, and the redemptive concern can seek a more inclusive community. Church strategy will focus, within this framework, on problems according to the sense of urgency, the accessibility of influence, and the stewardship of resources.

This discussion of social problems followed a presentation of theological and ethical guidelines and assumed the necessity of a normative frame of reference. Yet it has not outlined a distinctively Christian diagnosis of problems. The norms proposed for selection of and action upon areas of social concern are available to all men of good will; social pressures and cultural blind spots operate upon Christians as well as non-Christians; for all the identification of social problems is clouded by prejudice and vested interests. That which is special to Christians should be a genuine openness and a sense of responsibility as they share the life of the church. Those who have faced their own need and know the love of God in Jesus Christ should be more sensitive and more aware of the needs of others. Their gratitude should keep alive a deep sense of obligation. The quality of their commitment should enable them to deal with pressures from within and without. They possess resources within the faith and the fellowship both to know and to act in the area of social concerns. It is such resources, rather than any special diagnosis or solution, that distinguish the Christian in social action.

[47] "Robert Oppenheimer and the Iron Circle," The Progressive (September 1954), p. 17.

PART TWO

The Strategic Response of
Methodism to the Challenge

Synopsis

IN PART ONE METHODIST SOCIAL ACTION WAS INTERPRETED AS A response to the challenge that comes as the social situation is judged in the light of ethical norms. This response of the church is often without any underlying strategy. The church can deny or ignore its purpose, let the situation define its response, be preoccupied with inner tensions, or simply proclaim judgment.

An attempt is made in the chapters which follow to explore ways in which the response of the church can become strategic—rational, purposive, planned, and reflective. (1) In the strategic response persons apply rationality to both goals and situation. (2) They are deliberate in devotion to self-chosen purposes. (3) They allocate personnel and other resources according to a plan. (4) They engage in a continuing process, requiring research and evaluation. (See the chart following the Synopsis of Part One, page 26.)

Strategy is defined as the clarification of ethical norms, the appraisal of social needs, the assessment of costs and resources, and the deployment of energies to establish and accomplish goals. These processes are considered in Chapter IV.

In Chapter V social action is considered within the framework of the larger system of goals of the church. Concern for Christian action in society is a necessary dimension of the inclusive purpose of the church: the increase in the world of the love of God and neighbor. The tasks of maintaining the institution itself are essential but always instrumental to the larger purpose. This calls for critical self-awareness and the acceptance of diversity and disagreement as healthy and necessary. The church must become a community of trust in which differences are faced frankly to make possible a more creative strategy within the life of the church and in its relationship to other social institutions.

CHAPTER FOUR

The Strategic Response

A. The Nature of Strategy

1. THE NEED FOR STRATEGY

METHODIST SOCIAL ACTION FACES THE BASIC DILEMMA OF ALL social movements. It must gain and employ sufficient power and influence to affect the making of decisions in the direction of its goals. One horn of the dilemma focuses upon achieving loyalty to ultimate goals and principles (the purposes for which power is sought) to such an extent that the church is cut off from recruiting new members and from interaction with the society it would influence.[1] The other horn of the dilemma centers in stressing the instrumental goals of building membership and strengthening resources, so much that ultimate goals are compromised beyond recognition. As we have seen, it is within the framework of this general dilemma that the specific dilemmas of Methodist social action must be seen and within the tension of this dilemma that we must live and act.

Strategy, then, is not something which occurs in a vacuum. It is a response. But the action often involves something less than a strategic response. An institution may simply react to challenge on the basis of expediency with little conscious effort to relate purpose to social analysis. For example, Methodism's traditional position of abstinence from alcoholic beverages has been challenged by the explicit teaching of other groups and by divided practice within the denomination itself. The reactive level of response would reaffirm the traditional teaching without

[1] Failure to stress goals may also serve to reduce membership by breeding irrelevance and hence loss of appeal. The extreme case, however, would make membership requirements so stringent that there are almost no recruits.

serious attention to social changes or to theological and ethical bases of Methodist concern. The reaction may be somewhat more self-conscious if it adapts to the social situation, but this gives more importance to external pressure than to internal principle. This adaptive level of response would bring Methodist teaching into line with the practice of the world. If the response deals more with conflicts within the institution itself, it seeks adjustment or abatement of tensions caused by the challenge. This adjustive response might simply de-emphasize the matter of abstinence because it is dividing the church. The reaction becomes judgmental when attention is paid only to the ethical dimension without relation to the situation. Those who deviate from the traditional pattern are condemned. Each of these levels of response resolves prematurely the tension between social analysis and ethical judgment. None of them is itself strategic, although strategy often involves dimensions of adaptation, adjustment, and judgment.

By contrast, the strategic response involves four elements: rationality, purposiveness, planned allocation of resources, and continuing evaluation. It attempts to be rational in consideration of both goals and social situations. It seeks to bring self-chosen rather than imposed purposes self-consciously into relation to all decisions. Resources of personnel and material are allocated in accord with the planned action to achieve the purposes. Rationality is a continuing process, applying research and evaluation to goals, analyses and strategy itself.

A valid strategic response employing coherently the four elements just enumerated may be contrasted with less adequate efforts. The strategic response brings to bear the resources of the church upon a particular problem in the light of the church's goals and purposes. Such a conception of strategy is not entirely new to Methodism. But, as will be noted later, many of Methodism's supposed strategic efforts have been isolated responses to crises or particular problems. The church has had, for example, strategies in the education of children and youth, recruiting new members, dealing with problems of beverage alcohol, achieving a new world order, and strengthening Christian higher education. To be sure, it has not always known how to relate learning experiences in church schools to those in public schools and to the problems and choices faced each day. It has not always known how to orient new members in the theological and worship setting of Methodism, nor how to help them find their places of responsibility in its organizational structure. Methodism has not always seen social problems in relation to each other and tried to deal with the consequences as well as the causes of alcoholism, as it is now doing. Again, the church has been tempted to treat world order and higher education as urgent only for a quadrennium.

In short, the supposed strategic responses of Methodism have often been specific and *ad hoc*, unrelated to each other or to long-range goals. The church has seldom spelled out goals and kept account of results so that there could be an evaluation of effectiveness (except in terms of financial cost, numbers attending, and literature distributed). Many strategies have been devised administratively through bureaucratic processes, without adequate involvement of regional and local personnel. This is not to imply that bureaucracy is undesirable; it is, in fact, a necessity in modern organizations of the size and complexity of Methodism. Long-range planning cannot be accomplished without long-term appointments of "professional" personnel, trained to work within and through bureaucratic processes, and to involve local leadership, laymen, ministers, and specialists, in responsible two-way communication. Nevertheless, it is increasingly urgent that Methodism achieve democratically a coherent strategy, related to the planning of other groups, that it consider together both goals and tactics, and that it provide for continuing evaluation. What then is sound strategy?

2. THE DEFINITION OF STRATEGY

We have indicated that the idea of strategy is not new to Methodism. Whenever Methodists in committee or agency or conference session self-consciously consider the goal or goals they seek to achieve, take account of obstacles and costs, and then plan for collective or individual action, the church's response to the challenges facing it is given *strategic* form. Our concern in this study is not to set forth another strategy, nor to produce a quadrennial program, nor to provide an organizational chart or a handbook of committee procedures, nor even to blueprint "goals for a decade." Our concern is to enable the Methodist response to move from a casual and *ad hoc* crisis orientation to one which is increasingly self-conscious, deliberate, and long-range, yet flexible enough to meet crises as they arise. Our search is for methods and motivations, institutional understanding and dynamic forms that will help Methodism to think and act strategically.

111

The definition of strategy is usually given in military terms, as in *Webster's New International Dictionary:*

1. The science and art of employing the armed strength of a belligerent to secure the objects of a war. More restricted, the science and art of military command, exercised to meet the enemy in combat under advantageous conditions.

2. Use of stratagem, or artifice; planning; intrigue.

There are unfortunate connotations for church strategy in such a definition. The assumption is that goals are already fixed and that strategy is merely a technical matter of accomplishment. Such a conception lends itself to manipulation, removes goals from continuing re-examination, and overlooks the unity of ends and means.

The military conception organizes action against an "enemy," tempting the strategist to shift focus from solving a problem or resolving an issue to overcoming an opponent. One of the few explicit treatments of strategy presents its task thus: "to recruit and organize the strength on its side in the manner that will be most effective for assault and then seek out and strike at the weakest points of resistance in the enemy line.[2] There may be a sense in which Christians need to see their own attitudes and behavior, church practices, and even themselves as the enemy. It strengthens rather than weakens the strategic response when Christians are aware of their own involvement in evil, confess their sin, and seek reconciliation with other men and with God. Edwin T. Dahlberg has pointed out that the mission of Jesus was "not to destroy the enemy but to abolish the enmity." [3]

In this study, *strategy is defined as the clarification of ethical norms, the appraisal of social needs, the assessment of costs and resources, and the deployment of energies to establish and accomplish institutional goals.* The emphasis is not on technical harnessing of means to predetermined goals but on the continuing process of revising goals, confronting changed situations, weighing alternatives, and reconsidering institutional forms and procedures.[4]

[2] R. M. MacIver, *The More Perfect Union* (New York: The Macmillan Co., 1948), p. 82.

[3] "The Churches and the National Conscience," reported in *Information Service*, XXXVIII, 13 (June 20, 1959).

[4] C. E. Rothwell outlines four steps in the formulation and execution of policy: clarification of goals, evaluation of the situation, selection of a course of action by weighing

The strategic process includes elements of both proper timing and co-operation. There is a certain timelessness about goals and norms, but the social situation and the institution exhibit different degrees of readiness for change at different times. The phasing or timing [5] of action will need to take into account the stage of growth of the institution, the involvement of leaders in other tasks, the amount of stress or dissatisfaction, the ability to act in the direction of achieving goals, and the urgency of the task. Another aspect of timing is the calculation of which steps can be taken in which order; the initiation of certain tasks may await the accomplishment of others. For example, the determining of next steps for Methodism's Negro colleges depends upon both the improvement of instruction for Negroes in elementary and secondary schools and the pace of integration in other institutions of higher education.[6] Timing is crucial if strategy is not to become a rigid pattern of action to which all are expected to conform despite differences of approach and changes in the situation. There must be sufficient flexibility of planning to provide both for crises and for varying kinds of action, whether the difference be of appropriateness or scope of action.[7]

We have already noted the need for democratic planning that involves laymen and ministers as well as "professionals." Members must be a part of fact-finding and review procedures if these are to be accepted and effective. This is as true in the survey of a local church as in the evaluation of the jurisdictional system. Participation by many persons in "hearings," fact-finding, and educational preparation is important. Every member is a communicator whose information and feeling about the proposed action is as important to him and to his neighbors as is the opinion of the higher status group in the church.

The authors' principal concern is a strategy for the church and its members in social education and action. Social action always has actual

---

probable consequences of alternatives, and determination of optimum means. In D. Lerner and H. D. Lasswell (eds.), *The Policy Sciences* (Palo Alto: Stanford University Press, 1951), p. ix.

[5] See also Chap. VI.

[6] Illustrations will typically be taken from within the general framework of official Methodist positions, although the commitments of the authors will also be evident.

[7] Paul H. Nitze suggests that human freedom may be effective only at the margin. "At any given moment in time the margin of freedom left us may seem so small as to make it hardly worthwhile to exercise our will. But the narrow margin of today becomes the foundation of the broader possibility for tomorrow. . . . The decision of today makes possible, or forecloses, ten decisions of tomorrow." *The Recovery of Ethics*, p. 27. See also *A Case Book on Christian Responsibility for Freedom*, Chs. I-III.

or potential consequences beyond the immediate group. Its aim is to reform the institution and to change the relevant parts of its social environment. Social action is the organized participation of Christians in processes by which decisions are made and implemented in the church, the community, voluntary associations, the nation, and international bodies. Social education is the preparation for such participation and the continuing study which accompanies action. Evolving strategy includes the historical understanding of the church's interaction with society (hence Volumes I and II in this series), social and cultural analysis of need, working out policy within a framework of theological and ethical norms (hence Volume III in this series), and deepening motivation in the ongoing worship and other group life of the church.

When there is sufficient critical self-awareness, the church will itself be an *object* of planned change. The peculiar role of the unofficial social action agency and one role of any official agency is to speak *to* the church and to help the church find its true voice for speaking to society. The church is also an *agent* of planned change, for example, making pronouncements, working toward "Christian Responsibility on a Changing Planet," [8] or desegregating its own institutions. Again, strategy will be implemented as motivated and informed churchmen participate in social action organizations outside the church or make decisions in jobs, voting booths, and market-places.

Thus social education and action pervade the life of the church. They require renewal in the central acts of worship when self-awareness is sharpest and commitment is deepest. They need clarification in the study class seeking to wrestle with urgent problems in the light of Christian truth. They find expression at the mill gate or bargaining table or board room, at the seat of government or in the "smoke-filled room," and on the college campus when vocational decision seeks to relate talent and training to the world's need in the perspective of God's purposes.

3. STRATEGY AS A PROCESS

As we have noted, the elements in strategy include clarification of norms, appraisal of needs, assessment of resources, and deployment of energies. Ethical norms considered in Chapter II provide the yardstick

[8] National Council of Churches of Christ in America, Study Guide for Department of International Affairs, Nationwide Program for Peace, 1959.

against which institutions must be measured. Some institutions are then judged to frustrate the growth of persons, impede the realization of the responsible society,[9] or interfere with the proper functioning of religious institutions.[10] Appraisal of social needs, as dealt with in Chapter III, requires some understanding of the social situation. This involves more than attention to a list of recognized "social problems," for new "problems" emerge as old ones are dealt with and particular problems take on new dimensions and significance as other changes take place. We turn now to consider strategy as a dynamic process.

This study relies upon social science conceptions and is at the same time critical of explanations of social change and of analysis of contemporary problems. One difficulty with much social science thinking is its preoccupation with equilibrium models, with stability and how things fit together, rather than how things change. Such models slow down the process for more adequate analysis. There is danger only in so far as the model is assumed to be the real thing and the equilibrium becomes static. Then action consists in unfreezing the *status quo*, moving to a new point and refreezing. A closely related conception views religious institutions as contributing basically to the integration of society, as conserving traditions, and as resisting change.[11] These notions have offered little guidance to or hope for religiously motivated social action.

Recently social scientists have achieved new insights concerning social processes and the functions of religious institutions. When society is understood more as an organism than as a machine, change and growth are seen as normal rather than as exceptional processes. Man's responsibility is sometimes to get change started, but more often to guide change. Planned change is conceived as purposeful intervention to accelerate, retard, or direct processes that are already in motion.[12] Religion performs certain important integrative and conservative functions,[13] but

⁹ See Walter G. Muelder, *Foundations of the Responsible Society; In Every Place a Voice* (Cincinnati, Ohio: Woman's Division of Christian Service, 1957).

¹⁰ Although Protestant concern does not focus on religious institutions alone, there must be freedom for their functioning.

¹¹ See Elizabeth Nottingham, *Religion and Society* (Garden City: Doubleday & Company, 1954); Richard Hofstadter, *Social Darwinism in American Thought*, Revised (Boston: Beacon Press, 1955).

¹² The authors wish to acknowledge their indebtedness to the staff of the Boston University Human Relations Center for clarification of this issue and of the problem of conflict.

¹³ J. Milton Yinger offers a functional definition of religion as "a system of beliefs and practices by means of which a group of people struggles with the ultimate problems of

it also provides a transcendent reference for social criticism, a mission which includes social action as an essential element, and group life out of which can issue courage and willingness to sacrifice.

Rather than assume that social institutions and theological norms will continue as they are, relatively unmodified, we must deal with both stability and change. This study, while recognizing the necessity of conservative action in maintaining stability, will concentrate on the dynamic aspect of social institutions. There is always a danger of accepting the present level of practice without providing for new problems, new knowledge, new resources. The strategy proposed herein sees both theological insights and society interacting and changing, so that future projections take account of forces already at work. C. E. Rothwell urges that "the situation to be met is normally not static but involves a complex of moving forces" and that policy attempts to "shape the future by exerting influences upon trends that flow from the past into the present." [14]

There are several cautions related to long-range projections of changes and trends as the basis for devising of strategies. One is the danger of assuming that we control events. Another concerns the danger of miscalculation of events and reminds us of the necessity of flexibility in tactics and of continuing evaluation. A third is a reminder of immediate relevance, a caution that long-range planning should not divert the church from present responsibilities and needs. Truman B. Douglass writes: "Facing the possibility of humanity's total self-destruction in nuclear warfare, who can say what is 'long-range'? It is possible that the next decade is the longest 'range' we have." [15]

Not only must there be appraisal of needs; assessment of costs and resources is also required. Once an area for action is defined, what will the proposed program cost in terms of dollars and cents, energies of professional personnel and lay people, and spiritual resources? Each demand must be weighed against demands in other areas, as to urgency

human life . . . ultimate primarily because of their impact on human association." *Religion, Society and the Individual*, pp. 9, 12. See Herbert E. Stotts, *Introduction to the Sociology of Religion* (Boston: Wesley Press, 1958), p. 26.

[14] In *The Policy Sciences*, eds. Lerner and Lasswell, p. ix.

[15] "The Relevance of Long-Range Planning to the Task of the Church." He points to two "massive mistakes" in "betting on the shape of the future": one by Protestant home missions boards in the 'thirties deciding that church extension had come to an end, and one by foreign boards assuming China as the key area of work.

of need, uniqueness of contribution, and relative claim upon resources in hand or potentially available. A further consideration involves foreseeable consequences—the effects of the action upon the problem itself, upon other areas (as the effect of censorship of questionable publications upon the area of civil liberties), and upon the church itself (the cumulative effect of having acted or failed to act). In all of this there is implied some measuring of resources: what do we have or can we secure in money, power, leadership, unity of purpose, and enlistment of necessary support within Methodism and co-operating groups? With whom is the issue joined? What are the motivations and resources of the opposition, which may range from sincere disagreement to defense of "vested interests" and from deeply entrenched habit to million-dollar advertising accounts?

Deployment of energies suggests that strategy must proceed from study and planning into policy and then eventuate in action. Strategic thinking must always be done in the light of long-range goals and purposes of the institution, which hopefully overlap with long-range goals and purposes of members. But attention must also be given to the immediate satisfactions of persons involved (rewards such as involvement in a common cause, a sense of accomplishment, and so on) and to the immediate requirements of the institution (for participation of members, growth of constituency, continuity of institutional life, conservation of institutional resources). Here is the perennial problem of allocation of energies among maintenance, program, and service tasks.[16] Maintenance tasks are those necessary to keep the institution going as such. Program tasks involve carrying out the goals of the institution in its own life and in society. Service tasks designate meeting needs of members and non-members in such an agency as counseling center or hospital. Methodism has not always apportioned its resources among these tasks in accordance with its mission in the world, but it has seldom assumed that there were fixed limits to its resources, material or spiritual. J. H. Oldham has written:

It is of no small moment whether, when we speak of the church, we picture to ourselves the church as we have hitherto known it, or whether we think in trustful expectancy of the church which it is in God's power to

[16] See Chap. V.

fashion as the instrument for the fulfillment of his purpose in our time and in the days to come.[17]

Crucial to the Methodist strategic response is the assumption that neither the church nor society will remain what it is.

B. Establishing the Goals

The strategic response is a continuing one, cumulative in principle but providing for criticism and creativity. In the pages which follow attention is given to the phases of strategy: establishing the goals of action, assessing needs, costs, and resources, and deployment of energies. Each step is abstracted from its context in the process in which all phases intermingle and interpenetrate.[18]

The story is told of a marksman practicing his skill by shooting at the blank side of a large barn. After firing his shots, the marksman proceeded to paint the circles of a target, fixing the bull's-eye squarely upon the greatest cluster of holes. Such a procedure may provide considerable gratification of the moment, but it offers little test of accuracy or opportunity of improvement. H. Conrad Hoyer addressed an inquiry to several denominations asking about statement of purpose and outline of functions. He discovered that most stated purposes relate only to special emphases and that some church constitutions lack a statement of basic function. Many constitutions seemed not to have been reviewed since the establishment of the denomination. Mr. Hoyer offers "one gratuitous bit of counsel": that they review their statements and restate purposes and functions "in the light of the situation of church and society today." He concludes: "While there will always be a vast spread between affirmation and realization, the churches will more nearly achieve that which they have been called to do if these tasks are clearly stated.[19]

[17] Visser 't Hooft and Oldham, *The Church and Its Function in Society*, pp. 2-3.

[18] In recent years increasing attention is being paid to planned change and to evaluation. The authors are indebted principally to the following studies: Ronald Lippitt, Jeanne Watson, and Bruce Westley, *The Dynamics of Planned Change* (New York: Harcourt, Brace & World, Inc., 1958); Stanley K. Bigman, "Evaluating the Effectiveness of Religious Programs," mimeographed, 1958; H. Conrad Hoyer, "Criteria for Determining the Effectiveness of the Churches," mimeographed, 1959; Robert Lisensky, "The Methodist Church and War and Peace," unpublished Ph.D. dissertation, Boston University Graduate School, 1960; John Philip Wogaman, *Methodism's Challenge in Race Relations* (Boston: Boston University Press, 1960).

[19] Hoyer, *op. cit.*, a paper prepared for the National Council of Churches Consultation on Long-Range Planning, November 1959.

The need for clarification of goals already implicitly accepted and for clear statement of present goals is especially urgent in the area of social action. In the last chapter we noted Henry A. Kissinger's perceptive comment that "in the absence of well-understood goals each problem becomes a special case." [20] A fragmented approach to strategy precludes consistent and purposeful action and opens the way for ad hoc solutions. J. Milton Yinger indicates the mounting urgency of some problems seen in new settings: "To pursue goals that may have had meaning a century or even a decade ago may be to court utter failure in a world in which the aim of brotherhood has suddenly been transformed from an exciting vision to an absolute necessity." [21]

Some goals are normative guidelines, of necessity general and long range, little subject to change. Others are attempts to relate the more ultimate norms to immediate steps with varying degrees of attainability. Such a distinction might be drawn between the ultimate goal of world peace and the immediate goal of negotiated disarmament. A distinction also needs to be made between the goals that are ascribed or assigned to a board, agency, or local church by the General Conference (or to a local church commission by the official board) and those that are assumed voluntarily.[22] The latter are set by the board of the church for itself, within its framework of larger responsibility and in response to the challenge of the immediate situation. There may be modifications in intermediate goals as Methodists join in co-operative action with other institutions, but these are under continuing criticism in terms of the long-range goals.

The process of clarifying institutional goals for Methodism has several important results. Clarification is a valuable part of social education. Also, members identify more readily with goals they understand and have helped to formulate; they become publicly committed to the aims and so deepen their motivation to join in achieving the goals.[23] Finally, clear statement of goals involving commitment to Christian action in society puts the burden of proof upon those who oppose such action and

[20] "The Policymaker and the Intellectual," The Reporter, p. 32. This is the persistent peril of situational ethics. See Chap. II. The ordering of social action goals within the larger goals of Methodism will be treated in Chap. V.

[21] "The Function and Control of Power in the Church," a paper prepared for the World Council of Churches Commission on Institutionalism, June 1959.

[22] See Chap. VI.

[23] See Lippitt, et al., Dynamics of Planned Change, p. 202.

so releases persons with social concerns from preoccupation with defensive maneuvers.

1. INSTITUTIONAL GOALS

The importance of the process by which institutional goals are established has already been suggested. What Methodism becomes as it clarifies its purposes is as crucial as what Methodism affirms to be its purposes. Confronted with some particular issues, Methodism's decision may be spontaneous, on the awareness of moral principles involved, without debate. This will seldom be done in decisions concerning long-range goals. Democratic debate and provision for unpressured deliberation are crucial, but goal setting in Methodism can never be accomplished by a simple counting of votes or by the hurried legislation that comes as General Conference nears adjournment.

Reaching spiritual consensus must become a central concern rather than an incidental by-product of church action.[24] Much more attention needs to be focused on the ways in which consensus can be achieved; but especially within the church there must be, over and over, an appeal beyond the existing consensus to an overarching firmament of truth and right, however dimly perceived. Reinhold Niebuhr has phrased it thus: "Evidently there are limits to democracy in the church as in other communities, particularly when democracy means that a contemporary and local majority defies the moral standards set by a longer history and a more universal consensus." [25]

This consensus ultimately relates as much to worship as to deliberation and voting. Joseph Sittler, Jr. is convinced of the integral relation of "faith and order" and "life and work." He argues that "our immediate vexations" of corporate and social life must be placed in the context of worship, "the remembered and celebrated history of redemption," because "the problems of management and labor, . . . race, . . . knowing who one is, are not problems to be solved by one generation's experience." [26] It is possible for such appeals beyond present consensus to be

[24] See pp. 155 ff.
[25] "The Test of the Christian Faith Today," The Christian Century, LXXVI, 43 (October 28, 1959), 1239-43.
[26] "Some Concepts of the Church," a paper presented to the Division of Life and Work, National Council of Churches. Sittler refers also to a "liturgically built-in sense of humor, protective against . . . the current theological pattern which would urge that the only way to bring a man to confrontation of the Christian gospel is along the road of

appeals only to past history. But if the Christian would take full account of the continuing activity of God, he would have to provide for a process of achieving consensus and appealing beyond it, both to "a longer history" and to new understandings.

This emphasis in the strategic response is on deliberative consideration of values and principles and of relationships with groups which have competing goals. We have stressed the fact of change as ongoing, but we conceive of planning as more than precariously riding the waves of changes that occur without the impact of human choice. Strategy assumes that men can, by taking thought and by acting, affect the waves of change. It would confront the complexity of changes going on and the competing claims of ideologies with appeals for rationality rather than emotional response. Such an appeal to the rational capacity of man in no sense eliminates the appeal to values, the necessity of commitment, or the fact of involvement. Man is not a spectator but an actor, and he can become a thoughtful and deliberative actor.

What then are the tests by which Methodists can exercise their capacity for rational and faithful choice of goals? We would propose four larger tests, each inclusive of lesser ones: the coherence of goals, the acceptance of obligation to act upon goals established, the inclusiveness of concern, and the awareness of consequences.[27]

The test of coherence of goals involves first the *internal consistency of values and principles*. This is a principle of limitation, a requirement to examine each goal to see whether it contradicts another goal or the larger framework of goals. If we really mean that present consensus is not final, then awareness of inconsistency may constitute a demand to reconsider the previously accepted value or to restructure the constellation of purposes. This points to a second principle, that of adequacy or amplitude. Does the system of goals give expression to the full range of values and ideals of the Christian faith; does it do justice to such theologically

---

despair! Unless, so it is widely declared, one can be brought to a shuddering protoplasmic mass of negation, there is no way to hear the gospel." Worship is more than Sittler's incisive phrase indicates, but the phrase places Sunday morning in an inclusive context.

[27] The dependence of this section upon Edgar S. Brightman, *Moral Laws* will be obvious to many readers. Acknowledgment should be made to L. Harold DeWolf and Walter G. Muelder for extension and reformulation of the system of "laws." The authors are also indebted to Robert Lisensky for criteria developed in the dissertation referred to previously. Kenneth D. Benne points to the necessary establishment of conditions in education and research to make application of the criteria meaningful and possible.

rooted ideas as courage, love, and sacrifice? The inclusive social goal with which lesser goals must finally cohere is the kingdom of God.[28]

The second test deals with the acknowledgment by those establishing the goals of the responsibility to act in accord with the goals. The responsibility can range from a vague "some one ought . . ." to less general statements concerning the United Nations or the United States or Christians. Those goals which commit Methodism in some one or several institutional forms are more immediate: Methodist boards, church-related colleges, local churches, and so forth. The tone of the accepted goal can range from a permissive "It would be nice if . . ." to much more positive and urgent expressions. This test would also seek to balance the normative "best possible" with the relative "specific goals attainable." Recognition of the principle of relevance, while acknowledging that not everything can be done at once, should never be an excuse for inactivity or a justification of things as they are.

The third test has to do with inclusiveness of concern, the extent of community, asking who is considered as the "in-group" and who is excluded. Does the goal seek to enlarge the community of co-operation and to extend its application to an expanding fellowship? Reinhold Niebuhr interprets Jesus' saying: "If ye love them that love you, what thanks have ye?" as challenging every form of community that conflicts with a more inclusive community.[29] This criterion can ask too much of the sensitiveness of the isolated Christian or an individual church. It requires testing Methodist goals against those of the National and World Councils of Churches, and goals of the United States against formulations in the United Nations.

The final test proposed here is that of considering and accepting foreseeable consequences. The use of the word "foreseeable" implies that some consequences may be unanticipated, a matter that will be dealt with later. This test asks, not consistency among goals, but consistency of goals with methods chosen to achieve them. There is a sense in which principles of strategy are neutral as to goals sought, in which procedures

[28] See p. 76.
[29] "The Test of the Christian Faith Today." See also Walter G. Muelder, Foundations of the Responsible Society (Nashville: Abingdon Press, 1959), esp. Ch. II, "Mankind: The Unit of Co-operation." Paul Nitze holds that a basic question of politics and of ethics is that of the "we" and the "they," a question to be considered in the light of overlapping "we" structures and systems of value. The final judgment is in terms of a "'we' group virtually coterminous with mankind as a whole." The Recovery of Ethics, pp. 23-25.

can be used to seek or to oppose specific social action, can be made to serve "good" or "bad" ends. The authors trust the unity of ends and means, in which, finally, the use of "good" means for "bad" ends is self-defeating. They also trust that the democratic process of Methodism will operate, in choice of means as of ends, within constitutionally established limits, with consciousness of the Methodist and Christian ethical heritage, and with awareness that we act under the judgment and mercy of a transcendent God.

2. Goals for Whom?

One essential step in the establishment of goals is the specifying of audience: to whom is the statement of goal addressed (and by whom is it spoken). Without adequate representation and communication and lacking a clear understanding of audience, there is always the danger of "the fallacy of group soliloquy," of being misled by "the feeling of unanimity reached by a small minority unmindful of their relative isolation." [30] Methodism should properly have different goals for different groups within the church as they seek to relate the general goals to different aspects of institutional life in American society.

This study has chosen very deliberately to use the general term Methodism, within which may be distinguished several levels; the official action of the General Conference, the program of general boards, the policies of annual conferences, the decisions of episcopal leaders, the work of the local church, and the individual Methodist as he votes alone, or works through his church, or joins a voluntary group outside the church for social action ends. In interviews with board executives we asked concerning their image of Methodism, for whom did they speak, and their image of their audience, to whom did they speak. One leader disclaimed any particular image of the church, acknowledging: "While I usually try to speak for myself, I know that I am looked upon as a representative of a special interest of the church." Leaders in formulating church goals and policy need to be aware of such conditioning factors as their regional background, their educational attainments, and their present responsibilities as these influence their judgments. Does the leader know—and help others understand—when he speaks as a churchman, when as one with assigned responsibility, and when as one who

[30] J. Milton Yinger, "The Function and Control of Power in the Church," Yinger acknowledges the prior use of the phrase by Robert K. Merton.

seeks to articulate the voice of the church? What authority does he claim as he speaks? Another board executive saw his immediate "audience" as his own board, which, together with leaders in annual conferences, constituted almost a parish. He might look beyond this audience to the church at large or to public policy. Still another executive, operating in Washington, distinguished four audiences: the members of Congress (usually without reference to church relationship), the members of his board, Methodism at large, and the general public.

Whatever the level of work, it would seem vital for the social strategist to be aware of the audience for whom goals are formulated and to whom they are addressed. Some goals may be addressed to the churchman, in some one or more of his various roles *within the church:*

1. As an individual Christian, member of family, and so forth

2. As a church member, participating in the life of the church in its local expression

3. As a representative policy maker for the church, whether a member of the official board, or a board of directors of a hospital, or of an annual or General Conference, or of a general board, or of the Council of Bishops, or of some commission of the National or World Councils of Churches

4. As a "professional" in the church, whether minister in a local church, seminary professor, or board staff member

Other goals may be addressed to the churchman in some role *outside* the life of the church as such:

1. As a member of a voluntary association such as the Parent-Teachers' Association, American Civil Liberties Union, World Affairs Council, and so forth

2. As an employer, employee, consumer, stockholder

3. As a citizen, voter, member of a political party

4. As a policy maker in government, member of city council, judge, senator, or administrative official

Still other goals may have as their target the "general public." This may mean influencing public opinion so that responsible officials have support for action on goals addressed to them. It may mean participation in the process of helping the nation clarify its goals. It may mean taking account of special groups not now reached by the church, such as alcoholics, the mentally disturbed, radical nonconformists, persons with criminal records, and "those who are not disinherited economically but who are excluded from the community of the conventionally and piously respectable." [31]

Political leaders are often a target for church policy pronouncements, sometimes as if they were human barometers, expected simply to reflect the atmosphere generated by various pressure groups. There is an element of the "self-fulfilling prophecy" in such treatment. The policy maker treated as an object to be manipulated tends to become just that, rather than one who weighs rationally the various claims for his vote and influence and decides on the basis of publicly known values. Kenneth Underwood has argued that the American politician has the obligation (1) to exercise the full power of his office, to lead the people; (2) to express in policy the good of the whole society, rather than a special interest; (3) to encourage the critical judgment of the electorate.[32] It is in such a context that he serves as the responsible representative of his constituency.

If one takes seriously the necessity of specifying the target and evaluating results, then one is committed to the further specifying of action expected, whether acceptance of belief, modification of attitude, involvement in institutional life, adoption of a way of life (ethics), or some combination of these.

When a person becomes a Methodist, he commits himself to goals which are deliberately general rather than specific and which deal with individual repentance and obedience to God's commandments.[33] Goals more explicitly related to social action are dealt with in "The Methodist Social Creed," [34] adopted appropriately by the quadrennial General Conference. This conference is a delegated body, representing both laymen and ministers by election from an annual or provisional conference (and so, all local congregations of Methodism).[35] The overarching goals of Methodism are thus clarified and established by a body of responsible persons, removed from the pressures and provincialisms of local communities, operating in consciousness of their moral commitments. Within the framework of goals set by the General Conference, specific and

[31] Douglass, "The Relevance of Long-Range Planning."
[32] "The Social Responsibility of the American Politician," to be published, in *Politics and the Responsible Society.*
[33] See "The Order for the Baptism of Adults," *Doctrines and Discipline of The Methodist Church,* 1960, ¶ 1912; see also ¶ 1910-16.
[34] *Discipline,* 1960, ¶ 2020; see also ¶ 2021-2026, dealing with the family, temperance, world order, race, and so forth.
[35] *Discipline,* 1960, ¶ 5, 7, 8, 21.

local goals can be established by boards, agencies, annual conferences, local churches, and commissions on Christian social relations. This raises the crucial question of communication between local and national levels of Methodism, for communication lies at the heart of the process of establishing goals.

3. DEVISING CHANNELS OF COMMUNICATION

When voices are heard protesting that General Conference action or general board program does not reflect the sentiment of "grass roots Methodism," the appeal is for communication from the local to the national level. When lay groups in Texas organized action protesting the further participation of Methodism in the National Council of Churches unless the council repudiated the stand of its fifth World Order Study Conference on recognition of Communist China, the saddest aspect was that some laymen heard of the N.C.C. action through secular attacks upon it rather than through Methodist channels.[36] The need is for genuine two-way communication, not only by better reporting in news organs but also by the extension of participation of representative persons in the forming of policy and so in telling others about it.

There are at least four problems in improving the quality of the Methodist communication network. One is the pre-emption of usual channels with "promotional" material to the exclusion of background information, news of decisions reached and decisions pending.[37] A second problem centers in the process of representation, especially of the denomination in ecumenical meetings. The Reverend E. Jerry Walker, for example, writes of his experience on the General Board of the National Council of Churches that "virtually all the ministerial members ... held executive positions within their denominations [ten of our delegates are bishops] while I am just a local pastor." [38] There is a tendency, partly because of expense budgets and flexible schedules, and partly because of presumed competence, to overrepresent connectional officials, providing key leaders with multiplied opportunities to the neglect of broader participation by laymen and local pastors.

[36] For discussion of the N.C.C. action, see pp. 35 ff. For presentation of the Texas response, see the report by Das Kelley Barnett in *Christianity and Crisis*, April 27, 1959.

[37] An important exception is *Concern*, published twice each month by the General Board of Christian Social Concerns of The Methodist Church.

[38] "A Friendly Critic Looks at the National Council," *Christian Advocate* (January 21, 1960).

Regionalism in the church is a third barrier to communication. Because Methodist leaders in one area or jurisdiction tend to communicate more with each other than across regional lines (except at national meetings), stereotypes held of each region by the others are perpetuated without opportunity for correction. There is no guarantee that talking across lines will break down stereotypes, but one can rest assured that refusal to talk will reinforce barriers to understanding. This suggests that communication involves more than transmission of ideas, that it must also eventuate at some point in confrontation of persons. Regional lines are crossed as persons meet and work together in the general boards, in study commissions, and in special conferences such as those on family life, town and country work, and human relations. This problem poses special difficulties in ministerial education if tendencies toward regional seminaries prevent students from studying with their fellows in at least a national if not an international company.

A fourth problem can exist within as well as between regions; in fact, it can be found even within relatively small local churches. This is the phenomenon known as "pluralistic ignorance." [39] Members of a group in which there has been no real discussion of issues may have completely mistaken notions of the ideas and feelings of other members. Sometimes an opinion survey reveals that prevailing sentiment is quite different from what "everyone thought," and persons who have refrained from action because they were sure they were all alone have found they had many silent partners. Methodism can never truly find its voice in the establishing of institutional goals until it devises a current inventory of Methodist opinion with methods and motivations for overcoming pluralistic ignorance.

C. Assessment of Needs, Costs, Resources

1. AWARENESS OF NEED

The strategic response is always to some area of human need, actual or potential. It involves awareness of needs and balancing of urgencies over against costs and resources. Assessment alternates its focus between the human problem or area of need,[40] actual or felt, and the ability and willingness of the institution to respond. Many institutions employ out-

[39] See Lippitt, The Dynamics of Planned Change, p. 154.
[40] See Chap. III and pp. 114 ff.

side experts or consultants for one or both of these tasks. In a real sense Methodism is developing such experts within its leadership: technically competent staff members of boards; teachers and researchers in college, university, and seminary; laymen whose area of specialization can be utilized in the church; and ministers who are acquiring training in specific areas of social action. Certainly we need to extend the training of such persons and to provide for the systematic use of specialized knowledge and skills.

But in human relations the role of the expert is not to assess either outside problems or inner resources for the institution, but rather to help members achieve their own diagnosis. One aspect is thus the awareness of need, the sensitivity to problems, the sharpening of conscience or what Edmund Cahn calls "the sense of injustice." The other aspect is awareness of the institution itself, forces working for and against change.

In developing awareness, some writers have suggested the need for a "cultural island," with at least two meanings. One is the need for members, either by participation in other groups (councils of churches, national conferences, and so forth) or by help from a consultant, to see themselves and their institution somewhat objectively. The other is the need to withdraw for reflection on new ideas and actions. Such appraisal may not only heighten sensitivity; it may also awaken aspirations, and help members achieve new "images of potentiality" in areas in which they feel ineffective. Even the slowing down of ordinary group discussion may allow more reflective members to contribute to the group's awareness of problems and resources. This same process may enable the members to be aware of the problem of power in the group and so spread power more broadly. Certainly it directs attention to motivation, resources, and patterns of communication.[41]

2. Obstacles to Action

As we have noted, awareness of need must be balanced against costs and resources. Costs of social action are not calculated alone in terms of budget, although an adequate program will require allocation of money and personnel at each level of the church's operation. Costs also include perceived difficulty of action proposals, challenges to existing satisfactions, and choice among competing claims. Some obstacles will be irra-

[41] See Lippitt, The Dynamics of Planned Change, pp. 111, 150-51, 227, 31-33.

tional in the sense that their roots lie beneath the level of consciousness and will require more attention to emotions than to ideas. Other obstacles are less deeply emotional and more available to conscious consideration. Though nonrational they may become the objects of rational processes. There are also, of course, rational arguments and realistic obstacles to be faced.

Irrational obstacles to action often center in personal relationships, hostility toward the person proposing action, a remembered slight by a leader of the movement, the intrusion of bias so that decisions are made not on objective ground but on "Whose idea is it?" [42] There are in every church many persons who oppose action and change in general, who are reluctant to admit needs of themselves or others. Richard Niebuhr points to the individualism of middle-class religious ethics (peculiarly appropriate to Methodism) in a judgment which reflects both irrational and nonrational elements and which may be overly pessimistic:

Such an ethics is capable of producing a real heroism of self-discipline and, in its insistence on personal responsibility, the courage of resistance to the authority of state and church when these conflict with the imperatives of individual conscience. But this morality is incapable of developing a hopeful passion for social justice. Its martyrs die for liberty not for fraternity and equality; its saints are patrons of individual enterprise in religion, politics, and economics, not the great benefactors of mankind or the heralds of brotherhood.[43]

We have noted Muelder's judgment that Methodism has moved far from its earlier individualism, but, to the extent it still exists, it is an obstacle to social action, often lying just below the surface of rational discourse.

A crucial nonrational obstacle is the desire to preserve existing satisfactions, rational in so far as it is consciously acknowledged and irrational to the extent that real motives are hidden. Many persons have vested interests in "things as they are," and proposed changes in the institutional procedures may well be a threat to their leadership roles. The Negro ecclesiastic who recognizes that his personal participation in top policy decisions is probably due to Central Jurisdiction structures and

[42] See Chap. V.
[43] *The Social Sources of Denominationalism* (New York: Henry Holt and Co., 1929), pp. 87-88.

the lay leader who realizes his competence is in maintenance tasks are both threatened by proposals for action. Many Methodists are newly enough arrived in positions of prestige and influence that they feel quite insecure and so hesitate to test their leadership too far. The process of assessment itself, if prolonged without issuing in decision and action, can become an obstacle. Kenneth Burke names this attitude, when it is conscious rather than unconscious, the "Hamletic strategy," in which preparation for action is transmuted into devices for postponing action. Methodists have at hand several case studies of Burke's judgment: "For if you would forestall a final vote on a measure, and would do so in the best 'scientific' spirit, you need but appoint a committee empowered to find more facts on the subject." [44] In some instances the only approach to irrational and nonrational obstacles is pastoral and therapeutic; in any event the precondition of effective action is ability to deal with resistances and costs in a rational manner.

Rational obstacles often focus in a sense of inadequacy, in a lack of understanding of issues or of competence to deal with them. Campbell and Pettigrew indicate that there may be a mixture of questions of appropriateness and of competence when ministers consider their role as social action leaders.[45] The existing success orientation of ministers and of church groups (local church commissions and general boards) leads them to fear failure, to resist exposure of awkwardness, and therefore to minimize risks by focusing on safe programs. An irrational dimension intrudes, even here, as "Individuals and groups tend to dramatize their past experiences, insisting that something which has failed once can never succeed again or that something which has succeeded once must be repeated over and over." [46] Study needs to be made of the ways in which both members and groups can break free from the past rather than be victims of the past, unable to venture into new paths. The commitment of the Christian helps overcome the obstacles, whether of past failures or past successes.

Resistance to a specific program of action (as opposed to resistance to change in general) may be quite rational in so far as the goal is viewed

[44] *Grammar of Rhetoric* (New York: Prentice-Hall, 1952), p. 247; quoted in Alvin W. Gouldner, "Explorations in Applied Social Science," *Social Problems*, III, 3 (January, 1956), 177. Some illustrations reinforce the old comment that, if Moses had been a committee, the children of Israel would still be in Egypt.
[45] *Christians in Racial Crisis*, Ch. V.
[46] Lippitt, *The Dynamics of Planned Change*, pp. 249-50.

as undesirable, or the action seen as irrelevant to the central goals of the institution, or the task considered impossible of achievement. The first two factors are part of the process of establishing goals. The third involves in part rational calculation of energy and resources available, but Methodism can never afford to accept as final any present estimate of ability. If Lippitt and his associates can argue of secular institutions, "Faced with the right challenge, individuals transcend their measurable potentialities," [47] then institutions recognizing the power of God's grace can ill afford to make too pessimistic an appraisal. Even more, the church has a responsibility to develop in its members and leaders the willingness and capacity for sacrifice. This may mean the diversion of resources from personal pleasures or from institutional maintenance or it may mean acceptance of ridicule or suffering.[48] This suggestion that consideration of cost may be turned into a resource directs our attention to the next section.

3. RESOURCES FOR ACTION

Resources are usually thought of in terms of available persons, time, funds, or material. Strategy also takes into account those forces it finds operating for change as action is undertaken and those attitudes or capacities brought into play by the agents of change.[49] One initial force is a feeling of dissatisfaction, a sense of injustice. This feeling of pain is stimulated by the contrast between things as they are and as they ought to be, the awareness of poverty in an economy of abundance, the denial of voting rights in a land committed to democracy. This sense of discrepancy can be heightened by pressures external to the church (a Supreme Court decision, the airing of world opinion in the United Nations), or by some "inner requiredness" of the Christian message or of the nature of the church. John Deschner lifts this into focus as he argues that the race question for the Christian church is not "an expendable moral issue . . . , a matter of 'applying' the Gospel," but rather the inclusiveness of a community which is not our own invention. He concludes: "The race question challenges the Church not to enter a

[47] Lippitt, The Dynamics of Planned Change, p. 250.
[48] "A social revolution always involves suffering, even when it promises something better than the situation it seeks to change." Dilemmas and Opportunities, pp. 7-8.
[49] Lippitt, The Dynamics of Planned Change, pp. 73-89.

moral crusade, but to be the Church, not to do something extra, but to do the one thing essential." [50]

Actually this theological awareness of the nature of the church has grown as Methodism has faced social issues; it is both an initial force and an emergent resource. The tradition of Methodist social concern should serve as motivation for continuing action, as an investment in a task that must be carried forward.[51] Deeper involvement encourages more and more members to accept expectations of leaders, to see what was the response of a minority as the achievement and responsibility of all.

Another emergent resource is the realization that action in one area or one problem inevitably affects (as it is affected by) other problems; that in order to complete one task others must be taken on. Methodists are increasingly aware of the latent resources in a connectional system, both for support of prophetic individuals and for transcending provincialisms. John C. Bennett reminds us of other dimensions of the Christian life, "the spirit of the Christian citizen and the resources by which he lives."

He should be able to transcend partisanship without denying its proper place, to avoid bitterness and unfairness. He should not expect to find the perfect policy, but he should have the patience to seek the best available one with a mind that is open to new ways in which he may help to counteract the evil in it. He should be self-critical and aware of the bias in his own judgment that comes from his own social background and thus able to sense the moral limitations in all sides of a political conflict. He should be helped by his faith to combine contrition with resolute action. Always he should be aware of the consequences of his decisions in the lives of people and show a special concern for the weak and defenseless. He need not feel alone, not only because in the hardest and loneliest places he can know the divine companionship, but also because at all times he is a member of a Christian community which relates him to the sources of vision, of power, and of forgiveness.[52]

[50] "Segregation and the Minister's Faith," *The Perkins School of Theology Journal*, XI, 2-3 (Spring 1958), 4-9. See Chap. II.

[51] The series on *Methodism and Society*, of which this volume is a part, is intended to serve this purpose, not to encourage Methodists to "rest on their laurels," nor to substitute past achievement for present responsibility.

[52] *Christians and the State*, p. 297.

4. CLARIFICATION OF ALTERNATIVES

Thus far we have emphasized the importance of rational assessment of social processes and of the causes which underlie social problems. Focus upon the clarification of alternatives reminds us of several sources of insight that are not strictly logical, even though their results must finally be brought together in some rational framework. One of these sources is known in sociology as interpretive "understanding." The stress is on subjective factors such as meaning and motivation rather than on objective data and observed uniformities. Clarification is achieved through insight, feeling or empathy, "imaginative reconstruction." [53]

A second source lies in the recognition that factors which are crucial in historical causation may not be most important in strategy.[54] Economic competition may have been a potent factor in defining relationships between majority and minority groups in the past; now the economic competition is not directly operative and cultural factors are most powerful and most open to action. The fact that there are forces beyond present control, some of them irrational, does not prevent action upon forces that are accessible. This is related to the idea of "cumulative causation" formulated by Gunnar Myrdal.[55] This idea assumes that there is no such thing in social affairs as a single cause leading to a single result. It stresses the inter-relatedness of events as a result becomes in turn a causative factor, reinforcing its previous cause. This opens the way for action at any one or at several points, provided that the action continues over a period of time and that action is reinforced in so far as possible at other points.

A third element has been called verification. Here the emphasis is on action as an instrument of assessment. There is a danger of so setting the conditions of the experimental action that one's hypothesis becomes a "self-fulfilling prophecy." But in order finally to test one's assessment one must act on the best available hypothesis.

Such action may, at a given time, present an alternative that seems to be a move backward even when it is urged as preparatory to a forward

[53] See R. Bruce Raup, Kenneth D. Benne, George Axtelle, and B. O. Smith, *The Improvement of Practical Intelligence* (New York: Harper & Brothers, 1950), p. 44.

[54] See Robin M. Williams, Jr., *The Reduction of Intergroup Tensions* (New York: Social Science Research Council, 1947), p. 41.

[55] *An American Dilemma*, pp. 1065-70.

step. There would seem to be no way, for example, for communication patterns between members of majority and of minority groups to break through stereotyped expectations and rigid etiquette to a level of genuine intercourse without a period of conflict in which existing patterns are challenged and disrupted. The test of any such "retreat-in-order-to-advance" proposal is whether it is undertaken in good faith as a necessary step in order to realize the goal or is an attempt to postpone or resist its realization. It is necessary to "distinguish between resistance which is an attempt to defend unsatisfactory elements of the status quo and resistance which is an attempt to protect necessary and satisfactory elements." [56] "Dragging one's feet" may be either kind of resistance, but in any case it is a type of action.

D. Deployment of Energies

1. AGENTS OF PLANNED CHANGE

All social action is in one sense the action of individual persons directed toward social goals. Whether energies are conceived as action of a member, exercise of leadership, decision of a group, use of physical resources, or other means of power and influence,[57] it is persons who act. Our concern in this study is with individuals in so far as they are *representative* of Methodism in some way—citizens whose conscience is informed by church training, members exercising persuasion within and upon groups, or delegated representatives to an official gathering.

Even though action always begins with an individual, the change agent in social action can be either an individual member or a leader or an institution. On the one hand the individual must enlist others in his change efforts—in an expanding circle of informal gatherings of like-minded people, of more formal committees within a local church, of official church or community bodies (official board, annual conference, city council, state legislature), of unofficial or voluntary action groups (American Civil Liberties Union, Methodist Federation for Social Action, American Association for the United Nations), or of official groups at higher levels. Often he functions as an emergent leader, assuming the initiative in extending the acceptance of goals, exercising persuasion as a member of a group. At other times he serves as a more

---

[56] Lippitt, *The Dynamics of Planned Change*, p. 268.
[57] See Chap. VII.

formal leader, elected or appointed to an office or as a delegate to represent a group. Here his role is ascribed rather than assumed.

On the other hand the institution seeks to expand its constituency of informed and active supporters. This may range from the local Commission on Christian Social Concerns recruiting members or enlisting the concern and action of the total church membership, to the General Board of Christian Social Concerns seeking to develop local church commissions or working co-operatively with other general agencies of Methodism or the National Council of Churches on social action programs.

In principle there is no limit to the extension of co-operation (rather than opposition) if we accept the idea that we work not *against* an enemy but on a problem. The school committee may be enlisted as itself a change agent in securing better schools. The congressman may be persuaded to join in the fight for increased economic aid to other countries. In such cases the initiating agent expands the circle of action through intermediate change agents in action directed toward a common target or goal. The diagram on the following page illustrates the process.

The initiating change agent who originates the idea, develops a concern, or proposes a program may be an individual emergent leader such as a member of the Parent Teachers Association, a delegate to annual conference, a board executive as a member of the Council of Secretaries or a leader in an unofficial social action group. He may be a formal leader: chairman of the Social Concerns Commission or school committee, pastor, or executive of the Board of Education. Groups such as the M.Y.F., a ministerial association, a seminary faculty, or the General Conference may initiate the change process. Any Methodist, for example, may send a memorial to General Conference.

The initiating agent seeks to enlist the interest and aid of individuals or groups with varying degrees of influence as intermediate change agents: the Commission on Christian Social Concerns, the school committee, the platform committee of the political party. Together the initiating and intermediate change agents seek to affect institutional forms and processes such as jurisdictional structure, housing practices, and foreign policy. The target of change may be the local church, church patterns of organization or policies, groups outside the church, public opinion, or congress. In such areas there is always the possibility of en-

THE PROCESS OF PLANNED CHANGE

THE INITIATING AGENT

EMERGENT LEADERS:

1. Member local commission on Christian social concerns

2. Pastor as a citizen and member of political party

FORMAL LEADERS:

3. School superintendent

4. Board executive of TRAFCO

INSTITUTIONAL BODIES:

5. College faculty

6. Board of Christian Social Concerns

THE INTERMEDIATE AGENT

1. Persuades the various members of the official board who vote as a body to

2. Persuades the county party convention to

3. Persuades the churches to

4. Approaches the mass media executives to

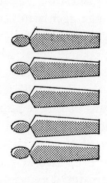

5. Sends resolution to Congress to

6. Approaches the Dept. of International Affairs of the National Council

TARGET OF ACTION

1. Recommend to the local council of churches that it come out vs. restrictive covenants in housing.

2. Oppose a state lottery.

3. Help with the education of migrant children.

4. Improve the quality of religious news coverage.

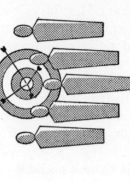

5. Repeal the loyalty affidavit in the National Defense Education Act.

6. Relative to a Protestant stand on disarmament.

listing the target group as a co-operating change agent seeking further extension of goals.

In practice there may turn out to be limits to the extent and scope of co-operation in devising and implementing strategy. These limits need continual testing rather than being permanently taken for granted. Methodists may assume that their circle of potential "friends" or intermediate change agents forever includes only one political party, only "labor" as opposed to "management," only certain Protestant churches to the exclusion of others, to say nothing of Jews and Roman Catholics. The fact that others are invited to seek common goals means that they must share in the deliberation concerning goals and methods, in the whole process of strategy, and are not brought in just to carry out tasks already decided. Thus the church is involved in continuing tension between carrying on its own goals with its limited resources and compromising its goals to secure the co-operation of others.

When the limits of persuasion and co-operation have been reached, there is a time for firm action, for clear formulation and statement of position (though always speaking the truth in love), for exertion of power, whether by writing letters, ringing doorbells, organizing informal meetings, or otherwise "getting out the vote." Ethical norms of fairness, honesty, and democratic procedures continue to govern as the mode of action shifts from what is ordinarily thought of as "human relations" processes to the arena of political decisions and power, whether inside or outside the church. The task of the church is not to avoid necessary conflicts of power when persuasive approaches have been exhausted, but to see that the conflicts are brought into the open and that procedures are subject to the moral requirements of maintaining community.[58]

2. CONFLICTING ROLES

No person operates with only a single loyalty or plays only a single role. It is obvious that the minister may at one time justify his stand on an issue by appealing to Methodism's constitution and play a conflicting role in relation to his church when he seeks to change its action on another issue. The roles of counselor and prophet present even more obvious conflicts. The board executive who, as the professional staff person, is a *formal* leader at the meeting of his board plays a different and

[58] See Chap. V.

perhaps conflicting role in the Council of Secretaries or as platform speaker in an annual conference. In one case he is the agent of the board, responsible for seeing that all facts are faced, all issues presented fairly, and all sides heard from, so that action can be taken and implemented. At the same time he is not a "taxi driver" who goes wherever the board directs; he must contribute substantively as well as procedurally, drawing upon his professional competence and his own commitments. He must face with the board both the frame of reference of church policy within which it acts and his own convictions as well as the limits beyond which he cannot continue as agent of the board. (The possibility of resignation is not a threat to secure conformity but rather a guarantee of freedom and integrity for staff and board.) In the other cases he is the informal persuader, with rights as a member or as speaker invited to state his own case.

Similar role conflicts face the layman. As a delegate to General Conference he is responsible to state his own conviction and argue for his position. As chairman of the committee on the state of the church he must represent the committee and its decisions (in which he has shared). The real estate dealer who is also a member of the Commission on Christian Social Concerns faces role conflicts as the matter of open occupancy housing becomes a community issue. The Methodist member of Congress who must vote on defense policies and appropriations operates, not with different convictions but within a different framework of responsibility from his action as a member of the national council of the Fellowship of Reconciliation. This does not necessarily mean that he fails to vote his convictions.

The assumption that all roles must be reduced to such consistency that there is no tension among them is a false assumption. Such integration of roles is not necessary, although there are logical and ethical as well as psychological limits to the role conflicts any person can stand. We have not, for example, chosen as an illustration the potential conflict faced by the Methodist (chairman of the Commission on Christian Social Concerns or not) who acts as sales representative for a liquor distributor or as lobbyist to defeat effective pure food and drug law administration. Each person must face for himself the conflicts inherent in the roles he plays in the light both of the ultimate purposes to which he is committed and of the circumstances surrounding each decision. He may well choose to continue in a role involving real tension with his professed ideals (such as ward chairman of a political party), recognizing the conflict but determined to exercise a responsible role in achieving better political processes.

It was noted in Chapter I that Christians must learn to live with the tensions of certain unresolved dilemmas. Just so the minister or layman must learn to live with and respond creatively to the tension that comes from playing both formal and informal leadership roles and from working in groups whose norms seem to conflict. To do otherwise is to resolve the tensions prematurely and to respond on less than the strategic level. Strategy is the clarification of ethical norms, the appraisal of social needs, the assessment of costs and resources, and the deployment of energies to establish and accomplish institutional goals. The process by which goals are established and assessment take place is as important as the goals actually sought and involves genuine communication. As individual strategists seek to extend the circle of action, the church itself becomes an agent of social change. That it finds itself facing tensions and choices within its framework of goals is the question to which we now turn.

CHAPTER FIVE

Social Action Within the Larger System of Goals

A. Larger Goals and Subordinate Goals

1. Concern for Social Action

METHODISM IS INEVITABLY ENGAGED IN SOCIAL ACTION, FOR, IN A very real sense, to abstain from action is to act—in terms of consequences. The question we now face is whether social action is a peripheral by-product of the church pursuing other purposes or is entitled to consideration in its own terms. Gustave Weigel, a leading Roman Catholic theologian, raises and answers the question for himself.

Religion can contribute to the welfare of the general community; it can help society. My only worry is whether it should.

It certainly cannot be the prime purpose of religion to make secular enterprise more satisfactory. That can indeed be the consequent of religion. But consequents are not the goals of deliberation; they are casual accretions to the proper goals of a planned effort.[1]

It is the position of the present volume that consequences must be given deliberate rather than casual consideration. Further, Methodism, lacking a hierarchical ordering of goals, can affirm its concern with society as a valid goal within a larger system of goals.

Methodism, in this as in other things, reflects the ecumenical consensus expressed at the time of the Oxford Conference:

[1] "The Present Embarrassment of the Church," in John Cogley (ed.), *Religion in America*, p. 224. Thomas F. O'Dea sees Roman Catholic intellectual life as inhibited not only by authoritarianism and clericalism, but also by formalism, the refusal to see "human fulfillment and Christian fulfillment . . . as interpenetrating processes." *American Catholic Dilemma*, pp. 155-59.

That, whatever limitations there may be on the action of the church as an organized society, Christians must give expression to their faith not only in what one may call the prepolitical sphere of the aims, standards and values that determine political action, but also in the field of concrete political decision and political struggle. To doubt this would be to deny the sovereignty of God over the whole of life and to surrender large areas of life to the unfettered control of the forces of evil.[2]

The "Study of Methodist Beliefs" revealed that members acknowledge a variety of goals, not always stressing social concern. To only 50 per cent of the respondents did salvation mean the "power to lead a new life in fellowship with God and man." Almost as many defined the "chief end of missions" in social terms.[3]

To the question concerning the responsibility of the church for social change, only 8 per cent replied that the church has no responsibility, but 40 per cent accorded only partial responsibility, leaving less than half accepting social change as at least equal to individual conversion in importance. Slightly over one third accepted the position of this study that there is finally no separation between social change and personal transformation as tasks of the church. When asked about how a more Christian society would be achieved, barely more than one fourth checked co-operative efforts in or out of the church (as opposed to individual conversion or the efforts of individual Christians).

2. VARIETY OF GOALS

Even casual observation suggests that persons may participate in the life of the church for many (and mixed) motives, seeking numerous

[2] Visser 't Hooft and Oldham, *The Church and Its Function in Society,* pp. 199-200. Waldo Beach seems to argue for an "indirect" approach to social problems in his stress on the nature of the church. "The church does not exist in order to produce racial justice, or to achieve racial inclusiveness in its own life. The Church [sic] exists to honor its Lord and Head, through a corporate life of worship and service. Its racial inclusiveness within, and its witnesses for racial justice without, are the inevitable by-products, not the intention, of this corporate life in Christ." "Ecclesiology and Race," *Union Seminary Quarterly Review,* XIV, 2 (January 1959), 22-23.

[3] The range of replies is as follows: The chief aim of missions should be: to save those who know not Christ, and who will be lost unless he is made known to them—19.9 per cent; to bring individuals to accept and live by the good news of the redemptive love of God revealed in Jesus Christ—42.9 per cent; to release in both individuals and society the redemptive power of God disclosed in Jesus Christ, so that all human life may be made whole—23.3 per cent; to improve the well-being of people by giving them new and improved methods of agriculture, industry, education, and health—8.5 per cent; write-ins—3.4 per cent; no reply—2.0 per cent. See Appendix B.

(and even conflicting) goals. For some persons the social function is primary, the desire to escape loneliness in making new friends, to find a marriage partner, or to engage in wholesome recreation. Some may even turn to the church to escape social responsibility and to find "peace of mind." For some the church offers comfort amid life's crises and answers to life's most puzzling questions. Some persons choose a church as they might an automobile, for its conferring of status or prestige, or as a means of upward mobility.[4] Very sincere members bring other cultural values into the church with them, including business-oriented standards and values; they tend to express their love of the church in their desire to see it "the biggest and best" in secular terms. There may be little relationship between increased participation in religious programs and acceptance of the church's ultimate goals. Hendrik Kraemer may not have been only jesting when he replied to a question whether a revival of faith was under way in Europe: "Why perhaps there is. Church attendance seems to be decreasing." [5] Certainly most Christians would assume that corporate worship is crucial to their life in the church, but this does not necessarily relegate social responsibility to the realm of the "extra-curricular." [6]

3. INCREASE OF LOVE OF GOD AND NEIGHBOR

One study of the church outlines its functions as: (1) a community of worship; (2) a community of love, including the forgiven, the forgiving, and those needing forgiveness, in different stages of growth in the Christian life; (3) a community of thought; (4) a social organism whose message can be seriously impeded when it conflicts with its institutional life; (5) the evangelization of persons; (6) the ministry of mercy and kindness; and (7) the witness to the community as well as to persons. "The church can fully serve men only as it helps them to see the whole of their life and all their activities in relation to the purpose of God." [7]

A more recent study asks explicitly what the purpose and objectives of the church are. H. Richard Niebuhr considers a wide range of responses, from cultivation of the Christian life, communication of the

---

[4] Bigman, "Evaluating the Effectiveness of Religious Programs," p. 13. Some persons, intentionally or unintentionally, use the church for goals other than religious.

[5] *Information Service*, XXXVIII, 14 (September 5, 1959), 3.

[6] *The Church Faces the Community*, ed. Das Kelly Barnett (Austin: The High Oaks Press, 1958), p. 11.

[7] Visser 't Hooft and Oldham, *The Church and Its Function in Society*, pp. 149-59.

saving doctrines of the Scriptures, preaching the gospel and administering the sacraments, developing the life of prayer, and increase in belief in Jesus Christ to building up the corporate life of the church. Then he goes on to ask whether there is one end beyond the many objectives, "one goal to which all other goals are subordinate, not necessarily as means to end, but as proximate objectives that should be sought only in relation to a final purpose?" [8] Niebuhr answers with a classic statement:

> No substitute can be found for the definition of the goal of the Church as the *increase among men of the love of God and neighbor*. The terms vary; now the symbolic phrase is reconciliation to God and man, now increase of gratitude for the forgiveness of sin, now the realization of the kingdom or the coming of the Spirit, now the acceptance of the gospel. But the simple language of Jesus Christ himself furnishes to most Christians the most intelligible key to his own purpose and to that of the community gathered around him. If the increase among men of love of God and neighbor is the ultimate objective may it not be that many of our confusions and conflicts in churches . . . are due to failure to keep this goal in view while we are busy in the pursuit of proximate ends that are indeed important, but which set us at cross-purposes when followed without adequate reference to the final good? [9]

The present study accepts this statement as its own, understanding that love is meant as that revealed supremely in the life and teaching of Jesus Christ and that it is never to be used instrumentally. The church fulfills its purpose when it embodies this love in its life and in its witness in the world.

The task of the church is not primarily in the church, except to see that its own life expresses its message, but in the world of which the church is part. It is within the framework of this larger goal that the subordinate goals find their proper place and their relationship to each other. In this perspective lay activities and evangelism are not separate and isolated tasks but are valid only as they serve the larger goal and are related to worship, education, and action.

[8] *The Purpose of the Church and Its Ministry*, pp. 27-30.
[9] *Ibid.*, pp. 31-32. Niebuhr insists that "the Church . . . loses its character as Church when it concentrates on itself, worships itself and seeks to make love of Church the first commandment." P. 30. The pastoral task of the church to all who are afraid, to those in whose hearts there is bitterness and hate, to those on both sides of social barriers, must never be forgotten. See *Dilemmas and Opportunities*, p. 28.

Certain alternatives are thus excluded from the choice of the Christian. He may not withdraw from the world to seek his own salvation. He may not conform to the secular world. He may not separate his life in the church and his life in the world into distinct spheres of activity. His life will be lived out in the continuing tension of reconciling the world to the love of God and man as known in the life of the church. Social action becomes not just an important task of the church but a necessary dimension of life in the redemptive fellowship of the church. There are, of course, difficulties in making this a part of the mutual expectations of the layman and the expert, the minister, the district superintendent and the bishop, and the board executive, whether of education or of missions.

4. CONFLICTING EXPECTATIONS

We illustrate such difficulties from a study of the behavior of ministers in a Southern city in a period of racial crisis. Campbell and Pettigrew [10] found three different sets of expectations influencing the decision of ministers to take action or remain passive during the crisis. (1) The first, and most influential, set of expectations was that of the membership of the church, or congregation. This group opposed ministerial action because members were conservative in their views on the issue and because they did not see such action as "appropriate" for a minister. (2) The second set of expectations was that of ministerial colleagues, the "professional reference system." These expectations came into focus as the minister identified with his image of his denomination as a whole, with the views of the local leadership and the local ministerial association, and perhaps with a special group with whom he had most in common. Here the expectation was of a "liberal" position expressed in action, but there was no basic challenge to conservatism because the minister was also expected to measure his professional competence in terms of harmony within his congregation and growth in membership and budget. (3) The expectations of the minister for himself (his own image of the ministerial task and the purpose of his calling) did not demand action, because of a stress on education, spiritual growth, and staying in touch with people. Thus all three sets of expectations mutually reinforced passivity.

[10] *Christians in Racial Crisis*, pp. 85-108. The authors treat the sets of expectations as "reference systems." Further discussion can be found in Wogaman, *Methodism's Challenge in Race Relations*, pp. 35-36.

Probably the modification of expectations should begin with the minister's self-image. Each man must come to terms with his own motivations as best as he understands them, reconciling his own needs for a sense of purpose and of accomplishment as well as for feeling accepted by his fellows, with his growing understanding of the larger purpose of the church and its requirements. Freeing himself from the threat of failure and loss of status will involve psychological adjustments, deepening of inner resources, and finally working out his own set of expectations in relation to the reference systems of church and colleagues.

As the minister helps his congregation to achieve a new set of expectations for his leadership, he also interprets his own expectations of them as fellow ministers in the ministering community. Too often laymen see their expected role only as usher or treasurer—related to the organization of the church rather than to its mission. The minister indicates the range of Christian social concerns and their relation to the Bible and church traditions, as he teaches through precept and example the value of a free pulpit,[11] and as he demonstrates the relationship of this task within the larger goal of the church through worship, education, pastoral work, and the whole gamut of personal ministry. Perhaps the greatest neglect of the ministry in social action is its failure to achieve a fellowship of shared concern, which could not only clarify mutual expectations in terms of the increase of the love of God and man, but could also provide opportunities for mutual support and common action. Ministers and laymen suffer from "pluralistic ignorance" of the real concern and convictions they share. As ministers in Atlanta, Dallas, and Houston have joined in statements to their communities concerning desegregation and law and order, they have found new strength to deal with pressure groups, new understanding of the issues involved, and new awareness of the different tasks that each may have in his own particular setting. Certainly the sets of expectations can be revised, if the larger goal is kept clearly in view.

[11] It is encouraging to recall this question in "The Beliefs of Methodists" study. A Methodist Minister should: be free to take a position on controversial issues if it is in accord with the Social Creed—9.7 per cent; be free to take a position on controversial issues as long as this does not interfere with his parish ministry—14.4 per cent; be free to take on controversial issues any position which he regards as Christian—68.4 per cent; not speak on controversial social issues—1.6 per cent; speak only on issues on which there is agreement in his local church—1.8 per cent; other—4.1 per cent. See Appendix B.

B. Maintenance, Service, and Program Tasks

1. PRIMACY OF PURPOSE

"A local church may be open seven days a week, with its furnace (or air conditioning system) going full blast, its lights on twenty-four hours a day, and its mimeograph machine humming and still not be doing the work of the Lord." Thus a pastor outlined to his congregation the danger of seeing maintenance of an institution as realization of its goals. There is a similar danger for ecclesiastical officials, district superintendents, bishops, or board executives—and for lay leaders. Board secretaries, whether liberal or conservative, can become protective of their agency and its budget, allowing the institutional response to take precedence over the program requirements. The tension between program, service, and maintenance tasks exists at every level of the church's life, from the member through the local official board to the regional, national, and even world-wide extension of Methodism.

Maintenance tasks are those necessary to the continued existence and functioning of the institution: the raising of budgets, the payment of professional salaries, the provision of facilities with adequate heat, light, and equipment, the travel of administrative officers, and the holding of many meetings. Some have distinguished these as "preconditions" to the achievement of goals. Raymond W. Miller has referred to the "edifice complex" with this question: "Are we, as laymen, so busy keeping up with the Joneses in building new church buildings that we don't have resources to do the real world-wide work of the church?" [12] He adds the warning that "all ancient and dead civilizations leer at the archeologist from the ruins of some form of temple." [13]

Service tasks are primarily pastoral in nature, aimed not at changing the conditions which damage persons but at ministering to the needs of these persons. One thinks of counseling services, homes for and services to the aging, hospitals for the ill, the global task of relief and rehabilitation, recreation facilities, and special ministries to working mothers, unmarried parents, alcoholics, juvenile delinquents, migrant

[12] "The Laymen's Orbit," Address at Lake Junaluska Assembly, 1958, p. 25.

[13] *Ibid.*, p. 7. He quotes the 1784 *Discipline:* "Let all our Churches be built plain and decent; but not more expensively than is absolutely unavoidable. Otherwise the Necessity of raising Money will make Rich Men necessary to us. But if so, we must be dependent upon them, yea, and governed by them. And then farewell to the Methodist-Discipline, if not doctrine too." The warning is against dependence upon any one group.

labor, and so on. In service activities "the churches bring light and help to men who live in an imperfect society." [14] Service may and should be rendered to those within and without the church. Service tasks are a valid expression of the larger tasks of the church; they have their own justification and are not means to other ends. For example, Methodists do not operate hospitals to engage in recruitment of members but as a genuine ministry to human needs. Service tasks require their own institutional maintenance operations and are seen in relationship to such program tasks as the search for justice in the responsible society.

Program tasks are those which are consciously an expression of the larger goals in the life of the church. In so far as any functions of the church, whether worship, fellowship, education and theology, evangelization, or social action,[15] serve to increase the love of God and man in the world, they are program functions. It is at least possible that any function may deflect energy away from rather than toward the central tasks and, in so doing, move from program or service to maintenance in an unjustified way.

2. NECESSITY AND DANGER OF MAINTENANCE TASKS

The above warning should not be taken as detracting from the necessity of maintenance tasks. Certainly maintenance is essential and an institution must operate efficiently. If one believes, as the authors do, that only through membership in the church are certain values for persons possible, then one must see maintenance functions as indirect forms of social action. Even a building campaign can focus on the purposes of the church and so serve as an instrument of reviving essential commitments.

Some ministers spend their lives in rebellion against the tasks of administration and all the other structured responsibilities of their work in the churches. Such rebellion is understandable, but it is futile. The need is for the breathing into administrative work such faith and love, expressed in such artful skills of organization, that administration itself becomes a means of grace.[16]

The danger is that things or activities worth doing as means-to-an-end

[14] *Policy and Strategy in Social Welfare* (National Council of Churches, 1957), p. 20.
[15] See p. 143.
[16] DeWolf, *The Case for Theology in Liberal Perspective*, p. 161.

become transformed into unjustified ends-in-themselves.[17] No discussion of Methodism can ignore its size or its spectacular success in raising funds and erecting buildings; but no consideration of strategy can overlook the price in the *preoccupation* of Methodists with what are essentially tasks of institutional maintenance; in the enormous amounts of energy consumed daily in what Truman Douglass has called "ecclesiastical lint-picking and salad-tossing." Part of this comes from the intrusion of cultural values into the life of the church, the judging of church success by secular criteria.

There seems to be an almost irresistible temptation to regard institutions and programs that are church related as automatically contributing to Christian goals. M. Moran Weston, in his study of Episcopal social policy, identifies five "heresies" that have come to be recognized as such in that church's Department of Christian Social Relations.[18]

1. That growth in size is necessarily growth in quality
2. That the chief function of a board of directors of an institution is to prevent deficits
3. That the words "church" or "Christian" are magic substitutes for standards of plant, personnel, or program
4. That institutions exist for their own glory
5. That any minister can make a good executive

A. Dudley Ward has noted Methodist organizational structure, trained leaders, and investments in buildings and has concluded: "There is no danger of Methodism going out of business as an institution; the danger is that it will become peripheral to the process of history." [19] It will be suggested in succeeding chapters that Methodism, having achieved its greatest growth in a period of the expanding geographical

[17] David L. Sills describes the same tendency in a national voluntary association: "In order to accomplish their goals, organizations establish a set of procedures, or means. In the course of following these procedures, however, the subordinates or members to whom authority and functions have been delegated often come to regard them as ends in themselves, rather than as means toward the achievement of organization goals. As a result of this process, the actual activities of the organization become centered around the proper functioning of organization procedures, rather than upon the achievement of the initial goals." *The Volunteers* (Glencoe, Ill.: The Free Press, 1957), p. 62.

In an interview, a national staff member of a political party described the continued tension between policy and principle and the view that "The main task of the party is to stay in office." Churches resist the idea that staff members are concerned with careers and with status; this failure to recognize the problem in ministers (or in lay institutional loyalties) complicates rather than eliminates the problem.

[18] "Social Policy in the Episcopal Church in the Twentieth Century," p. 67.
[19] Interview, October 30, 1959.

frontiers, now faces its greatest challenge in using its institutional resources in the challenging frontiers of politics, economics, and international relations.

C. Critical Self-Awareness in the Church

The next chapter deals with the church as object and as agent of
social change. Here we note that, if it would keep its actions related to
its larger purpose, "The Church must continuously scrutinize its own
life in the light of the gospel," [20] rather than simply reflect its community. The church, with other social institutions, faces the danger of
what Vidich and Bensman call "the falsification of memory and the
substitution of goals." [21] As aspects of the program of action are either
defeated when tried or not tried because of the press of maintenance
tasks, members tend to forget the proposed tasks and to ask only concerning the success of those now pursued. The church can become
captive to an economic class, a region, a nation, a tradition or its own
desire for unity. Against all these and other captivities, there must be
developed the capacity for and practice of critical self-awareness. This
reaffirms the need for establishing institutional goals.

This does not mean a perpetual state of anxiety, a feeling that "Whatever it is we are doing, it must be wrong." Such negativism is as paralyz-
ing to effective action as is complacency. Rather what is required involves
a certain sense of humor and relaxed attitude. This may provide sufficient security for learning from our mistakes, sufficient objectivity to
judge failure and success, sufficient sureness of goal to distinguish vital
from trivial issues (and vital from trivial mistakes). In this context,
research, evaluation, correction from others all are received with openness
and sensitivity, as contributing to rather than deflecting from ongoing
pursuit of goals.[22] Frenzy can drain more energy away from program
tasks than can maintenance.

The same capacity for critical self-awareness must be exercised in
ecumenical activities. It is, of course, easier to be committed to ecumenism in general than to work within a council of churches, but the
person working within the council must also be aware that the original

---

[20] "The Message from Methodist Conference on Human Relations," 1959.
[21] Arthur J. Vidich and Joseph Bensman, *Small Town in Mass Society* (Princeton, New
Jersey: Princeton University Press, 1958), p. 297.
[22] See Chap. XI.

ecumenical purpose may not be served by all council activities. Over and over one finds individual Methodists in crucial leadership positions in various levels of ecumenical activity. One senses a tendency to see such persons as even more in detached service than if they occupied similar posts within Methodism. This is only one indication that institutional Methodism has yet to trust its own resources fully in the ecumenical enterprise, within which it might well see itself more objectively and critically.

Another illustration of the need for critical self-awareness is in ministerial training. Here the focus is all too often upon institutional operation and church administration, with more help from pastoral counseling than social ethics in defining the task of the minister. And here is an opportunity for shifting the focus of training from the classroom to supervised field work in the community with its issues and problems. Critical self-awareness would reveal that most church-reporting sessions, from the fourth quarterly conference up, lend themselves to institutional achievements, to existing accomplishments and "progress" which can be measured, or to goals so unrelated to present fact as to seem utopian. Walter Muelder has pointed to the necessity of making the financial policy of the church an instrument of its larger goals.[23]

The above remarks should not be taken as condemning all institutional forms. Methodism, in pursuing its task, needs not less organization and more individualism but rather less individualism and more organization devoted to the larger purposes. Strategic thinking recognizes the necessity of maintenance tasks but insists that they should serve and not obscure program and service tasks, the increase of the love of God and man in the world.

D. Agreement and Disagreement Within Methodism

One potential for critical self-awareness in the church is its lack of uniformity, its disagreement. But this disagreement is all too often either denied (in the interest of presenting a united front) or glossed over (and so not used). The organic unity of Methodism is seldom treated as a goal in explicit terms; yet it operates powerfully as a sanction against controversy or action which might "split the church." This assumed goal of unity was probably determinative in the decision of the 1960

[23] *Methodism and Society in the Twentieth Century*, pp. 405 ff.

General Conference concerning the Central Jurisdiction. But Methodists are held together, not by uniformity of belief or complete agreement in policy, but rather by a conviction that their staying together in freedom is the best way of realizing God's purpose for their church.

If Methodism can use the diverse orientations of its members to focus significant controversy on important social issues, it may achieve both a richer community life in the church and a more effective social outreach. Better informed and disciplined Christians will go out to work on various causes, even on different sides of issues. But the battles over these issues outside the church should be seasoned and tempered by the trust and understanding developed in disagreement within the church. The role of the church is not to counterbalance the claims of practicality and realism by proclaiming ideal but unrealistic goals. The church rather must seek to relate its ideals to the possibilities of action within its own deliberations and then it can commend its views to those outside the church.[24]

1. THE SECTARIAN PRINCIPLE
IN A DENOMINATION ACCEPTING RESPONSIBILITY

Many of us operate with an image of a church speaking with one voice to the corresponding image of a Christian nation. Neither of these images takes account of the divided state of Methodist opinion (in religious beliefs and in social attitudes) or of the pluralism of American society. Much Methodist social action retains the assumption of a basic Protestant Christian orientation of American culture, without serious challenges. This ignores both the fact of Jewish, Roman Catholic, and secular challenges to a Protestant ethos and the potential richness of this diversity. Similarly, the image of the church may be of a like-minded and disciplined Wesleyan society. Both of these images may be seen as historic survivals, but they may also be interpreted as repressions of conflict in keeping with the religious emphasis on harmony rather than discord.

Ernst Troeltsch described two polar types of church groups as "church" and "sect." The "church" recognizes the strength of secular society and attempts to influence it by accepting its partial goods. Rather than a direct challenge, the "church" compromises and adapts; it helps hold society together and insure order. The "sect" is usually

---

[24] Nitze, *The Recovery of Ethics*, pp. 9-10.

small and voluntary rather than inclusive in membership. It repudiates the compromises of the "church," stressing obedience and discipline, and it may either flee the world in asceticism or fight it in radicalism.[25] F. Ernest Johnson calls the incorporation of sectarian protest and discipline within an inclusive church as the most significant development within the churches seeking to discover their social function.[26] Several writers have noted the puzzle of fitting Methodism into either type, since it exhibits features of both.[27] It has become a church almost by accident, retaining something of its sectarian character in its emphasis on moral character, prophetic movements, and social reform—even as it has appealed to human needs and become large and inclusive.

Methodism in many ways accepts responsibility for a society which includes other religious movements. This responsibility is, at its best, not an attempt to control or manipulate, but rather to persuade and influence, on the basis of genuine concern for every aspect of society. But Methodism also emphasizes for its own members the necessity of commitment, obedience, and discipline. While very few members have been read out of the church in over forty years, many persons are aware of Methodist demands (in ethics, not dogma) even when they dissent. The very openness of Methodism, ranging from its evangelical spirit to its lack of rigid creedal requirement for admission, means that many people come through the wide door of the church with very differing ideas on social problems. Thus Methodism faces a critical problem of keeping communication lines open and discussion going. The sectarian principle means that the growing edge of the church will be pioneering groups, willing to take risks and make mistakes, but unwilling to impose their views on the church save by persuasion, or to let the apathy of

[25] See J. Milton Yinger, *Religion, Society, and the Individual*, pp. 142-55, for a helpful discussion. Yinger expands Troeltsch's types to six: universal church, ecclesia, denomination, established sect, and cult. Franklin H. Littell has challenged Troeltsch's typology as being sociologically useful but theologically in error. For him sect and church are normative terms, with the sect a group that makes something other than loyalty to Jesus Christ central to its discipline and common life. The sect refuses to participate in the prayerful quest for guidance into unity. Littell describes the free church as a voluntary association of like-minded people with a strong structure of internal discipline. This is very similar to the sectarian principle as referred to in the text. See "Church and Sect," *Ecumenical Review*, VI, 3 (April 1954), 262-76.

[26] *The Church and Society* (New York: The Abingdon Press, 1935), pp. 82, 216-17. See also Bennett's normative conception which sees the sect as too exclusive and the church as too conservative, *Christians and the State*, pp. 201-2.

[27] See Albert C. Outler, "The Methodist Contribution to the Ecumenical Discussion of the Church." (Mimeographed.)

the church stand unchallenged.[28] Incorporation of this principle within a church rejects the idea of reform by separation, either of the church from society or from the church by a minority. It implies that there is both a loyalty that transcends any existing disagreement and a vision that bursts outside any existing agreement. Dr. Richard Cabot once characterized the ethical life as the making of agreements, the keeping of agreements, and the improving of agreements.[29]

2. UNITY AND DIVERSITY

Methodism has not taken full advantage of its sectarian principle, or of its diversity, because of its stress on unity, agreement, harmony, and peace. Many of us seem to assume that to get along in the same institution we must either all be alike or each ignore the other's differences. With rare exceptions we have not hunted heretics, but some have viewed persons who raised their voices on social issues as "troublemakers," upsetting a glorious concord. That Methodists differ from one another on social issues is evident to the casual observer, and even more so to the student of conference debates or of "The Beliefs of Methodists." General Conference debate in 1944 centered in the issue of whether the church as a church could be a participant in war. Later General Conferences struggled with the status of the Methodist Federation for Social Action.[30] More recently the church has been divided concerning the Central Jurisdiction. In the 1959 sampling of denominational opinion, Methodists split 65 per cent to 28 per cent over the issue of temperance (Question 26), 47 per cent to 41 per cent over whether to support their country in war "apart from considerations of justice" (Question 27), and three ways on the issue of racial segregation (Question 28).[31] Regional diversity is also apparent, with the South Central, Southeastern, and Central Jurisdictions showing a significantly larger proportion favoring total abstinence than the other three jurisdictions. The Southeastern Jurisdiction showed a willingness to support war "only for the preservation of justice" in some degree higher than the other five jurisdictions. There are, of course, marked jurisdictional patterns in the responses to the questions on race and race in Methodism. The

[28] Visser 't Hooft and Oldham, The Church and Its Function in Society, p. 214.
[29] The Meaning of Right and Wrong (New York: The Macmillan Company, 1933), p. 19.
[30] See Muelder, Methodism and Society in the Twentieth Century, pp. 216-26.
[31] See Appendix B. Percentages are combined in these totals.

two Southern jurisdictions were more willing to impose limits on school teachers' joining organizations but not on their ministers' freedom to speak.

We may often have acknowledged this regional diversity without being willing to open communication across regional boundaries or to welcome differences within regions. Wherever we have been afraid of controversy over differences, we have paid a price. One danger is that, by refusing to bring controversy into the open, we turn its resolution over to persons and groups willing to use the threat of controversy to achieve their own ends. Wogaman concludes, in his suggested strategy for desegregation in Methodism: "Where there is a majority within the church committed above everything else to unity and harmony, a minority which is committed above everything else to maintaining segregation can, by its threats, *determine the basis of institutional unity and harmony*." [32] By refusing to face issues, or by surrendering to a vocal or militant minority, the church may lose some of its most sensitive spirits, those whose leaving is accompanied by deep inner wounds rather than by loud protestations.

The ultimate commitment of Methodism cannot be to "unity at any price," but rather to faithfulness to the nature of the church and to frank facing of differences on the basis of this larger loyalty. But Raymond Miller reminds us that "reasonable men cannot agree until they know first upon what they disagree." [33] At least they cannot enlarge areas of agreement unless they are willing to explore the nature and causes of disagreement. This means that Methodists must learn to live in some degree of tension, to provide for and profit from controversy. Kenneth D. Benne has outlined various strategies used to deny controversy: keeping parties separated, labeling opponents as "evil" and ourselves as "holy," insisting that "we are all alike," punishing expressions of disagreement, refusing to recognize any loyalties other than those to the whole group (either to parts of the group or to groups beyond). [34]

But if Methodists recognize their differences and hold to their belief in freedom, then they must accept controversy. It may be that controversy, creatively used, is the essential condition of growth. Democracy

[32] Wogaman, *Methodism's Challenge in Race Relations*, p. 58.
[33] Miller, *The Layman's Orbit.*
[34] "The Significance of Human Conflict," address to Division of Christian Education, National Council of Churches, February 1960. (Mimeographed.)

requires that the minority be listened to. Dan Dodson insists that it is immoral to terminate controversy without resolving the issues involved.[35] So, too, it is immoral to engage endlessly in futile wrangling. If, then, our task is not to end differences, but to use them creatively, how do we provide for this?

3. CONDITIONS FOR CREATIVE USE OF CONTROVERSY

There are conditions for the creative use of controversy if we are to avoid both the repression of differences and endless arguing. Probably the most important condition is the acceptance of disagreement, the willingness to live with tension, the encouragement of honest expression of difference, the taking seriously of the convictions of others.[36] It is the genius of free institutions to be able to carry on continuing discussion among those who do not presently agree. Especially in the church is full, free, and informed discussion important; consensus can serve as a channel for the Holy Spirit only where there is also concern and moral earnestness.[37] Karl Barth emphasizes that participants do not simply express personal opinions or engage in tolerant chatter, but rather present their causes as true and binding. Each has to set his witness over against a firmly grounded opposing witness, both in the same bindingness. Members mutually rely upon the strength and rightness of the presentation of each cause and leave the way open for the witness of the Holy Spirit in the group.[38] When this happens, the church becomes a community of trust and interdependence, a fellowship within which competent and concerned persons can raise for and with each other the deepest commitments they have.

A second condition for the creative use of controversy involves the separation of realistic from unrealistic sources of conflict. Unrealistic conflict often stems from the misunderstanding of another's goals and

---

[35] "The Creative Role of Conflict in Human Relations," address to National Association of Intergroup Relations Officials, November 1957. (Mimeographed.)

[36] The 1956 Discipline, in the section on "Race," urges all racial groups to "be willing to admit their imperfections and seek to correct them." ¶ 2026.

[37] Franklin H. Littell, "The Work of the Holy Spirit in Group Decisions," The Mennonite Quarterly Review, XXXIV, 2 (April 1960), 75-96; see also The Free Church (Boston: Starr King Press, 1957). There is an apocryphal story of a board meeting that had reached an impasse. The chairman called for prayer to resolve the issue. One member replied: "Pray if you want to; my mind is made up."

[38] Karl Barth, The Church and the Political Problems of Our Day (New York: Charles Scribner's Sons, 1939). See also Larry Durgin, "Honest Talk in Churches," Social Action, XXIII, 7 (March 1957).

methods. Differences in both goal and method need to be faced in their complexity, with the effort made not just to "know" the other position but to "understand" why it is held. James Coleman has studied how, in community conflicts, specific issues tend to give way to general ones and disagreement tends to become antagonism. Almost involuntarily the following sequence seems to operate:

1. Initial single issue.
2. Disrupts equilibrium of community relations.
3. Allows previously suppressed issues against opponent to appear.
4. More and more of opponent's beliefs enter into the disagreement.
5. The opponent appears totally bad.
6. Charges against opponent as a person.
7. Dispute becomes independent of initial disagreement.[39]

The community of trust is violated when persons begin to ask "whose idea is it?" and to question motives. The supposition that things are not what they seem evades the necessary debate on the merits of the idea itself.

We must refuse stereotypes for ourselves and for others, accepting the dignity and the capacity for growth in both, and understanding the capacity of all for self-delusion. There is a certain openness and hope within Methodism that the lines are drawn differently on different issues, that "opponents" in one context are "allies" in another. This is also a basis for hope in the larger society, where religious loyalties do not coincide with economic and political allegiances. This helps us refrain from attacks upon persons and concentrates attention upon issues.

A third condition calls attention to substance rather than method. Controversy should not get bogged down in trivialities, but should deal with vital issues. Truman Douglass quotes a minister: "If people are to reject the Gospel in these days let it be for the right offenses, 'the foolishness of the cross' not the foolishness of the Ladies' Aid." [40] Real growth occurs when there is some imaginative reconstruction of issues and some exploring of alternatives providing for genuine reconciliation. This is accomplished not by expediency or by the simple adjustment of opinion but within a framework of ethical and theological concern,

[39] Coleman, *Community Conflict*, pp. 10-11.
[40] Douglass, "The Relevance of Long-Range Planning."

with an awareness of both the judgment and mercy of God. Given its theological and ethical frame of reference Methodism should have a firm position on some issues. One such would seem to be that "All discrimination and enforced segregation based on race should be abolished," [41] with the sanction that no benevolence funds shall go to discriminating institutions. Methodists should share a similar conviction concerning civil liberties, the rehabilitation of offenders against the law, and the equal rights of men and women. We may be moving toward more unity in our attitude toward war in the nuclear age, when many are convinced it can no longer serve the interests of justice. On issues such as those of economic justice, federal aid to education, and health insurance plans, a single viewpoint is not so important as the way in which the issues are studied, solutions considered, and opponents dealt with.

A fourth condition specifies the limits of debate; controversy proceeds most usefully within a framework of rules. Quaker procedures stress consensus and unanimity rather than majority vote. The *Discipline* sets for Methodists certain constitutional limits within which controversy can operate. Wogaman applies this to the matter of acceptance of minority group members in a local church. No one, he argues, is forced to belong to The Methodist Church; membership is voluntary. But once membership is accepted, the constitution is embraced in principle. Methodism does not define membership on the basis of race (see ¶ 105); so Wogaman insists that the racial composition of the local church is not a matter for consensus.

Nobody is "forced" to belong to The Methodist Church but . . . so long as one is a member he gives tacit assent to the church's Constitution, which nowhere defines membership or participation in the church on the basis of race. Democratic procedures are available for the amendment of the Constitution. But in the absence of constitutional sanction, the racial composition of the membership of a local church is not the kind of issue upon which consent or consensus by members of the local church must appropriately be obtained.[42]

In much the same way laymen, ministers and commissions may point

[41] See Appendix B. The convictions of the authors on similar questions are summarized at the end of Chap. IX.
[42] Wogaman, *Methodism's Challenge in Race Relations*, p. 40.

to actions of General Conference, pronouncements of the Council of Bishops, and statements of general boards to support a position that is unpopular locally. The disagreeing person or church is not obligated to accept the position thus presented as his own, but he is obligated both to work within the framework of constitutional requirements and established procedures and to accept the conflicts that are inevitable, given our diversity. Certainly no minister should be the victim of vituperation for taking his stand upon a position established by General Conference.

One the other hand, the minister or layman may seek to change the existing form of church polity (e.g., the jurisdictional system) or the character of church pronouncements (e.g., "right-to-work" laws) in the interest of conformity with the larger purposes of the church. Here he appeals beyond an existing consensus to the transcendent goals and norms.[43] Only by clearly understanding that defense of and challenge to existing policies and established forms must be both justified and criticized from a more ultimate perspective can such a dialectical process be accepted. This understanding is a first task of the responsible social action leader.

If the controversy is fruitful and changes take place, there will be costs involved. The church must both prepare its members to accept some sacrifices in the reconciling of differences and provide a context of repentance and forgiveness in which persons are caught up not only in controversy but also in a pastoral community.

Some such set of conditions would seem to be required if Methodism is to maintain its own critical self-awareness and its loyalty to the larger goal of the increase among men of the love of God and man. The frank facing of differences, the accepting of controversy as essential to growth, and the providing of limits within which persuasion, disagreement, and debate can operate to achieve growing consensus would make for a more creative strategy both within the life of the church and in its relation to other social institutions. In a Christian group consensus must be achieved and disagreements faced in the light of a transcendent frame of reference and of its larger purposes and goals.

[43] See Chap. II.

PART THREE

Methodism in Its Social Situation

Synopsis

THIS SECTION SETS FORTH THE SOCIAL SITUATION IN WHICH Methodism operates. It describes and analyzes the power of The Methodist Church and its resources as they relate to social action and strategic change.

Chapter VI focuses upon the role of Methodism as an object and an agent of social change. The schematic structure of its institutions, their component parts, and the basic needs which they serve are described in both a theoretical and an applied sense. The types of strategy which are effective are ranged according to their conservative, status, inventive, and religious functions and institutions. It is noted that every act of social change and each force of stabilization requires (1) an institution as its vehicle, (2) appropriate leadership, (3) social control techniques, (4) purposive goals, (5) an appropriate strategy, and (6) an appraisal of the appropriate time in the development of the institutions involved. Each of these components is related to Methodism.

From the discussion of Methodism's role in social change, the discourse moves in Chapter VII to the power structure of Methodism. In a constructive way, the power structure is discussed in terms of symbolic, physical, and technical assets, and in terms of strength and purpose. Each of these is related to the institutional power of American Methodism. The problems of initiating change in the power structures and of using them to creative ends constitute the closing sections of the chapter. The future use of Methodist power as an asset for the kingdom of God comprises the closing arguments as a prelude to an inventory of Methodists, their assets and liabilities.

This inventory comprises the burden of Chapter VIII, titled "Resources and Obstacles to Change Within Methodism." As such, it is a social description of the people called "Methodist." As a major segment of world Wesleyanism, The Methodist Church (as seen in the United States) is unique in form, structure, and function. Its flexibility, scope, and patterns of operation fit it for a major role in influencing the moral tone of America, and indeed of the world.

The organizational structure by itself, unique as it is, does not exist without its inner liabilities. These we presume to discuss and iterate. Many of them have become burdens which handicap the church in social and ecumenical leadership. Fortunately, there are major assets on the other side of the ledger to encourage us as we confront the challenges of Part Four. They include the prestige and status of our leadership, an increasingly competent group of specialists, and a basically ecumenical mood in the local churches of Methodism.

Finally, the economic resources and policies are reviewed. Here there is much to be desired. The *Discipline* of the church has not been implemented in its own fiscal policies and it must face its preachments to others with an awareness of this. However, the ingenuity of the Methodist system has produced the material resources necessary to do virtually anything the denomination agrees to do. The economics only wait upon the direction of the purposes of the church!

Methodism is itself in the midst of great social upheaval and change. While changing within, it is also the change agent for other institutions. The burden of this chapter is to help each layman and minister to understand the material with which he is working to achieve the purposes outlined in Part One through the strategy detailed in Part Two. In Part Four we shall move from theory to practice.

CHAPTER SIX

Methodism and Social Change

THE ANALYSIS OF METHODIST INSTITUTIONS HAS GENERALLY consisted of an inventory of static facts—numbers of church buildings, the net gains or losses in membership. The true genius of an institution, however, is to be seen in more dynamic factors. But this variability has rarely been made the object of empirical study.

In this chapter we focus on social change rather than the institutions which are modified by it. The effect of social change upon local churches, conference and general boards and agencies is more discernible than change itself, so the reception of that effect must be the focus of measurement. Social change may be defined as the dynamics of adaptability within and between social institutions, their component parts, their goals, and their leadership. When an institution makes this adaptability its purpose, it becomes an agent of social change. When the relationships of the recipient institution with others cause it to be modified, or when it is modified from within, it becomes the object of social change. When Methodism purposefully effects change, it functions as the change agent and social change grows out of social strategy.

A. Understanding Methodist Institutions

An institution may be thought of as any specified pattern of correlated human behavior. We are primarily concerned here with those institutions whose function is the embodiment of the gospel of Jesus Christ as they seek to increase the love of God and man in the world. This goal is accepted by each Methodist when he becomes a member of the church, and it becomes implicit in every pattern of behavior, or institution, he establishes as he co-operates with others to promote the work of his denomination.

The institutional forms and functions which have resulted from growth, social need, and inventions within Methodism are manifold. We are concerned primarily with those which support or which accrue from the General Conference of The Methodist Church. They include local churches, mission projects, general and conference boards and agencies.

While we are discussing particular kinds of institutions with specific purposes, it should be noted that most institutions have certain common characteristics and functions. Institutions, in general, tend to be similar because they are the organized efforts of human groups to meet common problems.

We would suggest that these similarities produce four basic types of institutions and institutionally oriented functions which are universal and transcultural. They are conservative, status-oriented, inventive, and religious institutions and functions. Each is a point of emphasis rather than an exclusive category.

Every effective institution, of whatever kind, must provide for its members certain basic functions: (1) immediate social satisfactions, (2) purposeful action in keeping with long-range goals, (3) a constructive attitude toward the traditional ways of doing things, and (4) technological innovations and skills for which society has respect. Whether an institution is conservative, inventive, religious, or status-directed, it still must provide at least these four basic functions. When an institution is observed to be declining it will usually be ignoring one or more of these necessary functions.

Let us now look at these four types of institutions and functions in general, and then as they relate to Methodism.

Conservative institutions and functions develop from the yearning of man for firm ground upon which to stand in his grasp of the future. Man's desire for a dependable universe leads him into such stabilizing activities as procreation and family welfare, and into the establishment of dependable factors of production, devices of social control, economic functions necessary to physical sustenance, and other devices in which societies seek to perpetuate themselves. Thus, conservation is a normal function of social institutions.

Status institutions and functions derive from the universal yearning of man for recognition and social position. Democratic processes are built upon this assumption and upon the concept of the dignity of man. The group is expressing this yearning corporately when it selects its leaders and expects them to embody the group ideals and purposes. Few human beings willingly accept a position socially inferior to that of all other persons. Institutions and individuals resist irrelevancy. They want to be wanted, to feel a sense of belonging and prestige, and to participate in decisions about themselves.

Inventive institutions and functions introduce the "new" and provide for society its teaching, research, and growth aspects. The challenges of the environment elicit from man and his institutions insightful responses which are fundamentally similar in all modern cultures. The questions "Why?" "How?" "When?" "Where?" and "Who?" typify the areas within which inventive institutions and functions operate. When an institution or group of institutions must answer these questions or teach the answers, inventive functions are exercised.

Religious institutions and functions emanate from that social yearning of man for harmony between and within the known and the unknown factors of his total environment. When this yearning has group recognition, the group in search of harmony elevates the most satisfactory habit systems into institutional form. We shall see later the further evolution of these religious institutions, but it is enough to say here that they are primarily responsible for fulfilling the tasks of reconciliation between man and his fellow men and with God.

It may seem anomalous to list religious institutions in four classifications, one of which is called "religious." The reader should keep in mind that we view the function of religion in its most general sense to be the production of harmony between and within the known and the unknown factors of man's *total* environment. When the central purpose of an institution fulfills this function, it is primarily religious. When another institution is primarily educative in its central purposes and indirectly concerned with reconciliation, we call it an educational institution. The difference is in point of emphasis. For this reason, a religious institutional arrangement like Methodism may have within it institutions whose functions are primarily conservative, or inventive, or status-oriented. Each has its home sponsorship in the religious purposes which brought it into being, but it functions practically and immediately to conserve, to educate, or to uplift. There is no inherent denial of the religiosity of the

163

educational institution or the historical society or the work of temperance when we fail to class them as primarily religious institutions in this frame of reference. The church-related university has more in common with other educational institutions than with the denomination which sponsors it. The church historical society is closest to other historical societies, but does not deny its subject matter nor its founding interest.

Under the umbrella of Methodism there are then four categories of institutions, each of which has a central function and purpose related to the basic needs of individual Methodists. We shall discuss these classes as they relate to the leaders of the church who are involved in social actions. These leaders have individual agendas and private purposes, and are often finally responsible for all decisions made. Individual leadership actions will first be correlated with the various types of Methodist institutions and their functions. Then we shall look at institutional actions before proceeding to the questions of social control and the appropriateness of strategy.

B. Methodist Institutions in Action

All social action involves groups of persons. The individual who directs action to achieve his own ends must involve the group. Even when his goals are selfish and relegate the group aims to a lesser status, the strategy and action for their attainment are social in character. The following discussion of the focuses of action implies, therefore, no false divisions between the individual and the group. Instead, our concern here is centered upon the individual as a basic factor in such action as he may direct, and upon the institution as the focus for such action.

1. THE INDIVIDUAL BASIS OF ACTION

Individual action in general is centered in experience and need. Whether it be the actions of the board executive who plans to transplant his own pastoral success formula into new soils, or the layman whose design is to obtain the removal of the present pastor, basic needs are at the root of action. The executive may have been selected because of the prominence of his success formula and may feel committed to sharing it with "the whole church." The layman may equally be driven by his feeling that the present pastor threatens the moral stability of his home church. In each case, group needs and sentiments focus in an individual who decides and plans action.

Religious leaders, then, may be thought of as those who embody in themselves the mores, principles, and aspirations of the religious institution in such a way that they are accorded the right to become the "community face" of the group. In each case of delegated authority, the group grants permission to the leader to act in its behalf. Even the tyrant acts with the submissive approval of those whom he directs.

In attempting to understand the role of religious leaders in such action, it may be helpful to look first at the types of leaders who control social situations, and then to consider the kinds of needs, drives, or functions which produce action on the part of these religious leaders.

A Typology of Religious Leadership

As in all social groups, leadership in religious institutions can be classified in four types: emergent, formal, crisis, and adjustive.

The emergent leader is one who, while holding no formal office, "speaks for a large number of people." Every local church has laymen who emerge as such informal leaders of groups within it. They may hold no official position but they control the basic decisions. They hold the influence which determines the direction of group thinking. They normally are persons of longer residence in the community than others. They spend a great deal of time in the church buildings. They have relatives who hold offices and who contribute to the church. They and their friends and relatives constitute the subgroups which, with other subgroups, form the cliques which "run" the church.

No Methodist minister can become an emergent leader within the church to which he is appointed. His primary loyalty is to the annual conference. His membership is not within the local church and the members know it. His emergent leadership is not at this level. For the minister, emergent leadership of another type exists within the annual conference, within the approved supply school, within the cabinet of an annual conference, and within the staff of a board or agency.

The formal leader is one whose directive relationship to the institutions in which he participates is explicit and whose functions are specified. Such leaders are likely to be found in the positions of administrator, pastor, and chairman of a committee or board. Any leader whose primary function is prescribed is a formal leader. In his position he functions on the basis of prejudgments and standards which he is expected to enforce and to which he must adhere in keeping with the requirements of his office.

In this sense, the minister functions primarily as a formal leader in his congregation. Because of his sympathy for persons, he is likely to feel that he is in fact "very close to his people," and thus a kindly cleric may influence his people to ends which they do not desire. In such instances, he usually finds "that even though he has lived there 25 years, he is the minister and they are the people." [1] The roles which he may play and the descriptions of his privileges are within clearly defined limits. He is selected because he is trained for his position, is accredited, has knowledge which the congregation does not have, and in fact enhances its standing in the eyes of the community.

The ideal formal leader, one who is singularly appropriate for the urbanized community, is a person of prominence who is conversant with the total community, makes a good appearance, and is in good health. He is capable of transmitting his attitudes and influences over a wide range, is optimistic, provokes emulation, and is humble in the sense of pointing beyond himself to group goals. He has technical proficiency in the ways demanded by the institution. He has a sense of social fitness and is experienced in democratic situations, with the ability to judge the mood of the group, to take it with him rather than to precede it, to communicate with clarity, to delegate authority, and to multiply self. Where crises are involved he has insight and prescience. [2]

For the Methodist leadership this means fraternity without lowering standards. It means impersonal judgments. It implies the communication of the highest goals, divine and human, without fear. It means a constancy of goals implemented by deep concern and sincerity. At all times the effective formal leader is aware of the possible consequences of his actions for his group. Humility and self-respect go hand in hand without contradiction in such ideal persons. In short, The Methodist Church, by its practical theology even more than its stated rules, demands unattainably high standards for its authorities. The highest status in the church comes to those who fulfill most nearly the group ideal.

The third type of leader emerges in times of crisis. Such leaders are

---

[1] Dwight Sanderson and Robert Polson, *Rural Community Organization* (New York: John Wiley & Sons, Inc., 1936), p. 380.
[2] Stotts, *op. cit.*, p. 176.

usually unexpected and often unprepared for their sudden burst into prominence. Martin Luther King, Jr., who became a key figure in the desegregation struggle in the South, did not know that Montgomery, Alabama, would be the scene of crisis.[3] Crises occur in unexpected places; and because they do, the recipient of such leadership status is tested in unexpected ways. He may be a layman whose church has burned, or whose fellow members are split into rival factions.

There are many natural crises over which the group has no control. They are the wars, floods, cultural revolutions, and disasters which pound upon the church from the outside. Coupled with them are those social crises which are the result of any sustained threat to the mores and purposes of the institution. Such social crises may be caused by the institution itself or by companion institutions with which it is related.

One may ask whether a professional "trouble shooter" is a crisis leader? He is not. His role is that of a formal leader. He is brought in from the outside to run the Red Cross services to the flooded area, to organize the local sentiment, or to add skills which are not held by local crisis leaders. Nor are those firemen, policemen, and others who stand by for emergencies the true crisis leaders of the group for the same reason. The leader who is already there at the time of crisis is the crisis leader. He may be any leader of any religious institution of Methodism at any time who is suddenly thrust into the crisis role.

The crisis leader is effective as he marshals the skills of the group in ways which are uplifting toward goals which they have espoused. The crisis leader never "betrays" his group or its ideals. He will make sacrifices because he dares to assist them. He may be forgotten and replaced when supplementary leadership arrives. His tenure is usually temporary. He may move on to another responsibility of higher status than he held before, since his effectiveness as a leader has been demonstrated, but he will rarely continue to be a crisis leader. The group may adjust to a recurrent crisis and classify it as "normal." In such a case, the crisis leader may continue in his new position, but as a formal leader.

Leadership in the church and on its doorstep is faced by many kinds of crises. The drama of war and the melodrama of natural crises seldom surround the "capricious and unpredictable behavior" of Methodists as they interact with one another. Yet these basic forms of crises are faced by the church in whole or in part somewhere in the world each

[3] See his book, *Stride Toward Freedom.*

167

day. For the facing of these crises, a tougher training of leadership than we generally practice is certainly demanded.

Adjustive leaders are those whose election comes through compromise and "deadlocks" in selection. They have few political enemies. They are relatively unknown prior to election, or if they are known they have the reputation of being kindly and effective persons whose elevation poses no threat to the electors. Often such status is obtained through family connections, proximity to a suddenly vacated office, personal popularity, or social extroversion.

In Methodism, adjustive leadership occurs most frequently in elective positions where continued balloting is practiced. Elections to General and Jurisdictional Conferences or to annual conferences, for that matter, seldom go to persons whose strong positions on given issues are known. Personal popularity or prominence through church activities often prove to be the device which projects one into such elective prominence. Adjustive leadership might be defined best as compromise leadership. In this sense it is clearly political. Opposing factions maintain the "favorite son" elective pattern until they are in an open or covert bargaining position. When it is apparent that they cannot win with their candidate, compromise candidates appear.

Fortunately for the church, this striving of interest groups with local leaders who cannot win their way into majority group acceptance eventuates in the kind of election in which a prominent person who has no enemies in either group, but is known to be capable, is elected. The very interesting pattern of lay elections during the annual conference sessions is a case in point. Many persons are elected because of groups they represent, such as the Woman's Society of Christian Service or Methodist Men. Others are elected simply because their names are known to voting laity. Lay electors receive little guidance from the clergy. It might very well be that Bishop Straughn's observation is correct that a clearer choice might be made if both clergy and laymen were voting for their delegates collectively instead of having the ministers voting for ministerial delegates and the laymen for lay delegates.[4]

Thus, we see that while emergent leadership is of the "grass roots," formal leadership is professional, and crisis leadership is tension-oriented,

[4] James Straughn, *Inside Methodist Union* (Nashville: The Methodist Publishing House, 1958), p. 161.

adjustive leadership grows out of compromise. This fourfold classification of leadership in no way invalidates the traditional concept of Christian leaders as prophets, seers, and charismatic persons. Emergent, formal, crisis, and adjustive leaders all may be prophetic. In times of crisis and challenge, where there are no guiding precedents, the leader must turn to moral authority and divine directives, and seek charismatic status for his new-found convictions. Prophets are not leaders solely because men so regard them, but because each prophet and each follower believes that the will of God is in such charismatic leadership.

Christian leadership, then, is not a matter of group striving and social pressures alone. Few social scientists would be naïve enough to describe it so. Each type of leader discussed is, in the field of religion, convinced that the responsibilities handed him have divine connotations. He is responsible to men, but also to God and his Church. While the method of his choosing may have seemed coincidental or directed by his own interests, he is usually driven by the rightness of the choice—by a sense of vocation.

Factors Influencing Individual Action

Although the individual leader is a basic factor in any kind of social action, the church has provided little or no training for specialists in its institutions, boards, and agencies outside the local church. This may be true in Methodism partly because of its relatively recent bureaucratic development. At any rate, increasing numbers of local pastors are being thrust into administrative positions for which they are equipped only with a growing interest and the most general training. Rare indeed is the strong leader who decides without committees and peer reassurance, the executive trained for his task from college days, and the administrator who is also a student of his institution.

Under these circumstances individual action is likely to be determined by functions inherent in the institution and by the predominant drives of the individual leader. It is influenced largely by conservative and inventive functions and by status and religious drives.

Conservative action is more widely understood in relation to the episcopacy and the office of the district superintendent—and aspirants for those offices—than in other administrative tasks. Here, as with many other administrators, many specifications are inflexible. The individual comes into a well-established framework of organization and pattern of

169

action and feels secure in a conservative strategy. He is employed to preserve, to protect, and to be loyal. His personal action must convince his staff, peers, clientele, and superiors that he is no malingerer in Methodism's cause. In his office hangs a portrait of John Wesley, an oil sketch of the church which "he" built, and memorabilia from the Uniting Conference of 1939. He commissions the writing of a history of his institution, the reconstruction of a Methodist shrine, and declares his undying loyalty to the rural church. Although he is self-conscious about these homages, he finally comes to see them as institutional counterparts to his demonstrations of loyalty to his family. For his family, he sets aside his "day off" and places their pictures on his desk. For the institution which he serves, there are other equally effective means of reassurance.

Much of the action of individual administrators and leaders is based on a drive for status. Many social scientists contend that status drives are the most constant individual motivation. Those who know Methodism, or any institutional arrangement, would privately endorse the view that status is a major professional goal of the clergy.

Laymen also perform high and low tasks, give of their time and money for recognition as prominent churchmen. It would be easy to misconstrue motives here, or to ignore mingled drives and concerns which hold leaders to their tasks. It would be more of an error to discuss individual action without recognizing the political aspirations, compensatory mechanisms, and personal motivations which create the agenda of many Methodist leaders.[5]

Each administrator, new staff head, lay leader, or president of Methodist Men must demonstrate to himself and to the organization that his status is commensurate with the position attained. His personal status is only part of the agenda. A familiar pattern in Methodism is the "showcasing" of newly elected bishops, executive officers and administrators, so that other jurisdictions, publics, and leaders may "get to know" them. The year following the General and Jurisdictional Conferences is largely devoted to this series of public introductions. This pattern is equally applicable to all forms of religious leadership, whether in the local church or at the district level.

[5] See James Gustafson, *Treasure in Earthen Vessels* (New York: Harper & Brothers, 1961), pp. 28 ff.

The drive for status has its effect in the mass identification of a congregation with a beloved pastor. Members of the congregation take pride in his successes and in the honors which he receives, and in turn feel a sense of fulfillment that he is "their pastor." Methodists within an episcopal area feel this way about their "own bishop." This is the heart of morale in a widely scattered institution.

From status needs come group demands for recognition, prestige, and fulfillment. Each group hopes to convey its idealized purposes, institutional image, and intentions to the several publics for which it is concerned, in ways which elevate its prestige.

Just as actions are required to fulfill conservative and status functions, the role of innovator has its function in Methodism. Out of inventive action come technological improvements, the educational institutions and devices of man, the curiosity-satisfying arrangements of the various cultures, and the general arpeggios of living found in the fine arts.

The administrator who is "always coming up with something new" fulfills his own needs for creativity and furthers the pioneering evolution of the institution he heads. As innovator he can be characterized by the inquiring mind that impels him into every nook and cranny of an administrative area; by the dreams which set high goals for staff or peers; and by acceptance of the discipline of advanced graduate study. His inventive action couples new media of communication with old truths, reformulates policy into crisp terms, modifies procedures for effectiveness, expands staff, and clarifies functions. Each is the proper and expected action of an administrator.

The ramifications of the action of individual religious leaders are endless. They explain the call to a ministry which drives a leader to second-mile stewardship, and the endless inner responses of laymen and clergy who fulfill the mission of the church in divers places. For Methodists, work is worship, and labors of supererogation are part and parcel of private strategy.

In a very real sense, many of our Methodist schools, missions, and settlements are synonymous with the individual religious motivation and actions of their founders or administrators. Think of Isabella Thoburn College in Lucknow without the name of its founder; or of Bingham Canyon, Utah, without Ada Duhigg; Pittman Center without Dr. Robert Thomas; Morgan Memorial and Goodwill Industries with-

out the Helmses; or the Department of Christian Social Relations of the
Woman's Division of Christian Service without Thelma Stevens! [6]

2. THE INSTITUTIONAL FOCUS OF ACTION [7]

As we have seen, any specified and predictable system of correlated
human behavior is an institution. In this sense, the cottage prayer
meeting and the local church are institutions. When such institutions
are grouped for mutual support they may be called institutional arrangements. If the focus of the discussion is the single agency (board, college, or church) we shall refer to it as an "institution."

Institutional action is collective. In contrast to individual action, the
committees, staff, board, or supervisors must approve the general policy
and intent of the institution. The bulk of such concurrence is tacit and
informal. Few local churches have a formal statement of purpose.
Conference boards rarely formalize policy and structure by legalistic
descriptions. Even agencies established by the General Conference
operate from directive as well as explicit legislation. Expressed as well as
tacit group policy then will be the concern of this discussion.

As we look at the institutional focus of action within Methodism it
will be helpful to make use again of the conservative, status, inventive,
and religious classifications. It will be helpful also to look at each of
these categories in the light of those roles which any institution plays,
at one time or another, in its social setting. In carrying out conservative,
status, inventive, and religious functions and actions, Methodist institutions are involved in adjustive roles, crisis roles, assumed roles, and
ascribed roles.

Conservative Action

Serves basic conservative needs. Purposive conservation which is tra-
dition-centered encourages stabilizing legislation; it also uses counter-

[6] It should be clear by now that we are concerned with much more than those institutions which the community clearly calls "religious." Many organizations of religious an-
cestry are now performing what the community sees to be secular rather than religious
functions. Frequently the social work agency or the fraternal group may become substitutes for clearly religious institutions in the lives of persons. Through a founder's interest,
we have a responsibility for many, many more institutions than those which are called
"religious." We cannot absolve ourselves from responsibility for the community by
changing the labels so that everything outside the church is "secular."

[7] Space limitations prohibit a discussion of the area of group life which is not institutional. Casual groups without predictable arrangements are not the focus of this volume.

measures to balance extremism. Likewise, the establishment of ritual, custom, and group mores fulfills this purpose.

Adjustive roles in conservative action come from the competitive–co-operative struggle of an institution with its environment. For example, parish planning must take account of its physical and cultural setting. A mobile ministry is necessary for migrant farm laborers, while an institutional church pattern may be required in the inner city. In the suburbs the lengthened week end and new leisure patterns may require major adjustments in the church calendar. On the national level, geographic pressures keep Methodist headquarters near the ports, investment centers, and offices of other denominations in the east.

In its conservative action an institution must compete and co-operate in order to retain the gains of yesterday. Financial investments, maintenance tasks, and service functions are essentially conservative in nature.

Conservative action usually accents the crisis roles played by all institutions. Agency responses to the challenge of unexpected situations seem the primary reasons for conscious policy change. Our staff interviews with board executives indicate that the majority of new and redirected policy comes from the crisis "demands of the churches." The Television, Radio, and Film Commission came from the social crisis of television's rapid growth. The westward shift of National Missions funds came from the crisis of the westward movement of the population.

An official of The Methodist Publishing House said: "Twenty-five letters of protest from an audience of six million users denote no crisis, but one thousand letters from one jurisdiction do." Changes in policy require the measurement of the importance of crises. Inexperienced leaders usually are disproportionately perturbed by one letter of protest or voice in disagreement. Persons inexperienced in social action or institutional leadership leap from crisis to crisis and are easily exhausted. The skill of judgment which puts social crises in proper proportion comes as much from experience as from wisdom and insight. Methodism's leaders are usually inexperienced in such judgments. One of the prices of a traveling ministry is inexperience in fields of specialization. A new and uncertain hand tends to be primarily conservative in crises.

When an institution begins the "First Annual" historic pageant, agrees to the erection of a new monument, or builds a memorial to religious martyrs, it fulfills "second-mile" strategic functions. Assumed

173

roles which respond to conservative needs are historic rather than temporal, voluntary rather than enforced, and creative rather than fixed.

Any role which is attributed to an individual or institution without prior consent is *ascribed*. The ascribed role of defending community morals is one function expected of every church. Social radicals may protest, extremists may dispute with its method, but all assign to the church the primary responsibility for a vigorous defense of mores and morals. The local church may not promote church lotteries. The community and the church have decreed the direction of action. The Board of Temperance does not choose whether it will approve social drinking. The institution, however, determines the vigor and volume of that action.

Status-Oriented Action

In broader strokes we shall examine the roles of status and inventive action. Each could be discussed extensively along the lines of the foregoing exposition. Status action is symbolic and easily illustrated.

Adjustive roles are seen in the "high-steeple" church which is the church of the town and in the board which scores a coup by holding a timely conference while an issue is at white heat.

Institutions maintain their *status* in crisis roles or attain a first reputation by the action they take when challenged. The program of the Board of World Peace in the Crusade for a New World Order or in servicing conscientious objectors during World War II illustrates this kind of action. The local church which bravely alters its program and leadership to meet a changing parish attains new status and respect as a by-product.

Assumed roles are usually a deliberate form of institutional action. The myopia of localism affects persons who inhabit a beautiful church, a new board building, or represent the largest district in the episcopal area. Each is likely to affect the posture of such an assumed status. Then Sidney Hook's "wish-fulfilling prophecy" becomes a reality. The institution which assumes its power to be great, acts as if it were and becomes thereby more prestigeful than before. The highest steeple becomes a meaningful symbol as the church accepts increasing responsibility and fulfills its own image of its power.

Ascribed status roles are most challenging in a day of racial and religious tension. The public platform which must have Catholic, Protestant, and Jewish clergy in evidence or the board which must have jurisdictional and racial representation is illustrative of artificially

174

ascribed status. In fact, ascribed representation is a central problem of Methodist institutional administration. Must it always do what it is expected to do and no more? Such ascriptions may become a fence which encloses the church.

Inventive Action

The excitement which comes from rational and purposive change has made social action popular. Persons who fear "social action" usually assume that basic structural changes may occur which will imperil the security of historic arrangements. This volume contends that inventive institutional action, the introduction of the "new," is only one of many threads of social change and should not be mistaken for the whole cloth. Educational functions, creative insights, and new programs are necessary to the ongoing life of any institution. New loyalties, leaders, and technologies determine its relevance to each new day.

Adjustive roles are most clearly seen in this need area in the strange alliances necessary for technological advancement. The coupling of Hollywood technicians with Methodist religious education, the use of Madison Avenue advertising by the Advertising Council, and the co-operation of the Board of World Peace with the War Department in World War II in providing assistance to conscientious objectors are the kinds of competitive co-operation which illustrate the institutional growing edge. The temporary alliances of church and secular agencies for common ends are seen at every level in Methodism. This is the epitome of adjustive action.

Crisis roles characterize "social action" at its best. Creative plans to meet crises are common in the United Nations. Several peace plans have been prepared for each potential trouble spot in the world by the Secretariat of the UN. It is customary in most boards and agencies to formulate responses to crises after they have arisen. In fact much strategic action grows out of crises. A local church reaches its working peak when a tragic fire forces rebuilding. A religious institution is always at its best in crisis if it reaches into its inner resources and formulates inventive strategy and action.

Assumed roles in this category are characterized by the educational functions which an institution initiates. The training of new and old leadership, the education of its several publics, the "brainstorming," freewheeling, idea sessions create new hope as well as ideas. In an

175

educational institution, much of this is ascribed. Even there, additional roles are assumed as confident and imaginative leadership permits creativity.

Ascribed roles are as variable as the spectrum of religious institutions. Each institution develops them in response to its own and to external expectations. The educational institution is expected to write new curricula. The church school is ascribed the task of preparing youth for new experiences. The Conference Board of Missions is expected to plan for the building of new churches. To the local church is ascribed the responsibility for a program of evangelism in its own parish. Failure to fulfill any of these ascribed roles causes the larger program of action to malfunction.

Action Specifically Religious

In religious institutions the religious interest is, or should be, paramount. The religious function per se is one of the many roles the institution fulfills, but it is the most important. There must be coherence between the general religious purposes of the institution and the specific religious functions it fulfills.

Adjustive roles evolve as the religious institution comes to face squarely its central religious function. The purposes of God, as interpreted by the leaders, become the norms for challenging accepted standards. Then actions are drastically reshaped.

Similarly, adjustive roles are in evidence in the competition and cooperation of denominational groups. As these adjustive roles have been carried out in ecumenical discussion and interchurch co-operation, there has developed in Methodism a new theological climate and a new sense of world responsibility.

Crisis roles which are clearly religious center around critical decisions, redemptive functions, and momentous moral judgments. In each case, the urgency of time and moment is central. Pronouncements of the church which challenge improprieties of the state, judgments which condemn transgressions of the morals, ministry to persons in mortal peril, and military chaplaincies are roles of strategic importance in this area of human need.

Perhaps the most graphic of these actions is that which leads to the development of schismatic groups within the denomination. Such actions led to the founding out of Methodism of the Nazarene and the Pillar of Fire churches. In each case, religious issues were central in the schism. The crisis action eventuated in the founding of new denominations.

Assumed roles in the field of religion include such diverse tasks as the maintenance of institutional purity and services of mediation. The tasks of "policing" the ministry, regulating deviant churches, and religious accreditation are assumed tasks. The church would go on without them, but purists in each institution demand the assumption of regulatory religious actions. The prophetic ministries of dedicated larger parish pastors who choose to be in difficult situations in remote rural areas or in the inner city, or elect to minister to miners or to the dispossessed on the migrant trail—these are such assumed roles.

Virtually any institutional plan which is above and beyond the basic program of that institution, is benevolent in character, and not ascribed to it by the community, may be called assumed religious action.

Ascribed religious roles include the functions of worship, devotion and unequivocally religious social acts expected of the institution by its publics. For the local church, such actions as providing sufficient services of worship are illustrative. Church boards and agencies are expected at least to be staffed by devout Methodists, to consider all problems in Christian love, and to present a calm appearance to the public. Many of these expectations are regional or local in character, and are virtually impossible ascriptions to a national board. Each conference, for example, expects that research and survey, church extension helps, or architectural advice will be immediately available upon request. Seldom does the annual conference leadership see the national picture and realize the slender staff, the many demands, and the limited budget with which general boards and agencies work. Such ascriptive roles and assignments are virtually impossible of fulfillment at the time and with the speed demanded.

The types of individual and institutional action discussed above may or may not involve the elements of rationality, purpose, and self-consciousness which we have indicated are essential to strategy. Action based on strategy calls for the appraisal of social needs, the assessment of costs and resources, and the deployment of energies to establish and accomplish institutional goals. We have seen that this has two primary foci. When an individual modifies institutional goals or uses them to achieve ends which are primarily his own, we have individual action.

177

This action may or may not have the approval of the group, but it fulfills the conservative, inventive, religious, or status concerns of the individual. When the individual involves the group in the modification of its goals and gains its consent, his action becomes strategic.

Institutional strategy marshals the social needs of the group and directs them toward the commonly desired goals of the group. These strategies may be classified according to the conservative, inventive, religious, and status types illustrated above. Since institutions are by and large the reflections of great leaders, all strategy may be said to be in a sense individual. But the obverse is also true. No individual goals are achieved by private strategy without the consent, collusion, and at least tacit encouragement of the group.

Social change introduced by one person or by a small group is not in the final sense a social change at all. It is an individual decision. At all points, social control is in keeping with group goals. The wider the group which accepts these goals, the stronger the social control devices.

C. Strategy Appropriate for Social Change

We turn now to a consideration of the kind of strategy which is appropriate for social change. This discussion will deal with the types of social control, the consistency with institutional purposes, and the timing of social action.

Social control may be defined as the sum total of the processes whereby society, or a subgroup within society, secures conformity to expectations on the part of its constituent units, individuals, or groups. Such conformity relates both to the institutional means and to the system of goals toward which the group desires to direct its members.[8]

1. TYPES OF SOCIAL CONTROL

Social control consists of two main forms: (1) coercive control and (2) persuasive control. They represent two of the major schools of social control theory. American law is established upon the first of these theories as set forth by Roscoe Pound.[9] Inherent in this view is the concept that all control contains within it force or the threat of force.

---

[8] Merton, *Social Theory and Social Structure*, p. 141.
[9] Georgès Gurvitch and Wilbert Moore (eds.), *Twentieth Century Sociology* (New York: Philosophical Library, 1945), pp. 320 ff.

Regardless of the gentle character of the rules, this school says, conformity through force is back of every regulation.

In contrast to this approach, the French School of Social Control holds that affirmative control with no implied force is equally valid in holding society within the socially approved boundaries. Contrary to the view of American law, this school holds that conformity comes equally through education, rewards, and noncoercive sanctions. Oddly enough, much of Canadian and British law today is based upon this theory of social control. The lack of firearms on the British police, the maintenance of "mass order," the rigorous regulation of Canadian highway patrols which may not violate the law in order to catch violators are cases in point.

A third view, which is really a combination of both the foregoing, might be called cultural control. Within this view an individual is encouraged to respond in socially approved ways because the total environment in which he finds himself encourages him to be consistent in his behavior. The strength of the control forces is directly tied to his family life and to his primary cultural contacts. Since for sincere Protestants the church is a part of daily life and practice, it may be said that "his is a Protestant world." His associates tend to be members of his own church, his prayers are in conformity with family and church goals, and his life is increasingly directed toward a corporate impression that the ways of the churchly institution and its goals are correct. If he feels that the goals are incorrect, he feels free to work toward improving them.

As we have indicated previously,[10] social change comes about by the operation of changing circumstances which affect or are affected by the institution and its members. Whether gradually by the drift of circumstances and changing cultural patterns, or suddenly through the changing environment and its demands, or deliberately through the choice of new goals, all institutions change and all change is governed in one way or another through social control.

In any planned social change there are at least four countervailing forces.[11] They are (1) the desire for change which stems from inventive needs, (2) the desire for maintenance of things as they are (the conserva-

---

[10] Pp. 86 ff.
[11] Lewin listed two: restraining and driving forces.

tive), (3) the sense of crisis if change moves faster than one's ability to comprehend or control (crisis), and (4) the state of tension which exists between the change and the restraint forces (adjustment or amelioration). The tasks of reassurance and consolidation of loyalties, as well as the inculcation of the new with its reorientations, are affected by various social control devices.[12]

The family pattern of control is typical of these culture-centered concepts. Within most families, the members come to have similar tastes, cherish the same family legends, and accept common patterns of restraint. Control here is both unconscious and conscious. Conformity brings acceptance and approval, but nonconformity seldom brings reprobation. Force and the threat of force are reserved for the most shocking affronts to the family code. This type of control exists in many small groups which characteristically discount the temperamental, short-range breaking of the group code.

Many physical sanctions could be listed if we were dealing with a more authoritarian church or institution. Such devices are expulsion, extermination, or physical punishment. The payment of penalties is still a prevalent pattern in some of the world's religions, but fortunately not among the Methodists.

Economic sanctions are much more common devices in The Methodist Church. The failure of a church to adopt an efficient and approved set of blueprints can disqualify it for church loans from conference and general agencies. The failure of a seminary to maintain its accreditation can result in the withdrawal of funds sent to it from the Board of Education. Many types of economic sanctions are used.

"The frame-up" occurs when members of any social group bring to the attention of the authorities the failure of a member to conform. "It takes only the breath of scandal to destroy the occupational status of a minister; while a gentle breeze . . . can often kill a physician's practice." [13]

Rewards as well as punishments can create conformity and the implementation of desired techniques. Economic rewards certainly come to those seminaries that accept increasing numbers of candidates for the Methodist ministry. Salary raises and incidental benefits encourage the

---

[12] Kurt Lewin, *Resolving Social Conflicts* (New York: Harper & Brothers, 1945), p. 56.
[13] Richard T. LaPiere, *A Theory of Social Control* (New York: McGraw-Hill Book Co., 1954), p. 235.

minister and administrators to continue doing well what they have been doing in behalf of the group.

Many types of group sentiment or psychological sanctions are effective in controlling religious institutions. Few churches have a merit system[14] for church attendance, the saying of prayers and attendance at communion; but each gives objective encouragement to those who adhere to its highest standards.

The punishment of persons by condemnation, threat and intimidation has largely faded into the frontier history of Methodist preaching. Yet some forms of it do exist. Repeated warnings to remain "true" prompt voluntary responses which may be classified as penalties for misconduct.

Those psychological sanctions which result in specific status awards are common in Methodism. Promotions depend upon conformity, and status is keyed to commonly accepted group goals. Only those whose future is relatively secure from problems of advancement are free from this temptation to be approved in all that they do and say. The unorthodox minister who figuratively "stands on his head on the steeple" may fill the church and revitalize it, but his aberrance is rewarded by the withdrawal of approval by his peers, if not his official board. Many official boards have resisted innovation as an alternative to the death of their church.

Many other kinds of anticipated sanctions hold one in line with the intentions of the group. They include the approval of superiors and the certainty that "this is God's will." They extend in fact to eternal life and its relationship to the good society here in this life.

In sum, there is nothing simple about social control. It is the total of the processes whereby society, or The Methodist Church in this case, secures conformity to institutional processes and approved goals. These controls are often ineffective, but they are always operative.

Social change then, with these correctives, is discernible *while* the institutions are in motion. One does not need to "freeze" institutions as if in suspension in order to analyze them. We simply ask what the forces are which militate for change; and recognize them as not only normal but necessary. Conversely, we accord deserved recognition to the conservative forces which are in fact equally necessary in order for

[14] Joseph Fichter, *Southern Parish* (Glencoe, Illinois: Free Press, 1957), p. 54.

change to take place. When either of these sets of forces destroy the normal equilibrium, and both do, the "panic button" is pushed by those who do not understand and a crisis is declared. Why is it, for example, that most surveys result in immediate changes which tend to slide back to old levels when the "police" aren't looking? Why does the pulpit get moved back into the center of the chancel as soon as the young minister moves on to another charge?

2. Consistency with Institutional Purposes

Previous explanations of the strategy of social action [15] prepare us for the correlative strategy of each type of institutional form and function. The basic form of social innovation and change is of course operative only in terms of the innovative, religious, and status functions of institutions. While techniques of conservation are used to strengthen the handmaiden functions of the institution, they are not basically dedicated to social change.

For strategy to be appropriate, it must be consistent with the prior purposes of the institution which it is to serve. Inventive institutions such as the church school, the colleges and seminaries, and the Board of Education demand a strategy which is primarily concerned with the new. The conservative functions of those institutions such as maintenance and service are not basic to their prior purpose, which is to teach. When teaching leads to research, and the research leads to change, that change is consistent with the prior purposes of the group! There may be cumulative and idealistic goals which are elaborated in the history of each institution, but basically its function is always to answer the questions of the oncoming generation.

Mediation and compromise are not the strategy of a defeated, but of a dynamic society. We will recall from earlier discussion in this chapter that an equilibrium normally exists between the inventive and the conservative forces operative within any institution. When these forces clash in crisis, there is need for a strategy of reconciliation. In Methodist institutions of any kind progress is made by strategic compromise. But a reconciliation of two creative points of view is not inherently a compromise of conviction.

Methodist institutions need a strategy for producing and reinforcing their own and their leaders' status. For example, each institution must

[15] Chap. IV.

confront and seek to impress several publics. Such impressions are directed by the goals of Christianity and their interpretation in The Methodist Church. Let no leader delude himself into thinking that the followers will long remain if they have reason to be ashamed of their relationship to the institution. A continued feeling of pride in the church (not carnal pride in the theological sense, but the pride "of good report" of which Paul speaks) serves to strengthen, to encourage, and to provide the social control that binds the institution together. Such strategies are as necessary as any other, both within the church and in the secular and interfaith press.

Any form of social strategy must utilize the existing social framework even though it may intend to change some of it in the process of implementing the strategy. The forms of social control available within an institution guarantee the implementation and stabilization of change. When an annual conference finally passes and formalizes a needed change in the social procedures of that body, it inevitably asks, "How will we enforce this?" or "How will we encourage the people to do what we have agreed is proper?" The accepted social control techniques within the experience of the conference will then be studied and one or more devices will be adopted.

3. The Timing of Social Action

We have discussed strategy, leadership, goals, and types of social control. Each of them, in addition to being mutually interdependent, is also dependent upon the field of experience of the institution in which change is desired. The *time* in which proposed change is introduced is a vital factor to institutional change as it is to everything else. This is variously called the "field," the "growing edge," the "place where the people are." Leaders in parliamentary affairs, through experience, come to sense and feel the propriety for introducing new legislation. Even for leaders with limited experience, there are ways of evaluating this dimension of time.

In the development of any institution there are the following descriptive stages: organization, consolidation, ritualization, crisis, decision, and dissolution. It should be noted that these do not necessarily follow a prescribed developmental pattern. If, however, we understand the stage of development reached by an institution at a particular time, we may be better able to help that institution engage in strategic action. We

183

now introduce these typical stages and suggest how each of the components of change and strategy may be utilized. These necessary components are (1) form and function, (2) leadership, (3) social control, (4) goals and purposes[16] and finally (5) appropriate strategy—which includes an understanding of the right time for the change desired.

The organizational stage of institutional life, or as Hertzler has named it "the incipient stage," [17] is one of fundamental simplicity. At no other period in its history does an institution function so directly and with such clarity of purpose. Every institution arises out of a basic need of the group. There is more than physical need involved in these beginnings. The congregation needs a church home, the denomination needs a radio and television center, the board needs a research department; and out of these needs come trial and error attempts to solve the problem.

An individual staff member feels the need for audio-visuals in his work and prepares his own materials in an amateurish way. This need spreads in trial and error fashion until the board itself has a department for audio-visuals and has institutionalized the lower level custom by their judgment of its worth.

Organically, the steps of organization are (1) individual need, (2) habits formed through trial and error, (3) a judgment of worth, need, and appropriateness, and finally (4) the birth of the institution.

We shall use a specific case history to illustrate this and subsequent stages. In one midwestern city in the early part of this century, the railroad yards dumped homeless men into the city each night. They were thought to be a disgrace to the community. From their presence came crime and a disturbance of the normal stability of this college town. Local Methodists saw the need, and in co-operation with students from the college, began helping these needy transients by placing them in temporary rented warehouse quarters. Out of this temporary solution, the Ladies Aid and the official board of first one church and then another accepted responsibility for the project. The mores of the community had approved it. The formal founding of the "H" Mission came when the Methodist churches of the city appointed representatives to a board of trustees and took over one store building in which

---

[16] Joyce O. Hertzler, *Society in Action* (New York: Dryden Press, 1929), p. 199.
[17] *Ibid.*

they might feed these needy men and provide housing for them.[18]

Structural analysis:

INSTITUTIONAL FUNCTION: A crisis was faced by the community in which the church effectively served as its conscience through crisis action.

LEADERSHIP: Emergent local leadership of a nonprofessional "grass-roots sort."

SOCIAL CONTROL: Familistic concern eventuating in direct action.

GOALS AND PURPOSIVE ACTION: "A neighborly concern for our fellow man. We couldn't see them suffer!"

APPROPRIATE STRATEGY: The formation of a conserving (conservative) institution.

It is worthy of note that the decision of the initial spontaneous group was not complex, but a simple decision that they must act in a crisis. Following that decision, the strategy involved was reviewed by each church, by the district, by the conference, and eventually by the Division of National Missions. At all points the decision of the group was that "it is good for Methodism to be involved in such a project." The goals of the denomination were held to be in line with those of the initiating group.

A period of consolidation usually follows the organizational stage. When a church has been formed and has its own building, it can be identified as an institution by certain objective characteristics: (1) it now owns material objects held in high regard by its members; (2) it abides by a newly formed code of action; (3) its members develop a set of acceptable attitudes and language characteristic of that institution; and (4) it has developed symbols which are distinctive.

When institution "H" had purchased its first building, it found that a pattern of communication with the community, the church and the

---

[18] This illustration came from a study of the institution. Its records are on file at the Division of National Missions and at Boston University School of Theology.

other agencies of the city had to be developed. In order to consolidate its gains, it purchased additional property. This period of success lasted for nearly thirty years. During that time, the property was in active use. First, it served as an openhanded mission. It gave away clothing; lodging was subsidized; and meals were provided for the needy. There came a time when the trustees and leaders became expert in representing the cause of the mission to those who could contribute to its sustenance. It was throughout most of this period an institution which served a social need in a socially approved manner.

INSTITUTIONAL FUNCTION:	Conservation and preservation dominant. Now functioning as a service institution without innovative drive.
LEADERSHIP:	Formal leadership employed by trustees. Some informal support from a congregation newly formed.
SOCIAL CONTROL:	An authoritarian agent providing economic sanctions and rewards for those who reinforced its rules.
GOALS AND PURPOSIVE ACTION:	A sincere concern for personal salvation to come to each person drawn into the agency for service.
APPROPRIATE STRATEGY:	All strengthening of gains came through institutionally approved means. Funds and goods collected from churches. Staff subsidized by the denomination.

In the life of any institution, this is its most fruitful period. There are evidences of physical growth; size and strength are supplemented[19] by purpose. The new church sees an increase in attendance, and consolidates its gains by the erection of a new religious education building. The social action group achieves its first goal and sets in motion devices to protect that gain. The consolidation period is a time of danger, but the institution does not know it yet. In this time of popularity, members are ignored who might be held. Simply because there are so many

[19] See Chap. VII.

members or so many possibilities, the institution cannot be alert to all of them. Herein lie the seeds of destruction.

A period of ritualization may, or may not, be the next stage. Merton has called this period the time in which cultural goals are sacrificed for institutional means.[20] When the early consolidation gains are observed by the members in retrospect, they may tend to freeze into ritual the means whereby the gains were achieved. It is widely observed in a kind of native insight that some churches which become "formal" and "ritualistic" are dying churches. There is no necessary connection between ritualization and archaism. The observations are based on the common coincidence of institutions which make ritual an end in itself and neglect the purposes for which ritual exists.

Ritualization occurs in an institution or institutional arrangement which becomes so concerned with its physical assets and technological holdings that they become its primary concern. Few Northerners realize the economic vastness of the Southern institutions which are based upon the principle of a segregated economy. Great colleges, country clubs, department stores, life insurance companies, churches and all forms of social institutions operated by Negroes exist to serve them. Most general agencies in the community would gain economically and socially from a free exchange of services across racial lines, but a ritualization of the means has supplanted the larger free goals of the nation.

Ritualization is in fact a means of defense against criticism. It is a self-protective device which is adopted by an institution when it wants self-assurance and it feels more secure in the repetition of proven ways. Mission "H" found its ritualization in the protection of established sources of income, the property held in hand and in the protection of the status of the trustees. Many of the leading supporters of the institution were prominent because of their identification with it. Since it had historically been efficient and approved, it was seldom questioned and rarely visited by most of the members of the conference who were putting money into it.

During this period of ritualization, the dormitories declined in quality and barely met the standards of public health. Other socially accredited agencies came into being in the neighborhood. At no time did the mis-

[20] Merton, op. cit., pp. 149 ff.

sion have an accredited social worker on its staff. It was "fighting for its life." During this period also, the community accepted an increasing amount of responsibility for its poor, unemployment declined and the number of persons served plummeted. Its congregation declined from a peak of one hundred eleven to twelve persons. As was the case in other cities with scores of social work agencies started by Sunday-school classes and church groups, the beneficent purposes of the church at the beginning were transmuted into an exclusive maintenance task. At the peak of this disparity, Mission "H" had a budget of $150,000 from all sources to service its twelve members and about twenty-five transients.

INSTITUTIONAL FUNCTION:	Conservation and preservation of institutional property.
LEADERSHIP:	Formal leadership in a self-perpetuating board of trustees.
TYPES OF SOCIAL CONTROL:	Anticipated sanctions from peers and fellow administrators.
GOALS AND PURPOSIVE ACTION:	Now transmuted into a primary concern for institutional means.
STRATEGY:	A "holding" action devoted to maintenance.

A *crisis period* may come at any time in an institution's life. The challenge which provokes the crisis may come from without or within. It may occur when it must face the fact that it has become more concerned with its own maintenance than with its prior goals.

It may be caused by irrelevance to the needs of the group which it should serve, as is often the case in the inner-city church. It may be caused by anachronistic techniques as in the case of the Anti-Saloon League. It may come from the failure or discreditation of its leaders, or disgraceful accusations believed by the public. No one can tell the extent of the damage done to Methodism by the irresponsible accusations of J. B. Matthews, Senator Joseph R. McCarthy, and Stanley High. Each leveled unproven slurs at Methodist ministers, accusing them of being Communists, "fellow travelers," and irresponsible persons.[21] The press carried the accusations, but buried the refutations.

[21] See Muelder, *Methodism and Society in the Twentieth Century*, pp. 205, 214, 220.

Mission "H" was forced to face its crisis period when it was confronted by the denomination with its inefficient administration record, by the community chest with questions about its procedures, and by the change agent [22] with a report on substandard health practices and a perversion of Christian standards.

The case of Mission "H" is typical of many other such situations.

INSTITUTIONAL FUNCTION:	Characterized by the imbalance of conservative and positive forces and a resultant state of institutional insecurity.
LEADERSHIP:	Crisis leaders performing mediating forms replace the enacted leaders.
SOCIAL CONTROL:	Psychological sanctions involving both reward and punishment, largely status-oriented.
GOALS AND PURPOSIVE ACTION:	Crisis and conservative goals dominant. Long-range goals of institution momentarily forgotten.
APPROPRIATE STRATEGY:	Ameliorative and conservative in practice. Inventive strategy needed.

The time of crisis is normally one of diagnosis, evaluation, and review. The alert leadership of an organization in crisis is not content to let the enemy furnish all the ammunition. An inventive strategy which prepares the institution for the decisive period of its history is necessary to life in the small agency and in the larger one, and should be present all the time.

The decisive period is the positive response to the crisis situation. Following the heat of the crisis period, each institution is confronted from within and without by the alternatives of *redirecting its goals and techniques so that they will be coherent*, or of *reaffirming the old goals and techniques*. In religious institutions, the ritualization period is in itself a time of crystallization and re-enforcement. It takes the shock of

[22] The self-study requested (on file).

crisis to force the leadership to ask objectively whether the same techniques and goals should continue. Occasionally, the denomination asks whether an institution should continue [23] but this is exceedingly rare, except in the case of local churches and colleges. Methodism has seldom abandoned a traditional system of institutionalized means or goals. Nothing is more persistent than a temporary agency.

Two major choices are confronted by the institution in this period, if it elects a new type of institutional means and goals:

Redirection of Goals

INSTITUTIONAL FUNCTION: Consolidation with other crisis-confronted institutions and the creation of different forms. Modification of material.

LEADERSHIP: New leadership of a new type, more experienced and perhaps more expert in the ways demanded of the new institution.

SOCIAL CONTROL: Through major modification of the ritual and procedure a continuation of old controls is made effective.

GOALS AND PURPOSIVE ACTION: Reviewed goals are modified in keeping with most urgent needs and purposes clarified acceptably.

APPROPRIATE STRATEGY: Innovation and status reinforcing devices characterize the new institution.

A period of dissolution follows if the institution elects to reinforce the old goals and techniques, and nothing more.

INSTITUTIONAL FUNCTION: Continue as conservative in character and face extinction rather than change.

LEADERSHIP: Formal leadership with followers impotent to provide emergent leaders.

[23] Especially those institutions which must be self-supporting, such as colleges.

190

SOCIAL CONTROL:	Members apathetic and resistant to traditional controls. Psychological sanctions ineffective.
GOALS AND PURPOSIVE DIRECTION:	Clouded and centered in maintenance of institutional means at a conservative level. "My family has always supported 'H' Mission and I always will."
APPROPRIATE STRATEGY:	Needed strategy; the creative redirection of the forces of the institution. Actual strategy: "We'll hold on as long as we live. There are a few old fellows who need us here." Fluttering attempts at review.

Mission "H" asked for a review of its situation in 1955. At that point it was in the period of crisis. It chose to maintain a stubborn adherence to the social work approach of the nineteenth century in keeping with its original goals. It never employed a social worker. It did not co-operate with other Methodist agencies nearby. It did not change its leadership. It chose to die. In the annual conference session of 1959, Mission "H" was sold by the remaining trustees and the funds returned to the trustees of the annual conference.

Methodism is confronted by many illustrations of social agencies which refuse to modify their approach to the people whom they profess to serve. In the inner-city church, in race relations, in temperance education, in church and state relations there are illustrations of institutions which are choosing to die, if by that choice we mean a refusal to redefine purpose and techniques. A thorough understanding of the constancy of change, the various stages of institutional change, and the ways of controlling both may help us to redirect that cycle.[24]

D. Methodism as the Object and Agent of Social Change

We have seen that every act of social change and each force of

[24] John Shope, A Strategy for Church Survival (Philadelphia: Research Monograph of the Evangelical and Reformed Church, 1959); Hertzler, op. cit.

stabilization requires (1) an institution as its vehicle, (2) appropriate leadership, (3) social control techniques, (4) an appropriate strategy, (5) purposive goals and (6) an appraisal of the appropriate time in the development of the institutions involved. It is not enough for Methodism to desire social change and express that desire through conference resolutions!

When Methodists are adequately self-critical they are aware of discrepancies between institutional goals and their embodiment in the life of the church. In a society marked by racial crisis, with the church consolidating its growth and unification, Methodism may be in danger or ritualization. In such a case the church itself becomes the object of social change with some part of the church serving as the change agent. The change agent may be the General Board of Christian Social Concerns or an unofficial social action group which seeks to enlist the General Conference, annual conference boards, the University Senate, or other agencies in vigorous change efforts within the form and function of the church.

At the same time the church may also have to serve as change agent itself, taking as object some pattern or unit in the larger society. Thus, again in the area of race, Methodism may speak and act concerning opportunities for housing, franchise, employment, and education for minority groups. In such change efforts the church seeks to enlist other institutions and citizens. It does not wait until its own house is in order to seek social changes, nor does it postpone indefinitely action on its own problems. Both proceed at the same time. Thus the church is both object and agent of social change.

Whether Methodism is the object or agent of change, its assets and influence make its actions of tremendous importance to the nation and the world. At the 1960 General Conference the church was made aware, as never before, of its influence in those countries where its churches are located. Delegates from India, Africa, South America, and the Philippines chided the delegates again and again for being concerned so much about the "church at home" that it forgets that Methodist inaction in the United States has the effect of social reaction abroad. There is no escape from the acceptance of the implications of the Christian message!

As a social force, Methodism cannot really choose to avoid responsi-

192

bility. Where it desires to serve as a stabilizing force in the cultures it serves, it has decided for a type of social change. When it accepts the responsibility for an enlightened strategy of social change, it has set in motion processes which affect uncounted millions of persons in many lands. Its leadership, techniques, strategy, and goals equip it for the countless times when time and the purposes of God call it forth to a new era of stewardship for all men.

CHAPTER SEVEN

The Power Structure of Methodism

A SECRET WEAPON OF METHODISM IS THE "CONFERENCE Journal." This publication of the annual conference is released each year and contains the appointments of ministers, their salaries, number of churches served, pastoral record, and more importantly a complete report of each of the churches. When a pastor, church, or district is being discussed, the appropriate journal is selected to ascertain ratings, status, and power. Minor augmentations of this journal appear, such as the *General Minutes*, which summarizes all conference journals, and *The Methodist Fact Book* which arranges high lights of the *General Minutes* and other Methodist data for summary perusal. Interestingly enough, these are the focus of attention of most Methodists when power and status are considered; but every leader is aware that these sources are unrepresentative and that they are only partial revelations of a status which runs more deeply.

What then is the power structure within Methodism? "Power" is not an epithet, nor is it used here in any derogatory sense. It may be defined as the discretionary control of resources and the exercise of influence over the decisions of persons and groups.[1] It involves the leadership, symbolic and physical assets, technology, and strength of an institution. Hence, for us "power structure" refers to that web of institutional arrangements within Methodism which denotes its connectionalism, official and unofficial, and which is devoted to the advancement of individual and institutional goals. It is the dynamo for the fuel of strategy. The institutional framework might be termed the housing, the power structure is the dynamo, and the strategy is the deliberate

[1] See pp. 31, 37, 219.

fuel of rational purpose and motivation. Hunter calls power "the word used to describe the acts of men going about the business of moving other men to act in relation to organic or inorganic things." [2] In this sense, power is synonymous with leadership. For us, leadership is a part of the power structure, but is important enough to be discussed separately.

We see, then, the importance of conceiving a structure within a structure. Power must have a residence. Its force depends upon the institutional framework. Each is necessary to the other. To carry our simile further, without aping its original form, let us fit our hypotheses into dynamic form. Three components are necessary to the power structure. *Assets* which determine its objective size combine with invisible, variable, *strength*, along with the basic *purposes* of the institution and its leaders to create power. The structure of power is capable of being diagramed, traced, and described even as the forces of electricity. It flows in much the same invisible way. Its lines of transmission and its field of force can be described and anticipated.

The size of an institution by itself is not a positive factor, nor is it negative. Each institution makes use of physical assets. "The church," in the mind's eye of the parish, is the physical building in which services are held. Its size is further measured in terms of the number of members, the size of its staff, additional properties which are "owned" by the congregation, and other things which it controls. A change in the basic purpose of or need for the institution can make of all these elements of size a hollow mockery if they stand alone. No community is composed of its buildings alone, nor is any institution powerful simply because it has buildings. However, those symbolic and physical assets which constitute its size are integral in its power structure.

Strength is the positive factor which makes hollow buildings, a large staff, and technological possessions hum with the promise of power. Its positive elements include (1) influence (discretionary power and authority), (2) value, and (3) perpetuative and dynamic motion. With influence, value, and motion, institutions come to possess vibrancy. The "things" which are possessed begin to have significance but are without direction and meaning until they are harnessed by the organizing force of power.

[2] Floyd Hunter, *Community Power Structure* (Chapel Hill: University of North Carolina Press, 1953), p. 6.

Institutional power is given purpose by human need and human aspiration. Human need may be primarily religious, inventive, conservative, or status centered.[3] Assets and strength exist to serve the social institution. They, in constellation with need, against the framework of the installation, constitute the power structure. To some exent they are negative, in the sense that a sea anchor or ballast is negative to the yacht or the balloon. Without oppositional drag or directional control, strength and assets mount endlessly to create inflated, purposeless, and short-lived power.

Purpose must be thought of as both human and divine. No small part of the power of The Methodist Church is that which is evidenced by "the way things work out." The direction of the Holy Spirit, and the deeper insights resulting from man's co-operation with it, explain in a major way the ability of the imperfect leader to maintain and extend the work of the church. There is reason, scientific as well as theological, to believe that the purposes beyond man's own are often the explanation for the power structure which succeeds despite human opposition and errors.

Purpose gives challenge as well as balance. It is the directive and corrective, the in-built compass. The inevitable question of the thinking man is "Why are we doing this?" "Why do we build skyscraper churches?" "Why do we pyramid executive leadership?" "Why are we strong where others are weak but weak where they prosper?" "Are we fulfilling God's purposes as well as our own?"

A. Assets as They Affect the Power Structure

We turn now to a consideration of those assets that determine the real "size" of an institution. They may be thought of in terms of the membership within the institution, its symbolic assets, its physical properties, and its technological knowledge and skills.

1. MEMBERSHIP

As American denominations go, The Methodist Church is large. Its ten million members make it one of the largest churches in the world. Since Methodist union in 1939, we have heard the boastful phrase "Nine and one-half million Methodists." Membership is vital to the

[3] See Chap. VI.

status of any institution. Without it, there is no institution. In a very real sense, the impression of size is as important as actual size in its effect upon power. The familiar phenomenon of "padded" church rolls is a specter which haunts each new pastor. Frequently, the inactive and unseen members were considered "active" by former leadership and were in fact loyal in their way. The vision of a church of one thousand members melts away (for the new pastor) to seven hundred but he seldom disturbs the fiction which is held by the conference public. He prefers for others to think of this institution as a church of "one thousand members" and the fiction continues. Seldom is "size" limited to the audited and inventoried statistics.

As an illustration of the developing size in an institution, let us look at the Board of Social and Economic Relations and the ways in which it has expanded since its inception in 1952. What are its "memberships?" They are (1) the commissions which are organized in the several annual conferences, (2) the persons involved in the strategies of those commissions which are effective and thus powerful, (3) the staff, (4) the number of persons involved in committees, commissions, boards, projects, and other activities, and (5) in a broad sense the entire membership of The Methodist Church. Each of these is measurable in numbers, hence is a function of size. Persons often fail to consider themselves members of the individual institutions of Methodism until they have voluntarily accepted membership in them. Hence, the "membership" of persons in missions, social and economic relations, education, stewardship and finance, membership and evangelism, and worship is so indirect that the local church member does not consider that he is a "member" of these activities unless he is "on" the commission in his local church.

2. Symbolic Assets

In the power structure of The Methodist Church, the "conference" or "convocation," called to fulfill a special function or need, is an increasingly valuable symbolic asset. Four quadrennial convocations on Town and Country Work, two on Urban Work, three on Family Life, and numerous conferences for Methodist Youth, the Woman's Society of Christian Service, Evangelism, and Christian Social Concerns are illustrative of a growing, expansive, and expensive trend in presenting

197

their corporate image and the endless efforts to communicate complex messages within a heterogeneous and dispersed church.

A second type of symbolic asset which adds to the stature of an institution is its research and survey commitments. In an increasingly technological era, when research is finally becoming accepted by the church as a means of inventory and evaluation, the very number of projects under way is a function of size. During its existence the Board of Social and Economic Relations sponsored many studies besides this one. The Board of Education is in a constant state of review and research in each of its divisions. The Publishing House has recently established its own research project to understand and evaluate the public it serves. The General Conference of 1960 added a Department of Research and Statistics to the World Service and Finance Commission and an Inter-agency Committee on Research to the Co-ordinating Council. The list of these projects is endless and each board is certain of added prestige as they mount.

A third category of symbolic assets is that of proved programs and procedures. Visitation Evangelism "belongs" to the Board of Evangelism. The Upper Room, an institution in its own right, "belongs" to the Board of Evangelism. The Group Ministry is a symbolic asset of the Department of Town and Country Work of the Division of National Missions; church extension and fund raising "belong" to Church Extension in that same division; the Methodist Youth Fellowship program and scores of others are a quantitative asset which can be counted in numbers, program, and efficacy.

The "special days" which are the intangible possession of many of the boards and agencies are a peculiar phenomenon of the church. Within the annual or General Conference a Sunday is set aside for special recognition of a given cause such as Rally Day, Student Day, Family Life Sunday, and so on. This becomes the vested interest of the board which is authorized to conduct such a recognition day. This usually eventuates in a special offering for that particular function of the church.

If the symbolic assets of certain boards, such as those in printed volumes, plays, literature, and similar creations, are taken by themselves as illustrative, they bulk large among its credits of power. Those materials written by the Boards of Education, Temperance, Evangelism, and Missions, for example, speak eloquently of their work. Add to these the printed publications they have sponsored or inspired and the symbolic assets which they have the discretion to use are tremendous.

The value of an address is the type of symbolic asset which cannot be ignored in presenting the public a dependable image of the institution. "475 Riverside Drive," "740 Rush St.," "100 Maryland Ave.," and "1701 Arch St.," are distinguished addresses which are in themselves a major asset.

Finally, and by no means last, are those symbolic assets which we shall call the collective skills of the institution. The process of working together over the years creates within a continuing staff a sense of rapport, ways of doings and a set of institutional mores which are often major assets in themselves.

3. Physical Properties

Physical assets are those possessions of the institution which are its distinctive tangible property. Each college, local church, annual conference and board has specific buildings "here" and projects "there." Highland Park Methodist Church in Dallas, Texas, has many buildings "there" in addition to its magnificent home edifice. The long-time Rankin Chapel project in West Dallas was an early manifestation of this sense of mission which each Methodist institution "must" have. To it have been added countless evidences of its physical stewardship.

Divers types of physical assets are in evidence among the prestige factors of Methodism. Planes, cars, and boats provide transportation and a more expeditious ministry in the Dakotas and in Sarawak. It is not enough to have modern portable equipment; it must have approximate equality to the standards set by the more aggressive economic world. Bookkeeping and research must be done by electric digital computers, in order to be as efficient as possible, as well as to command the respect and status integral to the desired public image of an efficient institution.

4. Technological Knowledge and Skills

In an increasingly complex society, where the standards of the urban world are becoming the standards of rural and town dwellers, an increasing respect for technological innovations is changing all local church standards. The church which utilizes new techniques, the board which is creatively concerned about ordering the future initiates new technological units regularly. A classic illustration of the technological alertness of the Methodist denomination is the Television, Radio, and Film

Commission. Here, under concerned leadership, new productions accumulate into such quantitative evidences as number of showings, copies, uses, and number of viewers.

It is not necessary that technological evidences be physical in nature. Skills and techniques, methodological achievements and abilities, are characteristic of such intangible technology. The skills in group dynamics, possessed by so many members of the staff of the Board of Education, the research skills of the Department of Research and Survey of the Division of National Missions, the Christian Social Relations outreach of the Woman's Division of Christian Service, the Boston Area Commission on Industrial Relations, and the intergroup skills of local churches illustrate this adaptability to change.

We see size, then, in terms of physical and symbolic assets, which are quantitative, measurable, objective, and socially evident. They are the "stuff" which people see as the physical evidence of an institution's existence.

B. Strength and the Power Structure

Another aspect of the power structure is strength. This positive element, qualitative in contrast to the quantitative nature of size, is the forward motion of an institution which gathers up the equipment, methodology, and persons and moves them.

Herein lies much of the secret ingredient of power and the creative movement of persons and things by other persons. Conference journals and their reports, statistics, and volume indicate the physical evidence of strength which we have chosen to call size. They are deceptive evidences however. We are familiar with the once popular church in the transitional area of the city, now relatively unused, but of great physical value. There are the interesting phenomena seen in the year of annual conference elections for General and Jurisdictional representation: the pastor of the largest church in the conference who is not elected; the nationally known and popular conference member who receives no local support; laymen known state-wide in agriculture, politics, or business who receive no votes. Conversely, a relatively unknown man may be elected as a reproach to the bishop or to some other conference member; one who has just delivered a popular sermon is elected; or "the same old gang" continues in strength and power.

What are the most significant factors in episcopal election? Here is

Wesleyan power at its peak. Even with the jurisdictional system, strange and unknown forces seem at work beneath the surface which erupt in unexpected directions with unexpected elections. The consistently high quality of the episcopal leadership of Methodism speaks for the quality of its pastoral leadership in general.

Why do these vagaries of leadership selection exist? Why are some leaders stronger than others? Strength is operative energy. It is the quality of an institution or individual which directs its matériel. It is this unexpected quality which places the "stranger" in a position of prestige, which generates status for the underdog, deflates the high and mighty, and lends perplexing importance to the commonalties.

1. INFLUENCE

Influence over others is the locus of power. Here is the heart of the power structure. No factor of strength is quite so significant in a connectional church. Votes for elective positions, "calls" to administrative positions and prominent pulpits, and prestige appointments are determined by this element. Methodism is still a rural church in its ideals, heroes, and mores. Those leaders who most closely follow the patterns established during the formative period of the church are most likely to become the centers of power. A rural church fellowship values highly the intimate traditions, the friendly camaraderie, the well-turned story, attention to the "little fellow," and similar family-like customs. Such Methodist traits have characterized the majority of our leaders. True, many persons change after having come to elected positions, but none are elected without this political identification with the majority. The emergent leader is the community face of the group. Hence, ministers in detached relationships, administrators, teachers, and board executives rarely qualify unless they wield influence which can benefit the group. Prominent pastors, fulfilling the ideal of identification, known to all members of the annual conference, affable to all ministers and laymen, and heading efficient local churches, generally qualify for elective positions and are the centers of power in each annual conference. For the local pastor, then, power comes through his friends and peers, in terms of the respect he commands and the way in which he uses his influence.

The district superintendent, in contrast to other administrators, follows a quite similar pattern. He is recognized by the "men on his district" to be a temporarily displaced pastor (the Discipline limits his

201

term to six years and he may not succeed himself) who will return to the local church as soon as he has completed his tour of duty. Due to his travels within the district, he visits every local church, knows each pastor personally, and commands respect by virtue of his office.

An interesting counterpoint to this high status of the local pastor is the omnipresence of administrators. In The Methodist Church it is primarily those who are the general employees who are provided with the budgets necessary for travel to the several regular and special conferences of the church. The expense of travel, the frequency of meetings, and their distance from the place of residence of laymen and local clergy make their regular attendance at such meetings exceptional. Similarly, ecumenical executive and board meetings are seldom attended by laymen and local clergy due to budget limitations within the boards or because of individual schedules. The result is that board staff personnel, district superintendents and bishops find their decision-making power increased by "the travel expense default." It is often true then, that "those who are seen are elected. Those who are not seen are forgotten." Here again, influence transcends tradition to create power.

In Methodism, the local church is the frame of reference which qualifies all leaders. Skill in the performance of the functions expected of the local pastor, fulfillment of the symbolic loyalties, and stability in their execution meet the expectations of the church. No teacher of religion, administrator, or pastor is exempt from these expectations. Each theologian is expected to have served a local pastorate successfully, or to be capable of stepping efficiently into such a position from the ivy towers. Lay administrators are few in the church because of this ideal. Rarely are the pastoral talents and experience of a local pastor used when he undergoes the metamorphosis of administrative selection, yet it is usually experienced pastors who are selected for the annual conference, jurisdictional, and general board positions. This proclivity for pastoral leadership in positions of power is in large part a projection of the self-image which each pastor has of his own role. Each leader must in fact be the image which the group desires the larger community to have of that group.

A scale of prestige could be developed with active service in a local church at the peak, ranked according to salary and size of church, temporary detached service such as the district superintendency next, and varying forms of permanent detached service farther down the scale. Perhaps no pastor rates so low in voting strength and influence as the military chaplain in peacetime. Interestingly enough, this scale is an unconscious one, and would be disavowed by the majority of "fair-minded" pastors. Yet the voting records of the annual conferences speak firmly to indicate the manner in which this judgment is made concrete in the mores of Methodism.

In the annual conference the executive session is composed entirely of ministers. Like an exclusive club, its members are intensely loyal to one another in basic matters. Critical in little things, they push up into leadership of the group those who are most loyal to The Methodist Church. Its leaders have power as they are identified with the welfare and mores of their peers. Few have come from other denominations into leadership of The Methodist Church. Many members, many ministers come from "outside" and are made at home in the fellowship. Rarely do they become prominent ministers, and even more rarely elected leaders. The Anglo-Saxon ring of the names of Methodist bishops speaks eloquently of this tradition.

Influence in the local church comes from this same identification with the mores of Methodists. The pastor of a powerful church asks the bishop to permit "his" church to raise the benevolence deficit of a neighboring conference. This offer is widely quoted and becomes a major factor in elevating him to a more responsible position. When the prestige of an annual conference is at stake, this second-mile loyalty to the mores of the denomination gives major prestige to the church and its pastor.

A district achieves prominence by becoming as loyal, or as "Methodist" as it can become. Many districts demonstrate fealty by becoming 100 per cent *Together* subscribers. Similar co-operation in conference programs, the achievement of evangelistic goals, and attendance at conference functions enhance the prestige of "the district" and the superintendent.

Influence for the individual comes in terms of votes controlled, loyalty to the mores of Methodism, skill and ability in the ways demanded by the institutions of the church, and the intrinsic contributions he makes. Church administrators strengthen this influence in much the same manner as a political leader strengthens his. Appointments which enhance prestige for the appointee, executive favors, recognition, and fame are the largess of bishops, district superintendents, and board executives. It is rare indeed for these forms of influence to be discussed, even in private. Certainly, no financial gains or admittedly undeserved favors are exchanged. The majority of annual conference members and administrators would be reluctant to notice that a system of influence exists. Such a recognition would be a denial of another basic system— that of self-effacement and humility—which is a professed standard of greatness in Methodism.

The influence of annual conferences and boards follows much the same pattern as that of the local church or district. Numbers, contributions, votes controlled, and the strength of local church as well as executive leadership, determine the reach of this influence. Size alone is no guarantor of power! We see that it must be coupled with influence directed toward values and purposes approved by the church at large.

2. VALUE

Another component of institutional strength is value. Its importance goes far beyond the physical factors of size. It is true that value comes from the investments of the Board of Missions, the presses of The Methodist Publishing House, and the beautiful buildings of the Board of Evangelism. But these are only physical symbols of more basic values. Value is used here to imply worth or relevance. In its preferred sense, to value means "to hold in high esteem."

"A valuable man" has no dollar price tag, despite crude attempts to label ministers as "$4,000 men" or as "circuit pastors." Neither does the phrase "a $10,000 church" produce basically descriptive symbols in the mind of one who knows Methodism. These are more superficial forms of value. Value is primarily a positive factor. However, there certainly exist negative values which detract from the status, prestige, and influence of institutions and individuals. Perhaps the following diagram may help to indicate the manner in which value increases or decreases. Certainly, dollars and cents, votes and size, have little to do with the central meaning of this kind of reasoning. As can be seen here, values increase and have greater influence as institutional needs and temporal relevance come closer together.

Illustrative of this convergence of recognized need and "the right time" are the frequent occasions when a regional technique will be adopted by the entire denomination because it is "just what we need." Such confluences have occurred with visitation evangelism, the move-

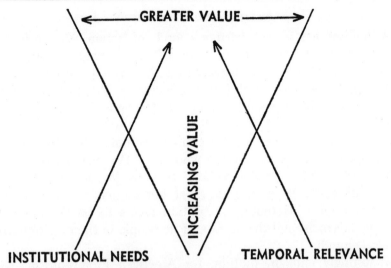

ment now called "Methodist Men" which began in California, *The Christian Advocate* "inserts" or area supplements which appeared first in Colorado, the Methodist highway signs which were first used in Michigan, and the rapid spread of conference radio and television programs and religious research. Value increases when technologies, manpower, and institutions are most needed and when they have demonstrated a workable solution to the felt need. The greater the pressure of group goals in terms of time and immediate usefulness, the greater the worth of social value facts.

Perhaps the classic illustration of temporal relevance in programing came when the Commission on World Peace stepped into the embarrassing vacuum confronted by Methodism on behalf of conscientious objectors at the start of World War II. No agency had been established to assist those Methodist youth who had decided they could not accept the call to military service and remain Christian in conscience and action. At first, the historic peace churches accepted responsibility for them. Belatedly, the task of establishing a liaison program was handed to the Commission on World Peace which executed a fulfillment of group goals at a time of great need. Similar cases could be cited in the history of every board. Bishop Oxnam's request to appear before the House Investigating Committee, the establishment of the Crusade for a New World Order, and Francis J. McConnell's action in the Steel Strike all demonstrate this conjunction of time and exigency with purpose.

3. CONSERVATIVE AND PROGRESSIVE MOTION

Methodism has always been a church of action. Variously called "activism" or "stewardship" or "works," this expenditure of physical and spiritual energies has characterized the church. Often the critics of Wesleyanism have used just this point as the fulcrum of their criticism. "Can it be possible," they ask, "to be holy when they are so busy?"

The happiest phrases in the church, as noted by the contented applause, are those by the layman who says, "We have a live church, a vital minister, and a good program." In sheer joy, he goes on to say, "things are *really* happening down at our church." One test of the effectiveness of a Methodist institution seems to be the amount of active involvement and the motion of its people in the organizations of the local church.

Interestingly enough, motion, for American Protestantism, is not necessarily creative or new, nor does it always redirect the group. The introduction of creative social change within the church is rarely the end result of this stirring up of the fellowship created by "a live program." In fact, two prominent Methodist executives pointed to the most prestigeful institution in the church, the morning service, and asked whether it ever introduces new ideas, creates change, or improves the social conditions of the church. Whether cynicism or creative insight, this question illustrates that there is no institution within the denomination free from challenge and review.

The morning service is often the kind of status-centered "proper thing to do" which does little to impel action. Some would contend that this is not social motion. Indeed it is! Admonitions to sobriety, to uphold local historic loyalties, to reflect faithfully the community mores are a form of social fence building. They are a form of conserving motion. The concerned "don't rock the boat" philosophy which surrounds the enthusiastic preacher is a form of conservative program. "We like things as they are!" is not necessarily an immoral statement, nor a withdrawal from civic responsibility. It may be, but the church may aggressively risk its prestige as well as its financial and physical security to preserve time-tested virtues and soundly conceived procedures. Reaction for reaction's sake is not of course a form of constructive conservatism.

The church that vigorously defends freedom of speech, that successfully fights a permit for a tavern to open across from the high school,

206

that defends the civil liberties of a stranger in the town jail, that courageously defends its traditional interracial policy, is in all these things exercising forms of conservative motion which enhance its strength in the community. Respect for it grows as it conserves those virtues and values which the church respects.

As opposed to conservative motion, progressive motion can be illustrated in the life-long creativity of Dr. John W. Shackford of Waynesville, North Carolina, begun when he was a concerned pastor in Norfolk, Virginia. Progressive motion carried the pastors under his leadership through a political and social regeneration of Norfolk which is of historic significance. He served to instill social concern in the Board of Education of The Methodist Episcopal Church, South, helped to form the Southern Regional Council, and still today serves as a symbol of prophetic forward motion.

Progressive motion is the spawning of new ideas, the development of new programs and the invention of "the new" which is demanded of all growing organisms. On the one hand, the conservation of yesterday's virtues may be a prime concern of the church. On the other hand, the church will die if it does not determine the morals of the morrow.

A classic indication of this concern for progressive motion in the business world came at the close of World War II when Lever Brothers summarily dismissed its popular president, Charles Luckman. An outstanding salesman, popular civic figure and capable administrator, he lectured regularly at schools of business where he was introduced as "the ideal corporation executive." Despite mounting sales, he was dismissed. Perplexed educators asked the board of Lever Brothers to explain. The reply was, "he gave us nothing new." At a time when other companies were introducing detergents and other new products, he ignored research. He simply sold soap! [4] Progressive motion is the encapsuling of a growing sense of proportion. Institutions which vibrate with life are constant in their research and in the spawning of new ideas.

The Roman Catholic Church is noteworthy in the manner in which it often tolerates internal criticism, rewards priests who are innovators and capitalizes indigenous cultures wherever it serves. The rise of Luigi Lugutti to Monsignor for his work in Iowa rural credit co-operatives and his establishment of the National Catholic Rural Life Conference is a

[4] *Fortune Magazine*, XLI (April 1950), pp. 81 ff.

case in point. The contribution of Ignatius Loyola to prayer and worship is another. The male saints of the church usually will be found to have made such contributions to progressive movement.

C. Purpose and the Power Structure

As we have seen, the third component of the power structure is the basic purpose of the institution and its leaders. The social purposes of an institution are not far removed from the philosophical or theological purposes. They are unique, however. We shall discuss social purposes here and the philosophical implications in the following chapter.

Social purposes, as we have said above, are the directional ballast, the practical reasons for the deployment of resources and the logistics of institutions. An institution may grow as it continues in time-worn grooves, simply because the society around it grows. It does not change location, build new edifices in distant cities, and deploy its personnel into new challenging areas without an emerging sense of purpose.

The church as a social institution faces daily new sets of social challenges. The theological purposes are said by some to be unchanging. But the social purposes change as the church realizes the implication of the theological purposes, and as it responds to social challenges and their urgency. The church should have a growing sense of purpose and a commensurate awareness of the emergent needs of its members and constituents.

We would suggest four aspects of this emerging purpose for our continuing consideration. They are: immediate social satisfactions; concern for ordering the future; technical competence; and respect for the traditional ways of the group. These but open the subject!

1. IMMEDIATE SOCIAL SATISFACTIONS

Let us consider first the problem of satisfying the immediate needs and lending proportional weight to their purposes. The daily housekeeping of a church brings forth the need for solutions to the little exigencies which were not or could not be anticipated.

The local church provides a meeting place for worship, study, and work. It must provide for its daily expenses, its outreach and service functions, and all of its ministry. Its pastor must make the calls and counsel those in need. Its church school must educate a new generation and re-educate an older one.

While the daily needs are clear, the purpose it not. When challenged with the query of purpose, many church groups are blankly puzzled. Does a janitor have a purpose? Does there need to be a purpose for a choir? Isn't it enough to say "We need money or time or leaders"? Must there be purpose too? No institution survives for long without conscious purpose. Size and strength wither away when they have no larger purpose to serve. The local church then must build for a reason. It needs guide lines for its daily chores.

To these old needs, familiar and chronic though they seem, are added new ones. The church that is dying does not see them, or seeing does not recognize, or recognizing does not possess the energy or sense of purpose to meet them. When a new ethnic group invades the geographical parish, the church faces a new need. When fire or obsolescence weakens the church's buildings, it faces emerging needs out of which must come new conscious purposes.

When the young people of the church laugh at the old morals, it is confronted by challenge. The spiritual Sputniks of our time have hurtled into the orbit of the church again and again to find it unaware of their challenge. Moral problems unknown to our spiritual fathers confront us now. On the American frontier, in the Indian mission field, and in the Puritan village a religion which was highly regulatory and moralistic had more acceptance than in the communities in this highly mobile and rapidly changing era. Answers which are more than manners must be found and effectively communicated to a generation which has become dissatisfied with yesterday's religious practices.

In the annual conference and the episcopal area, the housekeeping chores of present needs are equally important. There must be an awareness of the needs of the needy within this larger parish of the church. The Conference Moving Expense Fund, the establishment of minimum standards for parsonages and salary support bolster the conference members in their loyalty to this institution. In the episcopal area, creative administrative plans, concerned personal episcopal leadership and coordination may answer collective needs. An activist church is always in danger of belittling the maintenance tasks. They are in fact the "Martha" tasks which stabilize, regulate and maintain the home base from which the power emanates. The power structure would amount to little without them.

In the conference and the area, as in every institution, the "reasons why" are paramount in determining and retaining loyalties. When basic needs are ignored, when central purposes are obscure, when immediate concerns are frustrated, apathy intervenes in awesome ways.

Emergent needs at the conference level are illustrated by the response of the church to larger social challenges: the need for it to express its opinion relative to capital punishment, the displacement of citizens by unwarranted seizure, the suppression of basic human freedoms, the challenge of vocal opponents, religious and secular, and the relegation to a position of irrelevance.

An alert reaction to the unforeseen is expected of great institutions. This reaction must be correct but firm, just, and fair, dependable but not imponderable. Methodism has occasionally deserved each of these adjectives. Often, in the face of crisis, it has deserved none of them.

2. Concern for Ordering the Future

Each institution is expected by its members to be concerned for ordering the future. The family saves to send children to college. The church invests in its leaders of the future by providing colleges and universities. The conference builds a pension fund against the day of retirement of its clergy.

It is always difficult to peer into the future and to discern its form. Yet this is the task of leaders. Each must provide for the present, conserve the best of the past, and order the future if he is wise in the wants of his followers.

By its very name, the long-range planning committee in the church, the conference, or the episcopal area lends its own purpose to its existence. All groups have leaders who are planners. Their prescience and insight into the future may be great or small. Just so, the purposes of the institution become great, small, or irrelevant. Nothing is so deadly as the anachronistic purpose, or the horizon that all except the leader recognize to have faded into the group past.

Illustrative of the purposive means used by Methodism in ordering the future are the plans for the recruitment of ministers, a growing recognition of the ministry of the laity, a cognizance of the changing role of the bishop and district superintendent, and the recurring sets of quadrennial programs framed by each succeeding General Conference.

Slowly there is dawning upon The Methodist Church in the United States an awareness of age. Its church buildings are old enough to be discarded as congregations move on. Seldom has it ordered the future with a strategy for such evacuations. In an era of increasing mobility to the suburbs and from suburb to suburb, we have instituted mobile ministries to migrant people and even chaplaincies for polar expeditions. Is it not just possible that the rural patterns which dominate the urban church may have had their day and that wholly new administrative forms must come? May there not be a need for a ministry without a fixed building, a permanent congregation, or even a resident pastor? What of the future? Is it enough to describe the inner city as "Bohemian," "secular," and "irreligious"? Those who order the future must be a part of it if their institutions are to give it purpose.

This may be illustrated in the church's relation to labor. The concern of Methodism for its contacts with labor have had many expressions. Chaplains to industry have been appointed in North Carolina and in Massachusetts. The Board of Social and Economic Relations attempted to order the future through its appointment of Emerson Smith, who had served as Boston Area Director of Industrial Relations, as an Associate Secretary. As early as 1948, the Division of National Missions had appointed John Harmon as Director of Industrial Relations with the assigned responsibility of national and local contacts between Methodism and the labor movement.

3. TECHNICAL COMPETENCE

When an institution goes beyond its founding purposes into a new era and breasts the tide of the future, it consolidates its gains and establishes means of training leaders who are technically competent to direct purposes not yet formed.

High premiums of status and reward are placed upon the builder who organizes, leads, and consolidates new churches. The technician who brings the church into rapport with new techniques proved in the secular world is a prized leader. The writers, dramatists, financiers, accountants, hospital administrators, researchers, or church and community workers are illustrative of these specialists.[5]

The educators, technicians, and specialists in the colleges and seminaries labor to sharpen the tools of wisdom which will machine the future of the church. Their technical competence is guided by a more

[5] See above, p. 33.

self-conscious sense of purpose than is manifest in some other vineyards.

Technical competence, as we have noted, is most highly prized in the local pastor. As the line officer of the church, his competence is daily appraised, criticized, and explored. The church then, as other social institutions, prizes highly the technical competence approved by its institutional peers. Persons accredited by educational institutions are accepted by the church. Successful businessmen are sought as trustees. The obverse should also be true. The church should be developing its own technicians, ecclesiastical diplomats, and research personnel. It has the resources of its own colleges, universities, and seminaries with which to begin. The secular world should be following the church as it becomes again the pacesetter in matters of human relations and morals. The challenge to the church is that it may be failing to recognize the technical needs of the future because its ecclesiastical administrators have no time to dream of their purpose!

4. Respect for the Traditional Ways

In the midst of searching the power structure for signs of growth, for clues to leadership competence, for insights into planning, the principal purpose has been momentarily set aside. He who would move the world must have not only his fulcrum and lever, but a place on which to stand. The institution which moves the future of necessity stands in a stable present, firmed by a respected past.

The social purposes of the church are primarily revealed in the traditions which it has enshrined and the skills which it has kept. No mean part of the institutional purpose is the direct current of the ages. As a social institution, the church cherishes its ritual. When that ritual is executed meaningfully and reverently, its purposes become power. Preaching has always been central in Methodism. Even the most liturgical service is considered incomplete in many Methodist churches if there is no meditation, sermon, or "word" spoken outside the ritual. Even the funeral and the wedding ceremony, basically liturgical, are, in some sections of the church, merely a setting for "the spoken word." Hence the preacher in the local church and the evangelist are men of power. In a day when more and more churches prosper and demand their "own" minister, the necessity for and the status of the lay preacher are on the rise. These traditional skills and the mores which surround them, the congregational singing, the reading of the Scriptures, and voluntary

212

prayer augment and affirm the power structure of The Methodist Church.

Power is comprised then of size and strength combined with purpose. It is discretionary and directive. It controls and guides Methodism. When an institution or an individual is said to be powerful, each of these three components is present. The power structure of Methodism is seen in the institutional arrangements of the church and the manner in which these institutions and their leaders are interlocked. Illustrative power centers are those of the Council of Secretaries, the Council of Bishops, area delegations to the jurisdictional and General Conferences, the University Senate of The Methodist Church and, to a lesser degree, the related agencies and institutions of each of these. The power structure is guided by the full-time employees of the church and is structured through the agencies to which they are related.

D. Processes of Policy Initiative and Review

We have discussed the methods whereby the institution maintains itself and selects leaders and issues, as these methods relate to power structure. In addition to the maintenance tasks, however, there are the vital, indeed fundamental, tasks of diagnosis, initiative, and review.

This kind of assessment refers to the process of analysis of policy, personnel, and procedures by the members of the institution or their representatives. The informal diagnosis which characterizes the uninformed speculation of the nonmember is outside this discussion.

1. INSIGHT AND PRESCIENCE

Without discussing at length the merits of instinct, "hunches," and intuitive reasoning, we still must observe with appreciation that something like them exists in any experienced leader. He often "knows the reasons why" without being able to formulate those reasons verbally or to communicate them to the group.

When a leader is operating at peak efficiency, he can sense crises before they bear in upon his institution. The higher his status in the church, the greater the leader's responsibility to anticipate trouble and challenge. Similarly however, he must intuitively separate the imagined fears from the real ones and apply his insight with care.

Creative insights and diagnostic clarity usually come to those leaders who are not always under pressure. It is when they have periods of peak activity alternating with periods of relaxation conducive to creative thinking that leaders develop needed insight and prescience.

2. EXPERIENCE

Experience is the leader's best teacher. There is no substitute for it. When Methodism formed its new boards following the Uniting Conference of 1939, it created new offices and with them policies that were yet to be evolved. Out of The Methodist Episcopal Church, South, came such experienced leaders as John Q. Schisler, Nolan B. Harmon, A. J. Walton, and others to staff the new boards. Their regional experience in diagnosis was invaluable to the new church. None knew more than they about the South and in particular the needs of Methodism there. From The Methodist Episcopal Church, Earl Brown, Ralph Diffendorfer, John O. Gross, and Charles F. Boss added similar insightful experience about the regions which they knew best. The national scope of their combined leadership coupled with Methodist Protestant experience provided a full reservoir of national knowledge.

But all religious groups have much to learn about the experiences needed for the development of nonliturgical specialists. Ministers who are trained only for and experienced only in service to the local church are seldom technically competent for the increasingly complex tasks of board and agency administration. The executive secretary of a Washington agency who deals regularly with the church boards is quoted as saying: "There is almost a disdain for technical competence if an issue on which a declaration of any type is to be made offers the slightest opening for . . . a flood of emotional and moralistic oratory that can only be considered an affront . . . by those who must first politely listen and then decide a policy (congressional legislation) matter."

Impartial experts may be called in from companion boards in an exchange of services, though this is exceedingly rare in Methodism. A most likely procedure is that taken by the General Conference of 1948 which authorized the employment of a professional research agency to study the structure of The Methodist Church and make recommendations for its improvement. The story of the 1952 General Conference which handled the report would make a most exciting volume in itself. Although boards, agencies, and vested interests sidetracked and diluted some of the recommendations of the report, many of those recommendations are belatedly being accepted as more sound than the 1952 amendments which replaced them.

3. CLASSIFICATION OF PROBLEMS AND CRISES

In the process of diagnosis there are many ways of appraising the problems and crises which arise. One major board assesses problems which are reported from the "field" by returning staff in this fashion: (1) There is a tendency to discount crises unless they are persistent. (2) If they are persistent, board members within the annual conference are contacted for reactions and verification. (3) The staff member involved is not necessarily notified of such inquiries since the supervisory staff at present feels that such a notification might tend to unnerve the field staff member.

The Methodist Publishing House classifies its crises in terms of (1) the volume of mail received on given issues, (2) the influence and representativeness of critics, and (3) the instructions of the General Conference.

A major aspect of classification has to do with the level within the institution at which assessment is handled. Not all inventories and challenges are crises nor are they all external. Many matters of policy need assessment and review. Whether they are handled by field staff without reference to the division head, or whether they merit reference to the "General Board" is an operative diagnostic judgment of major importance. A hierarchy of reference might look like this:

A Suggested Hierarchy of Reference	
REFERENCE RANK	AGENCY TO WHICH DELEGATED
1	General Conference
2	Council of Secretaries
3	Council of Bishops
4	General Board
5	Executive Committee
6	General Secretary
7	Board Council (of Division Heads)
8	Division Head
9	Department Head
10	Field Staff
11	Annual Conference Officer
12	District Superintendent

The district superintendent is far from the bottom of the ladder in The Methodist Church. There are many who are responsible to him who might also merit the assignment of some analytic responsibility, but this scale of reference will illustrate the system of classification.

Each matter of policy which constitutes the guiding principles of an agency must be diagnosed at some time in its existence. Chapter II suggests the standards by means of which this assessment can be guided. In the assessment there exists (1) the policy, (2) the event which calls attention to it, (3) the staff affecting it, (4) the publics affected by it, and (5) the agency to which the diagnosis is referred. Of these aspects, none is as important to this analysis as the insightful, technically competent, and experienced analyst.

4. POLICY INITIATION

Following the analysis of policy and situation is the initiation of new and appropriate policy. In the local church, the minister may initiate policy through his "cabinet," official or unofficial, thence to the commissions and the official board. At the district level, policy is formed by the district, annual, and local quarterly conferences. In the annual conference, policy begins with an individual who presents his ideas to the appropriate committees and follows them through to the floor of the annual conference.

In the Division of National Missions, policy is initiated by the staff, which makes recommendations to the annual meetings of the General Board.[6] In the Board of Education, policy ideas and innovations are regularly tested against panels of critics which meet for that purpose. The recommendations are then either implemented directly by the staff or referred to the General Board for legislative action. In the Board of Social and Economic Relations, all policy matters were initiated by the executive secretary in co-operation with the executive committee or subcommittee. All resolutions and statements from the board to the public were written by members of the board and approved by the appropriate committee or subcommittee prior to acceptance by the board.[7] The Editorial Division of the Board of Education, against the backdrop of General Conference directives, utilizes the Curriculum

[6] Interview with W. V. Middleton, July 1959. Policy Manual, Division of National Missions.
[7] Interview with Dudley Ward, October 1959.

Committee as its principal policy-making group. All other boards are represented in it, hence interboard matters are automatically referred. "We set our guide-lines by the General Conference, but the staff determines the speed." [8]

Policy is changed in the regular disciplinary manner as well as within the intervening periods between conferences. The evidence of the General and annual conferences is interesting, but it is a matter of record and does not need to be discussed here at length. Some annual conferences are experimenting with a commission plan in which the conference is formed much as the local church or the General Conference with all members of the conference, lay and ministerial, assigned to working commissions which review and discuss all legislation prior to its introduction in the plenary session. At the other extreme are those conferences which do not seem to expect the laymen to be present except for "Laymen's Day," which implies that they do not participate in the decision making. [9]

At least four types of formal policy initiation seem apparent: (1) conference-initiated policy of a formal nature emanating from the quadrennial and annual conferences, (2) crisis-initiated policy such as the institution of a major radio and television agency through the Council of Bishops between the 1952 and 1956 General Conferences, (3) service-initiated policy which is an emergent response of the denomination to "the demands of the churches," (4) staff-initiated policy of the type which occurs between meetings of conferences and General Boards.

It would be hard to imagine policy being formulated without the initial advice of the executive secretary or staff. Even in those Methodist agencies where the General Conference has specified that they are not to initiate programs and policy, this pattern persists. Service agencies do initiate policy and implement it. Even interboard service agencies face this dilemma. [10]

Informal policy initiation occurs in the letters which are received by staff and board members in the general agencies. In the local church, nonattendance and disinterest herald changes in procedure or personnel. Many kinds of social pressure occur within the community which

[8] Interview with Walter Vernon, July 1959.
[9] Some conferences do not call the roll of lay members until "Laymen's Day" toward the end of the conference session.
[10] I.e., Commission on Promotion and Cultivation.

217

cause the church to react with changes in policy. The church may react against these pressures. Often it yields to them. Yet it is usually the agreement and acquiescence which is informal and the opposition which is formal and deliberate.

The challenges of other denominations and interests are responsible for many changes in policy which are never discussed in formal legislative procedures. Informal policy initiation comes to a denomination through those subtle changes in the culture which make acceptable and normal new ways of dress, modes of behavior, and architectural forms unfamiliar to preceding generations. We drift into social change without consent or opposition. No legislation initiated the renaissance of the divided chancel or the pulpit gown! No legislation encourages the increase in the number of supply pastors.

5. Policy Review

Much that has been said of policy initiation applies also to the review of present and past legislation and procedure.[11] Perennially, the Methodist conferences return to the familiar themes of smoking on the part of the clergy, lay temperance, and general social conformity. Regarded by some as matters of manners, by others as sacred, these admonitions of proper behavior for ministers and laymen are reviewed in each General Conference and with unique variations in the annual conferences. The 1952 General Conference, for example, saw a majority report of the Commission on Worship defeated because a militant and emotional minority saw in the proposed modification of the ordination ritual a possibility that the "smoking pledge" of the clergy might be modified. The rules of the conference were ignored and emotion reigned as the leader of the minority spoke again and again without intervening opposition speeches. The tradition carried the day! The modification of the ordination ritual was not accepted.[12]

Some tradition-bound and emotionally charged matters, although much discussed, do not get an objective review. In so large a church, with such infrequent general meetings, the emotion-charged symbol is often the rallying point of commonality while some basic issues are ignored because they tend to be divisive. For example, the provision for the Central Jurisdiction of The Methodist Church has been discussed

[11] See Chap. IV.
[12] Similar action was taken by the General Conference of 1960.

since its inception in 1939. Attempts at formal review in 1952 and 1956 resulted in the appointment of a study commission, thus postponing decisive action.

The weaknesses of such a procedure are evident. Within four years, the opponents to change have ample time to become entrenched while the advocates tend to become discouraged by the mass and inertia of so large an institution. The 1960 General Conference was still unable to take decisive action in spite of the fact that only 14.5 per cent of the total Methodist population approves of the Central Jurisdiction plan.[13] Change and review come very slowly in Methodism. When they do come, they must be charged with simple, communicable emotion.

E. The Future Use of Methodist Power [14]

Methodism is filled with a self-awareness of its power in numbers, skills, tangibles, and technology, but it has been as wasteful as any gross and complex arrangement of institutions. The evidence clearly indicates a variety of political office management and procurement procedures so diverse as to suggest that each board, agency, and commission is a law unto itself. The growth of these institutions has been so rapid and so startling that the denomination seems unaware of their value and size. A remarkable clientele seems to follow each board as though each were corporately a separate denomination. Policy is initiated by individuals within the agency, funds are expended by those executives, services are rendered to their provincial counterparts, buildings may be remodeled and expanded, offices relocated, automobiles purchased, delegations sent on distant journeys and other boards challenged . . . all within the self-sufficient umbrella of "Board policy and General Conference authorization." Note that ¶ 1115 restricts the initiative of the Co-ordinating Council. It may co-ordinate only "when requested." It has control over building expenditures only when "new buildings are contemplated" and it has no authority to initiate investigations or to control the expenditures of boards which overlap in function. Through action of the 1960 General Conference, the Co-ordinating Council now reviews major leases of these boards, but controls only the purchase of new property and the construction of new buildings.

Individual Methodists may resent the aloofness and separateness of

[13] See Appendix B.
[14] See pp. 31, 37, 194.

the boards and agencies, but they are the creation of our time and, through the annual conference, are the responsibility of each local church. Annual and General Conference boards and agencies are no more aloof than local churches within the same district or city. Methodism is a remotely delegated connectionalism. This remoteness in time and social distance may be its greatest weakness.

1. EVALUATION OF CENTRAL PURPOSE

Clearly then, the first step toward a more creative use of Methodist power has to do with an evaluation of central purpose within each board, agency, and local church. If The Methodist Church is to function as a powerful unit in behalf of the larger Christian goals, the centrality of purposive action must be constantly clarified and implemented. To glance at the Methodist *Discipline* is to be overwhelmed by the diverse purposes and points of view which have been officially endorsed.

The study of Methodist beliefs is a clear indication that Methodists are more characterized by diversity than unity. While the extremists are not predominant in any of the belief continua, every point of view is represented. The Methodist message, if there be one, is not discernible. A characteristic response among the pretest discussants who completed the questionnaires [15] was, "Just what is the Methodist point of view on this anyway?" While unity of belief may be expected, diversity on specific points is inherent in Methodism. This does not mean that there can be no unity of purpose. A primary task is that of developing central unified purposes in spite of diversity of points of view.

2. EVALUATION OF COST

A second major step is evaluation of cost. Methodism needs to know its resources, their value, and their availability. A general services administration of The Methodist Church would certainly begin with an inventory and a gigantic audit. The interwoven network of trails left by executive secretaries of the several boards and agencies as they cross the United States and its territories would be the kind of illustration which evidences the need for co-ordination. No simple listing of dollars spent for various items illustrates the duplications of manpower, travel time, research, physical and spiritual resources.

An operating economy of stewardship does seem to call for a general

[15] See Appendix B.

services administration of The Methodist Church to co-ordinate the use of (1) physical resources, (2) technological units and leadership, (3) travel and service, and possibly the establishment of (4) a civil service order or its equivalent into which lifetime Christian lay workers might move. Such a massive co-ordination certainly seems to call for the strengthening and implementation of the work of the Co-ordinating Council. Its program co-ordination now awaits the request of the several boards and agencies. It cannot initiate such co-ordination without further implementation and authorization by the General Conference. Co-ordination, centralization, and efficiency are now almost forbidden by the Methodist *Discipline* (¶ 1115).

3. SPECIALIZATION AND REFINEMENT

In the growth of any institution, there comes this time of specialization and refinement which Methodism is now entering. "Every last Methodist" must come to appreciate the need for the technicians, specialists, and "board people" who staff the many service agencies of the church. Not only must they be appreciated, but they must be used more creatively. The tension which exists between the executive secretaries and the annual conference cabinet, between the local laymen and the annual conference agency, between the pastor and the special appointment clergy comes from rapid growth without adequate explanation and communication.

Methodism is *no longer a rural church which can be run by pastors temporarily out of the local pulpit.* Perpetuative and dynamic motion demands an increasingly refined and trained type of administrator. Laymen increasingly are needed to staff and direct the power structure of Methodism. The traveling clergy are needed primarily in the local church. A dynamic program must be directed by skilled, experienced, and well-trained administrators who are permitted to stay in their positions of responsibility until they become the prescient, insightful leaders an urbanized and heterogeneous Methodism needs.

Since all the functions of the church are directed toward and originate with the individual worshiper in the local church, the development of the role of the laity is paramount. In the presence of God and the congregation, the minister's role of priest is to increase this confrontation of the layman with his Maker. The clergyman recedes into the background in this special focus and the layman assumes his true position. Although

221

only 24.9 per cent of all laymen recognize themselves in the phrase—
"the people of God called to a total ministry of witness and service to
the world." [16]

Along with his dignity and standing before God, the individual
layman is the indigenous leader of the witnessing community. It is he
and he alone who can lead his family, his coworkers, his Sunday-school
class, the church committee of which he is chairman. He is looked to as
"one of their own"; he is trusted and respected for his constancy in the
community. In contrast to him, the minister is a temporary resident
whose primary loyalty is to "the annual conference," to "others"; he
"won't be here long."

The continuance of policy in the local church and in the conferences
is in large part the responsibility of the layman. It is he who must "pay
the bills," "provide the troops," and convince the recalcitrant. If social
action is to be successful, it must not reside primarily in the hands of
the clergy. Any group of formal leaders is in danger of being considered
as "outsiders," of being treated with tolerance in areas other than their
traditional functions, and of being left alone in a crisis. The layman
can always say to the minister, "You don't have to live here! I do!"
and thereby disassociate himself from the cause which the minister has
expoused.

The layman in the local church who is committed to the church's
goals and purposes has many things in his favor besides his group
identification, but this is no minor asset. He serves as the group symbol,
educator, initiator, harmonizer, conservator, and administrator. In his
actions, he exhibits a willingness to aid in guarding the traditions and
customs of the local church and of the denomination. He, much more
than the pastor, has an almost innate sense of social fitness relative to
that which is appropriate and acceptable within the local church. He
possesses through cumulative experience an ordered skill in judging the
tempo of the group, and knows how to time the changes needed in the
church or the community. When changes are introduced, he is at the
center of things because it is his friends who suggest the changes. Seldom
does the group leader occupy the center of the stage without group
support.

Wherever Methodism is to move forward in refining its approach
toward the creative implementation of its theological convictions, it must

[16] See Appendix B.

move with laymen providing the advice, the initiative, and the followers. This is equally true in the boards and agencies, the General Conference, the subordinate conferences, and the local church in its community setting.

Increasingly, Methodism must be self-conscious about its influence on the American scene. There is ample evidence that its diversity is due to its representativeness. No level of American life, no region and no occupational group is without its Methodist contingent. As a representative denomination, it must increasingly be aware of the need to speak out on social and economic matters where the whole populace is affected. The interesting and provincial custom of appointing General Conference delegates almost exclusively to membership on the boards and agencies deprives Methodism of some of its most learned and influential leadership. The best informed Methodists in each field should be the primary constituency of all our boards and agencies. If they happen to be members of the conferences, well and good!

Legislative matters in each state and on the national scene illustrate the need for Methodism to become alert to its responsibility. Influential Methodist legislators and officials need the reinforcement of reasoned Methodist views. Prayers and letters to Congress are important, although eleven out of twenty Methodists never write.[17] However, a greater responsibility—the use, recognition, and involvement of responsible Methodist legislators, executives, and prominent officials—is almost totally missing from our present approach.

Finally, the clergy must become citizens of the world. A remarkable provincialism still exists among the clergy of Methodism. Repeatedly, in matters of Methodist belief,[18] the clergy were no more cosmopolitan than their laymen, no more cognizant of world need, no less indifferent to social responsibility. A new concept of brotherhood within the clergy is almost a prime requisite to the creative use of Methodist power in the world. At all status levels, in all types of responsibility, a new understanding of the role of the clergy is needed. The role of the distinctive "parson" in the local community must be earned today. It is not a foreordained position. Relatively speaking, bishops are not the men of influence outside the church that they once were. District superintendents, professors, missionaries, and board executives stand in need

[17] See Appendix B.
[18] Ibid.

223

of a new awareness of the world church and the mission of Methodism beyond all present churches and mission fields.

The future use of Methodist power then begins with a clearly defined purpose. Centralization and co-ordination of our connectional system is a foremost need. Greater efficiency in the stewardship of church funds and manpower will result. With this increased co-ordination a greater specialization and refinement of board and staff functions is a manifest and insistently real need.

Finally, the use of Methodist power will be in the hands of the present and future leaders of the denomination. Those leaders must become world citizens, appreciative of the diverse cultures, sympathetic with the problems of social groups and institutions less advanced than their own, and endlessly patient in the use of the power which is theirs to use.

In this chapter we have viewed the nature of connectional power in a major Protestant denomination. Methodism has been used illustratively. Size, strength, and purpose are the primary ingredients of all power structures. In religious groups such as Methodism, purpose is dominant. Through theological beliefs, norms, and convictions, the power of the church is directed by a leadership constantly being reminded of those dominant purposes. Policy initiation and review similarly are social processes applicable to any institutional arrangement which is concerned with ordering the future creatively. The Christian church has this as its primary purpose. Many of its branches choose to do this ordering through individuals only. Methodism has consciously chosen to be aware of its organization and a self-conscious use of its power to realize the central purposes of the kingdom of God.

CHAPTER EIGHT

Resources and Obstacles to Change Within Methodism

THE RESOURCES AND OBSTACLES TO CHANGE WITHIN METHODISM center around the people who make up The Methodist Church. They are at once its greatest earthly resource and the primary source of obstacles to their own improvement. Numerous stereotypes have swirled about the "people called Methodist." They have been called "blue noses," "psalm-singing Methodists," "teetotalers," and many other things. Due to the exclusion of religious affiliation questions from the United States Census, there have been no documentary data available to refute or redirect these caricatures. From the various segments of our research among Methodists, the following data and those in the appendixes may help to draw a more accurate picture.

A. People Called Methodist

Methodists tend to be older than the United States population average by nearly 15 per cent. The median age of 34.5 years is in marked contrast to the national median of 29.5 years. This presents a challenge, particularly in the young adult group which is being served least proportionally.

Educationally, "the people called Methodist" have four times as many college graduates as the national average. In all, 76.8 per cent of the Methodists twenty-five years of age and older have completed high school. The continued emphasis upon higher education, the universal religious education strength of the church, the economic and social groups represented combine to explain this sanguine educational picture.

Racially, it is difficult to appraise Methodism accurately. We know that it has a large nonwhite membership. The 364,689 members of the Central Jurisdiction are of course only a portion of the group served. Hundreds and perhaps thousands of nonwhites belong to Methodist churches where no separate roll is kept. There is no facile means of ascertaining the number of Negroes, Indians, Filipinos, Japanese, Koreans, and Chinese who have now been absorbed into multiracial Methodist churches and conferences. From the Indian, Spanish-American, Oriental, Japanese Provisional, Hawaiian, and Alaskan Conferences plus many integrated local churches, we can arrive at a rough estimate. A minimum of 47,964 are estimated to qualify as nonwhite Methodist in integrated church situations.

The total effort of the people called Methodist is not seen until we look at the independent Methodist churches which minister primarily to Negroes. Most of them have been aided in organization, counsel, and sponsorship by one of the three branches of Methodism. (In fact, only the Methodist Episcopal Church contributed any nonwhite churches to the union in 1939.) A total of 12,500,000 members of Methodist bodies are in the United States, including the Free Methodists and all the major groups. Serving Negro constituencies are three principal groups with a membership of more than 300,000 members each. They are the African Methodist Episcopal with 1,166,301, the African Methodist Episcopal Zion with 761,000, and the Christian Methodist Episcopal Church with 392,167 members. These, with the 47,964 nonwhites in integrated conferences and 364,689 in the Central Jurisdiction, make a total of at least 2,732,121 nonwhite Methodists. Thus, these groups represent 22.6 per cent of all United States Methodists. In contrast, only 11.5 per cent of the United States population is listed as nonwhite.

If the membership figures of those conferences which are predominantly nonwhite by United States Census definition are added to those of the Central Jurisdiction,[1] we get a total of 412,653, which means that The Methodist Church has 4.3 per cent of its 9,691,916 members in predominantly nonwhite congregations. Whether that many more are in multiracial congregations, we do not know. We do know that Methodism as a movement has included more nonwhite Methodists in

[1] It is interesting to note that 17.8 per cent, an exceptionally large nonrespondent group, failed to denote race and ethnic group.

separated organic units than have been included within The Methodist Church since 1939.[2]

If we may judge by the standards of income and occupation, Methodists are becoming increasingly higher-status persons. The correlations with length of membership indicate that this is not the result of a shift in emphasis, but of a process of family self-betterment. There are three times as many Methodists in the professions as the United States average, while there are only 37 per cent more farm operators, 14 per cent more sales workers, and 8 per cent more clerical workers.[3]

Craftsmen and operatives constitute 20 per cent and 70 per cent less than do those respective occupational groups in the total population. A similar failure to reach "blue-collar" workmen today is seen in the fact that 74 per cent fewer service workers and 77 per cent fewer laborers are Methodist than would be the case if Methodism were occupationally representative. Since two out of three Methodists studied have always been related to The Methodist Church, it is safe to assume that Methodism has climbed the social ladder along with its members. Those who were "blue-collar" workingmen twenty years ago, by their own report, were and are Methodist. They have changed location, saved their money, gone into business or a profession; but they are still Methodists. One of the major reasons for Methodism's change in emphasis is the changing character of Methodist families.[4] When we correlate length of residence with occupation, a different dimension is added. The Methodist Church is not evangelistically effective in reaching persons of lower-income status. Its new members tend to be similar to those who are now in its membership.[5]

Methodists are mobile today! A total of 51.2 per cent more respondents were reared in communities of less than 2,500 than are living in them at the present time. A total of 23.8 per cent more respondents are living in cities of 100,000 population and over than were reared in cities of the same size. It is important to note that 77 per cent of all Methodists today live in small cities and in town and country communities (less than 100,000).[6]

[2] Yearbook of American Churches, 1960, ed. Benson Y. Landis (New York: National Council of Churches).
[3] See Appendix B.
[4] Ibid.
[5] Ibid.
[6] Ibid.

What kind of church members are Methodists? Sorting out those in communities of less than 100,000, we see that 47.1 per cent of all Methodists actually live in communities of less than 10,000 population.[7] They attend 77.9 per cent of all Methodist churches. Since 63 per cent of all Methodist churches have less than three hundred members, it is not surprising that 53 per cent of all those small churches (less than three hundred members) are in town and country situations.

Thus, Mr. Methodist is likely to live in a small town, attend a church of 250 members, and at least once a month attend worship services (55.5 per cent every Sunday), and one other organizational activity. Eight of ten Methodists contribute regularly to their church. Their per capita annual gift is $48.70, although 47.1 per cent reported that they contribute over $3.00 per week.

Methodists live in each of the fifty states. Our best clue to the geographic distribution is the following table:

The Distribution of Methodists by Jurisdiction[8]

Jurisdiction	Per Cent	Members
Central	3.7	364,689
North Central	23.2	2,245,502
Northeastern	19.8	1,921,744
South Central	19.6	1,901,887
Southeastern	27.2	2,638,971
Western	6.4	619,342
Bishops	.1	81
Total	100.0	9,691,916

In no other region of the United States is the proportion of Methodists to the population as high as in the Southeastern Jurisdiction. With a total population of 26,066,000 in the states covered by the Southeastern Jurisdiction, 10.1 per cent of that total are in the active membership of The Methodist Church. Every tenth resident of Kentucky, Virginia, Tennessee, North and South Carolina, Mississippi, Alabama, Georgia, and Florida is a Methodist! And the proportion is much higher, of course, when constituency rather than actual membership is considered.

The national ratio of Methodists to the population is one in twenty

[7] Source Book of Town and Country Methodism (Philadelphia: Division of National Missions monograph, 1955), p. 98.
[8] General Minutes of 1958.

(5.6 per cent). Contrast this and the Southeastern Jurisdiction with the Northeastern Jurisdiction, where there are 44,628,717 residents in a heavily Roman Catholic and Jewish region. In the Northeastern Jurisdiction 4.3 per cent of the population are Methodists.[9]

In the Western Jurisdiction with a population of 25,820,000,[10] the 627,407 Methodists were only 2.4 per cent of the population. Great opportunities for growth are here also, although the ten western states constitute only one third as many persons in the total population as are residents in the states of the Northeastern Jurisdiction.

B. Unique Methodist Organization

Methodism is worth $3,277,335,576 in buildings and equipment. It contributes $539,506,175 per year for all church purposes. Of its 28,341 active clergy, 24,175 are serving 39,008 churches. Three thousand one hundred seventy-one serve as bishops, district superintendents, administrators, teachers, chaplains, and special service agents of Methodism.[11] How is this power deployed? How is it used?

The unusual connectional system called "Methodist" is characteristic, in whole or in part, of over a score of Methodist bodies throughout the world. Not all the following characteristics fit each of those Wesleyan bodies. They do describe the united body emerging from the Methodist Episcopal Churches and Methodist Protestantism which presumes to call itself The Methodist Church.

An itinerant ministry is a unique characteristic of The Methodist Church. It is described in ¶¶ 321 ff. in the Methodist Discipline as a "traveling ministry." In the Wesleyan tradition, this means the acceptance of responsibility to the duly authorized officers of the annual conference, the general superintendent, and the district superintendents. The Jurisdictional conferences elect, consecrate, and appoint the general superintendents (bishops) to whom each cleric is responsible. Each minister is to account to his bishop for the use of his time, for his

---

[9] In this connection it is interesting to note that in the Northeastern Jurisdiction there are more urban residents, more unchurched people, a greater heterogeneity in Methodism and less communication among its leaders than in any other jurisdiction in the church. There are no jurisdictional employees, little intra-jurisdictional communication of a formal nature, and no publications designed for use in the jurisdiction.

[10] U. S. Census Bureau, July 1, 1959.

[11] The Methodist Fact Book, 1960, ed. A. C. Hoover (Chicago: Statistical Office of The Methodist Church).

effectiveness and actions. The bishop who presides over the annual conference is the local minister's final ecclesiastical superior. Although each minister must be consulted by his district superintendent and bishop before appointment or reassignment, he is morally committed to accept the charge to which his conference, through the bishop and his cabinet, appoints him.

The consultative pattern along with equal lay representation ordered by the Uniting Conference in 1939 has guaranteed the church against the injustices of uncontrolled autocratic power. As Bishop Straughn has said succinctly:

The Methodist Protestant Church was organized 110 years ago on the basis of the rights of the local churches directly to participate in the legislative and administrative bodies of the church. . . . In setting up the Methodist Protestant Church, the founders swung completely away from the episcopal to the representative form of government wherein laymen shared with mutual rights all the prerogatives of church government. During these intervening years the Methodist Episcopal churches have granted increasing powers to the laity, and the Methodist Protestant Church has been extending its machinery in the direction of more centralized and closer supervision. In the new Methodist Church both theories of government were introduced and fully protected. Laymen elected by their churches to the annual conferences will sit in the body in equal numbers with the clergy and with equal powers; the same ratio will prevail in all the higher legislative bodies of the church. On the other hand, episcopacy remains and bishops will be continued as the great administrative officers of the church. We have, therefore, running parallel two great theories of church government: episcopacy and democracy. In their purest form they are incompatible and mutually exclusive. In their combination, they must of necessity condition each other. It will be impossible for episcopacy ever to appropriate unto itself exclusive authority over the churches in that it is directly responsible to bodies composed of an equal number of ministers and laymen. Nor can the churches ever become so independent that they may resist supervision and administive authority. But in their combination, wherein each surrenders certain privileges, we have remaining all the tremendous values of authority and cooperation.[12]

The stabilizing function in the Wesleyan itineracy is the guarantee of pastoral employment. By tradition, every Methodist minister in good

[12] Straughn, Inside Methodist Union, pp. 135-36.

standing is guaranteed a charge within the bounds of his own annual conference. Also because of the concept of the traveling ministry and the connectional system, no congregation is left without pastoral supervision. The guarantee of ministerial leadership which is inherent in the Wesleyan system in effect makes the district superintendent and the bishop pastors to every charge. In addition to the assigned local clergy, they and all other administrators are legally and by covenant pastors to each charge as needed.

Flexibility is another unique characteristic, and it is evident in many aspects of Methodist government and practice. Perhaps the flexibility of the traveling ministry mentioned above is the most important component. The old tradition of having all appointments read on Sunday afternoon of the annual conference session with no foreknowledge by the clergy of their appointments was modified by Unification. The drama of weeping and disappointed families or of those equally surprised by joy epitomized the expendability with which the clergy were viewed. Though this has been modified, the principle remains.

Flexibility in property and resources is much greater in a connectional system than in a form of congregational polity. The ownership of three billion dollars worth of material, with the theoretical possibility of deploying it as needed, constitutes a powerful potential. It is extremely rare to hear of a Methodist church that owns its own property free and clear of the denomination. The quarterly conference is the legal trustee of the property. Papers of incorporation must contain guarantees for the continuance of Methodist work in each local church building, and, in the event of discontinuance, all property reverts to the trustees of the annual conference.[13] In this way, an interest in the perpetuation of Methodist services in every property is a guaranteed benefit to the congregation and to the parish.

The acceptance by the conferences of Methodism of centralized trusteeship for all property of the church is unique in Protestantism. For example, Southern Methodist University is owned, not by the trustees of that school, but by the South Central Jurisdiction.

In addition to those institutions specifically controlled by Methodism, a major secret of its organizational strength is the manner in which it multiplies itself administratively. Many of the major institutions which

[13] *Discipline, 1960,* ¶ 176.

are called by distinctively Wesleyan titles were founded, directed, and wholly supported at one time by Methodists. The growth of some of these institutions had made such complete governance a practical impossibility. Methodism now assumes a benevolent system of *sponsorship rather than control* of great eleemosynary, educational, and service institutions. Such sympathetic support is a mutual reinforcement to the hospital or university—and to Methodism.

Flexibility in program is seen also in the specific deployment of such institutions as the Woman's Division of Christian Service, the Methodist Youth Fellowship, the Division of World Missions, and the Board of Evangelism. Constant evolutionary modification, growth, and development characterize these and other agencies.

The greatest evidence of modification lies in the historic record.[14] One need only mention the frontier circuit rider, worship services held in mining town taverns, missions on the frontiers of the world, and the mass migrations of clergy for evangelistic efforts, to illustrate the point. Institutionally, the union of the Methodist Episcopal churches, North and South, and The Methodist Protestant Church, and the resultant establishment of the unified or federated boards and agencies, demonstrates this adaptability on the grand scale.

There is also flexibility doctrinally in Methodism. Methodists represent the full scale of Protestantism. One may be immersed, sprinkled, or poured in a correct act of baptism by a Methodist clergyman. Views about the nature of the church range from the most conservative belief in apostolic succession (6.3 per cent) to the most liberal view that "the Christian church is a society of those who have joined together in their quest for the religious life" (30.4 per cent). A Methodist may believe that God is a "personal Spirit" (11.4 per cent) or a triune God (60.1 per cent). In creed and deed, the working Methodist is an independent, free-thinking workman in God's vineyard! [15]

Another factor in Methodism's uniqueness is its world-wide scope. No other major United States Protestant denomination has members and churches throughout the world. Many areas to which Methodist missionaries were sent are now completely indigenous in leadership, but still are organizationally one with American Methodism.

In another sense, Methodism is universal in polity. Independent of

[14] Cameron, *Methodism and Society in Historical Perspective.*
[15] Appendix B.

the state and voluntary in its membership, it is free to found, foster, and propagate Christian churches under diverse governments. Even where governments inimical to Christianity have come to power, individual Methodists, leaders, and sometimes churches carry on in independent faith.

Methodism asks the crucial questions of faith—in Jesus Christ, in fellow Christians, and in God. It *includes all* those who pledge their allegiance and devotion to this fellowship. It *excludes no man* who will "receive and profess the Christian faith as contained in the New Testament of our Lord and Saviour, Jesus Christ."

In brief, trained and supervised itinerant ministry, inherent flexibility, a connectional system, sponsorship of universal and inclusive polity, combine with representative government and an episcopal system to create the organically unique Methodist Church.

C. Resources in Administration

The resources of Methodism are found in the areas of strength, size, and purpose. Among these resources are many which extend beyond the skeletal organization and the theories of government seen in the foregoing section. Many of the aspects of organizational structure are classifiable as liabilities. Others are clearly assets which enhance the service and spiritual functions of the church.

One of the assets is the guidance and leadership expected of pastors. When 92.5 per cent of all Methodists expect their ministers to speak on social issues, their status is high indeed.[16] Not only are they respected as leaders in worship and pastoral functions, they are expected to speak freely. Nearly seven of ten Methodists feel that "a Methodist minister should be free to take on controversial issues any position which he regards as Christian." In the South Central Jurisdiction 72 per cent held this view, while the lowest proportion expressing an opinion (60.6 per cent) occurred in the Central Jurisdiction.

The prestige of Methodist clergy is safeguarded by a rigid set of academic, social, and physical standards and rules. Some of the latter smack more of a latter-day Puritanism than of a contemporary society. Methodist conference members resist change with asperity in such matters. Emphasis upon academic requirements is indicated by the

[16] See Appendix B.

233

standard of training in accredited seminaries which has been in effect since the formation of The Methodist Church in 1939.

Since Unification, the district superintendent has come to have an increasingly important, though increasingly complex, position in the church. The rise in the status of the district superintendent as a liaison person, the restriction of the episcopacy to regional status via the jurisdictional system, and the growth of the national boards have multiplied the functions of this position.

A Methodist superintendent is the only general officer [17] who is in every church with some frequency each year. He is the source of news and information and is the primary channel of authority in the connectional system. The pastor does not normally circumvent him.

As the co-ordinator of churches within the district and all with the church at large, the superintendent has a status commensurate with that of a Protestant Episcopal bishop. Both serve a similar number of ministers and churches, and both are primarily chairmen and liaison leaders. In many areas, the authority of the Methodist district superintendent exceeds that of the Episcopal bishop. In all, the superintendent is specifically charged with carrying out sixty-three administrative, ritualistic, and functional duties.

Fundamental to Methodism's administration is its unique episcopal system. The bishop is to "oversee the spiritual and temporal affairs of The Methodist Church," to preside at all annual conference sessions, to form districts and appoint district superintendents. He fixes appointments, is empowered to ordain and consecrate, and to travel throughout the connection at large.

The General Conference is authorized to define the powers, duties, and privileges of the bishops, but the bishops are directly responsible to the jurisdictional conferences which elected them. The bishops, however, hold their membership in the Council of Bishops, which is their only official membership in The Methodist Church. They are ineligible for membership in the General Conference, in the jurisdictional conference, or in the annual conferences, though the annual conferences may carry their names as honorary members. The General Conference may define their activities, but has no authority over their membership other than that which applies to all ministers of the church.[18]

[17] Straughn, *Inside Methodist Union*, p. 150.
[18] *Discipline*, 1960, ¶¶ 421-34.

Although bishops are now elected and consecrated on a regional basis, their national stature is insured by specific devices such as temporary courtesy exchanges of presidency over annual conferences, required travel to a mission field each quadrennium, and membership on general boards and agencies.

The general public recognizes the Methodist bishop as the voice of the denomination within his area.[19] His great stature as a symbol of Protestantism in ecumenical and temporal affairs is a decided asset to the denomination. Unmeasurable though this asset is, it may be the most indispensable one of this highest office in the church.

Many kinds of specialization are possible within the Methodist system because of respect for the traditional lines of authority. There are four principal categories of executive officers in Methodism. Three are relatively new; the fourth has evolved until it seems new. They are (1) annual conference officers and staffs, (2) episcopal area staffs, (3) jurisdictional staffs, and (4) the changing agency staffs. An important volume could be written in analysis of these four types of positions. Generic description is all that we have space to introduce.

1. Conferences are introducing such co-ordinative and supplementary officers as are needed within each conference. Board of Education personnel, church extension officers and other traditional positions are now being joined by Interboard Council staffs, public relations, research and survey personnel. Since each of these executives is appointed by the bishop, authorized by the conference, and personally known by each pastor, he has exceptional prestige and status.

2. In those areas where the jurisdictional system has been received with reservations, an intervening cordon of officers has appeared. The episcopal area staff has added to the prestige of the episcopal office. At the same time, they have shared the bishop's status. Outstanding illustrations can be seen in the Ohio, Indiana, and Iowa areas.

3. Jurisdictional boards and officers have been developed functionally only in the Southeastern and South Central Jurisdictions. Yet the efficacy of regional agencies has been proved. In large part, these officers have provided co-ordinative and public relations service to the general agencies and conference officers of the jurisdiction.

[19] Ralph Mirse, *Study of Ministerial Resources in Indiana Area* (Boston: Church Surveys, 1960), p. 77.

4. Increasingly important for their technical skills and creativity are those officers and staff members in the national boards and agencies. One asset of the jurisdictional system of episcopal election is that the national boards and agencies are not the political asset to aspirants for the episcopacy they once were. Tenure in those offices is longer and the skill of such executives is greater.

Methodism has yet to recognize with adequate funds, status, and control, the importance of career "civil servants" of the church. This is especially true of the "career" staff which constitutes an *invaluable reservoir of experienced bureaucrats*.

With the growth of the denomination since 1939, Methodism has recognized and implemented an increasing specialization of the ministry.[20] The executive officers mentioned above constitute but one aspect of this specialization. A list of the jobs within the Methodist ministry sounds similar to the roll call of community occupations. They serve as industrial, military, and hospital chaplains. They also serve as social workers, hospital administrators, teachers, technicians in agriculture and medicine, and veterinarians. Research, linguistics, statistics, architecture, finance, law, and politics now involve regularly appointed Methodist clergymen. In Methodist universities and seminaries, these and many other specialized applications of Christian ethics and service are being taught.

Another of Methodism's administrative assets is related to its publishing enterprise. John Wesley was intensely concerned for the printed word. He wrote and read constantly. Yet he could never have dreamed of the value, versatility, and scope of today's Methodist Publishing House. In a day when the printed word is yet the primary means of communicating educative ideas, it is the hub of the church.

The objects of The Methodist Publishing House shall be: the advancement of the cause of Christianity by disseminating religious knowledge and useful literary and scientific information in the form of books, tracts and periodicals; the promotion of Christian education; the transaction of any and all business property connected with the publishing, manufacturing, and distribution of books, tracts, periodicals, materials, and supplies for churches and church

[20] See F. Ernest Johnson and J. Emory Ackerman, *The Church as Employer, Money Raiser and Investor* (New York: Harper & Brothers, 1959), p. 106.

schools; and such other business as the General Conference may authorize and direct.[21]

Still another asset is its basic ecumenical mood. Methodism is a co-operative denomination in state, national, and world ecumenical circles. Here, however, an enlightened self-interest must be said to control many of its decisions. It does not co-operate without reservations and often feels that it is being exploited out of proportion to its size and numbers. Yet the local pastor who fails to co-operate with the council of churches, other ministers, and agencies would not stand in good stead with his fellow ministers. However, the ecumenical mood is limited when it comes to the possibilities of church mergers. The evidence suggests that Methodism has progressed little in its discussions with the non-Wesleyan denominations. Church union for the Methodists has meant "Unification of Methodists." The size and self-sufficiency of Methodism leaves the leaders with little feeling of need for denominational mergers.

In every jurisdiction the Methodists feel that their church "should co-operate with other Christian bodies in activities that can be done together better than separately." In all, 63.4 per cent of the church members endorsed this view. Only 1.5 per cent felt that their church "has the true gospel and should not jeopardize its witness by joint activities with other denominations."

There are scores of other assets which could be listed. The sacrificial spirit of the laymen, the tender loyalty of the aged, the enthusiasm of our youth and their spirited elders, and countless individual acts of devotion—these are the church and they are its chief assets.

D. Obstacles in Administration

Along with its resources Methodist administration has its liabilities which may serve as obstacles to change. Insurmountable handicaps and barriers are not the liabilities of which we need to speak. Geographical factors, major catastrophes, and crises over which we have no control are obstacles, but they are not subject to acts of will as are administrative liabilities. Our concern here will be those liabilities upon which the church can act with expected salutary effect.

[21] *Discipline*, 1960, ¶ 1122.

Some of these liabilities have to do with the present episcopal structure. Few persons are as well qualified to discuss the changing role of the Methodist bishop as he who has held the office. Bishops Francis J. McConnell,[22] James Straughn,[23] and John M. Moore [24] set forth many insights; others have come from interviews with active and resident bishops. Still others were offered by those who have worked most intimately with the bishops.

1. The failure of the church to define clearly the role of the bishop places him at a disadvantage. Certain of his duties are defined by the General Conference, but he is responsible to the jurisdictional conference which elected him.

2. The bishop is subject to constant pressure from national boards and agencies. More often than not, his responsibilities are controlled by General and Jurisdictional Conference directives. He is not the free agent in episcopal decisions which the public assumes.

3. Since bishops are ineligible for membership in any conference, their privileges of participation are curtailed and the church is denied their leadership where it is most needed—on the floor of the conference and in the committees.

4. Due to the regionalism of jurisdictional election patterns, the bishops are seldom national figures prior to election.

5. The episcopal address, by tradition (and not by instruction of the General Conference) speaks to the General Conference less precisely than is needed.

After reviewing the work of the church so beautifully, why, since the bishops are executors of the decisions of the General Conference and possess a knowledge of the church and its affairs beyond that of any other person in the church, why do not these addresses bring a program to the church with definite recommendations? Of all the papers I have heard, none has done it. . . . As I interpret leadership such is supposed to reside in the episcopacy, the General Conference and the church would appreciate such guidance.[25]

6. Since episcopal assignments are made by regional rather than

---

[22] Francis J. McConnell, *By the Way* (Nashville: Abingdon Press, 1952).

[23] Straughn, *Inside Methodist Union*.

[24] John M. Moore, *The Long Road to Methodist Union* (Nashville: Abingdon Press 1943).

[25] Straughn, *Inside Methodist Union*, p. 150.

national committees, the cross-fertilization of a true federal system is denied the church. The action of the 1960 General Conference may have improved this situation, but the evidence of its effectiveness is not yet before us.

7. Life tenure episcopacy does not need to be a liability. It tends to be so at the present time. Since episcopal areas are so large geographically and demographically, the bishop does not have the close relationship with laymen which guarantees full and free two-way communication. In an earlier day, an authoritarian episcopacy may have been more appropriate than it is in the era of well-educated clergy and laity. In present tendency, the privilege of interaction with fellow servants of the church is not utilized as it might be. Bishops seem to communicate almost exclusively with laymen who are leaders and perforce reflect their views and criticisms. Throughout a lifetime, a young bishop may grow so far away from his personal pastoral experience, that he no longer communicates with the "average" layman. The pressure on his time forbids it. The fortification and enrichment of testing and debate are denied him. Seldom do ministers or fellow bishops engage with the bishop in free debate and constructive criticism. He is even denied the privilege of knowing when he has preached an inadequate sermon unless his wife is an exceptional critic.

The Methodist bishop still wields considerable power over the ministers with whom he serves. This creates a social distance between himself and his fellow elders which increases his autocracy. Even members of the bishop's cabinet, district superintendents, often report that he is unwilling or unable to accept constructive criticism. How much more true this is of the local pastor with limited bargaining power of status!

Perhaps, if the jurisdictional system is to continue, a tenure episcopacy would be more effective. Certainly, the artificial limitation of electing men nearing retirement is not the answer! But, as Straughn suggests, there are other ways of closing the gap:

Here is a legitimate claim for the democracy of the church. Its polity has at last caught up with its doctrines and its preaching, although certain advances must yet come to complete the process. By this I mean lessening the finality of an appointment by the bishop; the granting to churches through its delegate or pastoral relations committee the same right of consultation in appointments

239

which is now granted to the ministers, and of giving further importance to the lay delegate to the annual conference.[26]

Still other liabilities stem from a lack of intercommunication nationally. The exchange of ideas is far short of being satisfactory in Methodism. Between the General Conferences, the local church has only ineffectual, opinionative communication with the church. Changes in the mood of the church are not communicable through orderly channels at present. If an annual conference desires to communicate with the entire church on a matter, it must wait from two to four years for the sessions of the General Conference.

Following the 1956 General Conference, The Methodist Church instituted for the first time a full-color monthly family magazine with popular appeal. Its subscription list has grown rapidly until it is seen regularly by the majority of active Methodist families. However, while the publication of *Together* magazine has greatly increased the audience of Methodist readership, it is not yet regarded as the general forum of Methodist opinion. Even if it were, the opinions would still be only that. Contrast this system to the political representation of the individual Methodist in his state or national legislature. (See p. 257.) There are recognized ways to communicate with his elected representatives, and they with him.

A second major concern in the area of communication is our *failure to assess and delineate the "publics"* which are to receive Methodist information. (1) Admittedly, nine of twenty Methodists attend worship infrequently if at all. It is doubtful that the majority of these persons are reached by any of our church-member-centered publications. (2) Research indicates that each Methodist church serves from 15 to 120 per cent more persons than it has in its membership.[27] That is, each church provides worship, program, and parish supervision for many more persons than there are in the membership of the local church. Aside from sporadic evangelism, how does Methodism communicate with this public? (3) The non-Methodist related "publics" are classifiable into several categories. Their misconceptions of Methodism are nothing short of amazing, but no more so than the indifference of church leaders to these misconceptions which they present.[28]

[26] *Ibid.*, p. 156.
[27] *Church Surveys*, Boston University.
[28] A case in point is the interpretation given to the report of the Committee of Seventy

The *lack of primary research in* Methodism is a fundamental liability. The whole structure of the church should rest upon it. New ideas and programs should evolve from it. Leaders should be equipped as a result. Now, no one knows whether the basic principles of church administration, for example, as practiced by local churches and annual conferences are valid. No general basic research has been done in this area. Nor, indeed, is there any agency which is authorized to do it. As can be seen through Volume III of this series, primary research into basic theological beliefs need not result in a commonly held theology. Constant evaluation and appraisal could do much, however, to help us see the effectiveness of our teaching and communication.

Surveys and research for specific *ad hoc* crises, preparation for conferences, administrative studies, and for effectiveness of program are beginning to dot the church. No agency has the authority, budget, staff, or mandate to co-ordinate them.[29] Pure research for the sake of research to unknown ends, as in science, industry, and education, simply does not exist.

Other liabilities are inherent in the rapid turnover of leadership, lay and ministerial, which characterizes the church and prevents continuing administrative policies at all levels. In the Indiana Area, for example, the average tenure for all pastors now serving, including district superintendents, is 2.5 years. 66.8 per cent have a lifetime record of less than three years. No national data are available on district superintendents, but their tenure is considerable less than the six years possible.[30]

The inadequate use of laymen is a major liability. Notable exceptions illustrate what could happen if leading laymen were given more opportunity to contribute their talents. Methodism has in its membership thousands of outstanding leaders in state and nation who, not being lay delegates to the conferences, are unused on its boards, committees, and agencies.

There are many conspicuous laymen whose abilities and loyalties should be

---

on the jurisdictional system in *U. S. News and World Report*, *The Drew Gateway*, and *The New York Times*.

[29] In 1960 the Commission on World Service and Finance was voted a research department with a general advisory board.

[30] Murray Leiffer, *Role of the District Superintendent in The Methodist Church* (Nashville: Parthenon Press, 1960), p. 49.

given recognition and under our present situation have little chance of consideration (election to General Conference). A combined vote [of laymen and clergy] would do much to condition the selection of representatives in both branches.[31]

Coupled with the foregoing is the companion weakness of naming almost exclusively the *membership of boards and agencies from conference delegations* to the General and Jurisdictional Conferences. Many lay and clerical experts in all fields are eliminated by this political practice. It is self-evident that persons trained to think at national and regional policy levels could constitute a major asset. Their disuse is a liability. One answer to this is the technique used by the Department of Church and Economic Life of the National Council of Churches. Its board is constantly on the alert for competent Christian laymen in positions of professional responsibility who can be recommended for appointment by their respective denominations.

The federated principle in board constitution is another deep-running barrier to efficiency. This administrative principle permits no central desk and is characterized by coaction rather than integrated action. The Board of Missions is actually three boards, not one. Its divisions operate autonomously. Similarly, the Board of Education is, operatively, three boards. The Division of The Local Church, the Division of Educational Institutions, and the Editorial Division are fundamentally parallel and are operatively autonomous. In both major boards, and these are merely illustrative, there is constant communication but no central desk, little common policy, and separate budgets. The Report of the Survey Commission of 1952 recommended their complete co-ordination,[32] but this has not been effected.

The duplication of publications constitutes a further liability. This is true particularly in the continued publication of house organs specifically curtailed by the action of the 1956 General Conference. This is in part due to the necessary time lag faced by the Commission on Promotion and Cultivation, but it exists in fact. Regional publications on an area or conference basis are still published generally.

The duplication of staff may be an insurmountable liability. Does it need to be? Why should each board need separate personnel, research,

[31] Straughn, op. cit., p. 162.
[32] Report of Survey Commission to the General Conference, 1952, p. 76.

library, and audio-visual staffs, for example? [33] Is it functionally necessary for every division of each board to be represented at each annual conference?

The General Conference curtailed much unnecessary duplication when it reduced the number of General Board meetings a bishop must attend. It has done nothing similar about board staff representation. This could be remanded to the Co-ordinating Council, but it is handicapped by the amendment which says that it may co-ordinate only "if requested by a board or agency."

E. Economic Resources and Policies

An economic determinism at times seems to control the thinking of Methodist leadership. Variously described as stewardship, tithing, proportional giving, "support" and offerings, the funds are always raised in the local church. They may be re-used through investments and earnings, but they originate with the contribution of the individual Methodists. Perhaps the stress upon the monetary values of property, programs, and the like stems from the fact that this is one common denominator which has an agreed meaning to the uninitiated and to the insider as well. There is no "double-talk" about the need for funds or their expenditure. Hence it is understandable that it is the core of much of the general conversation of the church. This does not make money the master of the church, but it provides most tangible assets and clearly understandable liabilities.

The Methodist Church is justifiably open to criticism from within and without for some of its economic practices. Similarly, some of what contemporary economists call "value facts" line up among the foremost constructive assets. Just a few of the favorable aspects of economic practice and policy will illustrate the need for a self-conscious strategy directed toward commonly agreed goals. Methodism certainly has:

1. Extensive physical assets[34]
2. An adequate manpower and talent pool upon which it can draw
3. Extensive assets for mission extensions
4. An international monetary status
5. Top credit rating

[33] Ibid.
[34] See Chap. VII.

243

6. The ability to marshal local funds
7. Church extension:
    a) ARCHITECTURAL SERVICE AT ALL LEVELS
    b) FINANCIAL ASSISTANCE THROUGH LOANS AND SHARED GIFTS
    c) FUND-RAISING LEADERSHIP AND ASSISTANCE
    d) CLARIFIED POLICIES OF CHURCH EXTENSION STRATEGY
8. Skilled advisors and technicians in most fields.

If there were a strong co-ordinate strategy for the resources Methodism already has, its effectiveness in Christian service could be appreciatively advanced at once.

Many aspects of constructive criticism have been noted above, but an iteration of these plus the consideration of some distinctive economic liabilities will aid us to clarify our understanding.

1. Inflexible investment policies. Methodism has been as conservative as the most conservative banks in its use of funds held for the church. Could there be a better use for those funds than church extension, for example? [35] Generally, our portfolios of investment are not as liberal as modern banking institutions or insurance companies.

2. The use of ministers instead of experienced laymen in economic posts.

3. The seeming inability to close inefficient and outmoded institutions.

4. The similar inability to modify redundant and duplicatory institutions and functions. The problems of the small Methodist college and competitive local churches are illustrative.

5. The failure to use governmental and secular resources and agencies through our indiscriminate fear of church and state entangling alliances.

6. The failure to review benevolent policies. This can be illustrated by the experience of many areas which suddenly find that they have "adopted" certain mission fields. At the conference level, the greatest reluctance is seen in reviewing sustenance funds. Many churches have been "mission churches" for years and are never asked to reconsider their status. Nationally, there is the unreviewed tendency of board executives to discriminate for and against favored or disliked Methodist

---

[35] The General Conference in 1960 authorized the Division of National Missions to use its invested funds for church extension loans.

institutions on theological or personal bases. The church does not allocate this right to an executive secretary.

Within any annual conference a series of economic "blind spots" could be named by conference members. Within the Western Conferences, they might be the aloofness of the churches from the problems of migrant labor and ethnic minorities, public power and reclamation problems, the plight of the small farm and similar problems. In the South, one could cite the relationship of Methodists to tenancy, investment practices, and soil conservation. In the Middle West, such economic problems as overchurching, a depression of pastoral salaries in town and country, and an identification with management might be selected.

Nationally, many economic blind spots could be cited. Methodists are consumers. Their economic position as individuals represents a socioeconomic problem for the church. If our ministry is gauged to serve some and ignore others, this may be a major economic "blind spot."

Methodists are not serving low-income groups proportionally. Only 6.6 per cent of the United States [36] population were earning over $10,000 in 1956, although 12.2 per cent of the Methodists were. In all, only 39.8 per cent [37] of the United States population earned over $5,000 while 45.1 per cent of the Methodists did so. Only 11.3 per cent of the Methodist reported family incomes of less than $3,000, but 34.5 per cent of the total population did.

Neither is Methodism serving its share of "blue-collar" workers.[38]

The General Conference does not have a clear policy on land reform in this or any other country. The rise of national interests in areas which are the church's mission fields brings this problem into sharp focus. The church's own land policy in every conference needs re-examination. Does the ownership of farm land by Methodist institutions encourage irresponsible tenancy? The Nebraska Annual Conference in 1948 held that it did.[39]

The failure to permit the free operation of national labor union activity in Methodist institutions has subjected the church to much external criticism.

[36] U. S. Department of Commerce, 1956.
[37] Ibid.
[38] See p. 227.
[39] Nebraska Annual Conference Minutes, 1948.

In brief, there should be a consistency between Christian ethics and church practice. As Bishop W. Vernon Middleton, formerly of the Division of National Missions, succinctly stated, "Our preaching is catching up with us. It did in China and it is happening here. We must stay to implement the principles we espoused when they were only principles. Now they demand courageous support." [40] The Methodist Church, since it is international, must have and hold universal norms and goals. Its standards of administration and practical government cannot be parochial. It must have an effective form of representative government. Its officials should have clear mandates of authority which do not duplicate functions. Its principles of administration must be consistent with agreed Christian precepts, and its goals must avoid ambiguity. If it is not afraid of self-criticism, and it does not need to be, it can become a sacrificial instrument in molding a more responsible social order.

[40] Interview, 1959.

From Theory to Practice

Synopsis

THIS VOLUME IS THE CULMINATION OF THE RESEARCH PROJECT on The Methodist Church in Social Thought and Action. Part IV constitutes the focus of the volume. One basic assumption in the early stages of research was that The Methodist Church is basically a conservative institutional arrangement which is not immediately interested in the social problems of the nation. This assumption has slowly cracked and dissolved under the research in which the members of the team have been engaged. It must now be replaced by a more hopeful assumption: The Methodist Church is composed of more courageous members than the individual annual conference and local church programs now reflect. They are anxious to have insightful and confident leadership in the Christian interpretation of the social problems confronting the American civilization. Methodism is asking for specific goals and guidance.

Chapter IX bridges the dilemmas of Chapter I into specific program suggestions and procedures at the national level. In this chapter, a social analysis of the assets and liabilities of Methodism prepares the way for frank appraisals within its fellowship. Here are the flaws about which little has been written. Many of the resources, unique assets, and characteristics have not been previously co-ordinated for analysis. Its purpose is the taking of a logistic inventory of the type necessary before planning any strategy, whether military, social, or religious.

Chapter X deals with ecumenical and social problems at the community level. It discusses the local church as the basic cell of the church universal and correlates its leadership with that fundamental nature. It suggests specific strategic responses to the dilemmas and challenges confronting the local church, including political, ecumenical, and educational crises. The task of the education of the parish in Christian love is the focus of the strategic response.

With the theory, historical development, research, and practical applications of each to the social problems behind us, we turn in Chapter XI to the summation of the volume. Guidelines for action are necessary whenever an institution is encouraged to become more active and to achieve certain goals. How far can it go? How do we regulate our social action machinery when it has been organized? How can the problems of archaism be anticipated and circumvented before they become barriers to the effectiveness of Methodism? These are some of the questions answered in the closing chapter. To the authors it and this volume are crowned with a sense of infinite faith in the wisdom of the Almighty in these matters. We must plan as well as humanly possible. We must prepare the finest strategic leadership and machinery that the human mind in co-operation with God and man can devise. We must work as hard as our theological beliefs tell us we must. But we cannot wholly anticipate the ends of God. His purposes may redirect our purposes. His intentions may be beyond our highest aspirations. Certainly we can prepare no less than the best of vessels to contain his goals for us.

CHAPTER NINE

Strategic Response on the National Scene

A. Dilemmas We Face

IN OUR OPENING CHAPTER, WE SUGGESTED THAT METHODISM IS faced with many dilemmas in those areas which might collectively be called its social conscience. Perhaps no more persistent or obvious dilemma exists than that between the need for power and influence on the one hand and the necessity of surrendering ideals in order to attain that influence on the other. The friends of the wealthy become church officials in every denomination. College presidents are often regarded as effective on condition that they remain unoffensive to the trustees. Boards and agencies are considered useful until they get into the headlines on debatable issues. Thus each leader is confronted with the choice of the roads toward temporal popularity or eternal verity and with the consequences of that choice.

The basis used in making these hard choices was tested through a series of discriminating questions in the MR-2 Questionnaire.[1] When asked to choose from four statements about the nature of the ethical teachings of Jesus, the following answer was chosen most frequently by Methodist ministers and laymen:

> The ethical teachings of Jesus provide basic principles which are just as valid now as when first uttered.

	Per Cent
Methodist Total	80.4
Central Jurisdiction	81.8
North Central Jurisdiction	80.3

[1] MESTA Research Project 2. Unless otherwise indicated, the data contained in this chapter are from MESTA Research Project 2. See Appendix B.

Northeastern Jurisdiction 78.4
South Central Jurisdiction 80.0
Southeastern Jurisdiction 81.9
Western Jurisdiction 82.6

If Methodists sincerely believe that the basic principles of Jesus' ethical teachings are as valid now as when they were first uttered, they are clearly faced with the practical problem of using or not using them as daily patterns of action. If they believe in the brotherhood principles, they cannot justify the common pattern of selective ministries to middle-income Anglo-Saxons. If they believe that "with God's help both individuals and society may progress toward the fulfillment of his purposes" (81.9 per cent), the continued practices which deny those purposes are unacceptable.

In the eighty-sixth Congress there were nineteen Senators and seventy-four representatives who were Methodist. They illustrate the problem of influence and ideals confronted by the administrators of the church. It is not our intention to advocate control of such legislation. However, they should know what their church believes about the principal social issues. They should be in regular communication with competent Methodist administrators in Washington and encouraged by their Methodist constituents. If a Christian consistency were evident, a new respect would come to them and to Protestantism.

How can a ministry of brotherhood, an enlightened social ministry, come from a denomination which is composed primarily of small-town businessmen, farmers, professional persons, and housewives? The Roper studies indicate that this is also the problem of Protestantism as a whole: When asked "Are you a member of a labor union?" the following replies by faith family accrued: [2]

Faith Family	Total	Yes	No
Roman Catholic	23 per cent	26 per cent	74 per cent
Protestant	68	16	84
Jewish	3	10	90
Other	3	20	80
None	2	21	79
Refused	1	40	60

[2] Williams College Roper Center, 1956.

It is quite apparent that Protestant churches are serving the labor union membership. Generalizations to the contrary are simply untrue. However, the Protestant proportion of labor union membership is not quite as large as the Roman Catholic. But it is formidable! Whereas 16 per cent of all Protestantism is labor union related, 25 per cent of the Methodists replying are in occupational groups where there is labor union activity. We do not know how many are union members. Unfortunately, the Federal Census does not ask religious preference and there is no public source of information about other denominations in this field. It is certainly apparent that the lack of concern for all groups within the social order is modified by the traditionally rural approach of Methodism. Various sections of Methodism have opposed labor unionism and chaplains in industry, and have only erratically favored openly the program, activity, and goals of the labor union movement, although Methodists generally are prolabor in their attitudes.[3]

The dilemma of lay control of the church has confronted The Methodist Church since the beginning of conversations about unification of the three branches of the church. Are we more fair and democratic as a church today than we were in the beginning? Prior to the first World War, the laymen of The Methodist Episcopal Church, South, organized an attempt to introduce a term episcopacy. The role of the layman in that branch of Methodism was symbolized by the prominence of the lay leader and many other functions in the local church.

In the Methodist Protestant tradition, the status of the laity was enhanced by the arrangement providing for a president who might be a layman. Their argument for lay representation in the annual conference had been won by their separation from The Methodist Episcopal Church. Laymen had come into the conferences of all three branches by the time of unification. With new power and prestige, the laymen have been a driving force of the church since the Uniting Conference.

A conspicuous example of this use of the laity and their capacity to understand and serve the church is seen in the fact that in the General Conference of 1952, which had before it the tremendous survey of the church with far-reaching recommendations, consideration and report on this document fell into the hands of a committee of six, five of whom were laymen.[4]

[3] See Appendix B, Question 43.
[4] Straughn, op. cit., p. 158.

251

Their responsibility is as great as that of the clergy in the General Conference and in all the subordinate conferences. The possibility of the abuse of power now confronts laymen as it has confronted the clergy all the while.

When laymen act alone as they have in some unofficial agencies, or as they have in caucus preparation for the conferences, their actions have tended to be characterized by a fear of the clergy. With responsibility increased, the Methodist laymen now could control the church. Though they seldom recognize it, they are the church in every local situation. They have equal representation in all the conferences, but do not participate proportionally. When they do, they are often so new to the procedures that they become discouraged. Methodism is faced with the need for the kinds of research and education which can provide for any Methodist layman the frame of reference for responsible decisions. At present, this is not the case. Ninety per cent of the Methodists do not look to the General Conference as their primary source of information for guidance on social issues.[5] Yet for the clergymen, church-related sources of information and advice are the primary determinants of Christian social decision.

Another dilemma arises out of present responsibility versus past commitment. Surprisingly few changes have occurred in the mores and traditions of Methodism in America. When they have been introduced, the modifications have moved slowly. To the majority of churchmen outside of Methodism, its taboos are better known than are its positive affirmations. These taboos are based on past commitments. A frontier church which served communities characterized by common drunkenness, killings, robbery, and debauchery had to have stern rules of conduct. These became the mores of each of its institutions. On many frontiers, Methodism is still judged by these standards of a withdrawn Christian community. The separation of Methodism from society in the eighteenth century [6] justified many stereotypes which are still held about Methodists. Can present responsibilities be faced by a denomination which clings to historic forms at the cost of souls? Wholly new religious forms must be developed to win the inner city. Methodism has usually approached the city with the same programs which were used

[5] See Appendix B, Question 56.
[6] See Cameron, *Methodism and Society in Historical Perspective*.

252

in the small towns of the frontier in the nineteenth century. Can Methodism be effective in any contemporary problem area if its standards are more provincial than ecumenical?

The refusal to discuss central issues or the postponement of them has characterized recent Methodist conversations on the jurisdictional system. Likewise, the problem of a term episcopacy, the election of bishops and their use of power, the problems of race in The Methodist Church, and the role of the denomination as it faces the union movement illustrate areas where conversation is discouraged. The contradiction of the need for debate on both sides of central issues as over against the refusal to discuss "hot" issues is a major institutional flaw. There may, in fact, be a weakness in the organization and structure which makes this discussion impractical. It was difficult enough to discuss the issues in the longer General Conference session. In 1960 even General Conference was abbreviated. What is to serve as the needed forum during the quadrennium between conferences?

Critical discussion of public issues is limited not only by Methodist structures but also by compromises of Methodist practices and the involvement of Methodist institutions. In some ways Methodist institutions are not different from state institutions in that they accept tax exemptions, federal loans for college dormitories, and government surplus products. Many Methodist institutions of higher learning have accepted federal scholarship funds which require a loyalty oath. Methodist clergy accept preferential treatment in income tax deductions and in military service, and they receive reduced fares on public transportation. Under such circumstances, Methodists may not be completely free to criticize the state. In some areas, gifts of town property to the church have been refused, as in Haverhill, Massachusetts, in 1957, where Methodist leaders refused the gift from the city of an abandoned hospital as a violation of church-state relations. More often than not, this expensive testimony to our convictions has been missing from the list of examples requested of conference leaders.[7]

Another embarrassment of Methodism relative to failure to discuss central issues is seen in the table that follows.[8] Both Roman Catholics

[7] MR-5, a project to discover annual conference action involving Christian social concerns through the solicited testimony of all Boards of Social and Economic Relations.
[8] Roper Research Center, Williams College, 1956.

253

and Jews have a more liberal attitude toward integration of public schools than do Protestants.

Faith Family	Favor Immediate Integration [9]	Favor Gradual Integration	Eventual Integration	No Integration	Don't Know
Roman Catholic	15 per cent	28 per cent	25 per cent	22 per cent	10 per cent
Protestant	11	21	24	38	6
Jewish	23	48	19	5	5
Other	19	21	22	26	12
None	8	15	30	40	7 [10]

Completing the list of the most obvious tensions is that of *institutional loyalties versus ultimate commitments*. Methodism is not alone in this inconsistency, but it is with this denomination that we are concerned. The older a denomination is, the greater its temptation to become concerned with ritualistic reversions to institutional loyalties. The ultimate commitments to the will of God often seem to be fused with these institutional mores in such a way that the physical church becomes holy, the "ways of doing things" become sacrosanct, and, in fact, every turn of a phrase seems inviolate. Ultimate commitments to the established Christian goals, to the will of God, are not really susceptible of institutional perversion. They only seem to be. When maintenance tasks obstruct new programs, when building and programs become ends rather than means, and when institutional forms are unquestioned, the tension is accentuated.[11]

B. Responses of Official Agencies and Leaders

In the course of this study thousands of Methodists have been interviewed. They include 3,208 college youth in Project MR-1; 15,000 in Project MR-2 (including the pretest publics); and, in the remaining

[9] In the public schools.

[10] From this same source of information at Williams College come these interesting reports relative to the self-definitions of Americans relative to their denominational preferences. The change between 1950 and 1956 is most significant. Data are not available for 1960, but the trend is apparent: In 1950, 27 per cent of those reporting were Roman Catholics. This proportion had diminished by 1956 to 22 per cent. The Protestant proportion had remained about the same with 68 per cent in 1950 and 69 per cent in 1956.

[11] See pp. 146-48.

primary research projects, leaders in every Methodist college, university, seminary, and conference Board of Social and Economic Relations. In addition, every major board and agency within the denomination has been contacted by the research team. *At no point* have administrative leaders expressed a desire for The Methodist Church to lessen its voice in the direction of its social conscience. Though many views were conservative, very few laymen and fewer ministers favor exclusively personalized religion. Instead, there is a remarkably consistent reverse impression which has come from every quarter.

An early project [12] of this study was an evaluation of the attitudes of Methodist college youth at the Lawrence, Kansas, Convocation in December 1957. The 3,208 delegates were asked to reply to a questionnaire which ranged their attitudes on twelve basic social problem areas on the basis of their personal willingness to accept responsibility. They were asked to agree or disagree on a four-point continuum measuring:

1. One's general attitude   "Somebody," "Protestants should"
2. One's denominational attitude   "The Methodist Church should"
3. One's local church   "My home church should"
4. One's personal responsibility   "I am willing"

Their attitude toward the responsibility of The Methodist Church in fields tested was affirmative and courageous. They personally accepted responsibility and felt that the denomination should act affirmatively in the areas of criminal reform, race and ethnic relations, economic planning, temperance, mental health, public education, acceptance of political responsibility, and improvement of public health standards.

Methodist young people seem willing and anxious to be challenged by a creative and courageous denominational leadership. They endorsed with the highest possible score each of the following statements which range from personal responsibility and involvement to the "somebody ought to" statement:

Modal Category—"Social Action"
I agree that I would join a group in my church that actually does something about the social problems in my community;

[12] MESTA Research, Project 1 (MR-1).

255

I agree that ministers should preach on the relationship of the Christian
gospel to current social problems;

I agree that The Methodist Church should have representatives in Washington to urge legislators to vote for social reforms;

I agree that this country needs people who will take more of an interest in
social problems.

It is clear that Methodist youth seem prepared to accept responsibility
themselves and desirous that their church act responsibly as well.

Let us now look at the responses of the denomination at large as discovered in the MESTA Research Project No. 2 (MR-2). When 64.4
per cent of the Methodists feel that politics "should call forth the
serious and intelligent concern of the conscientious Christian" and an
additional 29.4 per cent feel that politics "is an area which Christians
should regard as a special responsibility," there is little doubt as to how
they feel. Add to these findings the response about the freedom of the
pulpit, in which only 3.4 per cent would restrict it, and it is clear that
the denomination expects courageous leadership.

Methodism is disparate and diffuse, and widely misunderstood by its
leaders. It has much more social concern than conference records indicate. The difficulty may be due partly to the lack of effective communication between the rank and file members and the leaders. The majority
of meetings which Methodists attend give them little new information
or objective evaluation, and they rarely inform of the new discoveries,
theories, and developments within Methodist institutions. The tradition
of having pastors' meetings devoted to "good preaching" and the conferences devoted to "church business" stands in interesting contrast
to the conventions of other professional leaders. It is indeed rare for a
doctor to attend a professional meeting that does not provide him with
new insights and current reports on research. Each meeting of educators should provide informative papers to command attendance and
respect. It is self-evident as an initial principle that most pastoral conferences should be informative. Is it not just possible that objective education should have a similar place in the meetings of Methodist administrators?

This impression is heightened by a consistent feeling of separateness
between the agencies of the church and the local church. Perhaps it
could be said that no denomination tries harder than Methodism to

communicate with each local member. The introduction of *Together* magazine, the Commission on Promotion and Cultivation, the Television, Radio, and Film Commission, and recent innovations of the Board of Publications are long steps in that direction. The attempts of the church to eliminate regional publications which communicated immediately with each local church may have been a step in the opposite direction.[13]

Another point of breakdown is the elected delegate who often does not represent the people to his meeting nor report the meeting to his people. The election of annual, jurisdictional, and General Conference delegates carries little responsibility between conferences. In the political world, these delegates would maintain correspondence with their constituency throughout the quadrennium and represent them at all times. This may be impractical in Methodism. Almost universally, however, some two-way communication between the laity and administration is felt to be a need. The lack of effective communication may account in part for Methodism's conservatism in social action and her inertia in social crises.

When Christian ideals are applied to existent institutions which Methodists individually support within the United States, some of those institutions seem dispensable. Methodists do not believe that man is inherently evil, yet they support war as an institution.[14] They do not believe in segregation, yet are loath to eliminate it in the church.[15] When institutions become archaic and outmoded, they are permitted to continue beyond the time when it is wise stewardship to support them.[16] Four out of five feel that belief is determinative of conduct, yet seventeen out of twenty do not use Methodist publications regularly. Many of our present publications would appear to be expendable if judged by their effectiveness in reaching the whole church.

Readiness for social crisis contains a major challenge to Methodism. First of all, it is not geared for crisis. Its inflexible conference pattern forestalls the possibility of General Conference action within any given quadrennium. There is no agency to which is delegated general authority on its own initiative to act on behalf of the General Confer-

[13] See Chap. VII.
[14] See Appendix B, Questions 3 and 27. See also Appendix C.
[15] *Ibid.*, Questions 28 and 29.
[16] See Chap. VII.

257

ence. When Methodism has been faced with these inter-General Conference crises since 1939, its only answer has been an appeal from the Council of Bishops based upon ¶ 748 which permits modifications in the budget. No abuse of power has yet occurred in this arrangement. But it is illustrative of the reasons for the communication lag between the laymen in the local church and the administrators of general agencies. There is need for an integrative planning agency to meet crises! It would seem that each board might be served through such a co-ordinative function under the Co-ordinating Council.

Social action is always subject to shock. Emotional crises cause staid and dependable citizens to panic and abandon critical posts to which they have been assigned and to ignore principles to which they have been committed.[17] Within any large institutional arrangement, the danger of emotional stampedes is an ever-present one. Damaged reputations, vitiated organizations, and wasted resources follow in the wake of such man-made disasters. For example, no one can count the cost in manpower, leadership, and prestige which is following in the wake of the emotional crises within Methodism over the Central Jurisdiction issue.

Methodism must prepare a system of goals which are worthy of a Christian institution. They must be goals and standards which are shockproof. They must not be susceptible of misinterpretation. They must be as specific as the pledge which each minister must make relative to ordination and as definite as the vows of membership. When such standards have been approved, they may be disobeyed as with the foregoing vows, but at least there will be no question about the morals of Methodists in the area of social thought, education, and action.[18]

We have attempted to specify the levels of social change [19] in the life of religious institutions. The administration of an effective program by an administrator involves an awareness by the leader of the relevance of the social institution which he heads. The executive should be the first to call the attention of the denomination to the need for major changes in structure, form, and program of his agency. Social responsibility includes stewardship of the things of the church. Does any board have the right to retain an outmoded technology in a day when the

---

[17] Quarantelli, "Nature and Conditions of Panic," *American Journal of Sociology*, LX, 3 (November 1954), 267.
[18] See Chap. XI.
[19] See Chap. VI.

church is challenged on every front by the most modern techniques and equipment? An excellent illustration of this "growing edge" of the institution was evidenced by the Division of National Missions in 1952 when it elected John Harmon as Executive Secretary of Industrial Relations. He carried this office for a quadrennium and was an official representative of The Methodist Church to both management and labor.

Following Unification and prior to 1952, the Board of Education maintained a program of creative social action education under the leadership of Doris Dennison and Robert Eleazar. Miss Dennison served a co-ordinative function in setting up conferences on social relations all across the United States. Their content ranged from gambling issues to marriage and family relations and represented regional interests.

"INDICTING A WHOLE PEOPLE"

Burke Didn't Know How, But the Headline Writers Do.

R. B. Eleazer

"I do not know the method of drawing up an indictment against a whole people," said Statesman Edmund Burke, in a famous plea for conciliation with the American colonies.

There is such a method, however, and many American newspapers are demonstrating it in their handling of crime news involving Negroes. The fact that this is done without thought of injustice, merely as a matter of custom and convenience, makes its results no less serious.

Simple, but Effective

The method is simple—merely that of featuring race in the headlines of practically every story involving Negro crime or misdemeanor. Seeing these headlines daily, month after month, the public inevitably gets the impression that color and crime are closely related, if not synonymous. Thus is the whole race indicted, and, in the minds of the superficial, convicted.

As illustrative of this practice I think specifically of one daily which I know very well. This paper certainly is not hostile to Negroes. I would say, on the other hand, that it is essentially friendly, desirous of being fair and helpful. Yet a review of its headlines throughout a recent month (May 1947), reveals the unvarying pattern described above.

Dr. Eleazar served in human relations counseling and was responsible for many modifications in the church and secular press. His article titled "Indicting a Whole People" was widely reprinted in trade magazines and had much to do with removing the word "Negro" from the headlines of the city newspapers.

A heightened awareness of regional distinctiveness in planning seems to be one of the ways in which the boards might serve more effectively. The language and church traditions, for example, vary widely throughout the geographic regions served by the church. Effective communication and implementation of national programs demand an active awareness of the reality of these regional characteristics. The world of advertising uses from fourteen to sixty regional types of communication. Methodism has but five geographic regions (jurisdictions) and they are not culturally homogeneous.

It is widely held in the Southern part of the United States [20] that social action is most effective on a more dispersed and personal basis. Representative Southern leaders oppose "social action" committees and favor working through already established groups. "Church school classes, colleges, local churches, and other agencies should continue to carry the responsibility for the implementation of the social conscience of Methodism." [21] If this were done in such a way that social action workshops could involve these local church agencies in creative programs, a new respect for the connectional nature of the church might accrue.

The Social Creed of The Methodist Church and the Miscellaneous Resolutions of the General Conference contain statements which are the equivalent of the social views indicated to be liberal in Appendix B.[22] There is no lack of direction in these views. The lack is in their interpretation and implementation in specific programs within the church.

C. A Special Case: Methodism in the Nation's Capital

Interviews with the executives of the major religious lobbies and denominational agencies in Washington yielded a concurrent pattern of social action for the nation's capital. The largest of these agencies is

[20] Interview with Miss Louise Young, Executive Secretary, Tennessee Commission on Human Relations.
[21] Ibid.
[22] Questions 26-44.

the National Catholic Welfare Conference with a staff in excess of thirty persons in addition to the clerical employees. This staff includes four lawyers dealing with immigration problems, and four others who handle problems relative to education. Staff members deal with social action (3 persons), youth work (5), the women's council (6), the men's council (6) and an unnamed number in public relations.[23] This list does not, of course, include any of its staff outside of the National Catholic Welfare Conference office, nor does it include such staff as that of the National Catholic Rural Life Committee in Des Moines, Iowa. The Washington office does have a co-ordinative function in that all national Roman Catholic agencies are related to it. While this is the largest staff, it does not initiate policy or program, but serves as the intermediary for all Roman Catholic agencies which have business with the federal government.

The major Protestant denominations have representation in Washington under many names. There is a general reluctance to use the term "lobbyist" and their representatives do not register as such. They are called by such names as the Baptist Joint Committee on Public Affairs, Department of Social Education and Action of The Presbyterian Church, the Division of Public Relations of the National Lutheran Council, the Department of Public Relations of the Lutheran Church-Missouri Synod, the Council on Christian Social Progress of the American Baptist Convention, and the Friends Committee on National Legislation. Their functions include education and liaison.

Many denominations other than those listed are represented in Washington through other agencies. In some cases a local administrator, whose primary function is other than lobbying, as was the case with the Board of Temperance of The Methodist Church, exercises these functions. The central purposes of denominational representation in the nation's capital were well summarized by Raymond Wilson of the Friends Committee on Legislation:

1. To support the government wherever they can; wherever they feel that the policy is wise or appropriate or sound.
2. To oppose the government wherever they think the policy is outdated, inadequate or wrong.
3. To urge the government to do what it can do and ought to do but

[23] Staff Interview, March 25, 1959.

hasn't yet undertaken for one reason or another.

4. To supplement what the government should do by doing the kind of things that ought to be done privately.[24]

In every board or agency interviewed, a feeling of frustration with the present system exists. No denominational group feels that it is adequately staffed to do the many things its denomination asks of it. In addition, there is a lack of clarification of function. The Methodists, for example, have not seen the necessity of setting apart a bishop whose administrative duties could be lessened [25] in order that he might represent the denomination in the nation's capital. Nor has any agency been assigned the task of total co-ordination clearly needed in Washington.[26]

Social action in Washington might be handled in a number of ways which would be more effective than the present procedure. One pattern that has been widely discussed is the election of a Methodist bishop whose primary responsibility would be the representation of the denomination at the national level. His office would not be primarily responsible for the administration of the local annual conferences as has been the case in the past. Instead, he would have a new function in terms of the Methodist episcopacy. He and the members of his staff would represent Methodism in contacts with the federal government, with the corresponding status and prestige. There would be, in addition to interpretive functions, the responsibility of co-ordinating all Methodist contacts of an institutional nature. At present, each Methodist agency approaches the federal government individually and often at cross purposes with other agencies. A bishop as here proposed should be elected by the General Conference rather than by any one of the geographical jurisdictions.

One denomination acting alone is not of course as impressive as the concerted effort of many who unite to achieve common ends. In addition to the foregoing proposal, a plan for augmenting the work of the Washington Office of the National Council of Churches and for serv-

[24] Interview, March 25, 1959.

[25] Bishop G. Bromley Oxnam performed this function as a "work of supererogation" while administering the Central Pennsylvania, Peninsula, and Baltimore Conferences.

[26] The Board of Christian Social Concerns, centered in Washington, begins this process by co-ordinating the work of the former Boards of Temperance, Social and Economic Relations, and World Peace.

ing denominational constituencies through staff and financial resources was recommended by a consultation of denominational representatives on November 24, 1959. On January 26, 1960, the Washington Office Committee of the NCC amended and strengthened the recommendations to read as follows:

PREAMBLE These principles apply when a denomination makes a staff member available to the National Council Washington Office or otherwise augments the work of the National Council of Churches, Washington Office:

1) The denomination makes a properly representative contribution to the National Council Washington Office Program.

2) A participating denomination agrees to make available through the Washington Office a substantial portion of the time of its staff representative to work on commonly approved undertakings through the General Director.

3) Such denominational representatives would work with the National Council regulations affecting the Washington Office, as established by the General Board of the National Council of Churches.

4) The denomination would work under mutually satisfactory arrangements with the National Council Washington Office Committee in the selection of personnel, the allocation of time and responsibility, and the establishment of office arrangements.

A proposal to co-ordinate the facilities of those denominations which desire to co-operate with the Washington Office of the National Council of Churches would make it possible for specialists in the several fields of governmental contacts to be a part of a permanent co-operative staff. In such fields of technical competence as immigration, passports and travel, legislation, administrative reference, and national research a staff member in the office of one of the major denominations would carry the dual role of representing his own denomination and simultaneously all denominations in the area of his special skill and technical competence. A co-operative budget would be provided especially for this.

The alternative to the present unco-ordinated approach which might have most immediate backing would be the use of the new offices of the Board of Social Concerns in Washington, D. C., for the purpose of co-ordination and liaison of all Methodist approaches to the federal government. It would be the function of such an office to initiate programs as needed in its own areas of emphasis. In addition it might be responsible for program activity as requested by annual conferences, jurisdictions, and other General Conference agencies. These would include Washington seminars on the subjects confronted by the denomination, clarification of regional issues and problems, conversations with congressional and administrative delegations, and such other functions as are regularly needed by an international denomination such as The Methodist Church. It might very well be possible for this plan to be integrated with others which have been suggested, or it might be implemented through the activity of another of the existent General Conference agencies such as the Co-ordinating Council.

Finally, this illustrates one way in which Methodism could be heard before the publics which it hopes to serve. It is fair to say that Methodism is not now known, nor is it understood, by the general public. Its members know that there are often two sides to what seem clear public issues. No agency is now authorized to speak in behalf of the church to the nation between General Conferences. Public relations are well handled at present, but they could be incalculably more effective if they were channeled through an authoritative national office which could speak to the nation in behalf of any jurisdiction or of the whole church in cases of emergency.

D. Response of the Conferences

Extensive studies of the work of the annual conferences of Methodism indicate that they have been engaged in all types of creative social endeavor reflecting the social conscience of their churches. During World War II, the California-Nevada Annual Conference was one of the few religious organizations to protest the War Relocation Act and its wasteful imprisonment of Japanese-American families. Credit co-operatives, moving expense funds, and inter-racial churches have been started by many annual conferences. Such agencies as the conference Town and Country Commission, the Methodist Federation for Social Service Chapter, and the Methodist Youth Fellowship institutes have initiated programs, resolutions, and activities which have crystallized sentiment in behalf of Christian social causes. Conference Boards of Social and Economic Relations have been foremost in leadership since their initiation in 1952.

Many annual conferences studied [27] gave no evidence over a fifty-year period of having taken any action toward community betterment except a recurring condemnation of the liquor traffic and the support of educational institutions within their borders. Yet questionnaires completed by laymen within the bounds of those same annual conferences indicated privately that they were desirous of much more positive group effort than the conference leadership had provided.

In order to implement its own programs, answer its own needs, and supplement the work of the national agencies of the denomination, the annual conference will need to adopt specific goals. These, in addition to the national goals cited above, may point the way:

1. Each conference should establish indigenous goals which supplement, but do not contravene, the larger Methodist goals.
2. There should be a quadrennial planning meeting within each annual conference for the establishment of and later modifications of a concerted program in keeping with the conference goals.
3. Each conference should seek to strengthen local church, district, and conference administration practices in keeping with the conference goals.
4. Each should establish a co-ordinated research program to examine the work of social agencies and such other needs as may exist within each conference.
5. The creation of a social conscience within the annual conference should increasingly be the responsibility of every board rather than that of any one agency alone.

E. Response of Unofficial Agencies

Methodism has not been sympathetic toward its voluntary agencies in recent years.[28] It has disciplined such groups as the Circuit Riders, Inc. and the Methodist Federation for Social Action, following a national trend in such action.

But there are many indications that "unofficial" persons and groups play a needed role in the life of institutions. A creative criticism of the dangers of the committee system and volunteer advisory relationships is

[27] Names of conferences available on request. Many conferences which are known to have creative social action traditions did not reply.
[28] See Volume II.

voiced by Henry A. Kissinger in an article titled "The Policymaker and the Intellectual." [29] These excerpts will illustrate the point.

Committees are consumers and sometimes sterilizers of ideas, rarely creators of them.

. . . .

Policies developed with great inward doubt become almost sacrosanct as soon as they are finally officially adopted.

. . . .

Since individuals who challenge the presuppositions of the bureaucracy, governmental or private, rarely can keep their positions as advisers, great pressures are created to elaborate on familiar themes rather than risk new departures that may both fail and prove unacceptable.

. . . .

The "expert" not uncommonly is the person who elaborates the existing framework most ably, rather than the individual charting new paths.

We would suggest that representative officials do not feel free to make the unfettered suggestions, criticisms, and rebukes necessary to pure democracy—if, as in Methodism, they are subject to economic and status sanctions which may declassify them as "useful" committee members. From this hypothesis is derived the observation that the really distinctive contribution of the American way of life is in the work of its voluntary agencies. They, in this country more than in any other in the world, are its mark of character. Americans have been chided by some as "joiners," yet such voluntary organizations have kept the nation free of the necessity of becoming a Big Brother state. Charitable, service, fraternal, and all-purpose organizations may be formed with freedom when any community need arises. The McCarthy era did much to create a fear of the voluntary agencies. Membership in such unlikely organizations as the Masonic Lodge, the American Legion, and even professional societies dropped as a result of the scare era.

There must continue in Methodism the freedom to form voluntary unofficial agencies. At both extremes of the social continuum Methodism has had its unofficial political groups. Their function has been more than cathartic. They have been and will continue to be necessary. Yet in each General Conference there have been those who have attempted to

[29] *The Reporter*, XX, 5 (March 5, 1959), pp. 30-35.

legislate them out of existence. The tendency for individual Methodists to be disfranchised relative to national policy between quadrennial conferences can be overcome by the existence of the unofficial agency and those voluntary actions of all institutions, official and unofficial, which transcend the instructed program.

The unstructured freedom of the Methodist spirit has long been epitomized by John Wesley's greeting "If your heart beats as my heart, give me your hand." This spontaneity has found its focus in prayer meetings, barn-raising groups, song fests, testimonial meetings, and aspects of the mission field. How vital this voluntarism is to all of Methodism! Voluntary agencies rest on the theological beliefs of salvation through a community, the free witness of the Spirit, and inward and outward holiness. Social traditions which augur for such freedom include complete freedom of speech in the church, a tradition of personalized service, the admonitions of the Social Creed, and a tradition of voluntary works beginning with the Holy Club at Oxford.

There is a strong tendency within Methodism to "institutionalize" any voluntary program which is effective. This has characterized the long history of the Roman Catholic Church, and Communions in the Anglican tradition as well. One of the dangers of formally encouraging a voluntary organization is that such encouragement must soon take the form of financial support and, when it does, control of that movement is the next logical step. Very few Methodist organizations have resisted this escalator to institutional control.

Throughout this volume there has been a major stress on the group. We have been concerned with the responsible, established, controllable agencies of Methodism. The discussions, criticisms, suggested programs, and techniques of analysis have centered upon their responsibility. The denomination is also responsible to individuals and their right of individual expression. If there is any place in the institutions of the church which provides an opportunity for unrestricted freedom of expression, it is in the extemporaneous voluntary group. The literature of the denomination has long stressed the importance of action projects for church-school classes, adult and youth. Yet there is little evidence of any large number of unstructured, open-hearted unofficial groups. There must be official encouragement and tolerance for the activities which eventuate in organizations that desire to be unofficial. If there is any place where independent activity can be tolerated, it is within the church of a world-changing gospel!

F. Methodism and Ecumenical Responses

Nineteen out of twenty Methodists favor interdenominational co-operation. The majority (63.4 per cent) believe that Methodism "should co-operate with other Christian bodies in activities that can be done together better than separately." Another 30 per cent favor "union with other denominations willing to explore the possibility." [30] In such a climate, ecumenical activity should prosper.

With the free interpretation of the communion invitation, the baptismal ceremony and the administration of all rites which character-izes Methodism, there are few ritualistic barriers to full participation in interdenominational activity. In every ecumenical conference which has been held to date, Methodist leaders have participated actively and the denomination has given financial support as well. In addition, Methodism is concerned with the advancement of those causes which can best be handled ecumenically, continuing negotiations with those denominations interested in eventual merger, and the lessening of barriers between the several denominations and faith families.

Foremost among the ecumenical challenges in the immediate future is that of church and state relations. Increasingly, Protestantism is con-fronted with the possibility of a state dominated by powerful religious blocs. The use of the state by the church is as great a danger as the domination of the church by the state. During the month of February 1960, the United States Air Force issued a manual of instructions which informed Air Force officers without reservation that the Protestant pul-pits contained ministers who were "card-carrying Communists" and that they especially were a source of danger to the government. No mention was made of the Roman Catholic priesthood as an equal source of peril. The coincidence of pattern with that of the McCarthy era was reinforced with the statement of Chairman Francis E. Walter of the House Committee on Un-American Activities when he said: "The charges that were made are true." [31] Although legal evidence has dis-

[30] See Appendix B.
[31] U. S. News and World Report, February 22, 1960.

proved the charges [32] and it is generally conceded that they are more gossip than fact, this type of crisis emphasizes the need for a concerted plan of study and conversation on matters of church and state.

In an increasingly interwoven culture, the day of the provincial denomination which is primarily concerned with its own institutional form and the maintenance of its own agencies should be passing. There may be in the immediate future a need for the multilateral recognition of orders of ministers of all denominations which hold the same doctrinal (or religious) and educational standards. It seems unnecessarily legalistic that a minister cannot be ordained and recognized in more than one denomination. Why should it not be possible for a Methodist minister to be called to serve a Presbyterian church and be replaced by a Congregationalist without either losing his status in his "home" denomination? In any case, mutual respect for the denominations with which our future efforts must be pooled can grow only as we witness the increasing importance of the church-state problem.

G. Competing Strategies and an Over-all Strategy

The responsibility of organizing a compelling strategy is before Methodism. To ask each Methodist to dedicate his home, his worldly goods, his talents, and himself to the higher goals of Methodism is impossible with the mingled goals and competing strategies within the church today. There may be those who will be lost to the church if a firm set of goals of Methodism is impossible with the mingled goals and competing strategies within the church today. There may be those who will be lost to the church if a firm set of goals is established. The MESTA studies indicate that 8 per cent, or approximately one in twelve Methodists, believe that "social change is no responsibility of the church, since if individuals are soundly converted social problems will take care of themselves." Yet only one out of one hundred believes that "life is so complex and sin so powerful that advance in human righteousness cannot be expected in this life." Even these who see the possibility of social change to be a distant and unattainable goal may become a part of the militant majority if they see Christian goals which are definite and compelling.

[32] See The Truth . . . about the Churches . . . about the National Council of Churches . . . about the Revised Standard Version . . . about the noisy detractors (National Council of Churches of Christ in the U. S. A., 1960).

The redemption of society is a common goal which is seen clearly by Methodists of all theological types. To redeem one's own family and set it on the path toward Christian perfection is the individual's personal challenge when he has "accepted Christ." To redeem the family of the church and to set it on the road toward the goals of faith is the task of every agency, board, and commission of the church. Strategies in competition may be judged evil when measured by coherent goals. Defensive protection of vested interests becomes dispensable when the common goals are clear.

Developing common goals and an over-all strategy raise the question as to what Methodists would believe. This is a quite different question from that asked in the earlier volumes. Paul Schilling has suggested in Volume III a theology for Methodist social action. This volume has listed goals and ideals at a theoretical and ethical level. When applied to some of the leading social issues of our day, what is "right"? As Appendixes B and C indicate, Methodists hold a variety of views on each subject. While guidance is available in the Bible, the Social Creed, the Episcopal Addresses, and Methodist publications which we studied to discover explicit statements, there is no definite Methodist position on many issues. Our task, and one which we do not choose to avoid, is to give our impression of the application of the goals we have espoused and the strategic implications of this volume for specific issues.

We have selected those statements which we believe adhere most closely to the theological and social norms set forth in this volume. The first statement comes from Questions 17 and 18 combined. We believe that "a more Christian society will come mainly through the leadership of organized churches in advocating measures for social betterment, and that such betterment and social change is of equal importance with individual transformation." With this prelude, we shall list the "ideal" statements:

Question	Statement	Per Cent of Methodism Agreeing
26	"I, as a Christian, should totally abstain from alcoholic beverages."	56.8
27	"I, as a Christian citizen, cannot support or participate in war in the nuclear age, since war no longer serves the interests of justice."	3.2

270

28	"All discrimination and enforced segregation based on race should be abolished."	18.6
29	"Racial segregation should be abolished at all levels" (in The Methodist Church).	33.2
30	"Politics should call forth the serious and intelligent concern of the conscientious Christian."	64.4
32	"A Methodist minister should be free to take, on controversial issues, any position which he regards as Christian."	68.4
33	"The family may share some functions with other institutions, but should retain primary responsibility for moral and religious education."	60.1
34	"Public power projects like TVA greatly improve the total economic welfare of the nation."	41.0
35	"Economic and technical aid to other countries should be allocated on the basis of the needs of humanity as a whole."	45.1
36	"The United Nations deserves support as our best political hope for world peace."	80.4
37	"The main purpose of a prison should be the rehabilitation of offenders and their restoration to normal life in society."	69.7
38	"Occupations should be chosen mainly in terms of the use of personal capacities on the basis of stewardship to God."	36.0
39	"Men and women should have equal and identical rights in employment and education in both church and society.	34.1

271

40	"The Methodist Church should seek full union with all Christian bodies willing to explore the possibility" and	22.9
	"should co-operate with other Christian bodies in activities that can be done together better than separately."	63.4
41	"Public education should receive federal aid if parochial and private schools are specifically excluded."	12.0
42	"The federal public health program should be expanded in order that no citizen be denied adequate medical care because of financial limitations. At the same time, there should be a continuance of private medical practices and voluntary health associations." [33]	
43	"In labor legislation the federal government should protect labor's right to a union shop but limit the right to strike in the public interest,"	14.2
	and should control "unethical labor practices and racketeering."	44.3
44	"The federal government should act to stabilize farm prices, control surpluses, and conserve the soil."	47.5

Summarily, a national strategy of religious social action must, first of all, be self-conscious. It begins with an awareness of the challenges which the church confronts. They are not to be met by defensive rationalization, but by a responsible concern for the welfare of mankind as represented by those challenges. From this critical self-awareness, each institution must move through a reconciliation of its institutional and theological goals. Internal and interboard conflicts are inconsistent with the larger goals of the Kingdom. There must then be a confident evaluation of the obstacles, the phase in the development of each institution, an informed evaluation of the social situation and a preparation

[33] This position not in MR-2 Questionnaire.

of the leadership. When the resources for action have been arrayed, the alternative plans of action must be faced and ranked in order of priority and relevance to the larger goals. Finally, the church and its leaders become the agents of social change as they implement the plan of action which they and all available facts tell them to be closest to the demands of their theological imperative.

The purposes of God can become the purposes of the church if and when the leaders of its institutions learn to trust one another and courageously attempt to reconcile the differences between those categories of purpose. When the goals become clarified, their internal conflicts begin to disappear. The social and individual sins of mankind are at the root of each of these social problems. Without a recognition of these sins and the means of individual and social salvation, there is little hope of any national strategies becoming co-ordinated, or for that matter, successful.

CHAPTER TEN

Strategic Response in the Local Community

No MATTER WHERE CHRISTIAN SOCIAL ACTION IS INITIATED, IT must sooner or later find expression in and through the local church. Each congregation must be responsible for starting and implementing action. In each parish there are problems—problem institutions and persons—which demand the concern of conscientious Christians. A part of our task in this chapter is to suggest some of those problems and the ways in which a co-ordinated strategy can meet them.

We have defined strategy as the clarification of ethical norms, the appraisal of social needs, the assessment of costs and resources, and the deployment of energies to establish and accomplish institutional goals. A co-ordinated local strategy begins then with the clarification of those norms, goals, and purposes as they are confronted by practices in the local church and community.

A. Problems in "Our Town"

The local church is confronted by certain dilemmas which must be faced with frankness if it is to become the instrument of God which it was called to be.[1] The first challenge faced by Protestantism is the contrast between its stated desire to be of service to all and its practice of maintaining class churches. In the studies of 600,000 Protestants,[2] the modal occupation category and those immediately above and below it on the social scale constituted the majority of gainfully employed persons

[1] In each local church the Commission on Christian Social Concerns, the Woman's Society of Christian Service, The Youth Fellowship, and the Commission on Missions provide program opportunities for the implementation of the social conscience of the church. We shall not repeat their programs here for they are available to all and reiteration is unnecessary.

[2] *Church Surveys*, Boston University.

274

within each local congregation. For example, in churches where the professional group were the modal (most numerous) category, the next largest was the managers and proprietors class.

PROBLEM 1: SOCIAL SELECTIVITY

It would seem that Protestants illustrate the popular phrase, "birds of a feather flock together." We would add "when they are free to fly." This in part explains the fact that those churches which have a more authoritarian tradition are not so clearly stratified. The real and the ideal are bridged only by the attainable. It would be ideal for persons of all levels of society to attend our church. However, when potential church members have the choice of churches which do or do not represent their social status, they prefer to attend those in which they feel "at home." The key question for the local church to ask is this: "Does our church provide any opportunity through its program strategy and organizations where socially dissimilar persons can feel 'at home'?" While it is true that those who live "on the other side of the tracks" might be uncomfortable in the new high-steeple church, the congregation must still ask "what then?"

The purpose of the church is clearly not a segregated or stratified one. In considering strategy from the view of goals and purposes, the Commission on Christian Social Concerns will ask first of all whether it has educated the congregation to this larger responsibility for the spiritual welfare of the whole community? The social problem is clear then, is it not? Is the local church, by its standards, appearance, the dress and appearance of its members, plus their attitudes and behavior toward less fortunate or more highly placed persons in the community, denying those persons the opportunities of the church? From an acknowledgment of guilt and responsibility at this point come the next steps in strategy.

It has never been the practice of The Methodist Church to command all persons within a given geographical area to attend the church within that area. This parish tradition has wistfully been recommended by the Town and Country Commission and occasional annual conference cabinets, but it has never been a general practice. Most Protestants are free to choose the church which they prefer to attend. If they do not feel socially comfortable in a given church, it would seem socially improper to force them to attend simply because it is nearest their home.

If geographic attendance is accepted as the correct basis for a pattern of "churching" the community, the church is confronted with the embarrassing dilemma of providing only limited alternatives in most communities. If the church is to accept the responsibility for ministering to all peoples, it must either provide more churches with diversified program emphases or diversify its ministry within local church situations so that neighborhoods may be served with specific spiritual and service ministries appropriate to varying group needs.

In a previous listing of the principles of Christian ethics, the inclusive community [3] was highlighted. It is interesting to see however that a supposedly religious community which has as its primary purpose the demonstration of a human "cause" cannot hold its membership. In addition to the concept of inclusiveness, there must be in any church an awareness that the brotherhood of man presupposes the Fatherhood of God. Unless the local church, believing in the supreme worth and dignity of man under that Fatherhood, extends itself with purpose and Christian goals, its service to "the other side of the tracks" may never be nearer than the "foreign mission" field!

PROBLEM 2: THE PROUD CHURCH

Another contraposition which faces the church is the dilemma between the "status church" philosophy and the contrasting "suffering servant" concept. That sense of pride which often results in certitude and aloofness may be symbolized by the beautiful churches which stand at the head of the green in pristine New England white. It may be symbolized by the often-voiced desire that the church should be the "center" of the community. A certain haughtiness may beset a local church when it dedicates a new building, pays off a mortgage, or completes the payment of its annual budget. Each layman and every pastor can see the physical needs and is anxious to correct them. Each feels a sense of justifiable fulfillment when those needs are met.

The dangers are that the adequate facilities, the fulfilled budget, the efficiently run church business, that is, the maintenance tasks, may become "ends in themselves" and considered by the minister and the laymen to be the primary purpose of the church. Rather than a dilemma, this is a danger which the church must face in each local community

[3] See p. 75.

where the leaders are tempted to relax when the new building is dedicated.

PROBLEM 3: PROPHECY AND PERSONS

The sincere concern of the church for each soul within its parish presents one pole of another local contradiction. Contrasted to it is the traditional role of the stern prophetic voice. Perhaps no one is so likely to abandon the personal concerns as the prophet who sees in himself a great voice of truth. The avenging embodiment of the Old Testament prophet needs to remember that each of the true prophets was primarily concerned for persons before God, and, in each instance, spoke also as the voice of the people. One must not forget that Elijah represented the country vote before Ahab and spoke for his religion against the priests of Baal. Prophets rarely stand alone. They only seem to do so.

Methodists are rarely the stern prophetic judges they have been considered by those who know them least. The correlation of two questions will illustrate the point. In the question about the Bible, the most conservative position says "Every word is true because it came directly from God." Only 8.4 per cent of all Methodists [4] held this position, but when the same persons were cross-checked on another question (Ecumenism), just 3.9 per cent of the 8.4 per cent held that "The Methodist Church has the true gospel and should not jeopardize its witness by joint activities with other denominations." Rigidity is rare. This same 8.4 per cent when judged on a social issue, such as economic and technical aid to other countries, divided again until only 5.5 per cent of them felt that "Economic and technical aid to other countries should await our caring for our own needs and interests."

We must see that this austerity opposes the concept of the "people of God" or the chosen family of faith with the firm conviction that we are commissioned to convert those who have not shared in the redemptive love of Christ. For the theologian this may be resolved by the argument that men who are redeemed become a part of the chosen family, but this does not resolve the conflict in practice. There is a real sense in which Augustine's "City of God" dwells within each congregation and in which it is convinced, as he was, that there is something special and privileged about all who are called by the name of Jesus Christ.

[4] Appendix C.

277

When a local church has struggled through the hard years of privation, scanty attendance, and unmet budgets, it is tempted to believe that the Lord has blessed it in a special way as years become less hard. It is a continuing temptation to believe that personal financial success has come to us *because* we were more Christian than those whose progress is less marked. Just so with the church, this insidious form of temptation may cause a church to become smug and self-sufficient. Such a church has no desire to carry on an evangelistic program. New members might upset the balance of things! Perhaps this is what the critic of the church means when he speaks of "hypocrites within the church"!

PROBLEM 4: THE "PEACEMAKERS"

Social action such as the making of peace, for example, begins with the present congregation. It was startling indeed to see that persons of every theological tradition studied in this project chose the most militaristic positions on the continuum. This is a far step from the peaceful postures of the thirties! In all, 88.5 per cent of the Methodists endorsed views supportive of war. Remarkably, only 2.5 per cent said that they could "under no circumstances support or participate in war." Nearly one of two (47.2 per cent) feel they should "support (my) country in war when its continued existence is at stake, apart from considerations of justice." [5]

There have been many times when a local church has played the role of the peacemaker within the community. There is little reason to believe that the attestations of patriotism to the point of supporting war carry over into other phases of life. These same respondents, for example (90 per cent), believe that the United Nations is the best hope of peace.[6] War is not a way of life for Methodists, but, in the continued crisis of the present day, they seem sincerely to believe that they are in peril and that they must assume a nonpacifist posture.

Within each local church there are many opportunities for each congregation to assume the responsibilities of peacemaking. Is the church not responsible for its own inner peace and harmony? Is it not also morally responsible for the maintenance of fellowship between the contesting groups of the parish? In each town there are families, groups,

[5] Appendix B.
[6] Appendix B.

278

and even large institutions that play at their own kind of war. Deep-seated hatred that runs without examination or review, ethnic antag-onisms, interchurch strife, and cutthroat business competition are the crosses upon which the gospel is crucified. Does not the church have the responsibility here, where it is hardest, to make peace among neighbors?

PROBLEM 5: THE COMPROMISED CHURCH

In "our" town the state and the church are often represented by the same leaders. To think of Uncle Ben as the Sheriff on weekdays and as a church usher on Sundays poses no conceptual problems. Yet this same type of intermingling of functions in "our" town leaves the church handicapped when it is most needed. When brothers and cousins are the crowds which stir up hate, spread malicious gossip, run people out of town, vend venom, and degrade the Christian church by their actions, the gospel has ceased to be the primary code of the local church. When the church is not free to speak because its leaders have sold themselves and their standards short, church and state have become one in the worst way. The local church which is so compromised demon-strates at the local level what could happen in the nation's capital if there were a state church.

The courageous Christian who embodies in his daily activities the goals of his church and stands against the crowd, often finds himself surrounded by those who were "waiting" for his leadership. This inter-twining of the "Sunday" and the "weekday" selves makes the gospel a living thing and the goals of the church begin to have meaning. Some-times, this new courage will mean abstaining from an unthinking indictment of the leaders of the church. Again, it may mean intercession in behalf of freedom of speech. It may lead to racial or ethnic tolerances. Or it may lead to a whole new relationship between the church and its community!

When the church acts as the social conscience of the community, it does so as an institution under divine guidance. It is clear that each member should carry that conscience with him into every walk of com-munity life. But that is not enough. Community pressures may pull members of the Christian family out of the household of faith and force them to act in ways that hold the promise of shame. The agreed goals of the church, adopted by formally delegated representatives, are not dissipated so easily. How much more respected is the church which holds its own at all costs! It may do so by appointing representatives to the town meetings, to the United Fund, and to the Parent Teachers Association affairs. The church should be represented wherever moral decisions are made in the community. All institutions are based on those morals and mores which have to do with the total welfare. With representation and courage, the church does not need to stand aside in the posture of pathetic irrelevance which characterizes it in *Peyton Place, Our Town, "Regional City,"* [7] and other contemporary literature.

PROBLEM 6: FEAR OF DEBATE

"We can't discuss"—versus—"We *must* speak," the quotes from one annual conference indicate that religion *is* a disturbing influence. Many organizations to which Protestants belong have standing rules that forbid the discussion of "religion and politics." By refusing to discuss basic things, you see, we can retain "harmony" within the community! This dilemma confronts all faiths. It is confronted within the denomination as well when we come up against issues that we know to be raw and potentially troublesome. We do not discuss the families "across the tracks" because their problems added to our own would upset the church. Yet there is a need, God-driven and imperative, to discuss in loving concern our responsibility for them! [8]

As the entry of Paul into a community usually ended in a revival or a revolution, just so the Christian conscience of a local church knows no closed issues. The genius of Protestantism is in that privilege to discuss, to change, and to improve the church. How can this be done when local taboos prevent discussion in what could otherwise be a free church?

B. The Strategy of Solution

The existence of these dilemmas only emphasizes the human nature of the divine institution of the church. Basically, all of life is complementary and mutually balanced between that which we know we ought to be and that which we are. The ideal and the real are only bridged by the attainable. The resolution of a social dilemma is an orderly process. It *begins with the recognition that a contradiction between*

---

[7] Hunter, *Community Power Structure.*
[8] See pp. 150-58.

practice and purpose exists. Means and ends must be consistent. Their inconsistency may go unnoticed unless the group or its leaders examine the dilemma dispassionately and candidly. From this recognition, the second step is that of measuring each problem against the goals of the church. No double standards exist in Christ's way. When the dilemmas are recognized and measured against the goals of the church, their disparity demands that choices be made. These result in the third step —acceptance of responsibility by the whole church for the specific purposes, goals, and the methods used of attaining them. From an awareness through evaluation to the acceptance of responsibility is a long stride!

The implementation of the goals of the church by delegated and concerted action is the fourth logical step toward unity of purpose in the sight of God. Purposes without action are ideas without legs. Work has been an integral part of the Methodist ideal through all its history and certainly belongs to this level of problem solving. Finally, with this implementation in effect, each member walks in the new certainty of confirmed and resolute beliefs about the major social issues and embodies in his personal testimony of faith the church triumphant whenever and wherever he stands for the right!

C. The Church of the Holy Spirit

Christian social action centers ultimately in the local church. The grand strategy which moves the legislative assembly to action or encourages the state to accept responsibilities which it has ignored are ultimately directed from the communities where people attend local churches. Here is the locus of social action. It is as important that it be action for the purpose of retaining the basic freedoms, or conservative action, as that it be action for the purpose of directing, or reconstructing the social order.

One of the greatest contributions to the social conscience of the local church is the consistent pressure of indirect or incidental social action. The daily living of the exemplary life, the awareness of responsibility for good citizenship, the creation of good habits within the family are all indirect influences in behalf of the community welfare. And they are no small contribution! In every jurisdiction, except the Central Jurisdiction, more Methodists look to the church as a primary means of changing the social order. Central Jurisdiction Methodists believe that "social change is a partial responsibility of the Church, but secondary to the transformation of individuals."

However, only 7.6 per cent of all Methodists accept the statement that "social change is no responsibility of the church, since if individuals are soundly converted social problems will take care of themselves." Even this 7.6 per cent minority see that they must accept responsibility for social change when converted, since 85 per cent of them indicate an aggressive social conscience on the matters correlated.[9]

Methodism is not dogmatic. It has never been characterized by a narrow faith. Its critics from the beginning have sought so to classify it. Even though John and Charles Wesley and the members of the Holy Club were called "Methodists" in derision, they were seeking a larger faith. The questing spirit, searching and deliberative, has not always been the most common type of Methodist. Yet in every period of the church's history there have been those who sought the truth about contemporary problems and who sought to apply the teachings of the gospel in the most unlikely places.

How does a local church maintain this balance between certitude which breeds confidence and a fair and open mind which seeks the guidance of the Holy Spirit? Certainly a balance cannot be maintained if fear characterizes the relationships of the church with other churches in town and with all those citizens of the community who are not of our church. A church that is always asking questions and is unafraid of the right answers can be the kind of fellowship to which young people come for guidance, of which the old never tire, and where all ages can discuss in love.

To create a church which is constantly a part of the redemptive process calls for a reinterpretation of the relevant issues which affect the lives of the parishioners. Dr. C. M. ("Pat") McConnell used to say that "all the things which were a sin (when he was a boy) aren't sinful any more." Then in his jocular way he would comment that "What we need is a new set of sins."

Some sins grow out of economic change. This statement can readily be illustrated when we look at the kinds of occupations in which Methodists find themselves engaged. The engineer who designs rocket propellants, the operator of a Univac machine, the biochemist who abandons

[9] Appendix C.

cancer research for more profitable employment, and the Navy officer on the Polaris Project are Methodists. What does the church have to say to them? The moral decisions confronting them are new. The complex world of "organization man" is a new world. A growing Christian conscience should aid in vocational decisions as well as other "newer" sins.

The Puritan virtues which characterized Protestantism a generation ago centered around long hours of hard work, frugality, a canny wisdom about business affairs, and a temperate life.

American moral codes have been small-town codes, fixed in a simple agrarian society by the austere standards not of the dominant economic or social class but of the lower-middle-class "respectable" churchgoing groups. The wealthy and powerful did not shape the codes but lived largely on their margin. The business Titans whom I have called "The Puritans" shared the small-town morality, pay it at least lip service.[10]

Puritanism lingered on, not so much as a search for individual salvation or as a celebration of the virtues of thrift and industry, but as a recognition of the dignity of the individual and of his duty to achieve both spiritual and material prosperity.[11]

Recreation was considered sinful if it took place on Sunday and many entertainment forms were prohibited at any time.

With shortened hours of work the general rule, with a widespread acceptance of installment buying and a general dependence upon salaried situations limiting the proportional number of small businesses, these virtues are changed by the changing times. The church made little attempt to control the mores of making money. In fact, it generally approved the coup as an accomplished fact and welcomed the prosperous into the fold of respectability. The government has done what the church failed to do in controlling the excesses of manipulation, monopolistic control, and exploitation characteristic of much business in the last generation. While the Puritan virtues remain the core of the Protestant "way of life," they are anachronistic unless made relevant to the changing patterns of our culture.

[10] Max Lerner, America As a Civilization (New York: Simon and Schuster, Inc., 1957), p. 672.
[11] Henry Steele Commager, The American Mind (New Haven: Yale University Press, 1952), p. 410.

In all seriousness, we too must ask in each local church, "What are the moral problems confronted by the members?" Certain of the carnal sins still exist, and these are clear to the sinner as well as to the church. Less clear is the responsibility of the pilot who flies an atomic bomb-laden plane, the engineer who designs the rocket, or the physicist whose research is taken over by others to become an instrument of destruction. Christian vocational guidance is as important for the adult biochemist as it is for the college student! Just who helps the operator of the electronic brain to judge the morality of his work? Where in his world of business does the "man in the gray flannel suit" or "organization man" find Christian moral standards which are relevant to his daily decisions?

It is clear then that the challenge of the local church should be primarily at the level of the relevant issues for that community. To the farming community, the challenge may be in the prostration of the community farming patterns to the new ways of corporation farming. In the small town it may be the sin of permitting a high school to build its program exclusively around the tradition of shipping all the young people off to the city on graduation. In the college town, it may be the sin of focusing all the attention on the college students and ignoring the needs of the townspeople. In the military services it may be the sin of competing denominational interests which fail to transcend their differences and speak only of little things to men in the armed forces. The nerve endings of moral conscience leap to sharp relevant stimuli which are "close to home."

It is the church's responsibility when a child drowns in the river because there is no community swimming pool. The drunks who lie on the levee because the bars are open on Sunday are its responsibility. The carload of high school youth who are killed by the late train because they had no recreation center in their home town are its responsibility. The local church becomes relevant to all that happens in the community, when it is relevant to its own central purpose!

The church which is busily at work in study and education about its purpose becomes a growing church. On the other hand, our research has shown that those churches which abandon their study and education soon die. One of the reasons is that the smaller churches have a larger proportion of members in the church school than the larger ones.[12] It is

[12] *The Sunbury Study* (Boston: Church Surveys, 1959, offset).

clear that the studying church has hope for the future. When the key questions of "how," "why," "where," "when," and "by whom" are being asked, the churches are opening their doors to the future. Dying churches seldom call for a survey. Those who hope to build are much more concerned with counting the costs and assessing the possibilities. Interestingly enough, no study has ever been made in Methodism of the reasons for the death of churches now closed. They died without notice and often without any record of the closing being made in the conference journals.

Research marks the beginnings of things. Bible study and research, religious education and discussion, surveys and comprehension go together. Businesses, public schools, and agriculture wither without research. Growing minds are never satisfied with what has obviously been inadequate. A local church might wish to ask the following questions: How then can local churches keep having services at the same hour without asking whether it is the best and only possibility? Must all activities be held in the church building when other agencies are more effective through neighborhood meetings? Why does the "success" of a church hinge upon the quality of its preaching from the pulpit when there are more than enough qualified leaders, teachers, and speakers in the congregation? Why does the small church serve only "one family and their in-laws" when scores of people within walking distance of the church might be served? Why do we have four rural churches within one mile in an open-country community where everyone has automobiles? These are only the beginnings of the kinds of questions that can lead to dynamic research for a church really interested in serving its community. Particularly in the field of social action, we must be aware of the danger of using unnecessary and unneeded research as a form of delaying tactic. Brought over from the field of politics, such techniques have been used in many areas of church life at the expense of the larger community and immediate needs.

A church that is unafraid should provide opportunities for conflict. The pastor or some of the laymen may feel that only one point of view should exist within the congregation where theological matters are involved. On the other hand, any astute layman with a good memory can recall several theological perspectives within the history of the pulpit of his church. He has endured them all with patience. Why should there not be room within the same congregation for those who prefer a more formal service and those who prefer a more traditionalist type of evangelism? There is room in Protestantism for both in any local church. Methodist laymen obviously believe in freedom of the pulpit.[13] They also believe in freedom of expression for themselves. Does the church provide such opportunities? The cottage prayer meeting, evangelistic services, social study groups, the ritualistic service of worship and educational study groups not only can survive in the same church —they belong there!

The church of the Holy Spirit will provide in all that it does a place for the centrality of the gospel. The simple question, "What would Christ have us do?" applied to any problem the church faces will soon force that church toward the proper goals. The example of a Galilean who reformed his own temple, called his disciples from their first vocations to a life of stewardship, and who gave his own life in re-demptive love can lead each Woman's Society of Christian Service president, each pastor, each lay leader to a Christian spirit too! A reform-ing spirit, coupled with redemptive love in a life of stewardship can transform each leader and the group he leads.[14]

When the hard questions have been asked they come to a place of centrality in the life of the church. Each member of the congregation is busily seeking out the facts in creative research. There is room for the rainbow of ideas in creative discussion and programs are planned for them. Then the Christian spirit can pervade the whole life of the local church!

Common goals must guide the local church, but these goals must be the sort which gather up the whole range of mankind that ought to be served by that church. They must include those now within the family and those who ought to be. Even those institutions which the church means to change must be respected. Jesus accorded respect and concern to those condemned by the community and a church which would follow his example can do no less.

The primary responsibility for churchmanship rests with the local church. Through tradition, belief, and practice, it has become the key-stone of the whole church. All action begins and ends in it. As such, it provides the leadership, the inspiration and the basic membership which the boards and agencies exist to serve. The World and National Councils

[13] See Appendix B, Question 32.
[14] See p. 103.

of Churches are of highest value as they represent and speak to the local church. Just so, the national boards of each denomination exist to serve the local church and to act as its agents. It is the ultimate and the initial social institution for increasing the love of God and man.

D. Education for Leadership in Church and Community

We sincerely believe that there are no Methodists incapable of leadership. Their leadership may be on a local scale. It may even be restricted to one's own family and relatives, but it always should be a part of one's conscious effort as a Christian. One who lives his faith is always in training for and exercising leadership.

We have discussed the kinds of leadership [15] at length in a previous chapter. Each church has the responsibility for providing individual as well as institutional leadership for its community. A previous study indicates that as few as one fourth of the residents of a community provide all the membership of all its voluntary organizations, political officers, and church leaders.[16] Those who are officers and recognized leaders constitute an even smaller core. There seems to be positive correlation between home ownership, length of residence, church membership, and community leadership. Churches which are sincerely concerned about the total welfare of the community have a major task. They must provide skilled, professional (formal) leaders as well as crisis leadership. In addition, leaders of the "grass-roots" (emergent) and intermediate (adjustive) types come from the church for community service.

Leadership and strategy come *into* the church as well as *out of* it. The church must be in communication with other churches and agencies in the local community for this reason. There is much to learn from other faiths. They have plans for social action running parallel to our own. Their needs and concerns eventuate in strategy which must be taken into consideration in the planning of the local church. Through the council of churches or the ministerial association their interests are made known. It is here that our own plans and faith are broadened, tested, and reinforced.

From the political, service, and social work agencies of the community

[15] Chap. VI.
[16] H. E. Stotts, "The Platteville Study" (unpublished dissertation, University of Denver, 1950), p. 113.

come other beneficent programs and leaders with whom the church must coact. In the strengthening of church programs, we must be concerned that what we do is relevant to the community welfare, does not undermine its leaders, and respects the rights of other institutions as well as our own.

Leadership in practical politics must become the concern of Christian leaders. A church should honor those of its fellowship who have accepted community leadership. They should be made aware of the prayerful support of the congregation. The absence of these leaders from church affairs does not need to be a barrier. Busy leaders in community politics are perhaps more in need of the support of the church while absent at the courthouse or the capitol than those who man its church-school classes and serve on the official board. Indeed, we too often stand aloof from those who engage in the hard work of community service.

In addition to training persons for community leadership in other voluntary agencies, there is much that the church can learn from them about the operation of its affairs. The experienced juvenile court judge, the state legislator, the president of the farm bureau and the chairman of the local co-operative have much to share and should be asked to contribute to the church the skills which they know best.

The task of searching for and training leadership is a primary task of the educational program of the church. Church-school classes should be pointed toward this kind of responsibility. There are other kinds of leadership than that now envisioned in the leadership training courses in the religious education program, and there are more kinds than the Woman's Society of Christian Service provides, yet these are the primary training media now available.

Each church should develop an understanding that *the best leaders come from within the group*. They seldom move in the community without immediate group support. Yet it is customary in our churches to select as leaders those who have been church leaders elsewhere. Newcomers should continue to be utilized but, we repeat, the most effective emergent leaders are those who have lived within the community long enough to be known and to have a following. The place to search for leadership is within the family of the church. Just as the church is training people for other organizations, even so those organizations are training church leaders. One who has held office in voluntary organizations outside the church is often an ideal candidate for leadership.

Similarly, those who represent large families (as in a rural community) or idea groups (as "fundamentalists" or "liberals") have a following which they can bring into group activity if they are given a chance and kept in balance with others.

Every church should have leadership classes for persons who simply want to know more about group leadership. Such classes should instruct potential leaders in matters of tact, parliamentary procedures, organization of materials, multiplication of leadership, and the normal as well as the crisis forms of group process. The assumption that every registrant in a leadership class is going to become a "Sunday-school teacher" must be abandoned. Out of this class must come persons who work in double harness with other leaders. Each local church chairman, treasurer, or president should have an understudy who can replace him while he is on vacation or ill. Leaders grow in the church just as they grow in the family—slowly and with the patient oversight of an experienced leader.

As the concept of leadership is broadened and the leadership base of the church is shared with more persons, new facts and new issues will come into the hopper of the church's program. If there is no desire to change and better the church, avoid recruiting new leaders. They tend to change things for the better! The recognition of new leaders of necessity forces the church to recognize that social issues with which these new leaders are concerned often have importance equal to the old and outworn issues which have faded with familiarity.

E. The Place of Power in Strategy

Leadership and purpose are not the only resources which the local church has to use in its battle against social evil! There are also those complementary parts of the power structure—tangible and intangible assets and strength.[17] The numbers of friends of the church far outnumber its enemies in most American communities. This may be an indictment of the role of the church in the past. But, for the present, it is a valuable resource. The number of members in the church and church school and the many, many families whom the church has helped in crisis are also a part of its power.

The strength of the local church is as great as the purposes for which

[17] See Chap. VII.

its influence is used. The Commission on Christian Social Concerns will find its voice more persuasive than it had dreamed. If we can believe the data, most of the church is awaiting for prophetic leadership—especially at the level of the laity.

Assets, strength, and purpose, these three are the heart of the power structure of the church as an institution. When this power is led through purposive Christian action, the leaders as well as their community will be "new" in Christ.

F. From Problems to Action

In this chapter, we have discussed the representative major problems confronted by the church. The first group represents contradictions or dilemmas in which the church has been contravening its own nature and purposes:

1. The church was never intended to be exclusive. Its purpose is a ministry to all who need her!
2. There is no place for institutional pride and aloofness in a church of the Suffering Servant.
3. Austere prophecy fits uncomfortably upon a church which chooses to be controlled by the Holy Spirit.
4. The roles of peacemaker and intercessor become the Church and its leaders much better than that of gossip monger, belligerent, or militarist.
5. The local church which has compromised its right to criticize the government is not a free church.
6. The church that is afraid to speak about human problems for fear of offending has a low estimate of the dignity of man.

It is clear in each of the foregoing items that problems which have to do with the nature of the church and its ministry have clear goals and purposes with which they may be judged. These problems were anticipated in Volume III and made relevant to strategy in Chapter II of this volume. All that remains is the appraisal of the resources, the costs, and the leadership needed to change the local church to meet these problems.

The strategy for each of these six problem areas has been suggested in this chapter. It consists of the matching of the problem, dilemma, or contradiction with the purposes and goals of the church. This we have suggested in an introductory way. Through discussions, education, and research, the local church will develop its own strategy.

The strategy proceeds first to individual, then to group conversion. Neither is adequate unless coupled with the other. When the members of the local church are convinced that theirs can be a redeemed and redeeming church, the strategy has begun. Consistent with this new faith and the goals of the church, these steps should be taken:

1. Each church should have or organize a Commission on Christian Social Concerns.
2. This Commission might suggest these strategies to rectify the six illustrative problems.

PROBLEM 1: SOCIAL SELECTIVITY

Each church should provide a diversified program which is appropriate, helpful, and appealing to the total geographic community it is intended to serve.

This could mean services of worship and church-school activities at varying hours and in differing locations. It could mean a diversification of the program within the present church building. Its precise character, such as the language spoken or the form of service, may be determined by the unchurched group the local church seeks to serve. Normally, no change in pastoral leadership is indicated. The need is for improved attitudes on the part of those involved—ministers and laymen.

As with all creative strategy, these moves will need to be reviewed with regularity. The new people should be a part of any such review. Their insights, added to those of present leaders, may lead to major modifications in the strategy.

PROBLEM 2: THE PROUD CHURCH

The problem of an institutional pride which hinders the church from humble service defies strategy. The patient who will not be helped, cannot be helped. Similarly, the church which is convinced of its perfection is resistant to change. It may even be resistant to its own purposes!

A confrontation of the problem of haughty self-sufficiency begins the strategy. The answers lie in the confrontation of the leadership by the Commission or study group with such questions as these:

"How many young people have gone into full-time religious vocations from this church?"

"Do we serve the population residing within walking distance of the church?"

"Do we contribute as much to others as we spend on ourselves? Does our giving to World Service and Benevolences equal our current expenses?"

"Are our people personally engaged in meeting human need in our community?"

"Is our church building used each day for some good cause, if not in use for church activities?"

These questions contain their own plan of strategy. The community expects each church to serve, at least those persons who live near the church. The house of God is meant to be lived in. Each church needs to grow and recruit Christian leaders, else it is barren. Giving for others is the beginning of stewardship; not just giving for one's own family and one's home church.

A strategy which seeks to make the church relevant to human suffering and produced leadership for those beyond its doors will not remain aloof!

PROBLEM 3: PROPHECY AND PERSONS

The stern judges of local morals, the austere prophet or the avenger who hates the sinner as well as his sin are occasional but possibly dangerous opponents of the local church. When the church itself chooses austere prophecy rather than patient, loving ministries it is confronted by both a theological and a social dilemma.

We believe that it is a primary function of the church to be judicious without judging, to discriminate between the sinner and his sins, and to create Christian responsibility as its prevalent mood. This sense of responsibility extends to the last and the lost. The strategy must exclude no one as being beyond the caring of the church. This strategy becomes effective as it is communicated through teaching, preaching, and worship. It eventuates in a redemptive mood which needs little overt strategy.

PROBLEM 4: THE "PEACEMAKERS"

The most important social problem in the world today is the making of peace. There is within most congregations a reservoir of experience and conviction which can be counted upon to confront this problem.

Education for peace, as all Christian social action, begins with the individual in his home church. A peaceable church should be one in which the minister and the leaders conscientiously trust one another in love.

A deliberate strategy aimed at seeing that all criticism is constructive, that the highest motives are attributed and at promoting peace within the community, lends feet to the gospel. Knowledge of the problems of world peace, support of the United Nations, and a continuing study of the problems of war and its prevention are then the natural agenda of the congregation. They are a normal part of its way of life. Such a strategy must be a conscious group effort. It must transcend family ties, denominational and theological differences. It must regularly be under deliberate review.

PROBLEM 5: THE COMPROMISED CHURCH

The local church must decide which areas of community responsibility are its own and which are those of the government. The moral conduct of public agencies are its responsibility. If it is free from compromise, its criticism and help will have weight. The church must ask what "favors" it can accept and retain this freedom.

A strategy for church-state relations in the local community should be a responsible one. It should include the offer of assistance to the juvenile court, social welfare, and social work agencies. The local church needs to function as an institution with the corporate sense of responsibility it often accepted during World War II. When the church assists the community responsibility through a strategy of aid to the blind, foster-parent care, day nursery services, and a well-rounded program of recreation for youth, the community will respect its opinions.

PROBLEM 6: FEAR OF DEBATE

The final social problem area presented early in this chapter is that of a fear of discussion. The Commission on Christian Social Concerns may discover, in its survey of the situation, that this is well-founded. Many studies have shown that an unwillingness to discuss issues is caused by a lack of information on the part of the discussants.

A strategy in the local church must have as its goal a problem-solving atmosphere. Basic adult education, involving current social problems and

293

the means of studying them, is the beginning point. Folks must be taught to read comprehensively, to take notes succinctly, and to discuss with objectivity. This must precede the discussion of emotionally charged issues.

The principle to be held uppermost in this, and all strategy, is the imputation of the highest motives to others within the group. Within the Protestant tradition, freedom of speech is fundamental. The suppression of that freedom is at once a restriction of religious freedom and a denial of the importance of the human problems excluded from discussion.

An improvement of the social problems within the local parish then begins with a clear understanding of the purpose of the church. When it is seen to be a divine as well as a human institution, a self-conscious strategy is possible. The local church must begin with a frank evaluation of the obstacles to progress. Are they capable of human solution when buttressed by divine intervention? The channels of communication between men in the local church can be kept open provided they are in communication with God.

From the clear sense of purpose and commission comes an increasing awareness of need for resolving the social problems. The resources are available in the leadership of the church, their community connections, and the possession of the answers of the church. Each parish must be critically aware of its stage of evolution and its ability to change. It must see the alternative to its own present actions and prepare a strategy to which the church becomes dedicated. Provided continuing review and the establishing of new goals, there is no need for a church or its vision to die.

CHAPTER ELEVEN

Guidelines for Action

A. From Intention to Action

WE HAVE INTERPRETED METHODIST SOCIAL ACTION AS A RE-sponse to the challenge of the social situation judged in the light of the norms of Christian ethics. We have explored ways in which the strategic response is achieved through rational deliberation, loyalty to self-imposed ideals, and planned allocation of resources. We have defined strategy as the clarification of ethical norms, the appraisal of social needs, the assessment of costs and resources, and the deployment of energies to establish and accomplish social goals. This is a continuing process of analysis and decision, selection of targets, enlisting intermediate change agents and initiating action, with evaluation and reflection built into every step.

1. PREPARATION AND EDUCATION

The strategic process in the church begins with the clarification of norms and the assessment of social needs—facing the challenge. This means preparation and education, stimulation of awareness, sharing of information, recognition and definition of problems, and convergence of ideas. In this process the initiating agents gauge the readiness for action of other persons and groups. Who shares the concern? Who is motivated and at what level? How many are ready to share in preliminary decisions?

Initiators then move to the establishment of priorities: will energy and other resources be concentrated first upon those predisposed to act, or upon those uncertain of their motives and commitments, or upon those antagonistic to proposed action? An adequate strategy will have to deal with at least these groups on every level, or, in some cases, decide to ignore one element or to proceed despite its lack of readiness. At any rate, the educational program will be different in content and method according to the particular target given priority.

Goals must be distinguished from preconditions necessary for reaching the goals. "Preaching the gospel to all men" is probably a precondition rather than a goal.[1] There is a sense in which preconditions can be considered as instrumental goals or intermediate steps. Certainly preparation includes at least the following steps, phased somewhat differently according to the readiness of different target groups:

1. Exposure—attracting and holding attention
2. Understanding—securing and sharing information to correct errors, break down stereotypes, and awaken to need
3. Concern—appealing to conscience and value commitments to arouse intention and enlist motivation
4. Decision—exploring alternatives, relating proposals to other tasks, and formulating plans
5. Training of competence and providing realizable goals.

The "appeal to conscience" should arouse guilt feelings and may awaken resistance to influence. It would seem particularly appropriate in a church to help persons realize and deal with a real sense of guilt (whether from awareness of violation of moral standards or of disobedience to God) even while they are helped to overcome unrealistic guilt feelings and are supported in a fellowship of forgiveness.[2] The church has a special stake in the sharpening of the consciences of its members.

All preparation has a component of education, and all education deals, openly or covertly, with values. It is better able to deal with them frankly. Effective education enlists persons' loyalties as well as intellectual assent and has thus an emotional tinge. There is, in other words, a persuasive dimension to all education, and the educational aspect of strategy may well become a debate or a process of mutual persuasion. Such a process is most helpful if it is seen as contributing to an expanding consensus and if it is carried on within a framework of established rules, including respect for those in disagreement. Participants probably

[1] Stanley K. Bigman, "Evaluating the Effectiveness of Religious Programs," pp. 5-8.
[2] See Campbell and Pettigrew, *Christians in Racial Crisis*, pp. 4 ff.; Wogaman, *Methodism's Challenge in Race Relations*, p. 30.

learn very little when they feel they are personally attacked; somehow opponents need to feel that they are accepted even though their attitudes may not be.

Finally, although debate over some issues may and should continue, there come times when the achieved consensus needs to be given formal recognition, in policy or pronouncement of law. Since we are dealing with problems of ethics, it is well to note that many persons have opposed this kind of decisive action, arguing, "You cannot legislate morals." Kyle Haselden, dealing specifically with the problems of racial discrimination, replies that laws can restrain immoralities. "Laws are passed not to make bad people good, but to make innocent people safe." Haselden goes on to acknowledge that "legislation . . . too far in advance of the people loses itself." "If it precede public opinion, as in some cases it does and as in crucial cases it must, it must continually look back over its shoulder to see whether the people are following and whether it is still within the people's view." [3]

2. SUPPORTING SANCTIONS

Laws define rights, expectations, and obligations as well as provide procedural methods of settling disputes. Law is always an instrument of minimum rather than maximum justice. It is forever limited by public acceptance and by the quality of enforcement. In the last analysis law requires moral as well as legal authority, legitimation as well as power. Ideally there is an interacting process of raising the level of moral opinion so that a law can be passed to provide a still further tug on behavior, and then continuing education to bring about compliance with the law. Enforcement of law does not finally rest on the coercive power of the state or other law-making body, for the acceptance of coercive authority rests in turn upon a recognition of law as an instrument of right. Thus mediation, education, and conciliation are, along with force, all bound up in the law.[4] Passing laws and making pronouncements are valuable within the educational context, seeking to maintain

[3] *The Racial Problem in Christian Perspective*, pp. 111-15. Haselden concludes on p. 117 "that the hope of the Negro in America for an end to racial discrimination in our time rests primarily, not in a protracted program which woos the souls of men to good will nor in the coercive pressures which Negroes themselves may bring to bear upon the social order, but in a federal government which is increasingly disposed to establish justice."

[4] See Muelder, *Foundations of the Responsible Society*, pp. 87-100.

297

tension between practice and pronouncement rather than to reduce policy to the level of practice. The very process of seeking adoption of a policy statement by the church or of seeking change of church structure is itself an educational venture.

The quest for justice involves intrinsic rewards as well as legislative sanctions. Fellowship in a common task, action to reduce the gap between what is and what ought to be, the sense of bridging barriers of color and need—these surely should be added to Paul's list of the "fruits of the spirit" as applied to social action.[5] Goethe once wrote: "If we take people as they are, we make them worse. If we treat them as if they were what they ought to be, we help them to become what they are capable of becoming." [6] So, too, the church can never deal with its resources in terms only of a present inventory; it must take account of what it can become in faithfulness and obedience.

3. INITIATION OF DIRECT ACTION

The decision to take action is not in itself action. The integrity of an education program depends upon its issuing in action. "Education without action is sterile. Action without education is fanaticism; one of the arts of churchmanship is the lacing of the two together." [7] Formal instruction about prejudice and discrimination and about labor-management relations should issue in opportunities for youth to hold non-segregated meetings and investigate labor problems in church institutions and elsewhere.

We have examined the power structure of Methodism. Power, in church or in some other institution, rests on the implicit if not explicit consent of those affected by its exercise.[8] Power is seldom as unified and monolithic as some analysts have assumed.[9] Only as members challenge the holders of power to engage in new programs and to share their power can new leadership be developed and power be spread more responsibly through the group. Normatively, democracy in its Protestant conception

[5] Gal. 5:22.
[6] Quoted in Haselden, *The Racial Problem in Christian Perspective*, p. 137.
[7] *Contact*, I, 16 (September 15, 1959), 6.
[8] Alvin Gouldner writes: "Men in power are not merely technicians, concerned solely about the use of effective means to their ends; they are also politicians, committed to morally tinged precepts and symbols, and striving like all other men to maintain a decent self-image." "Explorations in Applied Social Science," p. 179.
[9] See, for example, James B. McKee, "Community Power and Strategies in Race Relations," *Social Problems*, VI, 3 (Winter 1958-59), 195-202.

challenges every allocation of power that is beyond the reach of persons affected by it.[10]

Some attention must be given to direct social action efforts, which have been implicit in the preceding pages. Church groups, pacifist and nonpacifist alike, have tended to shy away from coercive methods, except for violent coercion on behalf of the state in dealing with criminals or external enemies. Nonviolent resistance is itself a kind of coercion.

For many persons, perhaps to most, the word "coercion" has an ominous and odious sound; and this is especially true of those who might otherwise feel a special interest in non-violent procedure apart from coercion . . . there is a tendency to think of all coercion as necessarily involving the application of physical force. Such is not the correct interpretation.[11]

Haselden holds that "the history of human progress has been in part the story of the struggle of justice to have might as its ally; without its aid, justice has had no arm for its enforcement." [12] Is not much coercion within the church exercised through the social pressure of the threat of schism? Typically this kind of coercion is used more often by the opponents of social action than by the proponents. "Just take this action," so the argument runs, "and we will withdraw our support, or leave the church, or seek to form a new church and take over the property." Methodism lacks both the advantages and disadvantages of some authoritarian churches, in which coercion can be exercised through the threat or fact of excommunication.

The corrective spirit of early class meetings and the use of delegated groups to counsel with erring members may well have counterparts in today's church. Provision should be made for the realistic facing of issues on explicitly Christian grounds within the church. The Christian trusts in the appeal to conscience, enriched through the witness of Jesus and generations of his followers and inspired in the community of worship; in the pressure of community opinion achieved through the creative use of controversy; in the orderly rule of law both when there

[10] Harold A. Bosley, *Preaching on Controversial Issues*, p. 169.
[11] Clarence Marsh Case, *Non-Violent Coercion* (New York: The Century Company, 1923), pp. 402-3.
[12] *The Racial Problem in Christian Perspective*, p. 109. Others have noted that might exercised without an undergirding of right is ultimately self-defeating.

are threats of force and when he brings upon himself the sanctions of law as he is compelled to conscientious disobedience.

Mention should be made of one other method of direct action used especially in minority group relations, the *fait accompli*. In many programs it is assumed that changes in attitude must precede changes in patterns of behavior. When social action leaders have access to the requisite power or authority, they can establish new patterns as an accomplished fact, trusting that attitudes will adjust to the new patterns. Such action has been particularly effective when there were initial fears of desegregation which were not borne out when the desegregation process was actually experienced. The theory underlying this action would be that too much discussion can play on fears and increase rather than decrease resistance, and that in many situations the best way to alter stereotypes or other fixed attitudes is through contact or a carefully restructured situation.[13] Such a procedure must be within a framework of general consensus on goals and within a continuing educational process. It has possibilities for extension to learning and action situations other than desegregation.[14] When there is not yet general agreement on goals or on the pace of change, other types of direct action, such as vigils or sit-ins, may be called for.

4. DIRECTION AND PACE OF ACTION

The kind of action to be engaged in and the question of direction or indirection require attention to the direction and pace of changes already going on.[15] When the change is cataclysmic, there is an immediate crisis and the response must be immediate; there is no time for specific education except as this has already been incorporated in a general strategy of preparation. However, crises can be anticipated and planned for in general terms. Drift accounts for much social change and may be the most important, if not the most dramatic, form. When drift finds expression in serious changes in courtship patterns, for example, the church may well be concerned to slow down the pace of change, to redirect its movement, or to try to understand and deal with some of the

[13] See Gordon Allport, *The Nature of Prejudice* (Cambridge, Mass.: Addison-Wesley Publishing Co.), pp. 471, 510; George E. Simpson and J. Milton Yinger, *Racial and Cultural Minorities*, 2nd ed., rev. (New York: Harper & Brothers, 1958), pp. 501 ff.

[14] Wogaman, *Methodism's Challenge in Race Relations*, p. 38.

[15] See Chap. III.

causal factors—in other words, to play a conservative role in the interests of a larger strategy.

Directed change involves conscious and deliberate planning, whether by legislation concerning social security or by voluntary associations seeking extension of medical care. In a public relations-directed culture, private interests may seek to direct change by influencing drinking patterns, by keeping alive the conflict between East and West, or by securing privileges for sectarian groups. These may be oriented to economic, political, religious, or other ends, but they are typically in the interests of a part of the society rather than in the public interest. Other groups may be of a reform character, concerned with the public interest (at least as they define it) in seeking protection of civil liberties, preventing misleading advertising or adulteration of goods, or urging greater national participation in international agencies. In this field of competing forces, the church will find both allies and opponents, and it must make its judgments upon the basis of methods used as well as goals sought (as it must in its own strategy).

This study endorses the approach of R. M. MacIver, in considering direction and pace of change,[16] who distinguishes four kinds of situations in which forces are held in balance. (1) The first of these is the tense equilibrium, in which there is sharp opposition, emotional stress, and occasional violence. Outbreaks may be set off by chance or by a planned precipitant. Perhaps here all the church can do is to seek control of precipitants while it works at a gradual change of the balance of forces. (2) The precarious equilibrium is much like the first type, except that change is imminent in only one direction. The change may seem to be inevitable, but strategy can never assume either that a desirable change will come of its own momentum or that an undesirable change is impossible to prevent. (3) The indifferent equilibrium involves no clash of extremes, and action can either increase tension or reduce it. (4) The moving equilibrium is one in which changes are under way, for good or ill, the precarious balance of forces having been tilted. Strategy will vary from locale to locale and from period to period, depending upon the estimate of the balance of forces regarding a given problem. The program will be broken down into steps ranging from immediate action to long-range goals. This process enables members of the group to gain

[16] Robert M. MacIver, *The More Perfect Union*, pp. 52-61.

confidence as they make measurable progress; it also reminds them of goals yet to be achieved and provides natural opportunities for reflection on lessons learned from each step.

5. CONSOLIDATION OF CHANGE

There is always a temptation to assume that a force set in motion in the cycle of cumulative causation will continue in motion and that the change will be accomplished. Thus temperance forces relaxed their efforts following passage of the Eighteenth Amendment. And many peace-loving Methodists were tempted to do likewise as the Crusade for a New World Order was completed and the Charter of the United Nations was approved. Strategists must always deal with the problem of consolidation, of incorporating the change as a stable and permanent part of an ongoing process. The change must be worked out in the life of the institution and fitted into its various other parts of the institution. The setting up of a General Board of Christian Social Concerns calls for comparable agencies on the annual conference and local church level. The acceptance of American responsibility in international affairs requires more than a deluge of postal cards favoring the UN; there must be study, discussion, and action concerning elimination of trade barriers, opening the door to refugees, repealing the Connally Amendment (which unduly limits the treaty-making power of the President). An important way to institutionalize change is to build provision for it into the structure. If Methodism is to take seriously its responsibility for social action, and if it wishes to evaluate its effectiveness and improve its efforts, then it will need a department of research to develop criteria for evaluation and to execute studies of action projects attempted and new ones needed.

B. Evaluation and Review [17]

The persisting criticism of social action is that persons engaged in it are too frantically busy to face adequately the deep questions of faith. We dealt with social action in relation to the larger goals of the church in Chapter V, but the charge of busyness should occupy us now. Truman Douglass quotes a school administrator concerning his colleagues: "They are industriously learning the art of avoiding thought by immersion in

[17] See Chap. VII, "The Future Use of Methodist Power."

activities that do not require it." [18] Sometimes this weakness in institutional leadership is caused by the failure of the institution to provide leisure or reverie time for its executives. The executives who are close to the functioning dynamo of the institution are most insightful when the institution deliberately provides alternating periods of relaxation and peak activity. Continuing evaluation and review, both as a formal institutional process and as an informal aspect of all leadership and action, will help us face such dangers in the church.

There are several purposes of the evaluation process: (1) to test whether and how well goals are being accomplished; (2) to redefine goals, redesign means, and even to abandon some programs; (3) to discover reasons for successes and failures and so to build up a body of principles for effective strategy. All of these are set within the context of continuing worship and study in the life of the church, wherein we seek to clarify theological and ethical perspectives and relate them more meaningfully to social action. We evaluate, not to justify ourselves, but to guide us in obedience, not to rate institutions or programs but to learn how each may be more effective.[19] We should be able to learn from our failures as well as from our successes.[20] One difficult problem in evaluation of failure is discriminating between faults due to structure and organization, faults due to program, lack of skill of persons, and resistance in the area of change.[21] Confession and repentance prevent our seeing all obstacles as external and keep us open to new insights.

Evaluation may be either formal or informal. Formal procedures usually involve blocks of time set aside for a group of leaders, or a research team with developed skills and instruments, or an expert or experts who both aid in self-study and provide objective analysis. Certainly Methodism needs time in the institutional schedule for review on a systematic basis. One study of a General Board of The Methodist

---

[18] Douglass, "The Relevance of Long-Range Planning," p. 4.

[19] Hoyer, op. cit., p. 10. He notes that some of us will be disappointed not to have a meter to attach to churches to provide "progress readings" and warns against any mechanical ten-point score sheets.

[20] Abraham Lincoln wrote in a lecture on law: "I find quite as much material for a lecture in those points wherein I have failed as in those wherein I have been moderately successful." July 1, 1850. Library of Congress, Robert Todd Lincoln Collection, No. 455.

[21] Hoyer writes: "If the trouble be with the tool we can . . . improve it; and let us not be sentimental about it. . . . If the difficulty be in our lack of skill, then we must be better trained." Op. cit., p. 3.

Church [22] concludes that at the highest policy-making level there is neither time nor opportunity for serious and critical review of board policy and program. By default the evaluation becomes the function of the Commission on World Service and Finance, with efficiency of operation and other business criteria substituting for evaluation of goals and effectiveness in achieving them. This places the evaluation process back upon the boards and in some instances upon staff and precludes any reconciliation of goals and development of an inclusive strategy by a policy-making group. The same process of side-stepping policy review in favor of measurement of statistical items of membership and budget will be painfully familiar to the acute observer of the annual conference, the district conference, and the official board. It is essential that delegated bodies charged with policy decisions deal with goals and strategy as central to their agenda, not peripheral.

We have already suggested the desirability of the church providing a research office and staff, with specific assignments in the area of social action strategy, among others. Thus the church would develop its own experts and would be able to devise more sensitive criteria for measurement. But with or without research experts, there is need to train all leaders in certain specialist skills and research roles, so that study and evaluation become a continuing and informal accompaniment of all action. Methodist leaders share in the general critique Henry Kissinger provides of the policymaker:

> One of the paradoxes of an increasingly specialized, bureaucratized society is that the qualities rewarded in the rise to eminence are less and less the qualities required once eminence is reached. . . . The task of the executive is to infuse and occasionally to transcend routine with purpose.[23]

The process of selection of leaders is dealt with elsewhere in this volume. We point here to the need for so defining the role of our leaders that they have the skill and the opportunity for reflective thought and evaluation, for imaginative reconstruction of alternative proposals, for consideration of purposes that can and must infuse routine.

---

[22] See the excellent study by Joseph L. Allen, "The Methodist Board of Temperance as an Instrument of Church Policy." (Unpublished Ph.D. dissertation, Yale University Graduate School, 1957.)

[23] "The Policymaker and the Intellectual," p. 30. Kissinger adds that "Our executives are shaped by a style of life that inhibits reflectiveness."

We must deal with criteria of evaluation even though these can be refined in the process of study itself. Distinction has already been made between effectiveness and efficiency. The latter focuses upon means, the former upon the achievement of goals. Efficiency is a proper criterion only as it is judged in turn by the higher one of effectiveness. But how do we measure effectiveness? In actual practice we tend to rely on statistical devices: literature distributed,[24] literature paid for, use of staff time, calls for service, apportionment paid, and the like. No institution can fail to take account of quantitative criteria such as size in relation to potential, growth through time, turnover and continuity of membership, and so forth; but these are applicable in evaluation of social action strategy only as they indicate groups of people to whom the ministry of the church has not been extended with special relevance: to the labor movement, to the politicians, to the intellectual and power elites, as well as to the unchurched in rural and urban slums.[25] We may also seek to measure the participation of members in various social action programs within the church or in voluntary associations and the range of social issues dealt with.

More significant, and more difficult to measure, are the qualitative criteria. Is the depth of fellowship such that controversial issues can be debated and action agreed upon, with respect for both the majority and the minority? How well does the church (or board) achieve its own stated goals? In how far do members' lives and institutional practices reflect faithfulness and obedience to the purposes of the institution? Is there provision for confession of sin, for recognition of failure, for opportunity to renew resources and reformulate goals on the basis of new insights? To what extent do the various "audiences" of the institution reveal awareness of the program and goals? Is there measurable educational impact? Has legislation been secured? Has the process been democratic and means consistent with ends? Is there any discernible impact upon the audiences in attitude or practice? Is leadership in social action the exclusive prerogative of a chosen few, or is it shared,

[24] One ecumenical agency judges the success of its program in terms of denominational requests for and distribution of literature.
[25] Hoyer, op. cit., p. 5. He notes that there are one hundred counties in the United States in which four out of five people belong to no church. Relevant questions internal to the church concern income and occupational distribution of membership, ministry across barriers of class and color, positions of leadership occupied by members of minority groups.

305

with provision for the training of new leaders? Attention to such criteria does not guarantee success but quantitative criteria are helpful in dealing with the preconditions of action. Only qualitative criteria will enable us to judge in any way the extent to which our strategies serve to increase the love of God and man in the world.

C. Limits of Strategy

Strategy for social action is not in itself a panacea. Having a strategy may well have undesirable consequences. There is no intention in the preceding pages of forcing all of the rich diversity of Methodism into a single mold or of producing a social action "organization man" who conforms to a strategic blueprint. Within certain constitutional and ethical limits and within the framework of a community in which the truth is spoken in love, each Methodist is urged to express his own freedom and initiative. There is room for many different kinds of action within a wider strategy, especially for charismatic leaders who respond to immediate crises and also for those who resist strategic programs on rational grounds and grounds of principle. Conservatives are needed who can enter fully into the dialogue to prevent diagnosis and program from following their own "sociocultural drift" without correction. Again it must be noted that to be constructive the debate must be carried on within established rules, with awareness of common fellowship in a task whose bounds cannot be set by any one group, and with open facing of principles rather than discrediting of persons.

If there is need for conservatives, there is also, and probably greater, need for prophets, for men of conviction who do not court martyrdom but are willing to run the risks of becoming martyrs in working for "lost causes." We have indicated our concern that power and consequences be taken seriously, but there is also a certain recklessness and boldness in Christian social action, a willingness, having calculated consequences, to enter upon some ventures in which failure is probable. The diagnosis of strategists is always liable to rationalization or justification of cautious action in view of tremendous complexities, to being willing to settle for moderation and gradualism in every instance. The danger of the pragmatic orientation of much Methodist action is that it may miss deeper issues and fail to recognize the approaching crisis until the time for constructive action is far spent.

The strategic response requires a constant search for laymen with breadth of experience and depth of training. One board executive has indicated the rewards that have come as he has sought out laymen who possess technical competence in a given area and enlisted them in the area of the church's program in which their skills were most relevant. Many technically competent laymen may now be—or may become— theologically competent laymen as well. There is no guarantee that either technical or theological competence is undergirded with depth of religious commitment. What is called for is to provide opportunities for the interaction of theological and technical orientations within the frame of reference of Christian motivation. Laymen who are technically competent are often those who move from community to community over a period of years and who do not therefore have opportunity for selection through ordinary processes of representation. This may also be true of many persons of theological competence, who are not in strategic positions for conference elections. They may often be in detached service or in teaching. The church must set up special procedures of recruitment to bring its most sensitive members into policy-making groups.[26]

Strategists must also face the limitations of planning and the element of contingency in all human action. Man faces historical and environmental conditions not of his own choosing; he cannot operate with laboratory controls.[27] There is also what Robert K. Merton has called "The Unanticipated Consequences of Purposive Social Action." [28] Merton distinguishes the "self-fulfilling belief," in which confident error generates its own spurious confirmation; the latent or unconscious functions which an act fulfills; and the "self-destroying beliefs" which prevent fulfillment of what would otherwise happen. There are always unexpected events even though they may not be of crisis proportions. We can never predict the results of our actions with complete con-

[26] Kissinger applies something of the same danger even to experts: "And since individuals who challenge the presuppositions of the bureaucracy . . . rarely can keep their positions as advisers, great pressures are created to elaborate on familiar themes rather than risk new departures that may both fail and prove unacceptable." "The Policymaker and the Intellectual," p. 33.

[27] John C. Bennett notes the effects of past wrongs, vested interests, and accumulated disorders. Other problems of "applying" the Christian ethic include the mixed character of our communities, the impersonality of relationships, limitation of imagination because of position in society, the ability to cloak self-interest with idealism, and the dilution of personal responsibility. See *Christian Ethics and Social Policy*, pp. 15-24.

[28] *American Sociological Review*, I, 6 (December 1936), 894-904. See also his *Social Theory and Social Structure*, pp. 51, 128.

fidence. Some of these can be labeled "boomerang" effects, with the purpose of the action frustrated. Other effects are "windfalls," or pleasant surprises for which little credit can be taken (and which may not be directly in line with the objectives sought). There may also be irrelevant or incidental effects, in which opposition is aroused unintentionally.[29]

The elements of contingency argue not only for humility and flexibility, but also for providing adequately for "feedback." We have discussed three ways in which evaluative material can be fed back into the strategy considerations. One of these is provision of research procedures and for the inclusion of persons of technical competence in the process of strategy. A second device lies in corrective exposure to other viewpoints as the church becomes aware of and uses its own diversity, as it seeks to enlist other persons and groups in the change efforts, and as it works within the ecumenical movement. A third way is the recognition of the necessity of having an unofficial social action organization to speak to official boards and agencies, to the church at large, and to specific issues and groups outside the church. Unofficial bodies operate with fewer restraints than official agencies and also relieve them of some responsibility for venturing into new areas. The Fellowship of Methodist Pacifists has a limited focus; the Methodist Federation for Social Action was largely related to the Northern church and has been the object of vituperative debate.

Methodism needs a new unofficial membership body to play a decisive role that complements that of official boards in shaping the strategic response in social action. A fellowship based on voluntary membership and shared concern can embody the sectarian principle within the larger church and can acept disciplines of study and work difficult to achieve in more formal groups. It is also freer to experiment on the frontiers of action, probing beyond the borders of established policy. Such a fellowship does not detract from the responsibility of official groups but rather stimulates and enriches in terms of both leaders and insights.

The limits of strategy are best dealt with when they are recognized and when there is continuing assessment of crises, drift, and other groups seeking change. There must also be continuing review of policy and goals under the criticism of theological and ethical insights. No consensus

[29] Bigman, "Evaluating the Effectiveness of Religious Programs," pp. 11-12.

should ever be taken as final, for the consensus achieved must be extended to include new members and must be revised as members appeal beyond it. Methodist strategy proceeds from the achieved consensus and seeks to extend agreement and enlist action. But as J. H. Oldham wrote in one of the Oxford Conference volumes, "A consensus . . . cannot be genuinely prophetic. Prophets now as in the past are not banded together in commissions or committees." [30] True as this may be, the bureaucratic structure of Methodism can make a place for its prophets to be heard and its charismatic leaders to be followed. The reminder of the unexpected in the prophetic voice is also a reminder of another dimension of all Christian strategy, that noted by Thomas Kelly: "I am persuaded that religious people do not with sufficient seriousness count on God as an active factor in the affairs of the world." [31] This is a call not to quietism, but to awareness that "We are fellow workmen for God" (I Cor. 3:9, R.S.V.). This is the ultimate perspective within which we confront the challenge of social action and on the basis of which we seek to shape, in faithfulness and wisdom, our strategic response.

[30] *The Church and Its Function in Society*, p. xii.
[31] *Testament of Devotion* (New York: Harper & Brothers, 1941), p. 97.

Appendix A

Social Characteristics of Methodism, 1959

Sources of Information. TWO TYPES OF SOURCES HAVE BEEN utilized in an analysis of the social characteristics of Methodism. First, there has been a utilization of Methodist resource materials, both from official publications of the church and also from supplementary research studies. Official publications include: *The Methodist Fact Book, 1957,* the most recent issue at the time the study was made; and *The General Minutes of the Methodist Church, 1958.* An additional resource book used was *The Emerging Patterns in Town and Country Methodism, 1959.* Especially helpful have been the MESTA Inquiry on "The Beliefs of Methodists" [1] and the tabulated summaries from the project studies of *Church Surveys* of Boston University School of Theology. The MESTA Inquiry has been based on a representative sample of 5,020 Methodists. The *Church Surveys* studies have provided cumulative data and tabulated summaries from individual survey cards filled out for more than 600,000 Methodists within the past three years.

The second type of reference, the basis for comparison, has been summary data concerning the total U. S. population. The official reference for this has been *The Statistical Abstract, 1958.* Considerable use has been made of the monthly Current Population reports—Series P-20, No. 77, U. S. Bureau of the Census, Department of Commerce.

Sociological Definition of a Methodist. The point of reference will be the Methodist "parishioner" rather than "member" in order to have comparable data. Full members[2] of The Methodist Church would include only persons approximately twelve years of age and over, for the most part. Most U. S. Census data include reference to persons of all ages. A study based on Methodist parishioners rather than members obviates the difficulty.

A parishioner is defined as any person who is a part of the household

[1] See Appendix B.
[2] All persons responding to the MESTA Inquiry were members.

of a member family. A member family is a family which has at least one adult member of the church as a part of its household. Parishioners then would include not only all full members of the church in such a family, but also all unbaptized children, all children who have been baptized and who are preparatory members of The Methodist Church if they have been baptized as Methodists, and also any other person in a member household. The members of non-Methodist churches in such a household would be offset statistically by Methodist constituents who have not yet joined the church, and who are part of non-member households.

Median age of Methodists. The median age of Methodists is approximately 34.5 years, based on cumulative survey reports, with one-half the parishioners above this age and one-half below. A median age of 34.5 years is 15 per cent higher than the total U. S. population which had a median age of 30.2 years in 1950. The median age varies from state to state, with a low of 24 years for New Mexico and a high of 33.7 years for New York State. The median rural farm population age is 26.3 years. The median age has been increasing steadily in the nation from 22.9 years in 1900 to a high of 30.3 years as reported in Current Population Survey reports, 1956, U. S. Bureau of the Census.[3]

Sex Ratio. Eleven out of twenty Methodists are females. There are more females than males in the U. S. population at the present time, according to U. S. Census estimates, but the proportion of females is higher in The Methodist Church than in the total population. There are only 90 males per 100 females in The Methodist Church, as compared to 99.2 males per 100 females in the U. S. population as reported in the 1950 census. The ratio of males per 100 females has been gradually lowering since 1910, at which time there were 106 males per 100 females in the U. S. population. The decline in ratio of males has been attributed to various causes including wars, the employment of men in hazardous industries, and the general improvement in health and longevity for women.

Marital Status. Eight out of ten Methodists 25 years of age and over are married, according to an adjusted report of the MESTA Inquiry, approximately the same ratio as to be found in the total U. S. population. A total of 80.1 per cent of the Methodists 25 years of age and over are married as compared to 78.3 per cent in the total population.

One in ten Methodists is single, approximately the same ratio as found in the total U. S. population among persons 25 years of age and over. Only one Methodist in one hundred is divorced as compared to more than two per one hundred reported in the total population. However, in view of the opinion of census takers that a large number of divorced persons re-

[3] The median age was 29.5 in 1960.

ported themselves to be "single," there is a possibility that the divorce rate for Methodists is comparatively lower than the given figures would indicate. A greater degree of honesty would be expected for parishioners than for persons not affiliated with a church. Nine Methodists out of one hundred are widows or widowers among those 25 years of age and over.

Family Size. The average size of the Methodist family is 3.6 persons, identical with the U. S. average reported in the 1950 Census. The size of the Methodist family was obtained from the MESTA Inquiry, and compares favorably with the cumulative project studies of *Church Surveys, Boston University.*

The average size of the Methodist household, however, is only 3.1 as obtained from the cumulative reports of *Church Surveys* to date, compared to the average household size of 3.34 as reported in the Bureau of the Census estimate of March 1957. In The Methodist Church a large number of widows, widowers, and single persons have their own household. Many of these are elderly persons, as reflected in the higher median age for Methodists than for non-Methodists.

There is some evidence that Methodists may have a higher longevity record than the total U. S. population, due to a correlation of higher median age with an average family size. The percentage of Methodists 75 years of age and over is 40 per cent higher than the percentage of the total U. S. population in the age grouping, according to cumulative reports from the *Church Surveys* studies.

Education. The average Methodist replying has graduated from high school and has completed one semester of work in college. The median of educational attainment for Methodists is 12.4 years of schooling beyond kindergarten, with one-half of the Methodists having less education, and one-half more. This is somewhat higher than the median educational attainment of 10.8 years for the total population 25 years of age and over, from various reports of the U. S. Bureau of the Census studies as of March 1957. The educational attainment of Methodists has been obtained from the MESTA Inquiry.

The chance of a son or daughter graduating from college is at least three times as high if he or she comes from a Methodist family. More than one-third of the Methodists 25 years of age and over have graduated from college. As a denomination, Methodists have the highest percentage of students in the State Colleges and Universities of the U. S. in addition to having the largest number of church-related colleges and universities of all the Protestant groups.

Family Income. Methodists have a median family income of $5,329 per year, according to the MESTA studies, with one-half of the families receiving more income and one-half of the families receiving less. This is higher than the median family income of $4,687 for the U. S. total population of males aged 35-54 as reported in Current Population Reports, March 1957, U. S. Bureau of the Census.

This is especially significant in view of the large rural farm population in The Methodist Church. In a bulletin published June 1958, the Census Bureau reported the median money income of urban and rural nonfarm families in the United States to be $5,232 for the preceding year, as compared with the median money income of rural farm families at $2,490 for the preceding year.

Size of Community. Three out of four Methodist congregations are located in communities of less than 2,500 population, according to studies published in *The Emerging Patterns in Town and Country Methodism, 1959.* Six out of ten Methodists live in the "town and country," or rural areas of the United States, according to the definition of such areas as places of less than 10,000 population, as defined in the *1956 Discipline of The Methodist Church.* Approximately 33.3 per cent more Methodists live in rural areas than the proportion of the general U. S. population.

More Methodists were reared in small communities than live in them at the present time, according to the MESTA Inquiry. A total of 51.2 per cent more Methodists were reared in communities of less than 2,500 than live in them at the present time. And conversely there are more Methodists living in large cities than were reared in them. There are 66.7 per cent more Methodists living in cities of 10,000 to 99,999 than were reared in them. There are 23.8 per cent more Methodists living in cities of 100,000 and over than were reared in them.

Size of Church. One out of every five Methodists is affiliated with a church of less than 250 members. Nearly one-half of the Methodists are in churches of less than 500 members.

Twice as many Methodists were reared in small churches as are affiliated with the smaller churches at the present time. According to the MESTA Inquiry slightly over one-half of the Methodists were reared in churches of less than 250 members. And conversely the percentage of Methodists who are now affiliated with larger churches is much higher than the percentage reared in them. A total of 76 per cent more Methodists are now in churches of 1,000 or more members than were reared in them.

Denominational Background. Two out of three Methodists were reared in The Methodist Church. Of those reared in other churches, two-thirds came from one or another of these backgrounds: Presbyterian, Congregational, Baptist, Lutheran, or Episcopal. Less than two per cent of all Methodists were reared in a Roman Catholic background. Less than one out of ten Methodists was reared in any background other than those which have been named.

Length of Membership. One out of four Methodists has been affiliated with the church twelve years or less. The percentage of newcomers in The Methodist Church is low, however. A total of 14.5 per cent have been members of the church six years or less. From length of residence studies it has been estimated that a church needs to have 17.5 per cent of its membership composed of newcomers who have lived in the community six years or less, or who have been members of the church six years or less. The median goal of 17.5 per cent has been set for a normal church to keep pace with population growth. The Methodist Church is not keeping pace with total U. S. population growth.

Evangelistic Ratio. During the year 1958 one new member for every twenty-six members was added to the church on profession of faith. The evangelistic ratio is the number of full members of the church required to win one person to Christ and to membership in the church on profession of faith. The Board of Evangelism has estimated that one person should be received on profession of faith for every fourteen members. As a result of hardly more than 50 per cent efficiency in attaining the evangelistic ratio goal, The Methodist Church is growing slightly over half as fast as the total U. S. population. From 1950 to 1958 The Methodist Church has increased in membership from a total of 8,935,647 members in 1950 to a total of 9,691,916 members in 1958, a net gain of 756,269, or 8.5 per cent. From 1950 to 1958 the U. S. population has increased from a total of 150,697,361 persons in 1950 to an estimated total of 174,060,000 on July 1, 1958, according to Robert W. Burgess, Director, Bureau of the Census, Department of Commerce. This represents a gain of 23,362,639, or 15.5 per cent.

Correlation studies on the family size of Methodists and the net gain in membership would indicate that the church is not retaining its own constituency, and is not retaining its share of the total population. Most of the net losses are due to Methodists on the move, whose church membership has not moved to the new places of residence. One out of five Americans aged one year and over changes his place of residence each year, according to the results of a sample survey conducted by the Bureau of the Census from April 1956 to April 1957. The average American would be moving once every five years.

Church School. For every hundred members of The Methodist Church, there are seventy-four members of a Methodist Church School. Approximately one out of five members of a Methodist Church School is not a parishioner of the church, and is not affiliated with the church in any

315

other way than through a relationship to the church school. They are not in church member families or households.

Methodist Church Schools are becoming expanding frontiers of evangelistic opportunity. Some are located in areas not now served by a Methodist Church. Some church schools, formerly closed, have been reopened. From 1956 to 1958 Methodist Church Schools have increased from 37,923 to 38,350, a net gain of 427. During the same period of time Methodist Churches, or "preaching places," have decreased from 39,845 to 39,317, a net loss of 528.

Race. Less than one out of twenty members of The Methodist Church is nonwhite, but more than one out of ten persons in the total U. S. population is nonwhite. The Bureau of the Census reported a total of 11.5 per cent of the U. S. population as nonwhite in 1950. One out of twenty-five Methodists (3.9 per cent of the total) is a member of the Central Jurisdiction which consists almost entirely of Negroes. An estimated .7 per cent of the members of the other Jurisdictions are American Indian, Japanese, Chinese, or Negro, mostly the last.

Nearly one fourth of the members of all Methodist bodies are Negroes, however, and are members of the following four more or less segregated groups: African Methodist Episcopal Church, African Methodist Episcopal Zion Church, the Christian Methodist Episcopal Church, and the Central Jurisdiction of The Methodist Church.

More than four out of ten Negroes will be living outside the South in 1960, according to estimate reported in The Methodist Fact Book, 1957. The evangelistic ratio of the Central Jurisdiction is low at the present time. There has been an assimilation of six congregations over scattered areas from the Conferences of the Central Jurisdiction to the Conferences in various other Jurisdictions of The Methodist Church. In 1958 one person was received on profession of faith for every thirty-one members of the Central Jurisdiction. For the most part, Negroes are not being reached efficiently by the Central Jurisdiction.

Occupation. The occupational profile of Methodists shows a preponderance of professional men and women and managers, as compared to the total U. S. population, 1958 estimate from the Bureau of the Census. Conversely, the proportion of operatives, service workers, and laborers is very low compared to the total population.

Generally speaking, Methodists have a much higher percentage of persons in the professional, managerial, and so-called "white collar" occupations in urban life. Methodists have about the same percentage in the so-called "blue collar" occupations, meaning primarily the craftsmen.

The percentage of professional men and women in The Methodist Church is over three times as high as the percentage of professional men and women in the total population. This is correlated with the fact that the percentage of college graduates in The Methodist Church is three times as high as the percentage of college graduates in the total population.

The percentage of farm operators and various types of managers is approximately 6 per cent higher than the percentage of managers and farm operators in the total population.

The percentage of sales workers in The Methodist Church is less than one per cent higher than the percentage of sales workers in the total population.

The percentage of clerical workers in The Methodist Church is approximately 2 per cent higher than the percentage of sales workers in the total U. S. population.

The percentage of craftsmen in The Methodist Church is approximately 3 per cent lower than the percentage of craftsmen in the total population.

The percentage of operatives in The Methodist Church is 12.6 per cent lower than the percentage of operatives in the total U. S. population.

The percentage of service workers and laborers is 14.3 per cent lower than the percentage of service workers and laborers in the total U. S. population.

The percentage of private household workers in The Methodist Church is 2.9 per cent lower than the percentage of private household workers and domestic service employees in the total U. S. population.

Summary. In general it can be said that Methodists have characteristics similar to the total population in respect to family size. The median age is slightly higher than for the total population. The sex ratio of males per 100 females is slightly lower for Methodists than for the total population.

Characteristics which pertain to attainment find the Methodists far ahead. Methodism, then, reflects socially the configuration of the total population of the United States. In family stability, educational attainment, longevity, and occupational status, Methodism is exceptional. Its families stay together, its members are well educated and long-lived. In all other ways studied, the Methodists of the various census regions are truly representative of the general populace.

The Methodist Church is of service to persons in all occupational groupings, though not wholly adequate in serving the manually employed. There is sparse evidence that other denominations have been more effective here, but there is little comfort in this.

Perhaps the most dramatic social trend noted here is the migration of

Methodists from rural to urban areas. The sample clearly evidenced the earlier rural training of members who are now urban residents. The large number of urban Methodists in the next generation will constitute a major challenge.[4]

---

[4] This survey reveals the paucity of presently available information about the social characteristics of Methodists. Thus, for example, there are no data in Conference Journals which are comparable with Federal Census data classifications. Similarly, the Conference Minutes fail to indicate the physical location of Methodist properties, churches, and so forth. If such geographical (township, county, etc.) identification could be obtained, it would be possible to establish far more profitable correlations between census data and Methodist data.

318

Appendix B

An Inquiry on the Beliefs of Methodists

IN THIS VOLUME REFERENCES ARE REPEATEDLY MADE TO THE IN-quiry on "The Beliefs of Methodists." The committee realized at an early stage that its documentary research needed to be supplemented with an investigation of the actual religious beliefs and social attitudes to be found in American Methodism today.

The following account briefly explains the structure and form of the questionnaire, reproduces the questionnaire itself with the responses received in percentages by jurisdiction, and discusses the methodology of the inquiry and the representativeness of the responses.[1]

Structure and Form of Questionnaire

The questionnaire consists of four parts, covering respectively religious beliefs (questions 1-25), ethical and social beliefs (26-44), social action (45-58), and social background (59-78). Questions 1-20 and 26-44 offer a choice among four or five statements ranged on a continuum between poles. However, in the questionnaire as distributed the actual continuum was concealed by sequential rotation in order to avoid stereotyping of answers. Thus in question 1 the first statement represented position 1; in question 2 the first statement represented position 2, followed by positions 3, 4, 5, and 1; in question 3 the first statement represented position 3, followed by 4, 1, and 2; in question 4 the first statement represented position 4, followed by 1, 2, and 3; and in question 5 the order returned to that in question 1. This pattern continued throughout the questions listed. In answering questions 1-20 and 26-44 the respondent was asked to check under each heading the one statement which seemed to him to correspond most closely to his own belief, expressing better than any other what he regarded as centrally important. If he found no statement satisfactory, he was invited to write his own in the space provided.

---

[1] A comprehensive account of this inquiry and its results will be published separately in a technical monograph.

In Part I on religious beliefs, questions 1-10 represent more or less a common continuum ranging broadly from orthodoxy or conservatism to humanism. Position 1 reflects belief, for example, in the absolute power, sovereignty, and grace of God and the sinfulness and helplessness of man, while the other extreme stresses the freedom, ability, and potential goodness of man and, consequently, the central importance of human effort and achievement. The one pole is God-centered, the other man-centered; the one relies on the supernatural, the other on the natural.

Questions 11 and 12 deal with two historic Methodist emphases, the witness of the Spirit and sanctification or perfection. Question 11 therefore reflects the degree of certainty believed possible in religious experience; question 12, the degree to which holiness of life is regarded as normative for individuals and society.

Questions 13-20 attempt in various ways to relate theology and life. They have in common the fact that each indicates the degree to which the individual responding regards a particular reality, concern, belief, or action as relevant to his Christian responsibility or that of the church. Each of these questions has its own continuum from relevance to irrelevance, but they are too diverse in subject matter to scale meaningfully.

In Part II on ethical and social beliefs (26-44) each question presents a range of possibilities more or less evenly spaced between poles or a spectrum of the views most commonly held. The subjects are so diverse that no unified scaling is possible.

The last five questions (21-25) of Part I deal with the extent of the guidance which Christians receive from their religious beliefs with respect to certain social problems. Four possibilities are offered on a Likert scale, ranging from direct guidance to no guidance. Part III on social action (questions 45-58) seeks information on the nature and extent of expressions of social responsibility and sources of guidance and leadership in areas of social concern. Likert scaling is used here also, with choice of four positions ranging from "Regularly" to "Never" or "Much" to "None."

Part IV (questions 59-78) provides for a variety of information about the social background of the respondents, including such items as age, sex, education, occupation, income, size of church and community, church activities and contributions, and the like.

Questionnaire With Responses

The Board of Social and Economic Relations of The Methodist Church has asked the faculty of the Boston University School of Theology to make a comprehensive study of The Methodist Church in Social Thought and Action. The significance of such an enquiry at the present time is evident. Methodism has all through its history been noted for its intense social concern. Along with other Christian communions, The Methodist Church today faces the imperative task of rethinking and vitalizing its witness in a rapidly changing culture. It needs to ponder the lessons of its own heritage, to redefine its social motivations and ideals, to assess its present activities and resources, and to evolve creative strategies adequate for new advance in an increasingly complex society.

Your co-operation in completing this questionnaire and returning it to your pastor in a sealed envelope will aid Methodism in knowing for the first time the thinking of its total constituency on basic issues.

Under each of the following headings, please check the one (only one) statement which seems to you to correspond most closely to your own belief. By checking one statement you mean that it expresses better than any other what you regard as centrally important.

If no statement is satisfactory, write your own in the space provided.

* This and the following pages represent a reproduction of the MR-2 questionnaire, with the results given in percentage form.

I. RELIGIOUS BELIEFS

1. The Bible

	Total	C	NC	NE	SC	SE	W
Every word is true because it came directly from God	8.4	7.5	8.2	7.8	10.6	9.7	5.7
The Bible is the inspired Word of God, but not all parts are of equal spiritual value	32.0	33.4	30.7	30.0	33.6	36.0	30.8
As the unique historical record of God's revelation to inspired men, the Bible contains the word of God	49.7	48.4	51.7	51.2	48.7	45.3	49.2
The Bible is one of several records of man's religious search	7.0	7.6	6.7	8.2	4.9	5.1	11.9
Write-in	2.2	3.1	2.0	2.1	1.2	3.2	2.0
No report	.7	.0	.7	.7	1.0	.7	.4

2. God Is

	Total	C	NC	NE	SC	SE	W
the awesome being, wholly other than man and the world, whom we encounter only in Jesus Christ	10.0	4.5	10.7	10.9	10.8	7.7	9.7
the omnipotent Lord who exists eternally in three persons and whose righteous will rules his whole creation	60.1	62.1	61.3	57.1	62.5	64.0	50.9
the supremely personal Spirit who works in nature and history to realize his purposes	11.4	13.6	11.1	12.1	9.6	12.0	12.7
the creative, perfecting power in nature and history which supports and makes possible the realization of values	11.3	10.6	10.2	12.6	10.8	8.4	18.0
the name given to our highest human aspirations	3.0	6.2	3.3	3.2	2.5	2.3	3.5
Write-in	2.6	1.5	1.9	2.4	2.7	3.9	2.8
No report	1.6	1.5	1.5	1.7	1.1	1.7	2.4

3. Man Is

a creature of God who in sinful pride has rejected his Creator and deified himself	3.9	7.6	3.4	3.9	3.8	4.7	3.4
a being who has blurred and distorted the divine image in which God has created him	4.0	6.0	4.0	3.8	3.4	5.6	2.6
a rational being capable of knowing God and entering into fellowship with Him	78.2	81.8	79.3	75.4	81.5	77.3	77.0
a product of nature whose innate powers for achieving goodness, truth, and beauty are almost unlimited	10.5	3.0	10.3	12.9	8.1	8.1	14.6
Write-in	2.0	.0	1.6	2.3	1.3	3.4	2.0
No report	1.4	1.6	1.4	1.7	1.9	.9	.4

4. Sin Is

a corruption of man's nature inherited from Adam, and rebellious acts resulting from this condition	17.1	28.8	15.7	17.5	14.4	24.6	9.5
a condition of self-centeredness and pride which distorts the wills of men and affects even their best choices	21.5	25.7	20.0	18.3	21.3	26.4	24.5
voluntary attitudes and actions, partially due to our involvement in society, which are contrary to God's will	50.8	33.4	54.2	52.7	52.6	39.0	55.5
antisocial conduct caused by ignorance or bad environment	5.0	4.5	5.4	6.4	4.8	2.5	5.3
Write-in	2.8	3.0	2.2	2.4	3.2	4.1	3.0
No report	2.8	4.6	2.5	2.7	3.7	3.4	2.2

I. RELIGIOUS BELIEFS

Total Percentage

5. Salvation Means

		C	NC	NE	SC	SE	W
going to heaven and escaping hell	2.1	1.0	2.8	1.2	1.4	2.6	1.1
peace and joy with God through His forgiveness of our sins.	41.4	28.7	44.9	43.2	40.2	36.2	38.2
power to live a new life in fellowship with God and man ..	50.0	65.2	46.9	49.2	51.6	53.3	52.9
the integration and highest fulfillment of the self in harmonious social relations	2.3	1.5	2.0	2.4	2.0	2.1	3.8
Write-in	2.7	.0	1.7	2.2	3.5	4.6	3.0
No report	1.5	4.6	1.7	1.8	1.3	1.2	1.0

6. Jesus Christ Is

		C	NC	NE	SC	SE	W
God Himself, not subject to human limitations	13.7	10.6	14.4	11.9	13.6	13.3	12.4
both divine and human	37.5	53.0	34.3	36.4	35.7	47.3	29.8
a man uniquely endowed and called by God to reveal Him to man	36.4	22.7	38.7	37.2	39.6	26.6	43.3
one of the world's great spiritual teachers	6.6	4.6	7.6	8.5	5.4	5.5	9.3
Write-in	3.9	6.0	3.1	3.6	3.6	5.2	4.2
No report	1.8	3.1	1.9	2.4	2.1	2.1	1.0

7. The Christian Church Is

the custodian of the authority and grace committed by God to the apostles and their successors	6.3	6.1	6.9	7.0	6.3	4.3	6.5
the faithful congregation in which the pure Word of God is preached and the sacraments rightly administered	23.7	21.3	24.9	27.8	22.0	21.0	18.0
the community of those who have been renewed through Jesus Christ and empowered by the Holy Spirit	34.6	56.0	31.2	30.0	36.2	47.1	29.0
a society of those who have joined together in their quest for the religious life	30.4	10.6	32.5	30.7	28.6	22.3	41.5
Write-in	2.5	3.0	2.2	1.7	3.3	3.7	2.8
No report	2.5	3.0	2.3	2.8	3.6	1.6	2.2

8. Men Are Saved

entirely by divine grace	3.9	4.6	4.4	3.7	4.2	3.3	3.0
by believing that Jesus Christ is the Son of God	10.6	7.5	9.0	9.6	9.6	16.4	9.8
by divine grace when they respond in repentance and trustful obedience	54.3	66.7	55.5	50.4	55.0	55.6	52.4
by belief in Jesus Christ and upright living	24.6	15.1	25.0	28.8	25.0	18.2	26.8
by their upright character	1.5	1.5	1.5	1.9	.5	.8	3.2
Write-in	3.4	3.0	2.6	3.9	4.4	4.4	3.4
No report	1.7	1.6	2.0	1.7	1.3	1.3	1.4

I. RELIGIOUS BELIEFS

	Total					
			Percentage			
	C	NC	NE	SC	SE	W

9. The Chief Aim of Missions Should Be

	Total	C	NC	NE	SC	SE	W
to save those who know not Christ, and who will be lost unless he is made known to them	19.9	21.2	21.1	19.2	21.3	21.2	12.3
to bring individuals to accept and live by the good news of the redemptive love of God revealed in Jesus Christ	42.9	37.9	44.2	43.7	44.5	38.9	43.0
to release in both individuals and society the redemptive power of God disclosed in Jesus Christ, so that all human life may be made whole	23.3	31.8	21.6	19.7	22.2	30.9	23.3
to improve the well-being of people by giving them new and improved methods of agriculture, industry, education, and health	8.5	1.5	8.5	11.5	7.1	3.6	14.2
Write-in	3.4	3.0	3.1	2.8	3.1	3.2	5.6
No report	2.0	4.6	1.5	3.1	1.8	2.2	1.6

10. The Kingdom of God Is

	Total	C	NC	NE	SC	SE	W
the supernatural reign of God to be established wholly by divine action	12.7	12.1	13.8	12.7	10.0	11.8	14.2
the righteous rule of God which depends mainly on God's initiative, but requires man's co-operation	26.4	30.4	25.7	21.4	25.0	35.3	24.2
the fulfillment of God's purposes which depends mainly on the efforts of men aided by God	52.8	39.3	53.6	56.7	57.2	43.8	54.1
a name for the ideal social order to be built wholly by human wisdom and effort	1.8	7.5	1.6	2.1	1.2	1.4	2.5
Write-in	2.4	4.6	2.1	2.6	2.8	3.1	1.8
No report	3.9	6.1	3.2	4.5	3.8	4.6	3.2

11. Religious Experience

We cannot be sure whether our sins are forgiven; God alone knows	3.9	.0	4.8	4.6	3.7	1.4	4.7
By the inner witness of the Spirit, every Christian can have a sure trust that through the sacrificial love of Christ his sins are forgiven and he is reconciled to God	46.1	53.0	43.6	45.1	48.3	53.4	39.7
Christians may personally experience the presence and power of God in their lives	41.5	31.8	43.1	41.9	40.7	38.0	44.1
God revealed himself vividly to great souls in the past, but does so only infrequently to men today	.4	1.5	.5	.0	.2	.2	.6
We experience religion whenever we co-operate with our fellows in high ethical endeavors	4.0	6.1	4.2	4.4	2.8	2.6	6.9
Write-in	2.5	3.0	1.9	1.9	3.5	3.1	3.2
No report	1.6	4.6	1.9	2.1	.8	1.3	.8

12. Growth in Grace

Life is so complex and sin so powerful that advance in human righteousness cannot be expected in this life	1.0	3.0	.9	.8	1.9	.7	1.4
Only Christians who receive a second work of grace can live without sin	1.9	3.0	1.9	2.4	1.0	3.0	.3
Christians should expect through the power of God to attain perfect love in this life	11.3	13.6	9.3	10.1	10.7	18.8	7.0
With God's help both individuals and society may progress toward the fulfillment of his purposes	81.9	69.8	84.4	81.9	82.3	73.7	89.1
Write-in	1.6	3.0	1.2	1.8	1.7	1.7	1.4
No report	2.3	7.6	2.3	3.0	2.4	2.1	.8

I. RELIGIOUS BELIEFS

	Total Percentage	C	NC	NE	SC	SE	W
13. Belief and Conduct							
What one believes is all-important, because it determines conduct	43.3	40.9	44.6	38.7	46.3	44.7	41.3
Our actions are affected by our basic beliefs more than by anything else	37.2	39.4	37.9	36.0	34.5	36.2	42.2
Though some beliefs are essential, right conduct is much more important than correct beliefs	7.2	3.0	6.3	8.2	7.2	8.5	7.6
It doesn't matter what one believes—it's how he lives that counts	8.0	9.1	7.4	11.9	7.6	6.2	5.5
Write-in	1.7	3.0	1.4	1.8	1.7	2.0	1.2
No report	2.6	4.6	2.4	3.4	2.7	2.4	2.2
14. A Christian Should Live a Good Life Mainly Because							
it will win an eternal reward, and failure to do so will bring everlasting punishment	11.1	9.1	11.1	12.1	11.5	12.8	6.9
it is the will of God	36.6	28.7	37.7	34.9	37.4	38.7	32.6
all Christians should follow the example of Jesus	31.4	42.5	31.7	32.2	33.1	25.0	36.1
it works better than any other way, bringing more satisfactory results	14.9	12.1	14.7	15.7	12.5	14.1	18.4
Write-in	4.2	1.5	3.4	2.9	3.7	7.2	4.8
No report	1.8	6.1	1.4	2.2	1.8	2.2	1.2

15. The Ethical Teachings of Jesus

were suitable for a time in the first century for those expecting the end of the world, but have limited application to us	.5	1.5	.4	.6	.3	.8	.6
set up general goals for Christians, but cannot be achieved in this world	1.3	.0	.6	3.1	1.2	1.3	.6
provide basic principles which are just as valid now as when first uttered	80.4	81.8	80.3	78.4	80.0	81.9	82.6
are the most practical basis for human conduct	14.6	10.6	15.8	14.7	14.2	12.8	13.8
Write-in	1.1	1.5	.9	.7	1.9	1.6	.8
No report	2.1	4.6	2.0	2.5	2.4	1.6	1.6

16. Laymen Are

those who are ministered to by the clergy who are the true church	4.9	1.5	4.9	7.8	4.1	4.1	9.1
people in part-time Christian service	5.2	1.6	5.3	6.0	5.5	4.2	5.0
nonordained Christians whose function is to help the clergy do the work of the church	60.4	57.6	63.3	59.7	61.7	53.7	56.3
members of the people of God called to a total ministry of witness and service in the world	24.9	33.3	22.5	21.4	23.3	32.6	26.2
Write-in	2.5	3.0	2.0	2.6	3.0	3.8	1.2
No report	2.1	3.0	2.0	2.5	2.4	1.6	2.2

329

I. RELIGIOUS BELIEFS

	Total Percentage	C	NC	NE	SC	SE	W
17. Social Change							
is no responsibility of the church, since if individuals are soundly converted social problems will take care of themselves	7.6	15.1	7.2	6.0	7.9	9.7	10.8
is a partial responsibility of the church, but secondary to the transformation of individuals	40.5	16.7	39.7	38.2	40.5	46.4	36.4
is of equal importance with individual transformation	25.5	30.3	25.7	26.8	22.2	22.4	27.8
is even more important than individual conversion, since social conditions greatly affect individuals	9.0	7.5	10.1	9.9	9.6	6.0	11.7
is the all-important task of the church	11.7	22.8	11.9	12.2	13.0	9.5	9.1
Write-in	1.5	3.0	1.4	2.8	3.5	2.2	1.6
No report	4.2	4.6	4.0	4.1	3.3	3.8	2.6
18. A More Christian Society Will Come Mainly Through							
the conversion of individuals to Jesus Christ	44.1	39.4	44.5	41.9	47.9	53.0	34.0
the efforts of individual Christians for social betterment	23.1	16.6	22.4	22.3	22.4	19.9	29.6
the leadership of organized churches in advocating measures for social betterment	18.2	27.3	18.7	18.8	17.5	15.3	20.0
the co-operative efforts of socially minded persons and organizations in securing legislation to advance human welfare	8.8	12.1	9.6	11.4	4.6	4.6	11.2
Write-in	3.0	1.5	2.3	2.8	3.2	4.1	3.0
No report	2.8	3.1	2.5	2.8	4.4	3.1	2.2

19. Life After Death

Concern with life after death cuts the nerve of social responsibility	.9	1.5	1.2	.7	1.3	.6	.6
Concern with life after death weakens one's sense of social responsibility	2.0	6.1	1.5	2.1	1.4	2.9	2.6
Belief in life after death enhances one's sense of social responsibility	47.4	48.4	47.0	43.4	50.3	49.2	49.8
Belief in life after death is one of the strongest motivations for social responsibility	38.7	36.4	40.4	41.6	36.3	35.7	34.9
Write-in	3.8	1.5	3.5	4.0	4.4	4.3	3.4
No report	7.2	6.1	6.4	8.2	6.3	7.3	8.7

20. Human Rights Should Be Safeguarded Because

man is ultimately responsible to God alone, and must be free to fulfill his responsibility	27.0	12.1	28.3	27.1	27.9	25.8	25.5
people should have unlimited opportunity to develop their capacities as children of God	42.3	51.5	43.3	41.1	43.1	40.1	42.9
man by nature is a being of inherent dignity and worth	14.3	19.7	12.8	13.8	11.3	19.4	14.2
their recognition will lead to a happier society	11.3	12.1	11.7	12.9	10.8	8.0	12.8
Write-in	1.4	1.5	.8	1.1	1.5	3.2	1.4
No report	3.7	3.1	3.1	4.0	5.4	3.5	3.2

I, AS A CHRISTIAN, GET GUIDANCE FROM MY RELIGIOUS BELIEFS AS FOLLOWS:

	DIRECT GUIDANCE FOR MY OWN CONDUCT.	NO DIRECT GUIDANCE, BUT FIND MORAL PRINCIPLES TO GUIDE MY CONDUCT AND SOCIAL POLICY.	INDIRECT GUIDANCE FOR MY CONDUCT AND SOCIAL POLICY.	NO GUIDANCE BUT MAKE DECISIONS ON BASIS OF TASTE AND PRACTICALITY.	NR
21. Whether to drink intoxicants	42.9	36.3	6.3	4.9	9.6
22. What to do about segregation.	33.5	38.7	8.1	6.9	12.8
23. Whether to give economic and technical aid to other countries.	24.4	36.7	12.2	12.3	14.4
24. What the regulation of marriage and divorce should be.	42.2	33.7	7.0	4.1	13.0
25. Whether to participate in war.	28.4	37.4	10.2	9.0	15.0

II. ETHICAL AND SOCIAL BELIEFS

	Total Percentage						
		C	NC	NE	SC	SE	W
26. Temperance: I, As a Christian,							
may drink without reference to religious scruples	1.2	.0	.9	1.3	2.3	.8	1.1
may drink at social gatherings to avoid offending my host	1.0	1.5	4.6	1.0	.6	1.3	1.0
may use alcoholic beverages as long as I do so temperately and within reason	26.5	15.1	31.4	35.0	18.7	17.8	32.4
should totally abstain from alcoholic beverages	56.8	65.2	49.5	49.9	61.1	64.2	51.8
should work for prohibition	8.8	10.6	8.8	7.7	10.4	9.8	7.9
Write-in	3.9	3.0	3.4	2.9	5.6	4.6	4.2
No report	1.8	4.6	1.4	2.2	1.3	1.5	1.6
27. War: I, As a Christian Citizen,							
am obligated to support my country in war when its continued existence is at stake, apart from considerations of justice	47.2	50.0	47.7	51.3	48.1	40.7	47.2
can support or participate in war only for the preservation of justice	41.3	37.8	41.6	36.7	41.3	47.4	39.3
cannot support or participate in war in the nuclear age, since war can no longer serve the interests of justice	3.2	3.2	3.5	2.6	3.8	2.6	3.7
can under no circumstances support or participate in war	2.5	6.0	1.9	3.1	1.4	2.9	3.4
Write-in	2.6	1.5	1.9	2.4	2.4	3.2	4.6
No report	3.2	1.5	3.4	3.9	3.0	3.2	1.8

333

II. ETHICAL AND SOCIAL BELIEFS

28. Race

	Total Percentage	C	NC	NE	SC	SE	W
Some races are inherently inferior, and are not entitled to equal rights and privileges with those of superior capacity.	.6	.0	2.6	.7	1.2	2.9	.4
Members of all races should have equal opportunities, but segregation is desirable to preserve racial purity	24.3	1.5	17.7	19.8	26.5	41.2	12.1
Members of all races should have the same opportunities, but present patterns must be changed gradually	52.6	16.6	56.3	55.7	50.0	40.6	59.4
All discrimination and enforced segregation based on race should be abolished	18.6	80.4	20.2	19.7	18.3	8.4	24.9
Write-in	2.0	1.5	1.8	1.9	1.9	4.5	1.4
No report	1.9	.0	1.4	2.2	2.1	2.4	1.8

29. Race in the Organization of The Methodist Church

	Total Percentage	C	NC	NE	SC	SE	W
All jurisdictions, conferences, and churches should follow racial lines	14.5	1.5	10.2	9.1	15.5	34.1	6.4
The future status of the all-Negro jurisdiction and segregated Annual Conferences and local churches should be determined under permissive legislation	19.0	7.6	16.2	15.6	17.6	31.9	15.2
The all-Negro jurisdiction should now be abolished, and segregated Annual Conferences and local churches should be gradually eliminated by permissive legislation	20.4	16.6	22.1	23.7	23.8	9.3	24.7
Racial segregation should be abolished at all levels	33.2	72.7	39.1	39.5	28.0	10.1	42.0
Write-in	3.6	1.6	2.2	3.4	4.7	6.5	3.0
No report	9.3	.0	10.2	8.7	10.4	8.1	8.7

30. Politics

is of no concern to the Christian, whose citizenship is not of this world	.6	4.5	.2	1.1	.0	2.8	5.9
is a necessary evil, and Christians should be careful not to be contaminated by participating in it beyond necessity	2.4	13.6	2.1	2.2	2.8	2.1	1.8
should call forth the serious and intelligent concern of the conscientious Christian	64.4	50.0	63.4	64.1	63.6	65.0	62.0
is an area which Christians should regard as a special responsibility	29.4	30.3	31.4	28.7	29.6	26.8	27.9
Write-in	1.5	1.6	1.3	1.4	2.1	1.4	1.8
No report	1.7	.0	1.6	2.5	1.9	1.9	.6

31. A School Teacher Should

join no "cause" organizations	2.1	1.5	1.6	2.2	1.9	2.7	2.5
join only those organizations approved by the institution employing him	8.6	3.0	6.5	5.2	11.1	16.9	5.3
be free to join any "cause" organization (such as the League of Women Voters, National Association for the Advancement of Colored People, Citizens Council, Americans for Democratic Action, American Legion) so long as his membership does not interfere with his effectiveness in teaching	70.4	81.8	75.3	72.9	68.5	56.5	73.7
be able to join any "cause" organization	12.1	6.1	12.1	11.9	11.7	13.3	12.1
Write-in	2.9	4.5	1.7	3.3	2.7	5.0	3.2
No report	3.9	3.1	2.8	4.5	4.1	5.6	3.2

II. ETHICAL AND SOCIAL BELIEFS

		Total Percentage					
		C	NC	NE	SC	SE	W
32. A Methodist Minister Should							
not speak on controversial social issues	1.6	1.5	1.5	1.3	1.4	1.7	2.2
speak only on issues on which there is agreement in his local church	1.8	1.5	1.5	2.1	1.5	2.2	2.4
be free to take a position on controversial issues if it is in accord with the Social Creed	9.7	21.2	9.6	12.7	8.7	7.2	8.3
be free to take a position on controversial issues as long as this does not interfere with his parish ministry	14.4	12.2	14.5	16.2	12.4	12.7	16.4
be free to take, on controversial issues, any position which he regards as Christian	68.4	60.6	69.1	64.2	72.0	70.0	67.9
Write-in	2.2	1.5	2.0	1.5	2.5	3.1	2.2
No report	1.9	1.5	1.8	2.0	1.5	3.1	.6
33. The Family							
should seek to reclaim the whole range of functions once performed by the family	7.1	13.6	6.8	8.0	6.0	7.9	5.9
may share some functions with other institutions, but should retain primary responsibility for moral and religious education	60.1	48.5	62.9	57.1	63.0	53.9	64.7
should share with other institutions the responsibility for all of the functions	23.8	31.8	22.1	23.6	23.5	27.6	22.9
should accept the more limited range of functions left to it as other institutions now care for education, recreation, moral instruction, security for the aged, etc.	3.8	3.0	3.0	5.8	3.2	3.9	3.3

Write-in	1.0	3.1	1.0	1.3	.6	1.5	.2
No report	4.2	.0	4.2	4.2	3.7	5.2	3.0

34. Public Power Projects Like TVA

are a threat to our free enterprise economy	9.4	1.5	9.9	10.4	9.2	6.8	11.4
are questionable because they tax all our citizens to provide cheap electricity for a few	13.5	13.6	13.0	18.9	12.7	10.5	10.9
greatly improve the total economic welfare of the nation	41.0	48.5	41.2	35.5	39.3	48.3	38.9
provide worthy experiments in the extension of democracy	18.7	19.7	18.6	18.5	17.1	20.2	19.4
Write-in	3.0	4.5	2.6	2.7	2.7	3.9	3.9
No report	14.4	12.2	14.7	14.0	19.0	10.3	15.5

35. Economic and Technical Aid to Other Countries Should

await our caring for our own needs and interests	3.4	4.5	2.9	3.4	3.9	2.7	3.2
be granted only if it will advance our military objectives and economic interests	1.3	1.5	1.0	2.8	.9	4.9	.9
consider the welfare of the peoples involved as well as American interests	45.6	41.0	44.1	46.6	45.9	44.8	42.1
be allocated on the basis of the needs of humanity as a whole	45.1	50.0	47.5	42.5	43.9	42.7	49.8
Write-in	1.1	1.5	.8	.6	1.6	1.7	1.2
No report	3.5	1.5	3.7	4.1	3.8	3.2	2.8

36. United Nations

World organization involves dangerous infringement on national sovereignty; hence each nation should pursue its own course, making only such temporary alliances as serve its ends	2.7	3.0	2.5	2.2	8.9	5.1	2.2

337

II. ETHICAL AND SOCIAL BELIEFS

		C	NC	NE	SC	SE	W
	Total Percentage						
The UN deserves support as our best political hope for world peace	80.4	75.8	80.6	82.3	74.0	78.2	80.4
The UN deserves full support, but should be superseded as soon as possible by real world government	8.6	15.1	8.4	7.7	8.9	7.3	10.6
Full world government, abolishing national sovereignty, is the world's best political hope	1.5	1.5	1.6	1.6	1.1	1.0	1.4
Write-in	2.3	1.5	2.1	2.1	3.6	3.1	1.2
No report	4.5	3.1	4.8	4.1	3.5	5.3	4.2
37. The Main Purpose of a Prison Should Be							
the punishment of the enemies of society	1.2	.0	1.4	1.5	.5	1.5	1.2
the confinement of criminals whose freedom would endanger society	18.4	7.6	17.9	19.3	18.7	17.2	21.8
the cure of sick and maladjusted persons	4.7	3.0	4.3	5.6	5.9	4.9	2.5
the rehabilitation of offenders and their restoration to normal life in society	69.7	84.8	71.5	67.9	68.1	69.2	67.1
Write-in	3.6	3.0	3.1	3.3	3.8	4.1	5.2
No report	2.4	1.6	1.8	2.4	3.0	3.1	2.2
38. Occupations Should Be Chosen Mainly in Terms of							
income and social status	.7	1.5	.9	.6	.3	.6	.7
security in job and residence	4.8	3.0	5.1	5.9	4.4	2.8	5.8
personal satisfaction and meaning in work	37.0	27.3	40.1	39.2	35.5	26.9	42.9
use of personal capacities in the service of mankind	14.6	12.1	16.9	13.6	14.1	9.9	18.1

338

use of personal capacities on the basis of stewardship to

God	36.0	53.0	30.1	33.3	38.8	52.9	25.9
Write-in	3.2	3.1	2.9	2.9	4.7	3.0	3.4
No report	3.7	.0	4.0	4.5	2.2	3.9	3.2

39. Status of Men and Women

Woman's place is in the home	6.9	9.1	6.7	7.4	6.2	8.4	5.1
Men and women have complementary but different roles to play	23.7	18.1	23.3	21.5	24.1	27.2	23.3
The principle of full equality must be modified by woman's responsibility to home and children	30.6	27.3	30.8	31.4	31.0	28.5	32.0
Men and women should have equal and identical rights in employment and education in both church and society	34.1	45.5	34.3	35.2	33.9	30.5	36.2
Write-in	2.2	.0	2.5	1.9	2.4	2.3	1.4
No report	2.5	.0	2.4	2.6	2.4	3.1	2.0

40. The Methodist Church

has the true gospel and should not jeopardize its witness by joint activities with other denominations	1.5	3.1	1.1	3.2	1.1	2.3	.6
should co-operate with other Christian bodies in activities that can be done together better than separately	63.4	63.6	65.3	59.6	67.1	64.4	64.6
should, while co-operating with non-Methodist Christian bodies, seek full union with other Methodist bodies	7.9	6.0	7.6	7.0	8.6	7.8	6.3
should seek full union with all Christian bodies willing to explore the possibility	22.9	22.7	22.1	25.6	18.9	20.7	24.9
Write-in	1.6	1.5	1.5	1.9	1.7	2.2	1.4
No report	2.7	3.1	2.4	2.7	2.6	2.6	2.2

II. ETHICAL AND SOCIAL BELIEFS

	Total Percentage						
		C	NC	NE	SC	SE	W
41. Public Education Should Receive Federal Aid							
only if complete control remains with the states	21.6	9.0	21.1	16.7	24.2	29.3	18.4
only if parochial and private schools are specifically excluded	12.0	6.1	10.6	15.6	9.7	10.4	16.0
if parochial and private schools receive no direct subsidy but only such indirect aid as bus transportation	3.4	.0	3.6	4.0	3.4	2.5	3.4
on the basis of need	53.5	80.3	56.3	54.1	50.4	47.4	53.3
Write-in	4.5	1.5	4.0	4.9	5.5	5.1	4.1
No report	5.0	3.1	4.4	4.7	6.8	5.3	4.8
42. Health							
Socialized medicine would kill the individual initiative of doctors and the self-reliance of their patients	20.4	7.5	23.1	20.3	23.0	17.2	15.6
Health insurance is the best way for people to meet the costs of illness	54.0	59.1	52.2	53.5	53.4	56.5	56.5
The co-operative employment of physicians by voluntary health associations would provide adequate care at lowest cost	15.0	25.8	14.9	15.3	11.8	15.1	17.6
The government should provide free medical and dental care for all the people	1.8	.0	1.6	2.3	1.6	2.1	2.1
Write-in	3.9	4.5	3.9	4.0	3.4	3.8	4.6
No report	4.8	3.1	4.3	4.6	6.8	5.3	3.6

43. In Labor Legislation the Federal Government Should

pass "right to work" laws and curb the power of labor unions	29.3	16.7	29.6	29.3	33.5	28.3	26.7
aim primarily at controlling unethical labor practices and racketeering	44.3	51.5	44.0	44.4	43.2	42.5	49.0
protect labor's right to a union shop but limit the right to strike in the public interest	14.2	21.2	14.2	14.2	10.2	16.1	14.6
protect labor unions in provision for union shop, collective bargaining, etc.	3.4	6.0	4.0	3.0	1.6	3.1	4.3
Write-in	2.6	1.5	2.6	3.0	2.2	2.6	2.4
No report	6.2	3.1	5.6	6.1	9.3	7.4	3.0

44. The Federal Government Should

let the farmer care for himself and his soil	9.0	1.5	12.1	8.4	9.4	5.3	6.2
concern itself only with soil conservation	9.2	3.1	10.9	8.2	9.1	7.4	9.8
concern itself with control of agricultural surpluses and with soil conservation, but not with price support	24.4	18.1	24.8	26.8	22.1	21.0	28.4
act to stabilize farm prices, control surpluses, and conserve the soil	47.5	69.7	43.1	47.8	47.1	54.4	47.4
Write-in	2.9	4.5	2.8	2.2	4.4	2.7	2.2
No report	7.0	3.1	6.3	6.6	7.9	9.2	6.0

III. SOCIAL ACTION

HOW DO YOU EXPRESS YOUR SOCIAL RESPONSIBILITY?

	REGULARLY	FAIRLY OFTEN	SELDOM	NEVER	NR
45. By voting in national elections.	83.5	4.1	1.2	2.9	8.3
46. By voting in state elections.	79.6	6.9	1.3	3.3	8.9
47. By voting in local elections.	75.5	10.2	2.1	3.2	9.0

By participation in nonchurch organizations concerned with social problems:

	REGULARLY	FAIRLY OFTEN	SELDOM	NEVER	NR
48. On the national level.	16.7	17.2	21.8	18.0	26.3
49. On the local community level.	33.0	27.3	16.1	8.2	15.4

In writing letters expressing your concern:

	REGULARLY	FAIRLY OFTEN	SELDOM	NEVER	NR
50. To members of Congress.	3.5	11.3	29.4	41.0	14.8
51. To the editors of newspapers.	2.1	5.6	23.3	50.1	18.9

52. In the above areas, do you consider your action to be aimed in general at:

    a. Seeking social change?   34.1
    b. Conserving present traditions?   20.4
    c. No report   45.5

DO YOU LOOK FOR GUIDANCE AND LEADERSHIP IN AREAS OF SOCIAL RESPONSIBILITY FROM:

	MUCH	SOME	LITTLE	NONE	NR
53. Your minister?	33.5	36.8	8.4	6.0	15.3
54. Your local church commission?	10.8	29.7	16.3	18.1	25.1
55. General church boards and publications?	14.6	32.5	15.7	13.9	23.3
56. General Conference pronouncements?	10.1	22.9	19.3	20.1	27.6
57. National Council of Churches?	9.0	20.8	18.7	22.9	28.6
58. National publications other than Methodist, such as *Christian Century, Christian Herald?*	8.1	22.2	14.7	27.0	28.0

IV. GENERAL BACKGROUND

59. Age

10-24	8.1
25-44	40.4
45 up	48.0
NR	3.5

60. Sex

Male	45.6
Female	46.8
NR	7.6

61. Marital Status

Married	77.5
Single	10.7
Widow or widower	7.1
Divorced	1.2
NR	3.5

62. Education
  a. Elementary School:

ATTENDED	3.2
COMPLETED	5.4

  b. High School:

ATTENDED	10.8
COMPLETED	24.6

  c. College:

ATTENDED	19.1
COMPLETED	13.9

  d. Graduate School:

ATTENDED	6.2
COMPLETED	13.0

  e. NR   3.8

63. State Your Racial Background

a. White	81.8
b. Non-white	1.5
c. NR	16.7

343

64. State Your Exact Occupation

1. Professional — 15.3
2. Farm Operators & Managers — 9.4
3. Clerical Workers — 6.8
4. Sales Workers — 3.3
5. Craftsmen, Foremen & Kindred Workers — 4.7
6. Operatives — 2.3
7. Domestic Services — .2
8. Services Workers — 1.0
9. Farm Laborers & Laborers — .9
10. Housewives, Retired, Student, & Unemployed — 37.9
11. Ministers — 9.5
12. NR — 8.7

65. Family Income Per Year

1. Under $2,500 — 10.4
2. $2,500-4,999 — 28.7
3. $5,000-9,999 — 41.3
4. $10,000 up — 11.1
5. NR — 8.5

66-67. Size of Community in Which You Were Reared and Now Reside

	WERE REARED	NOW RESIDE
1. 0-2,499	56.9	37.4
2. 2,500-9,999	13.0	16.7
3. 10,000-99,999	13.5	22.5
4. 100,000 up	10.5	13.0
5. NR	6.1	10.4

68. In What Church Were You Reared?

1. Methodist — 66.6
2. Presbyterian, Congregational, Baptist, Lutheran, Episcopal — 19.5
3. Roman Catholic — 1.8
4. Other — 8.4
5. NR — 3.7

69.-70. Size of Church in Which You Were Reared and Now Belong

	WERE REARED	NOW BELONG
1. 0-249 members	52.0	26.0
2. 250-499 members	18.6	23.9
3. 500-999 members	10.3	17.6
4. 1,000 up	7.5	20.7
5. NR	11.6	11.8

71. How Long Ago Did You Join the Methodist Church?

1. 0-6 years	14.5
2. 7-12 years	11.8
3. 13 up	61.6
4. NR	12.1

72.-73. Estimate the Number of Sundays Attended During the Past Year.

	WORSHIP	SUNDAY SCHOOL
1. 1-4	7.6	5.1
2. 5-12	7.7	4.9
3. 13-24	24.8	6.3
4. 25-36	12.0	12.4
5. 36 up	39.2	45.3
6. NR	8.6	25.9

74. How Much Does Your Family Contribute Weekly to Your Church?

1. $ .00- 1.00	10.3
2. $ 1.01- 2.00	13.3
3. $ 2.01- 3.00	11.7
4. $ 3.01- 4.00	10.6
5. $ 4.01- 5.00	16.5
6. $ 5.01-10.00	13.8
7. $10.01 up	5.9
8. NR	17.8

75.76. Are You Related to Any of the Following Church Organizations?

	MEMBER	OFFICER
1. WSCS	1756	595
2. Methodist Men	793	111
3. MYF	325	168
4. Official Board	1520	464
5. Choir	605	65
6. Church-school Teacher	808	296
7. Other	1155	700
8. None	528	717
9. NR	398	2023

77. Check Your Political Preference

1. Republican	49.4
2. Democrat	33.1
3. Independent	11.4
4. Other	1.0
5. NR	5.1

78. Number of Persons in Household

1. One	6.5
2. Two	25.5
3. Three	18.7
4. Four	21.6
5. Five	14.2
6. Six up	9.5
7. NR	4.0

METHODOLOGY AND REPRESENTATIVENESS OF THE INQUIRY

To make possible a fair sampling of the total membership of The Methodist Church, every sixtieth church was selected electronically from an alphabetical list of charges. The pastors of these churches were asked if they would be willing to co-operate. Since the distribution of the favorable responses changed somewhat the character of the sample, replacements were sought according to the known control categories of (1) size of church, (2) size of community, and (3) jurisdiction. The co-operation of the resident bishops of the episcopal areas involved was also enlisted. Thus every effort was made to establish a sample which would represent the different sizes of churches and communities approximately in the proportion in which these sizes actually occur in each jurisdiction.

Altogether a total of 357 pastors agreed to co-operate. Each was requested to select alphabetically, without regard to age, sex, education, intelligence, social or religious attitudes, degree of church interest and activity, or similar factors, every tenth member of his church, asking him to complete the questionnaire and return it unsigned to the pastor in a sealed envelope. Questionnaires numbering 5,020 were finally returned from a total of 267 Charges. Since 12,000 schedules were mailed out, this represents a return of about 41.8 per cent.

At the minimum, these data represent adequately the 150,340 members of the co-operating churches. At most, they may be said to be the best possible sample of the entire church. Generalizations as to the beliefs of all of Methodism are safely supported by the tests and comparisons demonstrated below.

Table 1
Distribution of 22,435 Methodist Churches by Jurisdiction Compared with 267 Responding [1]

	JURISDICTIONS						
	Total	C	NC	NE	SC	SE	W
ALL CHARGES	100%	7.3	22.3	20.8	19.3	23.4	6.9
CHARGES SAMPLED	100%	3.3	27.7	31.5	12.4	16.1	9.0

[1] *Source Book of Town and Country Methodism*, ed. by Roy A. Sturm (Philadelphia: Division of National Missions of the Board of Missions of The Methodist Church, 1955), p. 147. Section quoted was by Herbert E. Stotts. The alphabetical symbols designate respectively the Central, North Central, Northeastern, South Central, Southeastern, and Western Jurisdictions.

Table 2

Distribution of 9,691,916 Methodists by Jurisdiction Compared to 5,020 MESTA Respondents.[2]

		JURISDICTIONS					
	Total	C	NC	NE	SC	SE	W
ALL METH-ODISTS	100%	3.7	23.3	19.8	19.6	27.3	6.3
SAMPLE	100%	1.3	37.1	20.4	12.7	18.4	10.1

Table 3

Distribution of 6,165,353 Methodists by Size of Community Compared to 5,020 MESTA Respondents.[3]

		SIZE OF COMMUNITY				
	Total	0-2,499	2,500-9,999	10,000-99,999	100,000 up	NR
ALL METH-ODISTS	100%	39.3	17.8	20.9	16.3	5.7
MESTA SAMPLE	100%	37.4	16.7	22.5	13.0	10.4

Table 4

Distribution of 9,691,916 Methodists by Size of Church Compared to 5,020 Persons Responding [4]

		SIZE OF CHURCH				
	Total	0-249	250-499	500-999	1,000 up	NR
ALL METH-ODISTS	100%	19.7	24.5	30.2	24.4	1.2
MESTA SAMPLE	100%	26.0	23.9	17.6	20.7	11.8

[2] General Minutes of the Annual Conferences of the Methodist Church, 1958.

[3] Source Book of Town and Country Methodism, p. 126. Data on distribution by size of community are not available for the other members of The Methodist Church. NR designates no response.

[4] Ibid., p. 127.

The judgment that these distributions are adequately representative is confirmed by Chi Square calculations made on representative questions as succeeding waves of schedules were returned and tabulated. A Chi Square of .05 means that each succeeding wave could be expected to provide the same distribution of answers in 95 per cent of the cases. Such patterns appeared at the .05 level, for example, on questions 6, 26, 32, 38, and 44, indicating that any number of additional returns would have yielded substantially the same results.

Table 5

Comparison of 121,188,924 Persons Aged 10 and over in the U.S. Population with the 5,020 Respondents [5]

Age Groups	U. S. Population	MESTA Sample
10-24 yrs.	27.6	8.2
25-44 yrs.	37.5	39.7
45 and over	34.9	48.6
No report		3.5

Surveys made in 1959 of the Methodist churches of five widely scattered districts[6] show that members aged 10-24 comprise an average of 21 per cent of the total membership of those districts. Thus the number of Methodist church members in this age-group is proportionately smaller and the number above 24 is proportionately greater than the numbers in these brackets in the general population. Many persons do not join the church until they reach adulthood. Yet the percentage of young people in these districts is still considerably higher than the percentage in this category in the MESTA sample.

Although pretesting showed that teen-agers were capable of answering the questionnaire under controlled conditions, it appears that Methodist youth did not respond in proportion to their probable numbers in the church. The research committee considered the possibility of removing from the total sample the 422 questionnaires returned by persons aged 10-24. However, though these are not adequate in number, they are probably not unrepresentative in character, and it is clearly desirable that Meth-

[5] U. S. Census, 1950, Vol. I.
[6] Fort Wayne, Bloomington, Fort Worth, Geneva, and Sunbury, located respectively in the North Indiana, Indiana, Central Texas, Central New York, and Central Pennsylvania Annual Conferences. These studies were made by the Department of Church Surveys of Boston University.

odist youth be represented. It therefore seems best to include them, while discounting the results accordingly.

Table 6
Marital Status of 111,703,400 U.S. Residents
14 Years of Age and over
Compared to 5,020 Methodist Respondents [7]

MARITAL STATUS	U. S.	MESTA
Total	100%	100%
Married	66.6	77.5
Single	23.1	10.7
Widowed	8.0	7.1
Divorced	2.3	1.2
No Response		3.5

The comparison of Methodists with the total population by marital status is in conformity with the experience and expectation of the research team.

The smaller percentage of divorced persons is probably a fair reflection of a lower divorce rate among Methodist church members than in the total population.

Among the Methodists surveyed are 479 ministers, 212 more than the number of pastors of co-operating charges. Sample comparisons make plain that the inclusion of these questionnaires does not produce distortion, and they provide valuable augmentation of the returns from this jurisdiction.

The following table illustrates that, with two exceptions, in each question sampled the position with the highest score (the "modal category") for the clergy is the same as that for the total number of respondents. Furthermore, with one exception the second rank in each case follows the same pattern of co-variance.

[7] U. S. Census, 1950, Vol. I.

Table 7

Modal and Second Rank Categories
Compared for 479 Ministers and 5,020 National Methodist Scores
* M designates ministers; T, the total group.

QUESTION					
Position No.	7 Christian Church	9 Religious Experience	13 Belief and Conduct	16 Laymen	18 Christian Society
1 M*			47.5		43.7
T			43.3		44.8
2 M	19.2	63.6	41.0		21.9
T	23.7	46.1	37.2		22.6
3 M	61.1	32.2		30.5	
T	34.6	41.5		59.9	
4 M	13.6			62.6	
T	30.4			24.8	
5 M					
T					

QUESTION					
Position No.	28 Race	32 Ministerial Freedom	38 Occupational Choice	40 Ecumenical Co-operation	67 Size of Community
1 M*					40.5
T					37.4
2 M				55.1	
T				64.2	
3 M	48.8		11.7		19.8
T	52.3		36.6		22.5

	QUESTION				
Position No.	28 Race	32 Ministerial Freedom	38 Occupational Choice	40 Ecumenical Co-operation	67 Size of Community
4 M	28.4	8.0		33.0	
T	18.9	14.4		22.4	
5 M		78.7	78.5		
T		68.4	33.2		

The two exceptions are questions 16 on the role of the laity and 38 on occupational choice, and in each case the divergence is what one would expect. Of the total number of replies 59.9 per cent view laymen as "non-ordained Christians whose function is to help the clergy do the work of the church," while only 30.5 per cent of the clergy themselves and 34.5 per cent of the southeastern clergy take this position. In contrast, 62.6 per cent of the ministers and 60.1 per cent of the ministers in the southeast, but only 24.8 per cent of the total sample, regard laymen as "members of the people of God called to a total ministry of witness and service in the world." Comparably, 78.5 per cent of the clergy and 77.3 per cent of the southeastern clergy maintain that occupations "should be chosen mainly in terms of the use of personal capacities in stewardship to God," while only 36 per cent of the total group make this answer. Of the total number of respondents, 37 per cent think that occupations should be selected chiefly in terms of "personal satisfaction and meaning in work," while only 11.7 per cent of the ministers and 13.1 per cent of those in the southeast hold this view. It is noteworthy that in each of these deviations the ministers of the Southeastern Jurisdiction are closer to the position of the total sample than are the ministers as a whole.

Although in question 7 on the church the modal category is the same for ministers and laymen, the percentages differ widely, and the second-rank positions also are different. Many more ministers (61.1 per cent) than laymen (34.6 per cent) view the church as "the community of those who have been renewed by the Holy Spirit," and many more laymen (30.4 per cent) than ministers (13.6 per cent) think of the church simply as "the society of those who have joined together in their quest for the religious life."

On the other questions of theology and socio-ethical belief the replies

351

of the ministers do not deviate sufficiently to justify removing them from the total sample. The divergences noted reflect differences which one would expect to find between clergy and laity in the particular areas concerned. They do inevitably change somewhat the character of the total results for those questions. However, even in these instances the removal of the 212 polled in the special study would change the score for any one position by less than two per cent.[8]

Further light is shed on the universe studied by the replies to questions 72 and 75 on frequency of attendance at Sunday worship and membership in church organizations. Of the total number of respondents, 55.5 per cent attended 37 Sundays or more during the preceding year, 18 per cent attended from 25 to 36 Sundays, and only 10 per cent attended 12 Sundays or less. The respondents also included 1756 members of the Woman's Society of Christian Service, 793 Methodist Men, 325 members of the Methodist Youth Fellowship, 1520 members of official boards, 808 church school teachers, and 605 choir members. In spite of the presence of overlapping memberships, these figures on church attendance and activity strongly suggest that the questionnaires returned represent the most loyal, interested, and active members of our churches, and therefore those most likely to have opinions which they are able and willing to articulate on questions related to Christian and church responsibility. It seems highly doubtful whether any other type of approach would have won a much more affirmative response from the nominal Christians who are so numerous in the average congregation.

When all factors are weighed, it can be said with considerable assurance that the results of the questionnaire represent adequately the views of the 150,340 members of the congregations sampled, with the possible exception of those aged 10-24. The tests and samples cited also indicate that generalizations may safely be drawn respecting the views of the membership of The Methodist Church as a whole.

[8] For example, in question 16, where the most extreme variation occurs, if the 212 ministers were omitted the percentage of the total sample for position 3 would rise from 59.9 to 61.2, while that for position 4 would drop from 24.8 to 23.1.

Appendix C

Correlation of Theological and Social Beliefs

INTERESTING INSIGHTS ACCRUE FROM THE MR-2 STUDY OF METH-odist Beliefs presented by the correlation of theological with social beliefs. The theological beliefs range from conservative to moderate conservative, to middle ground, to moderate liberal, to liberal. After this scale from "most conservative" to "most liberal" was built into the questionnaire, each of the statements included in the final form of the questionnaire was rotated so that the "most conservative" position, for example, appeared at

		Middle Ground		
C	MC	MG	ML	L
Conservative	Moderate Conservative		Moderate Liberal	Liberal

a different place in each of the succeeding questions. It was theoretically impossible for a reader to discover the "proper" place on the scale for his answer to fall, and mechanically to give that response on each question. Each question required a great deal of thought. It is encouraging to think that nine out of every twenty persons requested to complete this question-naire took the time to do so.

CONSERVATIVE This, as all the following terms, is scalar and rela-tive. This term denotes the upper range of choices on each of the first twenty questions. Its consistent meaning is that it is adjudged the opposite extreme of the liberal position on each issue. At times this position can correctly be called orthodox, Barthian, Catholic, or fundamentalist. Cer-tainly no one term covers the range of beliefs represented by the first position on this scale. Referred to as position 1, we think of this diagramati-cally as the left of center.

Illustration: Question 8   "Men are saved entirely by divine grace"
(3.8 per cent of total).

353

MODERATE CONSERVATIVE In the formulation of the questions, neo-orthodox, evangelicals, and neo-Barthians were asked to represent this view. Contained here are those views tending toward conservatism, but which lack the extremist overtones of the conservative position. In most questions no middle ground appears and it is likely that some MC positions in those instances will sound balanced between the two poles. It was the judgment of the theological panels that these statements deserved the position on the scale above between the MG and C positions.

Illustration: Question 8 "Men are saved by believing that Jesus Christ is the Son of God" (9.1 per cent of total).

MIDDLE GROUND Some questions actually contained a position equidistant between the two poles of liberal and conservative. This term applies to such a scalar position.

Illustration: Question 8 "Men are saved by divine grace when they respond in repentance and trustful obedience" (56.1 per cent of total).

MODERATE LIBERAL This position combines much of the conservative with the liberal but places much more emphasis on the ability of man to participate in the solution of his own and the problems of society. Those called "neo-liberal" or "evangelical liberal" are most often in this portion of the spectrum. They are, on most issues, the majority of Methodism.

Illustration: Question 8 "Men are saved by belief in Jesus Christ and upright living" (24.3 per cent of total).

LIBERAL The right extreme of the above scale denotes those liberals variously called religious humanists, immanentalists, and theological liberals. Nonreligious and secular views would be outside this scale. Primary reliance on man in the solution of society's problems characterizes this group.

Illustration: Question 8 "Men are saved by their upright character" (1.5 per cent of total).

Illustrative of these theological concepts are questions 1, 3, and 6, having to do respectively with beliefs about the Bible, beliefs about the nature of man, and the nature of Jesus Christ; in the following tables these three areas of theological beliefs are arranged with the most conservative view at the top of the scale and the most liberal at the bottom. A fourth category having to do with social change (question 17) is included because of its implication for the four volumes of the study. It, of course, does not follow the conservative to liberal scale, but contains its own scale of acceptance of responsibility.

The reader may profit from the following tables by following horizontally the views of the more conservative relative to temperance and the other issues listed. A universe of 100 per cent on the horizontal scale represents the beliefs of the more conservative respondents to each theological area. For example, in the area of beliefs about the Bible 0.5 per cent of those who believe that "every word is true because it came directly from God" also believe that they may drink without reference to religious scruples. Following horizontally on the same line it may be seen that 63.4 per cent of the more conservative in the area of beliefs about the Bible feel they as Christians "should totally abstain from the use of alcoholic beverages."

NOTE: The careful reader, comparing Appendixes B and C, will observe slight discrepancies (on questions 29, 35, 38, 39, 40) between Appendix B and the lines headed "Total Methodist Population" in Appendix C. The correlations which appear below these lines were computed at a later date when a larger number of questionnaires (5237) was available.

A COMPARISON OF THE RELIGIOUS, ETHICAL AND SOCIAL BELIEFS OF METHODISM

Q. 26 TEMPERANCE, I, AS A CHRISTIAN

Q. 1 THE BIBLE	MAY DRINK WITHOUT REFERENCE TO RELIGIOUS SCRUPLES	MAY DRINK AT SOCIAL GATHERINGS TO AVOID OFFENDING HOSTS	MAY USE ALCOHOLIC BEVERAGES TEMPERATELY AND WITHIN REASON	SHOULD TOTALLY ABSTAIN FROM ALCOHOLIC BEVERAGES	SHOULD WORK FOR PROHIBITION	WRITE-IN	NO REPORT
TOTAL METH. POPULATION	1.2%*	1.0%	26.5%	56.8%	8.8%	3.9%	1.8%
EVERY WORD IS TRUE BECAUSE IT CAME DIRECTLY FROM GOD	.5	.5	9.8	63.4	14.5	6.6	4.7
THE BIBLE IS THE INSPIRED WORD OF GOD, BUT NOT ALL PARTS ARE OF EQUAL SPIRITUAL VALUE	.5	.8	23.7	61.7	8.9	3.0	1.4
AS THE . . . RECORD OF GOD'S REVELATION TO INSPIRED MEN, THE BIBLE CONTAINS THE WORD OF GOD	1.0	1.0	29.3	56.3	8.5	2.6	1.3
THE BIBLE IS ONE OF SEVERAL RECORDS OF MAN'S RELIGIOUS SEARCH	5.7	1.6	45.1	37.9	5.7	2.7	1.3
WRITE-IN	1.7	.9	17.5	38.6	5.3	29.0	7.0
NO REPORT	0.	0.	19.4	41.9	6.5	9.7	22.5
Q. 3 MAN IS							
TOTAL METH. POPULATION	1.2%	1.0%	26.5%	56.8%	8.8%	3.9%	1.8%
A CREATURE OF GOD WHO . . . HAS REJECTED HIS CREATOR AND DEIFIED HIMSELF	0.	.5	16.8	63.8	13.8	4.1	1.0
A BEING WHO HAS . . . DISTORTED THE LIVING IMAGE IN WHICH GOD HAS CREATED HIM	.9	1.4	23.2	58.3	9.0	4.7	2.5
A RATIONAL BEING CAPABLE OF KNOWING GOD AND ENTERING INTO FELLOWSHIP WITH HIM	.9	.9	25.3	60.0	8.8	2.6	1.5
A PRODUCT OF NATURE WHOSE INNATE POWERS FOR ACHIEVING GOODNESS, TRUTH, AND BEAUTY ARE ALMOST UNLIMITED	4.0	1.3	43.9	38.8	6.4	3.6	2.0
WRITE-IN	1.8	.9	23.7	34.5	6.4	26.4	6.3
NO REPORT	0.	2.7	15.7	37.0	15.1	10.7	18.8

* HORIZONTAL LINES EQUAL 100%

SOURCE: MESTA
MR-2

356

Q. 6 JESUS CHRIST IS

TOTAL METH. POPULATION	1.2%	1.0%	26.5%	56.8%	8.8%	3.9%	1.8%
GOD HIMSELF, NOT SUBJECT TO HUMAN LIMITATIONS	.4	.7	22.1	60.9	10.9	3.2	1.8
BOTH DIVINE AND HUMAN	.9	.8	22.2	61.9	8.4	4.6	1.2
A MAN UNIQUELY ENDOWED AND CALLED BY GOD TO REVEAL HIM TO MAN	1.1	1.2	32.4	53.8	7.6	2.3	1.6
ONE OF THE WORLD'S GREAT SPIRITUAL TEACHERS	4.6	1.4	38.3	39.7	10.9	3.1	2.0
WRITE-IN	.9	0.	13.4	53.7	9.9	17.9	4.2
NO REPORT	0.	1.0	16.0	47.0	9.0	10.0	17.0

Q. 17 SOCIAL CHANGE

TOTAL METH. POPULATION	1.2%	1.0%	26.5%	56.8%	8.8%	3.9%	1.8%
IS NO RESPONSIBILITY OF THE CHURCH . . . SOCIAL PROBLEMS WILL TAKE CARE OF THEMSELVES	1.0	1.0	19.5	58.2	12.0	5.3	3.0
IS A RESPONSIBILITY OF THE CHURCH, BUT SECONDARY TO THE TRANSFORMATION OF INDIVIDUALS	1.1	1.0	25.9	59.9	8.1	2.8	1.2
IS OF EQUAL IMPORTANCE WITH INDIVIDUAL TRANSFORMATION	1.1	.9	30.6	55.6	7.5	3.3	1.0
IS MORE IMPORTANT THAN INDIVIDUAL CONVERSION, SINCE SOCIAL CONDITIONS AFFECT INDIVIDUALS	3.2	1.3	37.2	46.4	8.1	2.8	1.0
IS THE ALL-IMPORTANT TASK OF THE CHURCH	.6	1.0	20.9	60.6	12.0	3.6	1.3
WRITE-IN	0.	0.	15.6	35.1	7.8	36.4	5.1
NO REPORT	.9	0.	18.0	49.6	10.3	7.6	13.6

357

Q. 27 WAR: I, AS A CHRISTIAN CITIZEN

Q. 1 THE BIBLE	AM OBLIGATED TO SUPPORT MY COUNTRY IN WAR WHEN ITS CONTINUED EXISTENCE IS AT STAKE, APART OF JUSTICE	CAN SUPPORT OR PARTICIPATE IN WAR ONLY FOR THE PRESERVATION OF JUSTICE	CANNOT SUPPORT OR PARTICIPATE IN WAR IN THE NUCLEAR AGE, SINCE WAR CAN NO LONGER SERVE JUSTICE	CAN SUPPORT OR PARTICIPATE IN WAR UNDER NO CIRCUMSTANCES	WRITE-IN	NO REPORT
TOTAL METH. POPULATION	47.2%	41.3%	3.2%	2.5%	2.6%	3.2%
EVERY WORD IS TRUE BECAUSE IT CAME DIRECTLY FROM GOD	45.2	38.2	3.0	1.6	3.0	9.0
THE BIBLE IS THE INSPIRED WORD OF GOD, BUT NOT ALL PARTS ARE OF EQUAL SPIRITUAL VALUE	44.7	44.0	3.5	2.4	1.8	3.6
AS THE . . . RECORD OF GOD'S REVELATION TO INSPIRED MEN, THE BIBLE CONTAINS THE WORD OF GOD	48.5	42.0	3.3	2.4	1.9	1.9
THE BIBLE IS ONE OF SEVERAL RECORDS OF MAN'S RELIGIOUS SEARCH	54.9	31.4	4.6	4.0	2.9	2.2
WRITE-IN	39.5	34.2	2.7	1.7	13.2	8.7
NO REPORT	38.7	19.4	0.	3.2	3.3	35.4
Q. 3 MAN IS						
TOTAL METH. POPULATION	47.2%	41.3%	3.2%	2.5%	2.6%	3.2%
A CREATURE OF GOD WHO . . . HAS REJECTED HIS CREATOR AND DEIFIED HIMSELF	43.4	44.9	4.1	2.6	3.5	1.5
A BEING WHO HAS . . . DISTORTED THE DIVINE IMAGE IN WHICH GOD HAS CREATED HIM	42.3	42.6	5.7	2.8	3.8	2.8
A RATIONAL BEING CAPABLE OF KNOWING GOD AND ENTERING INTO FELLOWSHIP WITH HIM	47.0	42.5	3.3	2.4	1.7	3.1
A PRODUCT OF NATURE WHOSE INNATE POWERS FOR ACHIEVING GOODNESS, TRUTH, AND BEAUTY ARE ALMOST UNLIMITED	56.4	33.5	2.7	3.2	1.5	2.7
WRITE-IN	30.0	39.1	3.6	1.9	20.0	5.4
NO REPORT	41.1	19.1	1.4	2.7	5.6	30.1

Q. 6 JESUS CHRIST IS

TOTAL METH. POPULATION	47.2%	41.3%	3.2%	2.5%	2.6%	3.2%
GOD HIMSELF, NOT SUBJECT TO HUMAN LIMITATIONS	49.0	40.9	3.5	1.8	1.3	3.5
BOTH DIVINE AND HUMAN	41.3	47.3	3.4	2.6	2.6	2.8
A MAN UNIQUELY ENDOWED AND CALLED BY GOD TO RE-VEAL HIM TO MAN	51.6	38.6	3.0	2.4	1.9	2.5
ONE OF THE WORLD'S GREAT SPIRITUAL TEACHERS	58.0	27.5	4.9	3.2	1.3	5.1
WRITE-IN	35.3	44.3	3.0	2.5	8.5	6.4
NO REPORT	52.0	17.0	3.0	1.0	4.0	23.0

Q. 17 SOCIAL CHANGE

TOTAL METH. POPULATION	47.2%	41.3%	3.2%	2.5%	2.6%	3.2%
IS NO RESPONSIBILITY OF THE CHURCH . . . SOCIAL PROBLEMS WILL TAKE CARE OF THEMSELVES	58.0	31.2	2.5	.4	2.8	5.1
IS A RESPONSIBILITY OF THE CHURCH, BUT SECONDARY TO THE TRANSFORMATION OF INDIVIDUALS	46.2	45.3	2.3	1.9	2.4	1.9
IS OF EQUAL IMPORTANCE WITH INDIVIDUAL TRANS-FORMATION	41.6	44.7	5.1	4.1	2.2	2.3
IS MORE IMPORTANT THAN INDIVIDUAL CONVERSION, SINCE SOCIAL CONDITIONS AFFECT INDIVIDUALS	57.1	33.1	3.9	2.7	1.5	1.7
IS THE ALL-IMPORTANT TASK OF THE CHURCH	52.1	38.4	3.5	1.4	1.5	3.1
WRITE-IN	35.1	36.4	5.2	3.9	15.6	3.8
NO REPORT	41.9	27.0	1.8	2.7	2.3	24.3

Q. 28 RACE

Q. 1 THE BIBLE	SOME RACES ARE INFERIOR, AND ARE NOT ENTITLED TO EQUAL RIGHTS . . . WITH THOSE OF SUPERIOR CAPACITY	ALL RACES SHOULD HAVE EQUAL OPPORTUNITIES, BUT SEGREGATION IS DESIRABLE TO PRESERVE RACIAL PURITY	ALL RACES SHOULD HAVE THE SAME OPPORTUNITIES, BUT PRESENT PATTERNS MUST BE CHANGED GRADUALLY	ALL DISCRIMINATION AND ENFORCED SEGREGATION BASED ON RACE SHOULD BE ABOLISHED	WRITE-IN	NO REPORT
TOTAL METH. POPULATION	0.6%	24.3%	52.6%	18.6%	2.0%	1.9%
EVERY WORD IS TRUE BECAUSE IT CAME DIRECTLY FROM GOD	1.3	40.0	33.9	15.2	2.7	6.8
THE BIBLE IS THE INSPIRED WORD OF GOD, BUT NOT ALL PARTS ARE OF EQUAL SPIRITUAL VALUE	.6	25.3	55.0	16.1	1.1	1.9
AS THE . . . RECORD OF GOD'S REVELATION TO INSPIRED MEN, THE BIBLE CONTAINS THE WORD OF GOD	.3	21.9	55.2	19.9	1.6	1.1
THE BIBLE IS ONE OF SEVERAL RECORDS OF MAN'S RELIGIOUS SEARCH	1.4	15.9	54.6	25.9	2.2	0.
WRITE-IN	.9	29.8	21.9	19.3	17.6	10.5
NO REPORT	.0	29.1	32.2	12.9	0.	25.8
Q. 3 MAN IS						
TOTAL METH. POPULATION	0.6%	24.3%	52.6%	18.6%	2.0%	1.9%
A CREATURE OF GOD WHO . . . HAS REJECTED HIS CREATOR AND DEIFIED HIMSELF	1.0	29.1	43.9	20.9	4.1	1.0
A BEING WHO HAS . . . DISTORTED THE DIVINE IMAGE IN WHICH GOD HAS CREATED HIM	1.4	26.5	49.7	16.1	3.5	2.8
A RATIONAL BEING CAPABLE OF KNOWING GOD AND ENTERING INTO FELLOWSHIP WITH HIM	.5	23.9	53.7	18.9	1.5	1.5
A PRODUCT OF NATURE WHOSE INNATE POWERS FOR ACHIEVING GOODNESS, TRUTH, AND BEAUTY ARE ALMOST UNLIMITED	.7	23.8	55.7	17.4	1.7	.7
WRITE-IN	1.4	26.5	49.7	16.1	3.5	2.8
NO REPORT	.9	24.6	30.0	21.8	16.4	6.3

Q. 6 JESUS CHRIST IS

TOTAL METH. POPULATION	.5%	24.3%	52.5%	18.7%	2.0%	2.0%
GOD HIMSELF, NOT SUBJECT TO HUMAN LIMITATIONS	.6	28.9	48.7	18.3	1.7	1.8
BOTH DIVINE AND HUMAN	.6	21.7	54.7	19.6	2.1	1.3
A MAN UNIQUELY ENDOWED AND CALLED BY GOD TO REVEAL HIM TO MAN	.4	24.4	55.2	17.7	1.0	1.3
ONE OF THE WORLD'S GREAT SPIRITUAL TEACHERS	.9	28.3	48.4	18.7	2.3	1.4
WRITE-IN	1.0	23.9	37.8	18.4	12.5	6.4
NO REPORT	2.0	25.0	29.0	19.0	3.0	22.0

Q. 17 SOCIAL CHANGE

TOTAL METH. POPULATION	.5%	24.3%	52.5%	18.7%	2.0%	2.0%
IS NO RESPONSIBILITY OF THE CHURCH . . . SOCIAL PROBLEMS WILL TAKE CARE OF THEMSELVES	1.2	43.5	35.3	11.5	4.3	4.2
IS A RESPONSIBILITY OF THE CHURCH, BUT SECONDARY TO THE TRANSFORMATION OF INDIVIDUALS	.6	22.8	57.4	17.0	1.5	.7
IS OF EQUAL IMPORTANCE WITH INDIVIDUAL TRANSFORMATION	.3	16.3	57.3	24.2	1.1	.8
IS MORE IMPORTANT THAN INDIVIDUAL CONVERSION, SINCE SOCIAL CONDITIONS AFFECT INDIVIDUALS	1.1	28.1	49.6	19.1	1.3	.8
IS THE ALL-IMPORTANT TASK OF THE CHURCH	.8	30.9	48.2	17.5	1.8	.8
WRITE-IN	0.	26.0	26.0	22.1	20.8	5.1
NO REPORT	0.	24.3	36.5	14.9	4.1	20.2

Q. 29 RACE IN THE ORGANIZATION OF THE METHODIST CHURCH

	ALL JURISDICTIONS, CONFERENCES, AND LOCAL CHURCHES SHOULD FOLLOW RACIAL LINES	THE FUTURE STATUS OF THE ALL-NEGRO JURISDICTION SHOULD BE DETERMINED UNDER PERMISSIVE LEGISLATION	THE ALL-NEGRO JURISDICTION SHOULD NOW BE ABOLISHED. SEGREGATED ANNUAL CONFERENCES AND LOCAL CHURCHES SHOULD BE GRADUALLY ELIMINATED UNDER PERMISSIVE LEGISLATION	RACIAL SEGREGATION AND SEGREGATED ANNUAL CONFERENCES AND LOCAL CHURCHES SHOULD BE ABOLISHED AT ALL LEVELS BY PERMISSIVE LEGISLATION	WRITE-IN	NO REPORT
Q. 1 THE BIBLE						
TOTAL METH. POPULATION	14.9%	19.5%	20.2%	32.7%	3.3%	9.4%
EVERY WORD IS TRUE BECAUSE IT CAME DIRECTLY FROM GOD	20.4	16.6	9.5	26.4	6.0	21.1
THE BIBLE IS THE INSPIRED WORD OF GOD, BUT NOT ALL PARTS ARE OF EQUAL SPIRITUAL VALUE	16.6	22.5	21.2	29.5	2.7	7.5
AS THE . . . RECORD OF GOD'S REVELATION TO INSPIRED MEN, THE BIBLE CONTAINS THE WORD OF GOD	13.3	19.1	22.2	34.7	2.7	8.0
THE BIBLE IS ONE OF SEVERAL RECORDS OF MAN'S RELIGIOUS SEARCH	11.9	16.0	18.1	45.9	3.0	5.1
WRITE-IN	13.2	10.5	8.8	25.4	21.1	21.0
NO REPORT	18.8	9.4	9.4	15.6	3.1	43.7
Q. 3 MAN IS						
TOTAL METH. POPULATION	14.9%	19.5%	20.2%	32.7%	3.3%	9.4%
A CREATURE OF GOD WHO . . . HAS REJECTED HIS CREATOR AND DEIFIED HIMSELF	16.3	21.4	17.3	30.6	5.7	8.7
A BEING WHO HAS . . . DISTORTED THE DIVINE IMAGE IN WHICH GOD HAS CREATED HIM	17.1	24.8	20.0	27.6	2.9	7.6
A RATIONAL BEING CAPABLE OF KNOWING GOD AND ENTERING INTO FELLOWSHIP WITH HIM	19.9	19.6	20.7	33.2	2.7	8.9
A PRODUCT OF NATURE WHOSE INNATE POWERS FOR ACHIEVING GOODNESS, TRUTH, AND BEAUTY ARE ALMOST UNLIMITED	14.3	19.6	20.0	35.3	4.2	6.6
WRITE-IN	14.5	13.7	13.7	32.7	13.6	11.8
NO REPORT	11.0	13.7	9.6	15.0	5.5	45.2

Q. 6 JESUS CHRIST IS

TOTAL METH. POPULATION	14.9%	19.5%	20.2%	32.7%	3.3%	9.4%
GOD HIMSELF, NOT SUBJECT TO HUMAN LIMITATIONS	17.7	16.3	18.3	32.3	4.8	10.6
BOTH DIVINE AND HUMAN	14.0	22.1	22.3	30.3	3.3	8.0
A MAN UNIQUELY ENDOWED AND CALLED BY GOD TO REVEAL HIM TO MAN	14.3	19.6	20.5	34.7	2.1	8.8
ONE OF THE WORLD'S GREAT SPIRITUAL TEACHERS	16.5	13.9	15.9	40.7	3.2	9.8
WRITE-IN	14.4	14.4	13.0	33.8	11.7	12.7
NO REPORT	15.0	14.0	16.0	18.0	1.0	36.

Q. 17 SOCIAL CHANGE

TOTAL METH. POPULATION	14.9%	19.5%	20.2%	32.7%	3.3%	9.4%
IS NO RESPONSIBILITY OF THE CHURCH . . . SOCIAL PROBLEMS WILL TAKE CARE OF THEMSELVES	26.5	16.5	11.0	26.5	4.5	15.0
IS A RESPONSIBILITY OF THE CHURCH, BUT SECONDARY TO THE TRANSFORMATION OF INDIVIDUALS	15.2	20.6	22.9	30.8	2.9	7.6
IS OF EQUAL IMPORTANCE WITH INDIVIDUAL TRANSFORMATION	10.1	21.5	21.9	38.8	3.1	4.6
IS MORE IMPORTANT THAN INDIVIDUAL CONVERSION, SINCE SOCIAL CONDITIONS AFFECT INDIVIDUALS	16.6	17.4	20.9	36.6	1.5	7.0
IS THE ALL-IMPORTANT TASK OF THE CHURCH	17.7	19.9	17.0	32.0	3.7	9.7
WRITE-IN	15.6	15.6	15.6	27.3	19.5	6.4
NO REPORT	9.0	6.8	9.4	23.0	3.7	48.1

Q. 34 PUBLIC POWER PROJECTS LIKE TVA

	ARE A THREAT TO OUR FREE ENTERPRISE ECONOMY	ARE QUESTIONABLE BECAUSE THEY TAX ALL OUR CITIZENS TO PROVIDE CHEAP ELECTRICITY FOR A FEW	GREATLY IMPROVE THE TOTAL ECONOMIC WELFARE OF THE NATION	PROVIDE WORTHY EXPERIMENTS IN THE EXTENSION OF DEMOCRACY	WRITE-IN	NO REPORT
Q. 1 THE BIBLE						
TOTAL METH. POPULATION	9.4%	13.5%	41.0%	18.7%	3.0%	14.4%
EVERY WORD IS TRUE BECAUSE IT CAME DIRECTLY FROM GOD	9.3	10.7	36.6	16.1	2.3	25.0
THE BIBLE IS THE INSPIRED WORD OF GOD, BUT NOT ALL PARTS ARE OF EQUAL SPIRITUAL VALUE	10.9	15.5	40.4	17.9	2.2	13.1
AS THE . . . RECORD OF GOD'S REVELATION TO INSPIRED MEN, THE BIBLE CONTAINS THE WORD OF GOD	9.1	12.2	44.4	18.8	3.3	12.2
THE BIBLE IS ONE OF SEVERAL RECORDS OF MAN'S RELIGIOUS SEARCH	9.2	16.5	39.7	22.7	3.5	8.4
WRITE-IN	3.5	5.3	26.3	15.8	21.1	28.0
NO REPORT	6.4	9.7	32.2	9.7	3.3	38.7
Q. 3 MAN IS						
TOTAL METH. POPULATION	9.4%	13.5%	41.0%	18.7%	3.0%	14.4%
A CREATURE OF GOD WHO . . . HAS REJECTED HIS CREATOR AND DEIFIED HIMSELF	7.7	11.7	44.9	20.4	3.1	12.2
A BEING WHO HAS . . . DISTORTED THE DIVINE IMAGE IN WHICH GOD HAS CREATED HIM	8.1	12.8	38.9	23.7	4.2	12.3
A RATIONAL BEING CAPABLE OF KNOWING GOD AND ENTERING INTO FELLOWSHIP WITH HIM	9.8	13.4	42.1	18.4	2.8	13.5
A PRODUCT OF NATURE WHOSE INNATE POWERS FOR ACHIEVING GOODNESS, TRUTH, AND BEAUTY ARE ALMOST UNLIMITED	9.2	14.3	42.5	17.8	4.1	12.1
WRITE-IN	10.0	10.0	34.6	13.6	16.4	15.4
NO REPORT	6.8	5.5	27.4	11.0	1.4	47.9

364

Q. 6 JESUS CHRIST IS

TOTAL METH. POPULATION	9.4%	13.5%	41.0%	18.7%	3.0%	14.4%
GOD HIMSELF, NOT SUBJECT TO HUMAN LIMITATIONS	9.0	13.6	44.2	17.3	2.8	13.1
BOTH DIVINE AND HUMAN	10.1	14.5	40.0	20.1	3.6	11.7
A MAN UNIQUELY ENDOWED AND CALLED BY GOD TO REVEAL HIM TO MAN	9.8	12.7	43.5	17.3	2.4	14.3
ONE OF THE WORLD'S GREAT SPIRITUAL TEACHERS	9.5	13.2	40.6	20.8	2.4	13.5
WRITE-IN	7.4	7.4	37.4	13.4	12.6	21.8
NO REPORT	2.0	11.0	31.0	17.0	2.0	37.0

Q. 17 SOCIAL CHANGE

TOTAL METH. POPULATION	9.4%	13.5%	41.0%	18.7%	3.0%	14.4%
IS NO RESPONSIBILITY OF THE CHURCH . . . SOCIAL PROBLEMS WILL TAKE CARE OF THEMSELVES	14.5	11.2	34.5	17.8	2.5	19.5
IS A RESPONSIBILITY OF THE CHURCH, BUT SECONDARY TO THE TRANSFORMATION OF INDIVIDUALS	9.9	15.9	42.8	17.2	2.8	11.4
IS OF EQUAL IMPORTANCE WITH INDIVIDUAL TRANSFORMATION	8.7	12.3	45.7	21.3	3.8	8.2
IS MORE IMPORTANT THAN INDIVIDUAL CONVERSION, SINCE SOCIAL CONDITIONS AFFECT INDIVIDUALS	9.4	12.1	43.9	19.5	3.5	11.6
IS THE ALL-IMPORTANT TASK OF THE CHURCH	9.8	12.2	38.6	20.9	2.2	16.3
WRITE-IN	10.4	3.9	36.4	7.8	23.4	18.1
NO REPORT	2.2	6.8	25.6	7.7	1.4	56.3

Q. 35 ECONOMIC AND TECHNICAL AID TO OTHER COUNTRIES SHOULD

	AWAIT OUR CARING FOR OUR OWN NEEDS AND ECONOMIC INTERESTS	BE GRANTED ONLY IF IT WILL ADVANCE OUR MILITARY OBJECTIVES AND ECONOMIC INTERESTS	CONSIDER THE WELFARE OF THE PEOPLES INVOLVED AS WELL AS AMERICAN INTERESTS	BE ALLOCATED ON THE BASIS OF THE NEEDS OF HUMANITY AS A WHOLE	WRITE-IN	NO REPORT
Q. 1 THE BIBLE						
TOTAL METH. POPULATION	3.1%	2.1%	44.7%	45.4%	1.1%	3.6%
EVERY WORD IS TRUE BECAUSE IT CAME DIRECTLY FROM GOD	5.5	2.7	47.1	31.1	2.7	10.9
THE BIBLE IS THE INSPIRED WORD OF GOD, BUT NOT ALL PARTS ARE OF EQUAL SPIRITUAL VALUE	3.0	1.1	44.5	47.4	.5	3.5
AS THE . . . RECORD OF GOD'S REVELATION TO INSPIRED MEN, THE BIBLE CONTAINS THE WORD OF GOD	2.9	1.0	46.6	46.7	.4	2.4
THE BIBLE IS ONE OF SEVERAL RECORDS OF MAN'S RELIGIOUS SEARCH	4.6	3.5	44.3	44.1	2.1	1.4
WRITE-IN	2.6	0.	38.6	31.6	17.6	9.6
NO REPORT	6.5	0.	29.0	35.5	0.	29.0
Q. 3 MAN IS						
TOTAL METH. POPULATION	3.1%	2.1%	44.7%	45.4%	1.1%	3.6%
A CREATURE OF GOD WHO . . . HAS REJECTED HIS CREATOR AND DEIFIED HIMSELF	3.6	1.0	40.3	51.5	1.6	2.0
A BEING WHO HAS . . . DISTORTED THE DIVINE IMAGE IN WHICH GOD HAS CREATED HIM	4.3	1.4	43.2	46.4	1.9	2.8
A RATIONAL BEING CAPABLE OF KNOWING GOD AND ENTERING INTO FELLOWSHIP WITH HIM	3.1	1.1	46.0	46.0	.6	3.2
A PRODUCT OF NATURE WHOSE INNATE POWERS FOR ACHIEVING GOODNESS, TRUTH, AND BEAUTY ARE ALMOST UNLIMITED	5.2	3.3	47.9	40.6	.8	2.2
WRITE-IN	.9	0.	40.9	39.1	14.6	4.5
NO REPORT	0.	1.4	32.9	28.8	0.	36.9

Q. 6 JESUS CHRIST IS

TOTAL METH. POPULATION	3.1%	2.1%	44.7%	45.4%	3.6%	1.1%
GOD HIMSELF, NOT SUBJECT TO HUMAN LIMITATIONS	4.3	1.4	44.9	45.2	1.2	3.0
BOTH DIVINE AND HUMAN	2.4	1.1	46.2	47.0	.4	2.9
A MAN UNIQUELY ENDOWED AND CALLED BY GOD TO REVEAL HIM TO MAN	3.6	.9	45.8	46.4	.5	2.8
ONE OF THE WORLD'S GREAT SPIRITUAL TEACHERS	6.3	5.2	44.3	37.8	1.8	4.6
WRITE-IN	.5	0.	44.8	37.8	9.5	7.4
NO REPORT	3.0	2.0	37.0	31.0	3.0	24.0

Q. 17 SOCIAL CHANGE

TOTAL METH. POPULATION	3.1%	2.1%	44.7%	45.4%	3.1%	1.1%
IS NO RESPONSIBILITY OF THE CHURCH . . . SOCIAL PROBLEMS WILL TAKE CARE OF THEMSELVES	6.5	4.0	45.5	35.0	2.3	6.7
IS A RESPONSIBILITY OF THE CHURCH, BUT SECONDARY TO THE TRANSFORMATION OF INDIVIDUALS	2.8	.8	51.8	42.5	.7	1.4
IS OF EQUAL IMPORTANCE WITH INDIVIDUAL TRANSFORMATION	1.7	.8	41.2	54.3	.4	1.6
IS MORE IMPORTANT THAN INDIVIDUAL CONVERSION, SINCE SOCIAL CONDITIONS AFFECT INDIVIDUALS	6.0	1.7	41.3	47.0	.9	3.1
IS THE ALL-IMPORTANT TASK OF THE CHURCH	5.4	2.4	40.7	47.7	.7	3.1
WRITE-IN	2.6	1.3	37.7	31.2	24.7	2.5
NO REPORT	.9	1.4	37.4	27.4	1.8	31.0

Q. 38 OCCUPATIONS SHOULD BE CHOSEN MAINLY IN TERMS OF

Q. 1 THE BIBLE	INCOME AND SOCIAL STATUS	SECURITY IN JOB AND RESIDENCE	PERSONAL SATISFACTION AND MEANING IN WORK	USE OF PERSONAL CAPACITIES IN THE SERVICE OF MANKIND	USE OF PERSONAL CAPACITIES ON THE BASIS OF STEWARDSHIP	WRITE-IN	NO REPORT
TOTAL METH. POPULATION	2.8%	7.2%	36.6%	13.7%	33.2%	3.1%	3.4%
EVERY WORD IS TRUE BECAUSE IT CAME DIRECTLY FROM GOD	1.1	6.8	19.0	9.6	49.7	2.6	11.2
THE BIBLE IS THE INSPIRED WORD OF GOD, BUT NOT ALL PARTS ARE OF EQUAL SPIRITUAL VALUE	.9	4.1	35.7	14.6	39.7	1.7	3.3
AS THE . . . RECORD OF GOD'S REVELATION TO INSPIRED MEN, THE BIBLE CONTAINS THE WORD OF GOD	.6	5.2	39.6	15.1	34.0	2.6	2.9
THE BIBLE IS ONE OF SEVERAL RECORDS OF MAN'S RELIGIOUS SEARCH	1.6	6.5	45.7	21.9	18.9	4.0	1.4
WRITE-IN	.8	2.7	19.3	6.1	36.0	23.7	11.4
NO REPORT	12.9	3.2	29.1	6.4	16.2	0.	32.2
Q. 3 MAN IS							
TOTAL METH. POPULATION	2.8%	7.2%	36.6%	13.7%	33.2%	3.1%	3.4%
A CREATURE OF GOD WHO . . . HAS REJECTED HIS CREATOR AND DEIFIED HIMSELF	.5	3.6	32.1	15.3	45.4	1.6	1.5
A BEING WHO HAS . . . DISTORTED THE DIVINE IMAGE IN WHICH GOD HAS CREATED HIM	1.4	4.7	34.3	8.5	47.8	1.9	1.4
A RATIONAL BEING CAPABLE OF KNOWING GOD AND ENTERING INTO FELLOWSHIP WITH HIM	.8	4.9	35.8	14.3	38.0	2.3	3.9
A PRODUCT OF NATURE WHOSE INNATE POWERS FOR ACHIEVING GOODNESS, TRUTH, AND BEAUTY ARE ALMOST UNLIMITED	1.6	7.1	48.2	21.4	15.2	3.8	2.7
WRITE-IN	0.	.9	21.9	10.0	37.2	21.9	8.1
NO REPORT	4.1	5.5	24.7	6.8	23.3	1.4	34.2

Q. 6 JESUS CHRIST IS

TOTAL METH. POPULATION	2.8%	7.2%	36.6%	13.7%	33.2%	3.1%	3.4%
GOD HIMSELF, NOT SUBJECT TO HUMAN LIMITATIONS	.9	4.0	35.0	12.6	42.0	1.9	3.6
BOTH DIVINE AND HUMAN	1.0	3.6	33.4	11.7	44.8	2.1	3.4
A MAN UNIQUELY ENDOWED AND CALLED BY GOD TO REVEAL HIM TO MAN	.5	6.0	41.3	18.6	27.9	2.4	3.3
ONE OF THE WORLD'S GREAT SPIRITUAL TEACHERS	2.4	9.3	39.3	16.8	23.7	3.9	4.6
WRITE-IN	.5	5.0	26.4	11.4	33.3	16.0	7.4
NO REPORT	4.0	5.0	26.0	14.0	26.0	1.0	24.0

Q.17 SOCIAL CHANGE

TOTAL METH. POPULATION	2.8%	7.2%	36.6%	13.7%	33.2%	3.1%	3.4%
IS NO RESPONSIBILITY OF THE CHURCH . . . SOCIAL PROBLEMS WILL TAKE CARE OF THEMSELVES	1.5	10.3	32.7	9.3	35.7	1.8	8.7
IS A RESPONSIBILITY OF THE CHURCH, BUT SECONDARY TO THE TRANSFORMATION OF INDIVIDUALS	.9	3.6	38.0	15.6	36.8	2.5	2.6
IS OF EQUAL IMPORTANCE WITH INDIVIDUAL TRANSFORMATION	.5	3.2	37.9	15.1	39.5	2.8	1.0
IS MORE IMPORTANT THAN INDIVIDUAL CONVERSION, SINCE SOCIAL CONDITIONS AFFECT INDIVIDUALS	1.0	9.2	47.0	16.8	21.7	2.2	2.1
IS THE ALL-IMPORTANT TASK OF THE CHURCH	.8	6.9	30.0	14.1	42.3	2.0	3.9
WRITE-IN	1.3	5.2	11.7	15.6	31.2	32.5	2.5
NO REPORT	1.8	5.9	25.7	11.2	23.4	1.9	30.1

Q. 39 STATUS OF MEN AND WOMEN

	WOMAN'S PLACE IS IN THE HOME	MEN AND WOMEN HAVE COMPLEMENTARY BUT DIFFERENT ROLES TO PLAY	THE PRINCIPLE OF FULL EQUALITY MUST BE MODIFIED BY WOMAN'S RESPONSIBILITY TO HOME AND CHILDREN	MEN AND WOMEN SHOULD HAVE EQUAL AND IDENTICAL RIGHTS IN EMPLOYMENT AND EDUCATION IN BOTH CHURCH AND SOCIETY	WRITE-IN	NO REPORT
Q. 1 THE BIBLE						
TOTAL METH. POPULATION	11.6%	22.2%	30.5%	31.0%	2.2%	2.5%
EVERY WORD IS TRUE BECAUSE IT CAME DIRECTLY FROM GOD	20.5	13.4	19.3	36.3	3.1	7.4
THE BIBLE IS THE INSPIRED WORD OF GOD, BUT NOT ALL PARTS ARE OF EQUAL SPIRITUAL VALUE	6.9	24.9	32.6	31.2	1.9	2.5
AS THE . . . RECORD OF GOD'S REVELATION TO INSPIRED MEN, THE BIBLE CONTAINS THE WORD OF GOD	5.3	24.2	32.0	35.4	1.3	1.8
THE BIBLE IS ONE OF SEVERAL RECORDS OF MAN'S RELIGIOUS SEARCH	5.9	28.4	26.8	36.2	1.7	1.0
WRITE-IN	9.6	14.9	17.6	27.2	22.0	8.7
NO REPORT	9.7	6.4	22.6	25.8	3.2	32.3
Q. 3 MAN IS						
TOTAL METH. POPULATION	11.6%	22.2%	30.5%	31.0%	2.2%	2.5%
A CREATURE OF GOD WHO . . . HAS REJECTED HIS CREATOR AND DEIFIED HIMSELF	11.7	18.4	26.0	39.3	3.1	1.5
A BEING WHO HAS . . . DISTORTED THE DIVINE IMAGE IN WHICH GOD HAS CREATED HIM	11.3	24.2	35.1	26.1	1.4	1.9
A RATIONAL BEING CAPABLE OF KNOWING GOD AND ENTERING INTO FELLOWSHIP WITH HIM	7.0	24.6	31.2	33.5	1.5	2.2
A PRODUCT OF NATURE WHOSE INNATE POWERS FOR ACHIEVING GOODNESS, TRUTH, AND BEAUTY ARE ALMOST UNLIMITED	6.2	23.4	30.7	38.3	.5	.9
WRITE-IN	5.4	19.2	23.6	23.6	21.9	6.3
NO REPORT	15.1	6.8	20.5	26.2	4.1	27.3

Q. 6 JESUS CHRIST IS

TOTAL METH. POPULATION	11.6%	22.2%	30.5%	31.0%	2.2%	2.5%
GOD HIMSELF, NOT SUBJECT TO HUMAN LIMITATIONS	9.8	21.0	30.6	34.4	1.4	2.8
BOTH DIVINE AND HUMAN	6.7	27.1	31.3	31.7	1.2	2.0
A MAN UNIQUELY ENDOWED AND CALLED BY GOD TO REVEAL HIM TO MAN	6.3	23.3	31.3	36.3	1.8	1.5
ONE OF THE WORLD'S GREAT SPIRITUAL TEACHERS	10.6	20.5	25.7	38.9	1.8	2.5
WRITE-IN	7.9	15.0	26.8	30.4	15.5	4.4
NO REPORT	6.0	15.0	27.0	27.0	1.0	24.0

Q. 17 SOCIAL CHANGE

TOTAL METH. POPULATION	11.6%	22.2%	30.5%	31.0%	2.2%	2.5%
IS NO RESPONSIBILITY OF THE CHURCH . . . SOCIAL PROBLEMS WILL TAKE CARE OF THEMSELVES	17.5	15.5	23.0	34.7	3.8	5.5
IS A RESPONSIBILITY OF THE CHURCH, BUT SECONDARY TO THE TRANSFORMATION OF INDIVIDUALS	6.0	26.0	34.2	30.6	1.5	1.7
IS OF EQUAL IMPORTANCE WITH INDIVIDUAL TRANSFORMATION	3.9	28.7	30.5	35.1	1.0	.7
IS MORE IMPORTANT THAN INDIVIDUAL CONVERSION, SINCE SOCIAL CONDITIONS AFFECT INDIVIDUALS	7.4	20.9	28.7	41.3	.7	1.0
IS THE ALL-IMPORTANT TASK OF THE CHURCH	12.4	15.6	27.5	41.5	1.7	1.3
WRITE-IN	5.2	20.8	23.4	20.8	28.6	1.2
NO REPORT	8.6	14.0	24.3	28.8	3.2	21.1

371

Q. 1 THE BIBLE	HAS THE TRUE GOSPEL AND SHOULD NOT JEOPARDIZE ITS WITNESS BY JOINT ACTIVITIES WITH OTHER DENOMINATIONS	SHOULD CO-OPERATE WITH OTHER CHRISTIAN BODIES IN ACTIVITIES THAT CAN BE DONE TOGETHER BETTER THAN SEPARATELY	SHOULD, WHILE CO-OPERATING WITH NON-METHODIST CHRISTIAN BODIES, SEEK FULL UNION WITH OTHER METHODIST BODIES	SHOULD SEEK FULL UNION WITH ALL CHRISTIAN BODIES WILLING TO EXPLORE THE POSSIBILITY	WRITE-IN	NO REPORT
TOTAL METH. POPULATION	1.7%	64.2%	7.5%	22.4%	1.7%	2.5%
EVERY WORD IS TRUE BECAUSE IT CAME DIRECTLY FROM GOD	3.9	57.9	11.1	17.0	2.0	8.1
THE BIBLE IS THE INSPIRED WORD OF GOD, BUT NOT ALL PARTS ARE OF EQUAL SPIRITUAL VALUE	2.3	65.3	7.7	21.3	1.1	2.3
AS THE . . . RECORD OF GOD'S REVELATION TO INSPIRED MEN, THE BIBLE CONTAINS THE WORD OF GOD	.9	64.2	8.1	23.7	1.1	2.0
THE BIBLE IS ONE OF SEVERAL RECORDS OF MAN'S RELIGIOUS SEARCH	.8	56.7	5.1	34.1	1.4	1.9
WRITE-IN	.0	53.5	5.3	13.1	22.0	6.1
NO REPORT	.0	0.	6.5	6.5	51.6	35.4

Q. 3 MAN IS	HAS THE TRUE GOSPEL AND SHOULD NOT JEOPARDIZE ITS WITNESS BY JOINT ACTIVITIES WITH OTHER DENOMINATIONS	SHOULD CO-OPERATE WITH OTHER CHRISTIAN BODIES IN ACTIVITIES THAT CAN BE DONE TOGETHER BETTER THAN SEPARATELY	SHOULD, WHILE CO-OPERATING WITH NON-METHODIST CHRISTIAN BODIES, SEEK FULL UNION WITH OTHER METHODIST BODIES	SHOULD SEEK FULL UNION WITH ALL CHRISTIAN BODIES WILLING TO EXPLORE THE POSSIBILITY	WRITE-IN	NO REPORT
TOTAL METH. POPULATION	1.7%	64.2%	7.5%	22.4%	1.7%	2.5%
A CREATURE OF GOD WHO . . . HAS REJECTED HIS CREATOR AND DEIFIED HIMSELF	4.1	54.1	7.0	31.8	1.6	1.6
A BEING WHO HAS . . . DISTORTED THE DIVINE IMAGE IN WHICH GOD HAS CREATED HIM	1.4	64.5	10.4	21.8	.5	1.4
A RATIONAL BEING CAPABLE OF KNOWING GOD AND ENTERING INTO FELLOWSHIP WITH HIM	1.6	65.0	7.8	22.4	1.0	2.2
A PRODUCT OF NATURE WHOSE INNATE POWERS FOR ACHIEVING GOODNESS, TRUTH, AND BEAUTY ARE ALMOST UNLIMITED	.9	62.6	6.9	26.7	.6	2.3
WRITE-IN	.9	37.3	9.1	20.9	24.6	7.2
NO REPORT	.0	49.4	12.4	5.4	.0	32.8

Q. 6 JESUS CHRIST IS

TOTAL METH. POPULATION	1.7%	64.2%	7.5%	22.4%	1.7%	2.5%
GOD HIMSELF, NOT SUBJECT TO HUMAN LIMITATIONS	1.8	68.0	8.3	18.3	1.2	2.4
BOTH DIVINE AND HUMAN	2.3	61.4	8.3	24.4	1.2	2.4
A MAN UNIQUELY ENDOWED AND CALLED BY GOD TO REVEAL HIM TO MAN	.7	65.4	7.5	23.4	.8	2.2
ONE OF THE WORLD'S GREAT SPIRITUAL TEACHERS	1.7	58.8	8.4	25.1	1.0	5.0
WRITE-IN	.5	56.2	5.0	19.9	16.0	2.4
NO REPORT	5.0	51.0	11.0	11.0	0.	22.0

Q. 17 SOCIAL CHANGE

TOTAL METH. POPULATION	1.7%	64.2%	7.5%	22.4%	1.7%	2.5%
IS NO RESPONSIBILITY OF THE CHURCH . . . SOCIAL PROBLEMS WILL TAKE CARE OF THEMSELVES	4.0	62.0	11.0	14.2	3.3	5.5
IS A RESPONSIBILITY OF THE CHURCH, BUT SECONDARY TO THE TRANSFORMATION OF INDIVIDUALS	.9	67.4	8.5	21.0	.9	1.3
IS OF EQUAL IMPORTANCE WITH INDIVIDUAL TRANSFORMATION	1.6	59.9	7.1	29.8	.9	.7
IS MORE IMPORTANT THAN INDIVIDUAL CONVERSION, SINCE SOCIAL CONDITIONS AFFECT INDIVIDUALS	2.1	63.0	7.2	24.7	.9	2.1
IS THE ALL-IMPORTANT TASK OF THE CHURCH	2.6	64.4	8.0	21.6	1.5	1.9
WRITE-IN	2.6	42.8	3.8	23.4	27.2	.2
NO REPORT	.9	52.7	5.4	13.5	1.4	26.1

Selected Bibliography

Becker, Howard and Alvin Boskoff, editors. *Modern Sociological Theory*. New York: Holt, Rinehart and Winston, Inc., 1957.

Bennett, John C. *Christian Ethics and Social Policy*. New York: Charles Scribner's Sons, 1946.

————. *Christians and the State*. New York: Charles Scribner's Sons, 1958.

————. *Social Salvation*. New York: Charles Scribner's Sons, 1933.

Brightman, Edgar S. *Moral Laws*. New York: The Abingdon Press, 1933.

Cameron, Richard M. *Methodism and Society in Historical Perspective*. Nashville: Abingdon Press, 1961.

Campbell, Ernest Q. and Thomas F. Pettigrew. *Christians in Racial Crisis*. Washington, D. C.: Public Affairs Press, 1959.

Cogley, John, editor. *Religion in America*. New York: Meridian Books, 1958.

Coleman, James. *Community Conflict*. Glencoe, Illinois: The Free Press, 1957.

DeWolf, L. Harold. *The Case for Theology in Liberal Perspective*. Philadelphia: The Westminster Press, 1959.

Dilemmas and Opportunities: Christian Action in Rapid Social Change. Geneva, Switzerland: World Council of Churches, 1959.

Fagley, Richard M. *The Population Explosion and Christian Responsibility*. New York: Oxford University Press, 1960.

Foreign Policy and the Free Society. New York: Oceana Publications, 1958.

Galbraith, John Kenneth. *The Affluent Society*. Boston: Houghton-Mifflin Co., 1958.

Gustafson, James. *Treasure in Earthen Vessels*. New York: Harper & Brothers, 1961.

Harrison, Paul M. *Authority and Power in the Free Church Tradition*. Princeton, N. J.: Princeton University Press, 1959.

Haselden, Kyle. *The Racial Problem in Christian Perspective*. New York: Harper & Brothers, 1959.

Hofstadter, Richard. *Social Darwinism in American Thought*, revised. Boston: Beacon Press, 1955.

Hutchison, John A., editor. *Christian Faith and Social Action*. New York: Charles Scribner's Sons, 1953.

King, Martin Luther, Jr. *Stride Toward Freedom*. New York: Harper & Brothers, 1958.

Knight, Douglas M., editor. *The Federal Government and Higher Education*. Englewood Cliffs, New Jersey: Prentice-Hall, Inc., 1960.

Letts, Harold C., editor. *A Case Book on Christian Responsibility for Freedom*. New York: National Council of Churches, 1960.

Lippitt, Ronald, *et al*. *The Dynamics of Planned Change*. New York: Harcourt, Brace & World, Inc., 1958.

MacIver, Robert M. *The More Perfect Union*. New York: The Macmillan Co., 1948.

Merton, Robert K. *Social Theory and Social Structure*, revised. Glencoe, Illinois: The Free Press, 1957.

Mills, C. Wright. *The Power Elite*. New York: Oxford University Press, 1959.

Muelder, Walter G. *Foundations of the Responsible Society*. Nashville: Abingdon Press, 1959.

———. *In Every Place a Voice*. Cincinnati: Woman's Division of Christian Service, 1957.

———. *Methodism and Society in the Twentieth Century*. Nashville: Abingdon Press, 1961.

Myrdal, Gunnar. *An American Dilemma*. New York: Harper & Brothers, 1944.

Niebuhr, H. Richard. *Christ and Culture*. New York: Harper & Brothers, 1951.

———. *The Purpose of the Church and Its Ministry*. New York: Harper & Brothers, 1956.

Nottingham, Elizabeth. *Religion and Society*. Garden City: Doubleday & Company, Inc., 1954.

Pfeffer, Leo. *Creeds in Competition*. New York: Harper & Brothers, 1958.

Ramsey, Paul, editor. *Faith and Ethics*. New York: Harper & Brothers, 1957.

Sanders, Irwin T. "Approaches to Social Change," in *Education for Social Work*. Proceedings of the Eighth Annual Program Meeting of the Council on Social Work Education, New York, 1960, pp. 1-23.

Schelling, Thomas C., *The Strategy of Conflict*. Cambridge: Harvard University Press, 1960.

Schilling, S. Paul. *Methodism and Society in Theological Perspective*. Nashville: Abingdon Press, 1960.

Visser 't Hooft, W. A. and J. H. Oldham. *The Church and Its Function in Society*. Chicago: Willett, Clark and Co., 1937.

Ward, A. Dudley. *The Social Creed: A Living Document*. Nashville: Abingdon Press, 1961.

Ward, A. Dudley, editor. *Goals of Economic Life*. New York: Harper & Brothers, 1953.

Washburne, Norman F. *Interpreting Social Change in America*. New York: Random House, 1954.

Whitley, Oliver Read. *Trumpet Call of Reformation*. St. Louis, Missouri: Bethany Press, 1959.

Wogaman, J. Philip. *Methodism's Challenge in Race Relations*. Boston: Boston University Press, 1960.

Yinger, J. Milton. *Religion in the Struggle for Power*. Durham: Duke University Press, 1946.

———. *Religion, Society, and the Individual*. New York: The Macmillan Co., 1957.

General Index

377

378

Index of Persons